ESPN

LEGENDS
OF CRICKET

PROFILES OF THE GAME'S 25 GREATEST

ESPN
LEGENDS
OF CRICKET
PROFILES OF THE GAME'S 25 GREATEST

GEOFF ARMSTRONG

A Sue Hines Book

Allen & Unwin

First published in 2002

A Sue Hines Book
Allen & Unwin
83 Alexander Street
Crows Nest NSW 2065
Australia
Phone: (61 2) 8425 0100
Fax: (61 2) 9906 2218
Email: info@allenandunwin.com
Web: www.allenandunwin.com

National Library of Australia
Cataloguing-in-Publication entry:

Armstrong, Geoff.
   ESPN's legends of cricket : profiles of the game's 25 greatest.

   ISBN 1 86508 836 6.

   1. Cricket players – Biography. I. Title.

796.3580922

Cover design by Nine Hundred VC
Internal design and layout by Kirby | Jones Design
Printed in Singapore by Imago

10 9 8 7 6 5 4 3 2 1

CONTENTS

Photographs

The photographs in *ESPN's Legends of Cricket* are from Allsport and Hulton/Archive, two of the collections of Getty Images. Special thanks to James Nicholls, Ruth Gray and everyone in Getty Images' Sydney office. The images that open each chapter are as follows:

Page 13: **Don Bradman** during his then world record 334 against England at Headingley, third Test, 1930.

Page 23: **Garry Sobers**, bowling pace, on the West Indies 1966 tour of England.

Page 33: **Viv Richards** during his last Test series in England, 1991.

Page 41: **Shane Warne** spins his magic against South Africa in Adelaide, first Test, December 2001.

Page 49: **Jack Hobbs** in his batting stance, circa 1930.

Page 57: **Dennis Lillee** in Melbourne, 1979-80, wearing the one-day 'stripes' Australia wore for just one season.

Page 65: **Sachin Tendulkar** hooks during his 88 against England in Mohali, first Test, December 2001.

Page 73: **Imran Khan** bowls for the Rest of the World against the MCC at Lord's, 1987.

Page 81: **Wally Hammond** portrait, circa 1936.

Page 89: **Sunil Gavaskar** on the defensive during his 172 against England in Bangalore, 1981.

Page 97: **Ian Botham** against Australia at Headingley, 1981, arguably his greatest Test match.

Page 105: **Sir Richard Hadlee** appeals during his final Test, against England at Edgbaston, 1990.

Page 113: **Keith Miller** in the nets during the late 1940s.

Page 121: **WG Grace**, circa 1880.

Page 129: **Graeme Pollock** faces the rebel West Indians in South Africa, February 1983.

Page 137: **Malcolm Marshall** attacks England at Edgbaston, first Test, 1984.

Page 145: **Greg Chappell** at the MCG, third Test against England, February 1980.

Page 153: **George Headley** in 1939, part of the West Indies touring party.

Page 161: **Frank Worrell** walks out to bat during the West Indies' 1963 tour of England.

Page 169: **Len Hutton** hits out against South Africa at The Oval, fifth Test, 1947.

Page 177: **Wasim Akram** goes round the wicket against England in 1992.

Page 185: **Kapil Dev** with the World Cup at Lord's, 1983.

Page 193: **Steve Waugh** reaches his hundred at The Oval, sixth Ashes Test, 2001.

Page 201: **Barry Richards** batting for Hampshire in English county cricket.

Page 209: **Allan Border** at The Oval, sixth Ashes Test, 1993.

FOREWORD

By Bernard Stewart, ESPN International

ESPN PROVOKED AN ENORMOUS amount of debate with our SportsCentury series in 2000, when we counted down, from No. 100 to No. 1, to find the greatest North American athlete of the 20th century. We enjoyed our success with this Peabody Award-winning project, and soon set out to extend the experience — of a franchise that explores the highest levels of sports history — to other parts of ESPN's worldwide audience. Cricket — a sport with passionate fans across several continents — was a natural fit. From that realisation came the birth of the project, *ESPN's Legends of Cricket*.

If one would look to define the series, it would be as a celebration of history and tradition, and an exploration of heroes. Each sport has its great ones; cricket seems to have them in abundance. And when we talk of cricket's heroes, we talk not just of runs and wickets, but — much more significantly, I believe — of magnetic personality, of the ability to add considerably to the drama, to overcome adversity and break new ground. Featured here, for example, are stories of the South Africans — Graeme Pollock and Barry Richards — and how they reacted to the pressures of playing Test cricket at a time when their nation was being ostracised for the government's apartheid policies. 'If isolation meant changing South Africa's politics, if it played a part,' says Pollock today, 'Then I am quite happy that I missed out [on more than a decade of Test cricket].' Similarly, the stories of George Headley and Sir Frank Worrell in the West Indies, and Imran Khan in Pakistan, and the way their leadership and dignity altered the manner in which their national teams play their cricket, is simply inspirational.

We do not believe for a moment that the question of who are the greatest cricketers of all time has been resolved by *Legends of Cricket*. Every follower of the game — female or male, old or young — has an opinion on which cricketer is best, and inevitably the range of these views is broad. This is how it should be; this is how it is in all sports across the globe.

This is how it was when we first screened the SportsCentury retrospective — you would not believe the amount of letters and phone calls and faxes and e-mails we received telling us that we had got it right ... and wrong! I imagine similar disputes took place in Britain 80 years ago when cricket fans started arguing that Jack Hobbs might be better than WG Grace, and in Australia soon after when Don Bradman emerged to challenge the status of Victor Trumper. In this book we learn that in the West Indies, some still believe that George Headley was superior to The Don. I know that some Indians like to think that, day by day, their Sachin Tendulkar is edging closer to No. 1. The arguments must continue. Given that we assembled an esteemed and worthy panel of experienced cricket people to make the selections for the *Legends* series, we are sure we have added to the debate.

Please enjoy *ESPN's Legends of Cricket*. If the stories and opinions here change your view as to the quality of one champion over another, then we have done our job well. If you think we've got the rankings wrong, that's fine, too. We know that for so many people cricket is a passion. The game and its great players are well worth arguing over.

INTRODUCTION

By Geoff Armstrong

*P*ART OF THE APPEAL of sport is that it lends itself to arguments about who was better: today's champion or yesterday's hero, your favourite or mine? Whenever sports fans get together they delight in debates about one player or team's superiority over another, in which any or all of childhood memories, personal bias and fervent parochialism can play a part. Was Pelé a better footballer than Diego Maradona? Muhammad Ali a more accomplished fighter than Jack Johnson or Joe Louis? Who was the greatest driver: Juan Manuel Fangio, Ayrton Senna or Michael Schumacher? The better golfer: Jack Nicklaus or Tiger Woods? The best female tennis player: Margaret Court or Martina Navratilova? And the men: Rod Laver or Pete Sampras? Sachin Tendulkar might want to include one of his childhood heroes, John McEnroe, in that last one.

Cricket is no different, even if Sir Donald Bradman stands so far ahead of all other rungetters that conjecture must be about the *second-best* batsman. Still, if you were about to start one of those backyard cricket games — where one captain chooses first from all the available players gathered around, then the other captain picks second, and then the first captain picks again, and so on — and you had that first selection, who would you take: the phenomenal runscorer or a once-in-a-lifetime all-rounder? After that, would you rather a fast or a slow bowler, years of experience or youthful exuberance, a champion from the good ol' days or a hero of today?

Knowing the process would provoke more arguments than it would settle, ESPN set out to identify the greatest 25 cricketers of all time. To do so, a panel of eminent cricket authorities was formed — featuring a number of true legends of the game, esteemed commentators and writers, and a mountain of cricket knowledge and experience — and the result of their deliberations became the basis for *ESPN's Legends of Cricket*.

The panel was made up of Richie Benaud, Dickie Bird, Allan Border, Ian Botham, Ian Chappell, Tony Cozier, Martin Crowe, Sunil Gavaskar, Sir Richard Hadlee, Michael Holding, John Knowles, Robin Marlar, Christopher Martin-Jenkins, Mike Procter and Wasim Akram. Each was asked to nominate their top 25, in order, and then a second 25, in no particular order. The votes were then collated in the following way: the player nominated as No. 1 on a list received 26 points, No. 2 scored 25 points, No. 3 scored 24 points, through to position 25, who received 2 points. A vote for a player in the 26–50 positions scored a single point. In addition, to reward consistency in the judging, a point was scored for each vote secured; thus if all 15 panellists voted for a player he would score 15 'bonus' points, while if a player was high up on one list but did not appear elsewhere he would only get one additional point. The player with the most overall points became ESPN's No. 1 Legend of Cricket, the second highest point scorer became No. 2, and so on. First, *ESPN's Legends of Cricket* became a 26-part television presentation — one episode on the cricketers ranked 26 to 50, then individual shows on each of the top 25. Now comes this companion book.

Some might argue that the top 25 is a little skewed towards the players of the modern era, as only two players on the list — WG Grace and Sir Jack Hobbs — retired before World War II. Thus, old masters such as Victor Trumper, the 'Demon' Spofforth, SF Barnes and George Lohmann miss out. Spofforth and Lohmann don't even make the top 50 (the full list of those ranked 26 to 50 is listed opposite), when — in my view, at least — they might be entitled to a place ahead of a West Indian fast bowler or two. This said,

ESPN's Legends of Cricket Nos. 26 to 50

Rank	Player	Test Career	Rank	Player	Test Career
26	Sydney Barnes (England)	1901–1914	39	Curtly Ambrose (West Indies)	1988–2000
27	Everton Weekes (West Indies)	1948–1958	40	Michael Holding (West Indies)	1975–1987
28	Wilfred Rhodes (England)	1899–1930	41	Glenn McGrath (Australia)	1993–
29	Herbert Sutcliffe (England)	1924–1935	42	Jim Laker (England)	1948–1959
30	Bill O'Reilly (Australia)	1932–1946	43	Clarrie Grimmett (Australia)	1925–1936
31	Courtney Walsh (West Indies)	1984–2001	44	Javed Miandad (Pakistan)	1976–1993
32	Mike Procter (South Africa)	1967–1970	45	Ray Lindwall (Australia)	1946–1960
33	Fred Trueman (England)	1952–1965	46	Victor Trumper (Australia)	1899–1912
34	Brian Lara (West Indies)	1990–	47	Alan Knott (England)	1967–1981
35	Clyde Walcott (West Indies)	1947–1960	48	Allan Donald (South Africa)	1992–2002
36	Richie Benaud (Australia)	1952–1964	49	Alan Davidson (Australia)	1953–1963
37	Joel Garner (West Indies)	1977–1987	50	Bishan Bedi (India)	1966–1979
38	Andy Roberts (West Indies)	1974–1983			

a case can also be mounted for two stars of today — Sri Lanka's amazing Muttiah Muralitharan and the Australia's Adam Gilchrist — to be included, not in the top 25, but quite possibly in the top 50. Both Murali and Gilchrist suffer from the fact that the *ESPN Legends* voting was finalised in August 2001, as the 26 episodes of the series went into production. Since then Murali has become the seventh man to take 400 Test wickets, with strong prospects of reaching 500, 600, perhaps many more. And Gilchrist has taken his Test batting average to 60, establishing himself as arguably the most devastating No. 7 Test batsman in history, the most dangerous keeper-batsman of all time, and the best all-rounder Australia has produced since Richie Benaud and Alan Davidson, perhaps since Keith Miller.

One more thing: there is only one wicketkeeper, Alan Knott, in the top 50, and he's at No. 47. This surely can't be right. The absence of keepers is most likely a reflection of the fact that the best exponents of this art are the ones who are rarely noticed, rather than a statement by the panel that keepers aren't *that* important. The best indicator of the skill of Ian Healy, the outstanding Aussie gloveman of the 1990s, for example, was the way he so rarely erred when keeping to Shane Warne, rather than any of the spectacular catches he completed for fast and slow bowlers. In the statistical table at the back of this book, I have included a table listing most dismissals by wicketkeepers in Test matches. There is no doubt that at least two or three of the men on that list could easily be in the top 50.

All this said, if you add Spofforth, Lohmann, Murali, Gilchrist and a couple of wicketkeepers, then the top 50 is starting to blow out closer to 60. Especially with the top 25, it is so much easier to nominate cricketers who are not in who should be, than to identify those who are selected who might be left out. The thing I kept rediscovering, as I researched the careers of the *ESPN Legends* and listened to the opinions of the experts interviewed for the series, was just how magnificent each of these wonderful players has been. Their records are imposing, their influence on the history of the game profound, the respect they are given throughout the cricket world is deep and sincere.

Based on the judgment of ESPN's selectors, the best Test team of all time is as follows: Sir Jack Hobbs, Sunil Gavaskar, Sir Donald Bradman, Sir Vivian Richards, Sachin Tendulkar, Sir Garfield Sobers, Ian Botham, Imran Khan, Alan Knott, Shane Warne and Dennis Lillee. Wally Hammond would be 12th man. Some might prefer Sir Richard Hadlee (ranked No. 12) ahead of Botham (No. 11), on the basis that this best-ever XI needs a bowler rather than a third great all-rounder after Sobers and Imran. If you look at their entire cricket lives, you can argue that Hadlee was a superior bowler to Botham, but then again Botham did do some extraordinary things with the ball, especially in the first two years of his remarkable career.

Most would probably elect Bradman as captain of this team, but if I was in charge I'd go for Imran. The way he changed the face of Pakistani cricket in the 1980s is one of the game's most impressive stories, in my opinion close to, perhaps even the equal of, what Frank Worrell did for West Indian cricket in the early '60s. At the same time, Imran established his reputation as one of the greatest of fast bowlers, and was a batsman able to average nearly 40 in Test cricket. He has raised millions for charity, and now has set his sights on leading his nation. Nothing is beyond him.

OVER 60 DIFFERENT CRICKET identities — including former and current Test captains and players, plus commentators, writers and one very notable umpire — were interviewed for the *ESPN Legends of Cricket* television series. In this book, the careers of the top 25 *Legends* are studied at length, and these profiles are strongly supported by the views of many of those identities, with a selection of quotes from the experts highlighted in each chapter. The magnificent resources of Getty Images, through their Allsport and Hulton/Archive photographic libraries, complete the presentation.

The cricket identities interviewed for the series, whose quotes are featured in the pages that follow, are:

Paul Allott: Took 26 wickets in 13 Tests for England between 1981 and 1985; now a TV commentator.

Jack Bannister: Played 368 first-class matches for Warwickshire between 1950 and 1968; now a writer and commentator.

Dickie Bird: Umpired 66 Test matches between 1973 and 1996; also umpired in three World Cup finals, 1975, 1979 and 1983; played county cricket for his native Yorkshire and also Leicestershire; *Legends of Cricket* selector.

Allan Border: ESPN Legend No. 25; scored a Test record 11,174 runs in 156 Tests for Australia between 1978 and 1994; captained Australia in 93 Tests between 1984 and 1994; now a TV commentator and analyst, and an Australian selector; *Legends of Cricket* selector.

Ian Botham: ESPN Legend No. 11; scored 5200 runs and took 383 wickets in 102 Tests for England between 1977 and 1992; captained England in 12 Tests between 1980 and 1981; now a TV commentator; *Legends of Cricket* selector.

Greg Chappell: ESPN Legend No. 17; scored 7110 runs in 87 Tests for Australia between 1970 and 1984; captained Australia in 48 Tests between 1975 and 1983.

Ian Chappell: Scored 5345 runs in 75 Tests for Australia between 1964 and 1980; captained Australia in 30 Tests between 1971 and 1975; has been a TV commentator, writer and author for more than 20 years; *Legends of Cricket* selector.

Tony Cozier: The 'voice' of West Indian cricket; has been a leading writer, commentator and author for 40 years; *Legends of Cricket* selector.

Colin Croft: Took 125 wickets in 27 Tests for the West Indies between 1977 and 1982; now a commentator and columnist.

Martin Crowe: Scored 5444 runs in 77 Tests for New Zealand between 1982 and 1995; captained New Zealand in 16 Tests between 1990 and 1993; *Legends of Cricket* selector.

Alan Davidson: Scored 1328 runs and took 186 wickets in 44 Tests for Australia between 1953 and 1963; President of the NSW Cricket Association since 1970.

Tim de Lisle: Former editor of *Wisden Cricket Monthly* and *wisden.com*.

Andy Flower: As at 1 May 2002 had scored 4655 runs, and completed 149 catches and nine stumpings, in 61 Tests for Zimbabwe; captained Zimbabwe in 20 Tests between 1993 and 2000; International Cricketer of the Year in 2001.

David Frith: One of cricket's finest authors and historians, who writes from the unique position of having spent many years living in Australia, before moving to the UK; edited *Cricketer* magazine before establishing *Wisden Cricket Monthly* in 1979; is the author of over 25 books on cricket.

Sourav Ganguly: As at 1 May 2002, had scored 3454 runs in 55 Tests for India, after making his debut in 1996; became India's captain in late 2000, and soon after led his team to a series victory over the No. 1 side in the world, Australia.

Sunil Gavaskar: ESPN Legend No. 10; scored 10,122 runs, including a world record 34 centuries, in 125 Tests for India between 1971 and 1987; captained India in 47 Tests between 1976 and 1985; *Legends of Cricket* selector.

David Gower: Scored 8231 runs in 117 Tests for England between 1978 and 1992; captained England in 32 Tests between 1982 to 1989; now a TV commentator.

Sir Richard Hadlee: ESPN Legend No. 12; took 431 wickets and scored 3124 runs in 86 Tests for New Zealand between 1973 and 1990; *Legends of Cricket* selector.

Roger Harper: Took 46 wickets in 25 Tests for the West Indies between 1983 and 1993; later a West Indies team coach.

Michael Holding: Took 249 wickets in 60 Tests for the West Indies between 1975 and 1987; now a TV commentator; *Legends of Cricket* selector.

Carl Hooper: As at 1 May 2002 had scored 5325 runs in 94 Tests for the West Indies, having made his debut in 1987; named Windies captain in 2001.

Dean Jones: Scored 3631 runs in 52 Tests for Australia between 1984 and 1992.

Gary Kirsten: As at 1 May 2002, had scored 5671 runs in 83 Tests for South Africa, after making his debut in 1993; captained South Africa in one Test in 1998.

Denis Lindsay: Scored 1130 runs, completed 57 catches and two stumpings, in 19 Tests for South Africa between 1963 and 1970.

Clive Lloyd: Scored 7515 runs for the West Indies in 110 Tests between 1966 and 1985; captained the West Indies in 74 Tests between 1974 and 1985.

David Lloyd: Scored 552 runs in nine Tests for England between 1974 and 1975; later the Lancashire and England team coach and a TV commentator.

Steven Lynch: Was a writer with *Wisden Cricket Monthly*, now managing editor with *wisden.com*.

Glenn McGrath: As at 1 May 2002 had taken 389 wickets in 84 Tests for Australia, after making his debut in 1993.

Maninder Singh: Took 88 wickets in 35 Tests for India between 1982 and 1993; now a TV commentator.

Sanjay Manjrekar: Scored 2043 runs in 37 Tests for India between 1987 and 1996; now a columnist and TV commentator.

Robin Marlar: Played first-class cricket for Cambridge University and Sussex (taking 970 wickets), before becoming one of the UK's most respected cricket correspondents; *Legends of Cricket* selector.

Christopher Martin-Jenkins: For many years was the BBC's cricket correspondent, and remains a regular in the commentary box; also an editor of *Cricketer* magazine and a prolific writer on the game; *Legends of Cricket* selector.

Arthur Morris: Scored 3533 runs in 46 Tests for Australia between 1946 and 1955; captained Australia in two Tests, one in 1951–52, the other three seasons later.

Mark Nicholas: Played 377 first-class matches for Hampshire in English county cricket between 1978 and 1995, many of them as captain; now a writer and TV commentator.

Graeme Pollock: ESPN Legend No. 15; scored 2256 runs for South Africa at 60.97 in 23 Tests between 1963 and 1970.

Shaun Pollock: As at 1 May 2002, had scored 2242 runs and taken 261 wickets in 63 Tests for South Africa, after making his debut in 1995; was named captain of South Africa in 2000.

Mike Procter: Took 41 wickets in seven Tests for South Africa between 1967 and 1970, before South Africa was banned from international cricket; *Legends of Cricket* selector.

Ramiz Raja: Scored 2833 runs in 57 Tests for Pakistan between 1984 and 1997; captained Pakistan in five Tests between 1995 and 1997.

Jonty Rhodes: Scored 2532 runs in 52 Tests for South Africa between 1992 and 2000; still playing one-day internationals for South Africa, and is recognised as one of cricket's best-ever fieldsmen.

Barry Richards: ESPN Legend No. 24; played four Tests for South Africa in 1970, before his country went into Test exile for 22 years; played many years for Hampshire, also a record-breaking season for South Australia, and two seasons in World Series Cricket; now a TV commentator.

Ravi Shastri: Scored 3830 runs and took 151 wickets in 80 Tests for India between 1981 and 1992; captained India in one Test in 1988; now a TV commentator.

Ian Smith: Completed 168 catches and eight stumpings in 63 Tests for New Zealand between 1980 and 1992; captained New Zealand in one Test in 1991; now a TV commentator.

Keith Stackpole: Scored 2807 runs in 43 Tests for Australia between 1967 and 1974; now a radio commentator and analyst.

Sachin Tendulkar: ESPN Legend No. 7; made his Test debut for India in 1989, and as at 1 May 2002 had scored 7869 runs in 93 Tests, including 29 centuries; also scored 31 centuries and 11,069 runs in one-day international cricket; has captained India in 25 Tests.

Jeff Thomson: Took 200 wickets in 51 Tests for Australia between 1972 and 1985.

Max Walker: Took 138 wickets in 34 Tests for Australia between 1972 and 1977.

Wasim Akram: ESPN Legend No. 21; as at 1 May 2002, had played 104 Tests for Pakistan, after making his debut in 1985; captained Pakistan in 25 Tests between 1993 and 1999; is the leading wicket-taker in one-day international cricket, with 459 wickets; *Legends of Cricket* selector.

Bob Willis: Took 325 wickets in 90 Tests for England between 1971 and 1984; captained England in 18 Tests between 1982 and 1984; now a TV commentator.

Ian Wooldridge: A sportswriter for more than 40 years, award-winning columnist with the *Daily Mail* for 30, and a renowned maker of sporting documentaries; was a cricket correspondent for eight years through the 1960s, today he is recognised as one of the world's finest sports journalists.

John Wright: Scored 5334 runs in 82 Tests for New Zealand between 1978–1993; captained New Zealand in 14 Tests between 1988 and 1990; now the coach of the Indian national team.

Bruce Yardley: Took 125 wickets in 33 Tests for Australia between 1978 and 1983.

Two Legends in battle at the 1996 World Cup. Sachin Tendulkar attacks Shane Warne in Mumbai, in a match in which the Indian maestro scored 90 but Australia won by 16 runs.

OF ALL THE QUOTES featured in this book from all these outstanding cricket personalities, in my view one of the most telling comes from the celebrated sportswriter Ian Wooldridge. He is talking about Shane Warne, and I think he identifies something about the great legspinner that has been crucial in Warne becoming the most influential slow bowler in cricket's history.

'The first time I saw Warne was down in the nets in Sydney,' Wooldridge said. 'He must have bowled in the nets for an hour, and what intrigued me was that this was no work for him. This was what he loved doing. He loved spinning the ball.'

Of course, Shane Warne is about a lot more than just passion for the game. He possesses rare natural talent, enormous powers of concentration, courage, focus, pride, confidence and a propensity to work extremely hard. He knows the game, inspires teammates and brings drama to his sport. But — above all else — he loves the game.

All the *Legends* are like that.

Geoff Armstrong
May 2002

SIR DONALD BRADMAN
Legend No. 1
The Boy from Bowral

*A*S PART OF ESPN's SportsCentury celebrations in 2000, an extensive retrospective of 20th-century sport, the company assembled a panel of 48 experts to determine, in order, a cavalcade of the 100 greatest North American athletes of the century. Like *Legends of Cricket*, this list of champions became the basis for a documentary series, which generated immense interest in the US when it was originally screened, starting with No. 100, the great boxer Jack Johnson. The countdown worked down to three absolute icons — Muhammad Ali, Michael Jordan and Babe Ruth — but very few people were sure as to whom of this celebrated trio should be named at No. 1. When the experts leant to Jordan, arguments were inspired rather than settled. The race was that close.

For cricket, the choice is more clear-cut. There are a few students of sporting history who argue for WG Grace, on the basis that he made the game in the 19th century, leading it from its pre-1860 status as a pastime for the gentry to it being a sport of the masses by the turn of the century. Some push for Sir Garfield Sobers, who seemed to influence just about every game he played with his batting, his bowling, his fielding, his personality, his everything. However, most experts strongly

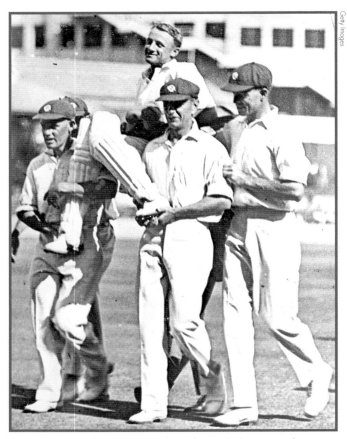

Bradman is chaired off the SCG by his exhausted Queensland opponents after scoring a world record 452 not out for NSW in January 1930.

support Sir Donald Bradman, the greatest batsman who ever lived. And so it is with *ESPN's Legends of Cricket*.

The thing about Don Bradman is that he didn't just break batting records, he obliterated them. There are few things in sport more engrossing than when an athlete is in pursuit of something that has never been done. Think of the four-minute mile, or Tiger Woods' grand slam of golf's majors. With 'The Don', it seemed that during nearly every week, month and year of his cricketing life he was

Mark Nicholas: We can pontificate about others — whether it be Richards or Hobbs, Hutton, Gavaskar or Sobers — we can talk about anybody, but the fact is the average of 99.94 is so far ahead of what anybody else achieved. You can talk about the standards of the time, you can do whatever you like, but just imagine playing a season for your school side when you're an international player and trying to get 100 every time.

rewriting the record books. For cricket fans, this meant that when he went out to bat there was *always* the chance they were going to see something that had never been seen before.

Further, Bradman — through the huge threat to opponents he represented and the runs he scored so rapidly — brought much drama and entertainment to his sport. Whenever he took guard, for the bowling team the game was on the line. Unconventional methods had to be considered. If you didn't get him out immediately, more than likely he'd get a hundred. And win the game.

For those trying to measure his greatness, the statistics are compelling. Bradman's Test batting average, built over 20 years, 1928 to 1948, is 99.94. As at 30 April 2002, next best of those to play 20 Test innings is Graeme Pollock, at 60.97. Four batsmen — Pollock, George Headley, Herbert Sutcliffe and Adam Gilchrist — average between 60 and 61; another 10 average between 55 and 60. Of the 66 batsmen to make more than 10 Test centuries, only Clyde Walcott (15 centuries in 74 innings) and Arthur Morris (12 in 79) played fewer than Bradman's 80 Test innings, yet only Sunil Gavaskar (34 in 214) has scored more hundreds than The Don. Bradman averaged a century every 2.76 Test innings, a double century every 6.67 Test innings. He scored 12 double centuries in Test matches; next best is seven by Wally Hammond, who played 60 more innings. Perhaps most importantly of all, only twice did Bradman score a century in a Test that Australia lost, and these were his first and third Test hundreds.

In Sheffield Shield cricket Bradman's average is an amazing 110.19. He scored 36 centuries and 20 half-centuries in 96 innings, 15 of those 96 being uncompleted. Only Darren Lehmann (37 in 215 innings) has made more Shield hundreds but a whopping 93 Shield batsmen have been dismissed between 50 and 99 more often than Bradman, a telling tale of his appetite and ability.

It is true, as some observers in Australia have noted over the years, that Victor Trumper was a more *stylish* batsman. This could also be said of Hammond, Frank Worrell, Greg Chappell and Barry Richards. And of Brian Lara today. But to suggest that any of these superb players was or is in the same class as Bradman is to suggest that cricket matches are won in the same manner as gymnastics or diving. Batting is about runs, and over his career Bradman averaged substantially more than half as much again per Test innings than any other cricketer in the game's long history. No other sports figure — not even Jordan, Ruth or Ali — has ever been that far ahead of the rest of the field.

LIKE WG GRACE, BRADMAN practised relentlessly as a child. He was born on 27 August 1908 in Cootamundra, in southwest country New South Wales, but his family moved to Bowral, closer to Sydney but still in the bush, in 1910. There, one of cricket's most popular folk stories was played out — that of the young Bradman time and again throwing a golf ball against a bricked-up leg of an old water tank and then time and again hitting it unerringly with a cricket stump. History proved that Bradman had a rare natural gift for batting, and this repetitive drill very effectively honed that talent. As well, the young Don would throw his trusty golf ball at an old fence, and catch and field the rebounds, a practice that helped turn him into one of cricket's finest outfielders.

ARTHUR MORRIS: He could never figure out how someone could get 60 or 70 and not get a hundred. That was his attribute. He was able to concentrate so well, which kept him going and going and going. And, of course, he had all the shots, quick reflexes, and fast footwork, which is so important for a great batsman, particularly someone who scores quickly.

Bradman's father was a senior figure at the local cricket club, which gave young Don an early insight into the spirit of cricket, a chance to observe the most capable players at the club, and the occasional opportunity to field as a substitute or even bat down the order. At the same time, he was proving a somewhat prolific runmaker at Bowral High School, despite often giving away years in age to his opponents. And in early 1921, Don's father took him to a crowded Sydney Cricket Ground for the fifth Ashes Test of the summer. They saw Charlie

The Don at Trent Bridge in 1930, during his first Test century in England. He finished with 131, and went on to total 974 runs in the series. Wally Hammond is fielding in the gully.

Getty Images

ALAN DAVIDSON: One day I wagged school and came down with my uncle from where I lived on the NSW Central Coast. I saw him score 12. It's funny, at the time, the thing that stood out for me was his footwork. He had the supreme footwork of a boxer. Bradman's feet were absolutely magical.

Macartney make a big hundred, and the future champion reputedly said to his father on the long trip home, 'I shall never be happy until I play at that ground.' One can imagine the 12-year-old keenly observing accomplished players and then going back home to rehearse, with stump and golf ball, all that he had seen.

Bradman left school at 14, was playing grade cricket in Sydney at 18 (initially travelling to and fro' Bowral), Shield cricket at 19 and Tests at 20. He came into international cricket as something of a prodigy, having made his name with some big scores in country cricket, a century on his Shield debut, against Clarrie Grimmett in Adelaide, and

The Australian captain walks down the Strand in London in 1938, as always the centre of attention.

two more unbeaten hundreds in his next six first-class matches. Two failures in his debut Test (the first Ashes Test of 1928–29) and he was dropped to 12th man for the second Test, in Sydney, but was brought back for the third encounter of the series, made a hundred, and was never left out again.

At this stage, while many prophets believed he would become one of Australia's finest players, no one could have foreseen that the 'Boy From Bowral' would be regarded, at the time of his death 70 years on, as the most famous and distinguished Australian of them all. He became clearly the best exponent of Australia's national game, doing so without ever besmirching his own name or publicly belittling others (except, of course, bowlers with his bat), confident but never deliberately brash, with a beautiful and devoted wife by his side and usually wearing a cheerful, modest smile. Being from the bush and working class, he played out the dreams of thousands of Australians. At just 173cm, slim but wiry, first impressions suggested perhaps a frailty, but his athleticism in the field and the fours careering from his bat revealed he was a tough and surprisingly powerful competitor. Australians love an underdog who wins through, and Bradman won through time and again. When he made a duck in his final Test innings, when four would have given him a century career batting average, he finally proved he was fallible. It completed the legend.

Like the revered racehorse Phar Lap, Bradman emerged as Australia plunged into the Great Depression. At a time when there were precious few positive certainties in most Australian lives, it seemed as if Phar Lap always won and Don Bradman always made a hundred. In 1932, just as the worst of the crisis seemed over, Phar Lap died in mysterious circumstances in California. Many reckoned it was deliberate poisoning and blamed the Americans; despite strong veterinary evidence clearing them, some still do. Eight months later, Bradman was set upon by bodyline. This time it was the Poms attacking Australia's own, and the result was little short of an imperial crisis.

BRADMAN'S FIRST-CLASS SEASONS before bodyline were dominated by his runs, always scored quickly and bountifully. The first indication that he was a runscorer *par excellence* came in January 1929, when he hit 340 for NSW against Victoria. Twelve months later, against Queensland, he smashed a world record 452 not out in just 415 minutes, after 22 wickets had fallen in the first day and a half of the match for 495 runs, suggesting the wicket wasn't that perfect. Then, on his first Ashes tour, Bradman went on an orgy of rungetting, starting with a double century at Worcester, scoring 1000 runs before the end of May (the first overseas player to do so in an English season), and finishing with an unprecedented 974 runs in the Test series and 2960 first-class runs for the tour. His series aggregate broke the Test record set by Hammond in 1928–29, and made a mockery of critics who had suggested his technique was too unorthodox for English conditions. Bradman still played many of the cross-bat shots he'd learnt on Bowral's matting wickets, and some had theorised that he'd be in trouble trying them on the seaming English wickets. But these knockers had underestimated Bradman's extraordinary eye, his quick feet and perfect balance, and also his remarkable cricket intelligence, which gave him the ability to unerringly select the right shot for every ball.

Bradman's scores in the 1930 Ashes series were 8 and 131, 254 and 1, 334, 14, and 232. The 334 at Leeds was a Test record, and featured 309 made on the first day, still the only instance of a Test batsman making three hundreds in a single day. If one thing emphasised his impact it was that famous newspaper poster: 'He's Out!' Everyone knew who 'He' was; the fact he'd been dismissed was so unexpected, so astonishing, that the public needed to know at once.

When the new hero arrived back on Australian soil after the tour, he jumped off the ship in Perth and set off on a heavily sponsored 'welcome home' adventure that had him, thanks to trains and the wonders of air travel, arriving in Adelaide, Melbourne and Sydney before his naturally aggrieved team mates. When the rest of the party finally arrived in Adelaide, vice-captain Vic Richardson reflected their feelings when he quickly told reporters that the only truly indispensable member of the team was Grimmett, who'd taken 29 wickets in the series.

Relations between Bradman and his colleagues had already been strained by a number of episodes that led to some concluding that he played chiefly for himself. Adding to this conflict was the sectarianism rife in Australian life at the time, which sometimes left Bradman, a Protestant, at

Bradman, later a scratch golfer, takes to the fairways during the '38 Ashes tour.

odds with a few of his Catholic team mates. Chief among the unhappy moments came at Leeds, when he received a gift of £1000 after making his 334 but refused to put any of it on the bar. Instead he spent the evening in his room listening to the gramophone. The next day, it should be emphasised for the sake of his upset colleagues, was the rest day.

Bradman argued that he was only being himself. He wasn't a fellow who ever spent much time sharing stories over a pint or a schooner. An English paper reinforced this point when it wrote during the tour: 'Don Bradman is the most elusive man of all, preferring to write letters in his room or get away to a show. He also has a habit of going off sightseeing alone, or with only one companion.'

DICKIE BIRD: The story goes that when he used to play at Headingley at Leeds, that a lot of people from Barnsley — what, 30 miles away from Headingley — used to walk it to watch Bradman bat. That's the great attraction he was.

There is no doubt, though, that the Bradman of the early 1930s was a young man of contradictions, and this sometimes put him offside with confused friends and foe. When he made his big scores he did so with a buoyant grin, which annoyed beleaguered rivals, who assumed, wrongly, that he was cocky. He was simply enjoying himself and never thought to suppress that joy. Off the field, Bradman was a private man, but countering that was his conviction that he should try to make as much money out of his phenomenal ability and popularity while he could. The Depression showed him the devastating impact of poverty, and while he might not have yearned for exorbitant wealth he certainly wanted comfort and security. If that meant putting his face in the public eye then he did so, but only for a price. A hefty part of that price was having some of his comrades tagging him as greedy.

'To the last ounce, he knew his value, not only as a cricketer but as a man,' commented Ben Bennison, who helped Bradman with *Don Bradman's Book* in 1930. When the Board of Control fined him £50 after extracts from the book were serialised in a manner contrary to that allowed in his tour contract, Bradman was appalled. In 1931, he was offered the then considerable amount of £1000 a season to join the Lancashire League club Accrington, and thought seriously about going, despite the fact that it would have meant the end of his Test career. His decision to decline the offer only came about after Sydney business interests cobbled together a two-year package that at least matched the Accrington offer. That deal included writing and broadcasting opportunities with the Sydney media, plus appearances for a local sports retailer, and gave him the security he craved. For Bradman, the only negative was that everything revolved around cricket; soon to be married and looking long term,

he wanted a career outside the game, a desire that led to him moving to Adelaide in 1935 to begin life as a stockbroker.

BODYLINE WAS CREATED TO counter Bradman, and there is no doubt that it did bring him back to the field. This said, it should be stated that, despite the English faster men aiming endless bumpers at the Australian batsmen and specifically him, with a platoon of close-up catchers on the legside in support, he remained atop the batting averages. But he averaged only 56.57 runs per innings for the series. In England in 1930, he'd averaged 139.14; against South Africa at home in 1931–32, the return was 806 runs at 201.50.

The fierce English assault on him spawned perhaps his most dramatic hundred, an unbeaten 103 in the second Test at the MCG during Australia's only victory of the series. He had missed the first Test, after three doctors nominated by the Board of Control ruled him to be 'rundown'. This was a peculiar affair, because Bradman had signed that deal to write and broadcast on the Tests, but the Board was adamant that only *full-time* journalists (such as the opening bat Jack Fingleton) could write and play. Bradman said journalism was his career, the Board said it was not, so the impasse remained. There is no question that the people's hero had been 'off colour'(his own words), but it was also true that he learnt he was out of the first Test not from Board officials but from Claude Corbett, a journalist with the Sydney *Sun*. Up until then, Bradman had seemed willing to play — if officials would let him. Was the Board, knowing how public opinion would turn if they barred him, buying itself some time? In fact, the dispute was not settled until the day before the second Test, when Bradman reluctantly accepted Associated Newspapers' offer to release him from his writing contract. In one last bitter swipe, he released a statement condemning the Board for its intransigence, and then went out in the first innings in Melbourne and was bowled, first ball, after aiming a wild pull at a Bowes bouncer and dragging the ball onto his stumps. The silence as he walked off was stark. Fingleton, who was at the non-striker's end, later called it 'an unbelievable hush of calamity'.

In the second innings, after again being cheered all the way to the centre, Bradman was as purposeful as he had ever been. He worked his way to a century

---

ALAN DAVIDSON: He showed me a bat he had in his den downstairs in his home in Adelaide. It was the bat he got 254 against England, which he always reckoned was his greatest innings.

He said that during that innings he hit every ball in the middle of that bat. And, honest to goodness, there was a dent in the middle of the bat. You couldn't believe that a bat could have a hole in the centre of it from making that constant contact in exactly the right place.

ARTHUR MORRIS: I remember in the fifth Test at The Oval in 1948, when we got England out for 52, Denis Compton came out to bat. Bradman said I was to field just slightly fine of the square-leg umpire, he moved me about five metres. And Ray Lindwall bowled Denis a bouncer and he hooked it and I caught it. I went up to Don and said, 'Why did you move me?' And he said, 'I remember in 1938 Ernie McCormick bowled him some bouncers and Denis used to hook down that particular line.'

from 146 balls — staid by his standards — the final runs coming to wild acclaim with the No. 11 Bert Ironmonger at the other end. Jack Hobbs, on the tour as a newspaper correspondent, wrote of this innings, 'Instead of playing ordinary defensive back shots, as most first-class batsmen would, Bradman, by quick footwork, retreated slightly and either placed the ball hard past the bowler, or, when it pitched outside the off-stump, cut it brilliantly.'

Hobbs' words offer an indication of Bradman's unique response to the bodyline assault. Australian skipper Bill Woodfull had asked his batsmen to stand in line, but Bradman decided to step away from the short stuff and try to force it through the vacant offside field. This worked in Melbourne, where the pitch was relatively slow, but was less successful elsewhere. Critics within and outside the team were angry that he had gone against the captain's orders, and deplored what looked like a retreat. Others thought the strategy an innovative 'least-worst' solution. Wally Hammond, who was part of that legside field throughout, wrote afterwards that 'those who said that Bradman was afraid of bodyline don't know cricket as it was played on that tour'.

What is beyond question is that Bradman's cricket soul was irreversibly hardened by his bodyline experience. When he hammered into his young Australian team after World War II that Test cricket was a game in which you give your opponents nothing, some — most notably Keith Miller — felt he was being too tough, too unbending. But they had never faced bodyline.

In England in 1934, an ill Bradman struggled in the first three Tests, the worst run of his career, before scores of 304 and 244 in the final two Tests helped Australia win back the Ashes. Before the team left England, Bradman was felled by an attack of acute appendicitis and then peritonitis that almost claimed his life. As writers prepared obituaries and rumours were about that he had indeed perished, his wife Jessie (whom he'd married

in April 1932) set sail for England, arriving three days after he was released from hospital. Such was the need for a full convalescence, it was more than two years before he returned to Test cricket.

When he did, he was a resident of Adelaide, delighted to be learning the stockbroking business, and the Australian captain. Unfortunately, his reign began with a stutter, as he lost his first two Tests. However, the Australians fought back to win the next three — Bradman leading the way with 270, 212 and 169 — and the Ashes were retained.

His leadership in the third Test, when he shrewdly outmanoeuvred England captain Gubby Allen to gain advantage from a wet wicket,

Getty Images

Footwork as perfect as ever, Bradman hits through the offside during the 'Invincibles' tour of England in 1948. Godfrey Evans is the wicketkeeper.

Getty Images

Bradman looks back after being bowled second ball for a duck in what proved to be his final innings in Test cricket.

established his reputation as a strategist. Off the field, four Catholics in the team — Bill O'Reilly, Stan McCabe, Leo O'Brien and 'Chuck' Fleetwood-Smith — were summoned by the Board of Control to respond to suggestions that some players weren't supporting their new leader. Fingleton, another Catholic whom Bradman years later described as 'the ringleader', was not invited, perhaps because he was a journalist. Bradman had no knowledge of the meeting, which was instigated by the Board in response to rumours and press speculation that the team was split, but the four players could hardly have believed that and were bitter that their captain did not attend. Bradman's relationship with O'Reilly never recovered, while Fingleton carried an anti-Bradman obsession for the rest of his life that marred his otherwise excellent cricket commentaries. Whether Bradman was ever spurred by sectarian prejudice is not known, but there is no doubt that at times as captain before the War he was gravely disappointed by the lack of support he received from some of his men.

Having scored three hundreds in the final three Tests in 1936–37, Bradman scored three more in the first three Ashes Tests of 1938. At The Oval, when England scored 7–903 (declared), Hammond did not declare until Bradman badly damaged an ankle while having a rare spell at the bowling crease. Without their captain, Australia crashed to the heaviest defeat of its cricketing life.

DURING THE WAR, BRADMAN enlisted with the RAAF but was invalided out within a year. One of the myths of Bradman's life is that the War years cost him many hundreds — in fact, such was his ill-health through this period that he would hardly have played. If anything, the War prolonged his career, because between 1946 and 1948 he played in 15 more Tests, all as captain, as Australia enjoyed three of its most profitable years. This golden age culminated in the tour of the 'Invincibles' to England in 1948, when for the first time an Australian team went through an Ashes

SACHIN TENDULKAR: Meeting Sir Donald was the most thrilling moment of my life. I remember Shane Warne and I were driving down to Sir Don's house, we were excited, but we didn't know what to say. So we both decided, OK, we'll just go and stand next to him and listen to what he has to say.

I was so glad to hear that he followed most the games. He thought the standard of fielding was much better, the general standard was much better. When we asked him in today's era, what would you have averaged, he said, 'Round about 70.'

I said, 'Why Sir Don, why do you think 70?'

He said, 'I'm 90 today and that's not bad for a 90-year-old man.'

tour without losing a game. The Tests series was won 4–0, with Bradman scoring two centuries, the second a brilliant 173 not out as Australia became the first team to ever score 400 in the fourth innings to win a Test.

He chose to resume his career because, in his own words, 'Cricket badly needed a good start in the post-war era, and I was anxious to assist in that direction if it lay within my compass.' He was a different batsman to that of the '30s, less exuberant yet perhaps even more sure. Like Grace and Hobbs, he was — technically at least — at his best in his latter years, because he understood batting and what he was about. Again like Grace and Hobbs, despite his advancing years and reduced flexibility, his balance at the crease, ability to pick the right length early, skill and placement were such that he still scored quickly and with certainty.

England's Alec Bedser, who bowled at Bradman from 1946 to 1948, summed the older Don up this way: 'He was always looking to score. He didn't necessarily hit the ball for four every time you bowled, but he would push it for twos and threes, run every run quickly. He always tried to dominate when he was batting, which he did, of course.'

Almost to a man, the cricketers of Bradman's post-war teams spoke highly of him as a captain and mentor. Take these examples …

Neil Harvey: 'Bradman was a far less emotional leader than Richie Benaud; he rarely proffered advice to his players and stayed more aloof from the team than has been Benaud's policy … But make no mistake, Bradman was a great leader. He directed his side on the field with great strategy and understanding.'

Colin McCool: 'I liked the bloke. As far as I was concerned, he was fair, just and very human. In fact, the more I remember Bradman the more I remember his warmth and understanding.'

Ray Lindwall: 'From my earliest days as a devoted Bradman fan on the St George ground he had remained a hero to me, but from the first time I met him as a cricketer he treated me exactly as an equal. I never heard him say a word of criticism about anyone else in the game, player or official, and I never heard him complain about an umpire's decision. His knowledge of the game could not have been surpassed …'

In contrast, for Fingleton and O'Reilly — both working as journalists during the '48 Test series — the pre-war enmity still burned. When Bradman walked out to the middle for what was to be his farewell Test innings he was accompanied by a sustained standing ovation, after which the England captain led the England team and the Oval crowd in singing *For He's A Jolly Good Fellow*, followed by three cheers for Don Bradman. 'I was up the other end,' remembers Arthur Morris. 'Eric Hollies bowled him a beautiful leg spinner. Then he bowled him the wrong 'un in about the same spot and Don played forward, he might have got the tiniest bit of an edge, but it was well delivered and it hit the off-stump.' In the pressbox, Fingleton and O'Reilly couldn't contain themselves. 'I thought they were going to have a stroke,' the veteran English writer EW Swanton was quoted in Charles Williams' outstanding 1996 biography, *Bradman*, 'they were laughing so much.'

'With these fellows out of the way,' Bradman wrote in a letter to Williams in 1995, 'the loyalty of my 1948

SIR RICHARD HADLEE: I have never forgotten the words of Bradman, when he said that everyone is a 'custodian of the game'. It is up to each player, it is up to the media, it is up to the administrators, to perceive the traditions, the values, the heritage of the game and play it in its fair spirit. Be competitive, go out there to win, of course, but do it the right way.

side was a big joy and made a big contribution to the outstanding success of that tour.'

Of that dismissal, one of the most famous ducks in Test history, Bradman commented in 1996, 'I'm very sorry I got that duck. Some people said I got out because I had tears in my eyes, and that's rubbish. Obviously I was very emotionally concerned, but I wasn't that bad. I think I used the expression, "Well, fancy doing that." And that's all there was to it.'

DON BRADMAN BECAME SIR Donald Bradman on 1 January 1949, the only Australian to be knighted for his services to cricket. However, his contribution to the game was hardly over. First appointed a selector in 1936, he stayed in the job, bar for two brief interruptions, until 1971. A long-time South Australian delegate to the Board of Control, in 1960 he became the first former Test player to be appointed chairman. He was a pivotal figure in the resolution of the chucking controversies of the late 1950s and early 1960s and in the abandonment of the 1971–72 South African tour of Australia, and had a strong influence on the Board's strategies during the World Series Cricket split of 1977–79. In most cases, he appeared to handle crises and routine matters with a shrewdness and commonsense that made him arguably cricket's best ever administrator.

He seemed to have an uncanny sense about what was good for the game. His influence in 1960–61, for example, encouraging the Australian and West Indies captains, Richie Benaud and Frank Worrell, to have their teams play aggressive, entertaining cricket, was a critical factor in how that most famous of series panned out. However, some cricketers of the 1970s found him intractable when it came to the question of increased player payments, which was ironic given his feelings in the early 1930s about top cricketers being paid what they were worth.

As he gradually removed himself from the official cricket stage, he remained a clear thinker on the game, refusing — unlike some of his contemporaries — to pine for the good old days. He lauded the wonderful abilities of modern champions such as Wasim Akram, Shane Warne and Sachin Tendulkar, recognised the value of one-day cricket, but bemoaned negative practices such as sledging and match-fixing. He craved privacy, yet his fame and legend continued to grow. Grandstands were named after him in Sydney and Adelaide, a Museum was built in his honour at Bowral, a Bradman memorabilia industry exploded in the 1990s, prime ministers sought private audiences, biographies of varying qualities all sold exceedingly well, the number of letters arriving each day grew and grew. Still, he tried to answer personally as many as he could. When Bradman was interviewed on television in Australia in 1996, the ratings were extraordinary.

News of his death in February 2001, aged 92, was received with enormous sadness across the cricket world, especially in India, where he never played but was revered for what he meant to the game. The pride Indians felt when Bradman had compared his batting style to that of India's modern hero, Tendulkar, was immense. In Australia, newspapers were filled with Bradman tributes and memories for many days.

At his private funeral in Adelaide, people lined the streets to quietly watch the cortège go past. Everywhere, Bradman was seen as the embodiment of all that was good about the game and his country. In his tribute, Richie Benaud described the late Sir Donald as 'probably the most important Australian of all time', while the much-respected Australian Governor-General Sir William Deane said, 'His wonderful qualities as a man, combined with his pre-eminence as a cricketer, make him the most admired Australian of our times.' In South Africa, Nelson Mandela commented, 'In the 1930s we regarded Sir Donald Bradman as one of the divinities, so great was his impact on cricket.'

As a sportsperson, Don Bradman was a unique combination of supreme dedication, desire, physical prowess for his chosen endeavour, natural talent, efficiency, positive thinking, common sense, a bit of stubbornness and, perhaps most important of all, total concentration. This all sounds a lot, but you need a lot to explain his total dominance. If you go right though his cricket career, inning by innings, it is very rare to find an instance where he threw his innings away, rarer still to find a suggestion that he 'lost concentration'. It just didn't happen. When asked in that 1996 interview why his records have remained unchallenged, initially Bradman struggled for an answer, before remarking: 'I saw much better batsmen than I was, lots of them …

'They just kept getting out.'

SIR GARFIELD SOBERS

Legend No. 2

Five Great Cricketers in One

SOME VERY NOTABLE CRICKET people are prepared to argue that while there is no doubt that Don Bradman was the game's greatest batsman, he wasn't cricket's No. 1 legend; that in terms of who was most likely to win you a game, Garry Sobers was superior. Certainly, Sobers was more than an all-rounder, more the ultimate all-round cricketer who was good enough to average over 57 with the bat, win Test matches whether bowling left-arm fast medium, finger spin or wrist spin, and a fieldsman of the highest quality in any position. If Bradman's supreme quality was that he was all but guaranteed to score more runs than anyone else, Sobers' unique appeal was that he was going to have an influence on any game he was involved in at some stage, in some way. Despite losing his father when aged five, thus having to go out to work when 13, he still found time to excel at soccer, basketball, water polo and tennis. And, best of all, at cricket. Later, his golf handicap would all but disappear. He did this without coaches, just keen observation and abundant natural talent. Had he been born in NewYork, he would have been a baseball pitcher, a slugger, or a wizard shortstop. Or, more likely, all three.

SUNIL GAVASKAR: Without doubt, Sir Garfield Sobers was the greatest cricketer I have seen. He was a genius. He could do everything. He could bat, he could bowl, he could field. And when bowling he could bowl spin, he could bowl quick, he could bowl swing, he could bowl back-of-the-hand Chinaman stuff. I dare say that if he was asked to keep wickets he would have done a very good job with that as well.

Surprisingly, although Sobers was something of a boy wonder, gifted enough to be playing in the Test arena against England in 1954 before his 18th birthday, he was hardly an overnight sensation once he got there. Whereas Sachin Tendulkar, for example, would make five Test hundreds in 25 Tests as a teenager, Sobers averaged 29.33 with the bat in nine Tests, with a highest score of 64, his only half-century. By the end of his first tour of England, in 1957, by which time he was 21 years old, his Test

Sobers at The Oval in 1957, standing firm against England while his more experienced teammates falter.

batting average had climbed to 30.55, with no hundreds and three fifties. His bowling average was in excess of 40 runs per wicket, a little better than one wicket per Test.

The first signs of Sobers' genius at the highest level came in the final Test of that England series, at The Oval. There, the West Indies were swept aside by the famous spin pair, Jim Laker and Tony Lock, on a pitch Everton Weekes described as a 'beach', being bowled out for 89 and 86 after the home team had made 412 (Sobers: 44-6-111-1). In the Windies' two disastrous replies, Sobers, batting No. 3, made 39 and 42. None of his comrades reached 30 in either innings.

To this point in his career, Sobers had constantly frustrated his admirers by getting out after making a start; he reached double figures 18 times in his first 22 completed Test innings without ever going past 66. However, in The Oval dressing room after that final Test of 1957, an old Englishman walked up to him and said quietly, 'Well played, son. It needed something special to bat the way you did on that pitch. You will go from strength to strength, I am sure of it.'

That man was Frank Woolley, the 'pride of Kent', one of cricket's all-time great left-handers.

Another Frank, Frank Worrell, saw Sobers as something of a protégé. In fact, through the Sobers story much is revealed of the influence of the most distinguished of West Indies cricket statesmen. Like Worrell, Sobers was born in Barbados, but whereas Worrell was so dismayed by the race and class prejudices on the little island that he felt obliged to move to Jamaica in his early twenties, Sobers remains a Barbadian. Politics were never for him; he was a cricketer.

Of his relationship with Worrell, Sobers wrote in 1966: 'Frank helped shape my career. He helped a lot on my first tour in England [1957] and, afterwards, when I followed him as a professional for Radcliffe in the Central Lancashire League, we lived near each other. I spent most of my time with him then, and we became very close friends. He encouraged me when I was low, advised me when I was bewildered, blasted me when he felt I was getting a bit too big for my cricket boots. Always he was there, with a well-timed word, when I needed him.'

In the three years after that 1957 England tour, Sobers set off on a Bradman-like runscoring explosion. In 24 Tests, he scored 2250 runs at an average of 93.75. Included in this sequence was Test cricket's then highest score — 365 not out — made in Kingston in early 1958 against Pakistan during a series in which he smashed 824 runs in five Tests. In a run of 10 innings, against Pakistan and India, he made six centuries. Against England at home in 1959–60, he hit three more, while scoring 709 runs in five Tests. Yet Sobers arrived in Australia in October 1960, with his life, and hence his cricket, in turmoil, and would need all of the great influence of Worrell to give him back a genuine sense of purpose.

Sobers' mindset, indeed his life, had been shattered a bit more than 12 months earlier when a car he was driving was involved in a collision in the north of England. Also in the car were Collie Smith and Tom Dewdney, two West Indies Test players who, like Sobers, were playing in the Lancashire leagues. Smith, Sobers' closest friend in cricket, broke his back in the accident, and died three days later in hospital, leaving Sobers, who could remember little of the actual crash but was later fined £10 for driving without due care, abjectly guilt-ridden. He began drinking heavily; every day were to be lived as if it was his last. Though he made all those runs against England in 1959–60, months after the tragedy, his mind kept spinning. The 1960–61 Australian tour was crucial. Worrell knew it and Sobers probably knew it too …

Sobers played one or two majestic innings, chief among them his famous 132 in Brisbane on the first day of what became cricket's first Tied Test. 'That 100 he scored in the Tied Test is easily the best Test hundred I have ever seen,' says Alan Davidson, 'because he didn't just beat the field, he bisected the field. He just played some of the most incredible shots. And his timing! When Garry was going, basically there was nothing you could do about it.'

However, as the series went on, Sobers also frustrated his fans by sometimes attempting shots that were overly ambitious at best, irresponsible at worst. In his book of the 1960–61 tour, AG Moyes wrote of Sobers: 'So often he touched greatness shared by few of the present generation. His finest innings bore comparison with anything we have seen for many years and yet somehow he did not inspire the same confidence as [Rohan] Kanhai, who reached Australia with a lesser reputation but increased it immeasurably by so many grand innings. The truth was that Sobers had not matured and he failed far too often for one of his quality …'

True this was, but there is no doubt that Sobers learnt plenty about his game, and how best to consistently make runs, during this tour, lessons he would apply in the seasons that followed. Away from the batting crease, Moyes called Sobers' fielding 'simply magnificent', while his bowling was 'more than useful', especially his spinners. This description of his bowling reflected the fact that at this point in his career, Sobers was not a prolific wicket-taker. In the '60–61 series he took 15 wickets, his main asset being his versatility, which allowed Worrell to play an extra batsman in the final three Tests. He had taken four wickets in the first Test innings he ever bowled in, back in March 1954, but by the end of the series in Australia he had only 55 Test wickets, at an average of more than 43. By the end of his Test career he would get that average down to 34, mostly through his faster stuff.

As well as providing some important cricket lessons, the Australian tour gave West Indian cricket, and Sobers personally, a greater sense of worth. For a man still struggling with the memory of that tragic car crash, the significance of the respect and acclaim he received cannot be underrated. 'It was, in every respect, an experience which had a tremendous effect on my cricket and my life generally,' Sobers wrote of the tour in 1984. The team's faith in Worrell was total, and they believed, with much justification, that they were unlucky to lose the series. With luck, they could have won 4–1, rather than lose 1–2. Still, they revelled in the celebrity status their play earned them — at tour's end, the Melbourne public gave them a ticker-tape farewell — and Sobers was flattered and excited to receive an invitation from Sir Donald Bradman to return to Australia in 1961–62 to play Sheffield Shield cricket for South Australia.

For the next decade, Sobers was clearly the dominant all-round cricketer in the game. In his first season in the Shield, South Australia had their best season in 10 years, with their star import topping the batting and bowling averages. At home against India, he dominated a five-Test series,

ALAN DAVIDSON: I could name a hundred shots that he played off me that were incredible. I bowled a slower ball to him in the Tied Test in Brisbane and he creamed it. Colin McDonald was in the covers and it hit him in the shins before he started to bend and still hit the fence and bounced back 10 yards. It was fortunate it didn't hit Colin flush on the leg or he wouldn't have played again that season.

DICKIE BIRD: If there has been one better I would have loved to have seen him play. He had this great gift. Not only was Sobers the greatest all-round cricketer that has ever lived, I think that he is the greatest athlete that has ever lived.

scoring 424 runs (including two centuries), and taking 23 wickets (including his first five-for) and 11 catches. And so it continued for the next decade, as he justified time and again the tag Bradman had given him — the 'five-in-one cricketer'.

The Batsman

The finest Sobers innings Bradman ever saw was the 254 made for a Rest of the World XI against Australia at the MCG in the first week of January, 1972. Indeed, The Don described it as 'the greatest exhibition of batting ever seen in Australia'. This opinion put Sobers knock ahead of the best of Trumper, Macartney, Jackson, McCabe, Miller and,

of course, Bradman, but rather than bringing the cynics out in droves, for the most part the praise was echoed across the country. Sobers had struggled in Melbourne in the past, and this time he was up against a young tearaway called Dennis Lillee, who had taken 8–29 in the previous encounter between the two teams and dismissed Sobers first ball in the first innings of this match.

Lillee was fired up by a bouncer Sobers had bowled at him, but when he charged in seeking revenge in the World XI's second innings, the great West Indian hooked him, second ball, for four. Instantly, the game was transformed. 'In almost every over before Garry's arrival, Lillee had looked like taking a wicket,' wrote Ray Robinson in *The Cricketer*. '[Now] cuts began scudding past point so rapidly that a third-man posted almost square on the wide boundary could not intercept them.'

When Lillee took the second new ball, Sobers immediately drove him straight, rocket quick, for four. Twenty-nine runs came from the quick's first three overs with that new ball, Sobers raced to his

The famous finish to cricket's first Tied Test. Sobers is at the far end, next to a leaping Rohan Kanhai, as Australia's Ian Meckiff is run out by more than a metre. Closest to camera, West Indies captain Frank Worrell is the calmest man on the field.

Getty Images

century from 129 balls, and then, after a rest day, continued on to 254 from 326 balls. 'Some of the shots he played off Dennis Lillee in that game were just unbelievable, especially the straight drives,' says Alan Davidson. 'Dennis hadn't even got through his follow-through and it went back past him.'

'It was a tremendous innings, just poetry in motion,' remembers Clive Lloyd. 'This guy was something else. I'm not too sure if we will see someone like him again. I hope we do, but that would be some player.'

Style-wise, Sobers was the Tiger Woods of batting — a fearless, aggressive, powerful hitter whose game was built upon a textbook technique. There was no slogger in Sobers, just as there is no wildness in Tiger's game, yet Sir Garry gained and Tiger gains great advantage from hitting the ball harder and further than others. In describing Sobers' batting, Bradman talked of his 'high backlift and free swing' and his 'strong, steely wrists'. Davidson says he had 'the fastest hands, the best hands I have ever seen on a batsman'.

When Sobers famously hit Glamorgan's Malcolm Nash for six sixes in one six-ball over while playing for Nottinghamshire in 1968, he did so without even once resorting to a slog. The first four went over various parts of the legside boundary, from just wide of straight hit to square-leg, and the fifth was semi-mishit, but still had enough muscle to clear the rope at long-off. Amid great excitement, with almost all the fieldsmen out on the boundary, Nash fired the sixth in at middle and leg and Sobers smashed it clean out of the ground. Someone found the ball far away, rolling down the street, and it was returned to the ground the following day.

The Bowler

It would be wrong to suggest that Sobers was a phenomenal Test bowler, in the manner of a

Sobers at The Oval in 1966. At the time he was probably the best batsman in the game, one of the best spinners (finger and wrist spin), an effective fast-medium bowler, the best all-round fieldsman, and captain of the No. 1 Test team in the world.

Marshall, a Hadlee, a Warne or a Wasim Akram. His uniqueness lay in his versatility — no other bowler in Test history has been so proficient in three contrasting forms of attack — and the fact he was doing this while scoring mountains of runs as well.

One spell of a year and a half proves the point. In Brisbane in November 1968, against Australia at the Gabba, Sobers spun the West Indies to victory by taking 6–73, bowling orthodox front-of-the-hand

IAN CHAPPELL: I had the very good fortune to bat with Garry a few times when he was playing for South Australia. In the first innings of a match against NSW I scored my first first-class 100, against Richie Benaud and Johnny Martin, but by the time I came out in the second innings the pitch was really turning. This was the first time I'd ever faced a leg-spinner coming around the wicket and bowling into the footmarks.

I was batting at No. 7 for South Australia in those days, and we needed about 40 or 50 to win outright. And where I felt that I'd handled Richie Benaud reasonably well in the first innings, suddenly facing this ball spinning out of the rough, I didn't know what had hit me. Anyhow, I managed to survive the over, at the end of which Sobers came down to me and said, 'Don't worry, son, we'll fix this in a hurry.' And he went down to the other end, and hit four fours off Johnny Martin's next over. Then he got the strike and banged a couple of fours off Richie. He was dead right. The game was over in a *big* hurry.

Getty Images

Sobers bowls at Arundel in 1966, at the start of what proved to be his greatest tour.

wrote the former England all-rounder Trevor Bailey of Sobers' quick bowling action, 'classically perfect, head looking over the outside of a high right arm, left arm completing a full arc before chasing the right across his body in a full follow-through'.

Inevitably, his bowling suffered to a degree because his batting was so important. And, because he was a support bowler to Hall and Charlie Griffith in the pace department and Lance Gibbs with spin during the Windies' great days in the 1960s, he rarely bowled downwind with his quicks or into the breeze with his slows. And later, after Hall and Griffith faded from the scene and the team's overall bowling power was diminished, Sobers was obliged to bowl long, defensive spells. Despite all this, he finished with 235 Test wickets, which at the time of his final Test, in 1974, ranked him seventh all time, and the leading left-hander.

One occasion that tells plenty about Sobers' bowling gifts occurred during the 1963 series in England, a thrilling five-Test rubber in which he was clearly the pre-eminent all-round player, scoring 322 runs and taking 20 wickets. In doing so, he became the second man, after Keith Miller, to do the 300 runs/20 wickets double in a series twice (three years later, again in England, he would become the first — and to 2002 only — player to achieve this feat three times). In the fourth Test, at Headingley, while Hall was warming up to bowl the opening ball of England's second innings, Sobers walked up to Worrell and said, 'I've got a hunch I can get Micky Stewart out.'

Stewart was preparing to face the first ball. Worrell didn't blink. 'Okay,' he said, 'you can have the first over.'

What Wes Hall thought of this is not recorded. The fact that Sobers knocked over Stewart's stumps immediately most certainly is.

The Fieldsman

Like so many of the truly great players, Sobers was an extraordinarily gifted fieldsman, capable of blinding catches in the slips, in close and the outfield and with a brilliant throwing arm. In the exciting fourth Test

spinners. In 1970, at Lord's, captaining a Rest of the World XI against England, he took 6–21 on the opening day, swinging and seaming the ball at pace. Not done yet, he scored 183, and then helped his team to victory bowling back-of-the-hand wrist spin.

Sobers came into Test cricket as a spinner, but became most feared as a bowler when he came off his paceman's run, a skill he had developed at Radcliffe, and progressed further when playing for South Australia. Once he recognised he could fill a void in Worrell's Test team as a regular first-change bowler, he quickly absorbed the subtleties of swing and seam, while retaining the ability to fire down the odd ball as rapid as anything the side's classic fast spearhead, Wes Hall. 'His speed derived from a beautiful body action,'

ROGER HARPER: Garry Sobers was the man. In the '60s, when I was born, and early '70s everybody aspired to be a Garry Sobers, because he was always involved. He was the main batsman, he was a quality bowler and a high-class fieldsman. He was the man who really inspired me.

of 1968–69 in Australia, at the Adelaide Oval, Aussie keeper Barry Jarman was run out by Sobers in exhilarating style. The home team was 6–322, chasing 360, when Paul Sheahan called Jarman for a sharp single to Sobers, fielding about 15 metres from the bat in the gully, on an angle of 45 degrees behind the wicket. Jarman was running to the far end, the bowler's end, as Sobers dashed four paces to his left, gathered the ball, steadied and threw …

'I was about three yards short,' Jarman said ruefully afterwards, 'when the stumps exploded.'

Perhaps his most famous fielding exploit in England came in the first Test of 1966, when he caught the English opener Eric Russell off the bowling of Lance Gibbs. EW Swanton described the dismissal this way: 'Then Russell fell, likewise to Gibbs, thanks to a superb piece of anticipation by Sobers, who crept almost up to Russell's hip-pocket, as he saw Gibbs' slower one in the air, and picked the ball virtually off the bat.'

'Lance Gibbs, of course, was a great off-spin bowler,' says Tony Cozier, 'and Sobers fielding around the corner to him was absolutely magnificent, snapping up balls that were a couple of inches off the ground. Gibbs would say that Sobers anticipation in that short-leg position was something incredible, that as the batsman was playing the shot, Sobers knew exactly where the ball was going to go …'

Another classic catch — the one Sobers says 'pleased me most' — came at a critical time on the last day of the Tied Test at the Gabba. Australia were chasing 233 for victory, but collapsed to 5–57, with a key wicket being Australia's best batsman, Neil Harvey, caught at second slip by Sobers, who had to dive sideways *and* forward to make the grab. Many great slip fieldsmen in cricket history have gone sideways to take spectacular catches, but very, very few could go forward, especially when fielding to a bowler of Hall's lightning speed. In the process Sobers dislocated a finger, but no problem, Gerry Alexander, the West Indies keeper and a trained veterinarian, pushed and pulled the angry joint back into place and Sobers stayed on the field for the remainder of that memorable day.

The Six-in-One Cricketer

As we have said, Sir Donald Bradman called him the five-in-one cricketer (batsman, fieldsman and three-in-one bowler), but in England in 1966

> **CLIVE LLOYD:** Once we played at Sabina Park when the cracks in the pitch were about an inch-and-a-half or two inches wide. I top-scored in the first innings with 34 not out and I thought I played extremely well. The cracks got much bigger in the second innings and Garry made 113 not out and turned the Test on its head. Everyone else was looking for the ball to do something, but he came out and smacked it around.

Sobers was even better. He led the West Indies superbly to a 3–1 series victory, scored 722 runs including three centuries, a 94 and an 81, at an average of 103.14, took 20 wickets and 11 catches, and won all five tosses! At Lord's he hit 163 not out in the West Indies second innings, after he and his cousin, David Holford (105 not out in his second Test), came together with their side effectively 5–9 and added an unbeaten 274. Sobers always rated this his greatest Test innings, because of the state of the game, the fact he had to guide his inexperienced partner and because he prevailed in a tactical battle with his opposing number, Colin Cowdrey. At first, the England captain crowded both batsmen, and Sobers counter-attacked. Cowdrey then chose to defend against Sobers and attack Holford, so Sobers kept attacking, but also took the easy singles, making no attempt to monopolise the strike. Holford's confidence grew, and in the end he was batting as vibrantly as his much more illustrious relative.

Tony Cozier tells of a mid-pitch exchange between the cousins: 'First couple of deliveries, Sobers could see that Holford was a bit nervous, and he came down the pitch and said, "Look, this is just like Spartan (which is a club team back home), the bowling is no better than the club bowlers we have at home. Look at the conditions, look at the pitch, just play as if you are playing club cricket at home."

'And that relaxed Holford right away. This is the way Sobers played cricket — Test cricket, club cricket, division-one cricket, first-class cricket — it didn't matter to him. He played it as if it was just a game. He was so relaxed, had no nerves whatever.'

At Headingley, Sobers hit 174, including 103 between lunch and tea on the second day, and then — bowling fast and slow — took 5–41 and 3–39 as the Windies won by an innings and 55 runs. Away from the Tests, he took 9–49 in a tour match against Kent. Throughout the series, he marshalled his men with verve and still had time to lecture sections of the English press about their treatment of Griffith, who some observers had labelled a chucker.

AS THINGS TURNED OUT, that series was the highpoint of Sobers' captaincy career. Soon after, the West Indies won decisively in India, but in March 1967 came the ghastly news that Worrell had died from leukaemia. In early 1968, England won a controversial series in the Caribbean, after a reckless declaration by Sobers in the fourth Test handed them victory. The first three Tests had been drawn, as it became increasingly obvious that the once-feared Windies pace attack had lost its spark, and in the fourth, for which Hall had been dropped, the visitors were asked to score 215 runs in 165 minutes, which turned out to be 53 overs. Sobers was heavily criticised for his charity, and responded in the fifth Test with another stirring all-round performance, scoring 152 and 95 not out and taking 3–72 and 3–53 from 68 overs. But England held out by one wicket to draw the Test and take the series.

The West Indies never won another series under Sobers' captaincy, and from this point on his career — which still had another six years to run — was marked by controversy and criticism. In Australia in 1968–69, a tour that followed his first season of county cricket with Nottinghamshire, he often travelled apart from the team and was seen more often on the golf course than at fielding practice, at

The West Indies in England in 1966. Back (left to right): Basil Butcher, Jackie Hendriks, Joey Carew, Rawle Brancker, Peter Lashley, Seymour Nurse, Joe Solomon. Front: Rohan Kanhai, Wes Hall, Garry Sobers (capt), Conrad Hunte, Lance Gibbs.

Sobers at Edgbaston in 1973, during his final Test series in England. Alan Knott is behind the stumps.

a time when it seemed his men needed strong leadership. Sobers pointed to his 497 runs, 208 eight-ball overs and 18 wickets, but the series was lost, in the end decisively. In 1970, after captaining that Rest of the World XI in England and playing his third season of county cricket, he was castigated in the Caribbean for participating in a double-wicket competition in Rhodesia. The racist policies of the white Rhodesian government were deplored throughout the West Indies, whose governments had cut all contact, but Sobers seemed oblivious to the politics. In the process, he proved himself naïve in the extreme, and though he apologised once he understood what he had done, the damage to his reputation was irreversible.

Sobers went past 7000 Test runs in the home series against India in 1971, but more and more he was coming across as a 'soldier of fortune', playing everywhere and anywhere. On the field, his unique talents allowed him to score runs and take wickets, but he seemed perennially exhausted, contained by a succession of injuries. In 1972, Sobers finally had the major knee operation he had been putting off, which revealed damage much worse than had been expected. He resigned as captain, Rohan Kanhai took over, and Sobers was forced to miss the

TONY COZIER: I'm of the firm belief that people are put here to do certain things, like Pelé to play football and Muhammad Ali to box. Sobers was put here to play cricket and he played it magnificently. He was a tremendous sportsman. He enjoyed life to the fullest, yet it had no effect on his cricket; perhaps it had a beneficial effect on his cricket. He just went out there and was very relaxed in everything he did, no matter what the situation. He could do anything on the cricket field. I haven't seen anyone since, and I don't think there is anyone before him, who would compare.

1973 home series against Australia. Thus his extraordinary run of 85 straight Test appearances, which had started against Australia back in 1955, came to an end.

Unfortunately, his continued absence from that series against the Aussies had a bitter edge. Though unfit for the first Test, Sobers believed he was right for the remainder, but officials wanted him to confirm his good health, either in a match for Barbados or via a fitness test. Sobers, indignant that he wasn't allowed to measure his own fitness, refused to obey, arguing that no one had asked him to undergo a test when he was carrying the side through the previous five years. Instead, he went back to resume his county career in Nottingham, and then made an emotional return to the Windies side for three Tests against England in England in 1973. In his final Test innings at Lord's, he made an unbeaten 150, his 26th and last hundred in official Tests, before returning to the Caribbean for his farewell series, against England. He retired as the

only man to complete the treble of 8000 runs, 200 wickets and 100 catches. In fact no one else had scored 8000 runs, or done the double of 3000 runs and 100 wickets, or the treble of 1000 runs, 100 wickets and 75 catches. In February 1975, he was knighted by Queen Elizabeth II.

Yet these statistics, while momentous, do not do him total justice. It's the stories told by admiring teammates and rivals that reveal his unique genius …

'I don't think anyone can compare with Sir Garfield Sobers,' says Mike Procter. 'He was captain of the Rest of the World side that toured England in 1970 and I remember a practice we had at The Oval. The first Test was scheduled for the following day at Lord's, but we were at The Oval. Eddie Barlow was the vice-captain and he got us all together, and being an enthusiastic guy he had us all running and fielding and batting and bowling. Garry hadn't arrived yet.

'Eventually we saw his famous walk, coming across the ground. He just said, "Hi, carry on, I'll see you tomorrow."

'We saw him tomorrow. He scored 183, took eight wickets, and then we moved on to the next match.'

Eight and a half years earlier, South Australia were playing a full-strength NSW, which meant the attack was led by Alan Davidson, who was in the absolute peak of his form. But when he started a spell with the second new ball his foot slipped in the bowling footmarks and he accidentally bowled a beamer that flew at Sobers' head. Of course, Davidson was immediately down to apologise, but Sobers wasn't happy. Straight after, the bowler tried the slower one, which fooled Sobers for a moment. Then, in Davidson's words, 'He rocked back to start with, but then, when he realised it wasn't coming on to him, he came forward and hit it on the up and picked it up. It finished up in the bar under the scoreboard on the Hill of the Adelaide Oval.' The hit, which went beyond and between deep mid-wicket and long-on, was measured at around 150 metres. And this wasn't a case of helping a fast ball on its way; Sobers had to meet the ball with a mighty whack and hit it a distance that science and logic say cannot happen.

This might have been the biggest six belted in big-time cricket, not hit off a spinner, but smashed off the great Alan Davidson. It's possible that no other cricketer who ever lived could have done it.

Two great West Indian left-handers. Sobers with Brian Lara after Lara had made 375 against England in Antigua in 1994, breaking Sir Garfield's old Test record of 365 not out.

SIR VIVIAN RICHARDS
Legend No. 3
The Intimidator

IAN CHAPPELL TELLS THE story of the first time he ran into Viv Richards: 'He was playing for the President's XI at Montego Bay in 1973,' the former Australian captain recalls. 'Jeff "Bomber" Hammond was bowling and Viv whacked him down the ground three times in a row — bang! bang! bang! — just straight back over the bowler's head. And then he edged the fourth one and he was out caught behind. And we all gathered around to say "Well bowled" to Jeff Hammond, and I remember Jeff looking at this guy as he left the field and saying, "That'll teach the so and so, you can't keep playing like that, that's bloody ridiculous batting."

'I didn't think much more about it at the time but when I saw a couple of Viv's innings later on and we were on the receiving end, I thought back to those words of Jeff Hammond and I thought, "Hey, Bomber, you can play like that and get away with it."'

Almost seven years later, the West Indies were batting in a Test at the Adelaide Oval. 'Lenny Pascoe was bowling to Viv, and he's bowled him three bouncers in a row,' Chappell remembers. 'After the third one, Len was walking back past umpire Max O'Connell and Max said, "Len, that'll be enough for this over."

'And a voice came from the other end: "Max, please don't stop him."

'It was the voice of Viv Richards. Intimidation is a two-way street.'

IN IMRAN KHAN'S VIEW, the thing that separated Viv Richards from all others was his reflexes, which 'enabled him to get into position so quickly that bowlers never quite knew what length to bowl to him'. Like all the game's truly great hitters, such as Hammond, Sobers, Pollock and Botham, Viv Richards was able to combine timing with savage force, which meant he was lethal on all surfaces. But perhaps only Sobers could match him for reflexes. A slow wicket never stopped him, nor his habit of initially moving straight onto the front foot, which often gave the illusion that he had committed himself too early. Just when a bowler thought Richards might be in trouble, the champion would move sweetly back and play the right stroke with time to spare.

For a player who liked to plant that front foot, it is astonishing that no fast man, however rapid, was ever able to surprise him with a bouncer. Pause a video of him batting at the moment just after the ball was delivered and you might think him technically deficient, incapable of keeping his balance to play a decisive shot; fast forward to the moment he hit the ball and everything seems right, even if he was hitting across the line.

His teammate at Somerset, the England off-spinner Vic Marks, called his measured walk to the wicket to begin an innings a 'declaration of intent'. So assured was Richards at the crease that throughout his career he considered a helmet superfluous, an admission of fear, and though very occasionally he was struck on the cap, he was never ruffled. And never put off. For a decade, he was the best hooker in the game, perhaps the greatest of all time. Richards v Larwood bowling bodyline would have been thrilling theatre. In World Series Cricket, which featured a bevy of fast bowlers bouncing and bumping on some

suspicious surfaces, Richards was supreme, taking the quicks on while others were trying to survive.

Richards was a big-match player who revelled in a challenge. He saw his role as being to stride out at No. 3 and take the attack to his opponents, with a special assignment being to destroy his rivals' spearhead. 'He didn't fear anyone, he just felt he was the master when he went out there,' says Clive Lloyd. 'And he proved it so many times.' For Ian Smith, Richards brought more than just his bat out to the middle: 'Very few batsmen make as big a statement with their presence as Viv Richards. He'd come to the wicket and the score might be 3–30, but sorry the rules are about to change. That was the way he approached every innings that he played.' Current West Indies captain Carl Hooper says simply, 'He'd walk out there and it would look like a totally different game.'

In 1980, Richards tore at England's Bob Willis to the point that the bowler, in his own words, 'felt utterly helpless and depressed'. *Wisden* called the assault in the third Test a 'vendetta-like attack', in which Richards crashed 53 of his 65 runs from England's then No. 1 bowler. Willis was dropped after one more Test and didn't recover his confidence for 12 months. When the pair next faced each other in a Test match, four years had passed, but the attack continued. Richards played a significant part in ensuring that Willis' final 85 overs in Test cricket brought a return of just six wickets for 367 runs.

The value of such offensives, on the bowler, the bowler's colleagues and Richards' teammates, cannot be understated. Few fighters come back from first-round knockouts. With his mission accomplished, and the field placings now more suited to a one-day game than the first morning of a Test match, Richards would relax and pick off his runs. His fellow batsmen, ever grateful, would face demoralised bowlers who were no longer thinking aggressively. The pressure was off. The crowd, meanwhile, was abuzz. When Richards was due to bat, the first session was not to be missed.

> **DICKIE BIRD:** If I was picking the World XI of all the great players that I have seen in my time as a player and an umpire, Viv would be my No. 3 batsman, without a shadow of a doubt. He used to murder the attack once he got in.

VIVIAN RICHARDS WAS A hero of the tiny Caribbean island of Antigua long before he made his name across the cricket world. In 1969, aged 17, he was the star attraction of a game against the neighbouring island of St Kitts, a match that lured 4000 people to the local ground. Richards sauntered in at No. 3, but was immediately given out, caught at short-leg. He refused to go, staring at the umpire, stamping his foot, then gazing contemptuously into space before slowly, very slowly, heading for the pavilion. His supporters were outraged, and soon a chant of 'No Vivi, no match!' was reverberating across the field. Spectators ran towards the pitch and the game was held up, until local authorities astonishingly ruled that Richards must be allowed to resume his innings. This was done, and Richards, now contrite and embarrassed, straightaway got himself out. In the second innings, he made another duck — three in one game! — but the real pain came afterwards, when he was suspended for two years for the petulant display that initiated the ugly demonstration.

Despite this setback, by 1972 he was playing for the Leeward Islands. He'd grown into a natural athlete good enough to play World Cup football for Antigua and with a physique not too dissimilar to one of his idols, the great boxer Joe Frazier. A year later, local subscribers sent him and a promising fast bowler named Andy Roberts to England for a coaching course, after which both were signed by astute counties — Roberts by Hampshire, Richards by Somerset. Richards made his Somerset debut before he'd made even one century in first-class cricket back home, but such was his ability that by year's end he was in the West Indies Test squad for a tour of India.

Within two years, Viv Richards was the leading batsman in the Caribbean; within three arguably the best batsman in the world. That he — and Roberts — were from Antigua was to the rest of the world a source of wonder. Antigua had never produced a Test player until Roberts' debut in March 1974; then came Richards, then others, Curtly Ambrose, Richie Richardson and Ridley Jacobs among them. For a decade the island's inhabitants were able to revel in the fact that the world's greatest batsman came from their shores. Today, Antigua's capital, St John's, is a regular Test-match venue. And Viv is Sir Vivian, Antigua's first cricketing knight.

BACK IN 1974, THE West Indies team that toured India was in the process of rebuilding. Garry Sobers and Rohan Kanhai were gone, the outstanding off-spinner Lance Gibbs was going.

Richards in England in 1976, where he scored 829 runs in four Tests, including two double centuries.

There was a new captain, Clive Lloyd, a new fast bowler, Roberts, and two batsmen would make their Test debuts in the opening match of the series. One of these batsmen, Gordon Greenidge, began with a bang, becoming the first West Indian to score a century in his maiden Test match, that Test being away from home. The other, Richards, was not so successful with the bat, seemingly bamboozled by the spinners, especially the outstanding, quick leg-spinner Bhagwat Chandrasekhar. Richards made just 4 and 3. He was, though, a hit in the field,

MICHAEL HOLDING: One day, Rodney Hogg bowled him a bouncer, actually hit him in his jaw. No helmet, Viv Richards never wore a helmet. Hit him right on his jaw. Rodney Hogg was no slow coach but Viv just massaged the jaw a bit. And the very next ball, Rodney Hogg thought to himself, well, I'm going to bounce him again. Well, the next ball went for six …

PAUL ALLOTT: From the moment Viv Richards walked to the crease, you knew you were in the presence of somebody special. He was the hardest man I ever had to bowl at, in county or Test-match cricket, because you just didn't know where you were going to bowl the ball. You felt, especially at my pace, that he was quite capable of hitting every ball you bowled for four.

taking two brilliant catches at the start of India's first innings, and the team was successful, winning by 267 runs.

Two weeks later, Richards came to the wicket on the second morning of the second Test with the West Indies at 3–73, pursuing India's 220. Almost immediately, joyous Indian fieldsmen were shouting for a caught behind. The umpire thought otherwise (a decision Richards is sure was correct), but the close shave exacerbated his self-doubt. Fortunately, Lloyd was at the other end. He showed Richards that the Indian spinners

were not as huge a bogey as his young colleague believed, and gradually an important innings evolved.

Richards went all the way to 192 not out, hitting six sixes in the process, then a record for a West Indian batsman in Tests. 'Once past my fifty, I felt invincible,' he recalls. 'Now even those spinners could not contain me. It was during that innings that I realised the true possibilities of my game …'

In the 1975 World Cup final, Richards failed with the bat but was still almost man of the match purely because of his central role in the run outs of three of Australia's top-order batsmen. First, opener Alan Turner was caught short by Richards dashing in from mid-wicket, picking up and throwing side-arm without breaking stride to shatter the stumps. Then Ian Chappell pushed a ball square on the offside, where neither Greenidge, running in from backward point, nor Richards, the cover-point, could quite reach the ball. As the ball trickled past Richards (who had been put off by his teammate), the batsman called for a single. Richards, however,

Another boundary during the 1979 World Cup final. Richards was at his greatest in the big matches.

recovered in a flash, pivoted, and threw the keeper's stumps down with Greg Chappell many metres from home. It was an astonishing piece of athleticism; to criticise the batsmen would be to suggest that such a fielding effort was even remotely possible. Not done yet, Richards then broke the crucial Ian Chappell–Doug Walters fourth-wicket stand, at a time when it seemed Australia were just starting to get on top. Chappell clipped a ball to a gap between mid-on and mid-wicket and set off for a run, but Richards was patrolling the region and his bullet throw to Clive Lloyd at the bowler's end was sure. Chappell was out by a metre and the final was lost.

As an all-round fielder, Richards was probably the best of his time, high praise given that this was an era in which fielding standards reached new heights. In the slips he was a sure catch, with a goalkeeper's ability to dive sideways. At mid-wicket or in the covers his range was many metres wide, and he could conjure spectacular catches such as the running grab that dismissed Ian Botham in the 1979 World Cup final. Bob Willis called that one 'a masterpiece of nerve, athleticism and judgment'.

The Australians in 1975 quickly came to the conclusion that Richards was a powerful and gifted, if nervous, young talent. During the first half of the '75–76 West Indies tour of Australia, he played some wonderful cameos, and hit a remarkable 175 in a touch over three hours against Western Australia, but after failing to reach fifty in any innings in the first four Tests, his place in the side was in jeopardy. The tour selectors promoted him to open the innings for a two-day non-first-class game in Canberra and he made 93, followed by a century in each innings as an opener in a tour game in Tasmania. With regular opener Greenidge horribly out of form, Richards was given the job for the final two Tests and responded with scores of 30 and 101, 50 and 98. Going in first left him less time to be anxious, and also gave him first shot at the quicks. For the home series against India that followed he was moved to No. 3, with Lawrence Rowe and Roy Fredericks opening. He scored big hundreds in the first three Tests, and arrived in England in April 1976 confident of his place in the side and the game. By series end, he was recognised as being just about the best batsman in the world.

In the lead-up to that series, England's South African-born captain Tony Greig told the media that

Richards at Bridgetown in early 1986. The West Indies won this third Test against England by an innings, on the way to their second straight series cleansweep against the Englishmen.

it was his team's intention to make the West Indians 'grovel'. For anyone to say that was provocative; for a South African to do so to a side made up of black cricketers who represented nations opposed to the racist policies of South Africa, was appalling and stupid. Richards' response was to say flatly, 'Nobody talks to Viv Richards like that.'

To prove the point, on the very first day of the series, Richards attacked the English bowlers, making 143 not out. The following day he went on to 232, the start of an extraordinary sequence of rungetting that culminated in the final Test at The Oval with a magnificent 291 and a series aggregate of 829 runs, at an average of 118.42. Rarely has an opposition captain had to choke so hard on his

SACHIN TENDULKAR: I always really flipped over Vivian Richards' batting. His effortless batting was something that I was so fond of.

ALLAN BORDER: In a one-day game at the MCG, we had an attack that included Dennis Lillee, Jeff Thomson and Rodney Hogg, a pretty formidable pace attack, and Viv made 153 not out. He just bludgeoned it and smashed it and whacked it to all parts of the MCG. We had the field spread when he was on strike but he still managed to hit boundary after boundary after boundary. At the time I never thought anyone could bat better than that.

words. And to think Richards missed the second Test because of a bout of influenza! No man has ever scored more runs in one series while playing in only four Tests. For the year of 1976, he scored two double centuries, five single centuries and 1710 runs, still the most runs ever made by one batsman in a calendar year. In *Wisden*, the veteran editor Norman Preston wrote, 'Richards was exceptionally brilliant and must be ranked among the finest West Indies batsmen of all time, worthy to be coupled with the great George Headley of pre-war fame … Mere figures cannot convey his perfect style and stroke play. His cover driving was superb and with his feet always in the right position the way he flicked the ball on his leg-stump to square-leg had to be seen to be believed.'

For the next decade, Viv was king. And let's remember, these were the days of pace, starring bowlers of the ilk of Lillee and Thomson, Roberts and Holding, Snow, le Roux, Willis, Hadlee, Garner, Croft, Hogg, Lawson, Botham, Imran Khan, Kapil Dev, Daniel, Patterson, McDermott and Wasim Akram. If anyone was going to be in charge, it should have been a fast man. While Richards didn't face the West Indian quicks, he did have to face the others, all of them seeking retribution, and so well did he respond to this challenge there is a strong case to argue he was the greatest player of pure pace bowling in cricket history. In both Tests and the burgeoning one-day international arena he was the man, producing a succession of innings that only he

could play. 'There were times when, of all the players I have ever seen,' Mark Nicholas says, 'Viv would be the most unbowlable to.'

In the 1979 World Cup final at Lord's, Richards made 138 not out from 157 balls, an innings emphatically underlined by a spectacular six, off the last ball of the innings, that went deep into the crowd beyond backward-square. With Collis King, he added 139 for the fifth wicket in 77 minutes, after the West Indies had stumbled to 4–99. Two years later, in the first ever Test played at St John's in Antigua — and only three days after his wedding (a very major event for the island) — Richards painstakingly scored his sixth hundred against England in 12 Tests. Clearly, marking this historic event with a hometown hundred meant a great deal to him. But if that was one of his slowest hundreds (305 minutes), five years later, again against England and again at St John's, he made a completely different style of century, the fastest in Test history in terms of balls faced. He scored 28 before tea from 14 balls, reached his fifty in 34 balls and his hundred in 56, hitting seven sixes and seven fours. One hit off Botham landed in the 11th row of the top deck of the grandstand beyond extra cover, a carry of around 110 metres. Another six, off a low full toss speared in by the off-spinner John Emburey, was slapped with colossal strength back over long-off's head. Of his fellow Antiguans' reaction when he reached his century, Richards wrote, 'I began to realise what it must be like to score for Liverpool at Anfield.'

Another astonishing innings was his 189 not out in a 55-over one-day international against England at Old Trafford in 1984. Made from 170 balls, it featured an undefeated last-wicket partnership of 106 runs in 14 overs with Michael Holding, who scored 12 of them. One of Richards' five sixes went clean out of the ground.

So many of his statistics are impressive. His eight hundreds against India has been matched only by Sobers. He reached a fifty against India at Kingston in 1983 in 32 balls, the third fastest in terms of balls

CLIVE LLOYD: He was a great inspiration to all, young and old. He gave 120 per cent, 130 per cent. He just gave his all every time he went out there. I remember once he had a back problem in Trinidad. A doctor gave him some cortisone, he could hardly walk but he took the injection, went out and batted. That's how much he loved West Indies cricket and this game of ours. He was just a great ambassador for the sport.

faced in Test history. In New Zealand in 1987, he scored 119 and took 5–41 in a one-day international in Dunedin, the only instance of a player achieving a century/five-for double in a ODI. Between 1979 and 1986 Richards played in 12 Test series and scored at least one century in 11 of them, the only miss coming in a three-match rubber in Australia in 1981–82. In 1988, he became the first West Indian to score 100 first-class centuries. His career average in one-day internationals of 47.00, from 187 matches, is the highest of anyone to score 4000 ODI runs.

Forty-seven of his first-class hundreds were scored for Somerset, including nine in 1985, but during the 1986 season the county made the stunning decision to dispense with his services, and those of fellow West Indian Joel Garner. Richards went back to league cricket, before making a comeback with Glamorgan in 1990. The split with Somerset caused great divisions — Ian Botham walking out of the club — but Richards, though bitterly disappointed, kept his dignity better than most. Botham recalls that when Richards called him to explain what had happened, it was Richards who had to calm him down, rather than vice versa. 'Somerset meant everything to him,' Botham says. 'That was his first big chance, as it was with me, so it meant a great deal to him and we learnt a lot. We learnt about life together, and the two of us grew together. It was magnificent to watch his career — and I would take as much interest in what he was doing as he did in what I was doing.'

There is a perception that the West Indian teams Richards captained were not as all-powerful as the sides led by his immediate predecessor, Clive Lloyd. But the record book suggests this is not true. Not counting the times he filled in prior to Lloyd's retirement in 1985, Richards led the West Indies for six years (1985 to 1991), during which he never lost a series, and beat England and Australia home and away, and India and New Zealand at home. Certainly, the team was much less dominant in one-day internationals, but the team's defeat in the 1983 World Cup final suggested this decline might actually have begun under Lloyd. Richards captained the West Indies in 50 Tests, for 27 victories and 15 losses. Lloyd, in contrast, had 36 wins and 26 losses from 74 Tests. If Richards had a fault as a captain, it was that he could be impatient,

MARK NICHOLAS: When Viv arrived at the crease he looked six inches taller than he was. He looked six inches wider than he was. He has this strong presence in his face, the Roman nose, the brilliant bones. There was an emperor-like feel about Viv. Still is, actually.

even indignant, with people who made mistakes. This seemed especially true near the end of his time in charge, when he was getting old in cricketing terms and so were many of his comrades.

'In the dressing room Viv was always looking for a way to win, always trying to gee the guys up,' says Michael Holding. 'Even after he got out he would go around the dressing room, saying listen, you have to win this game, try to do this, try to do that. He was so competitive, that is why when he took over the captaincy sometimes people thought he was a bit hard on his players. And he was, but that was because he was so competitive. He always wanted to

Richards hooks his great friend Ian Botham in a Test at The Oval. The pair were teammates at Somerset in English county cricket for more than a decade.

MICHAEL HOLDING: If Viv was the type of batsman who cared about records he would hold every record in Test cricket. When Viv was out there he was trying to entertain the public and also trying to win for the West Indies. Viv was never one to go out and just bat and bat and bat and bat. He would get a hundred, perhaps go on and get a big hundred, but he was not one to sit around and think, 'Oh, the world record is 365, I'm going to get 366.' Because I am absolutely sure that if he sat down every time he went out to bat and thought like that, he would have got it eventually.

win, always wanted to make sure that the West Indies were winners.'

Those closest to him believe his onfield persona did not accurately reflect the real man. No doubt, he is a proud individual, as keen as any to reverse

Richards rounds off his magnificent career by leading Glamorgan to victory in the 1993 AXA Equity & Law League. In the crucial final match of the season against Kent, in front of a crowd of 12,000, Richards scored 46 not out to give his team victory with 14 balls to spare.

the sense of inferiority blacks in the Caribbean feel after decades of white colonialism. Hence he took great delight in resoundingly defeating England and Australia, and felt real hurt when the Australians inflicted that heavy defeat in 1975–76. That was, he said years later, 'the hardest, meanest cricket tour that I have ever been involved in'. The Australians, he said, 'would take every opportunity to humiliate and ridicule us'. On the field, Richards would exaggerate his swagger, appear arrogant and often wear a snarl. Away from the action, many thought him reserved, open only with those he knew well, still capable of a piercing stare if his blood was burning, but loyal, compassionate and honest. His friendship with Botham is one of cricket's most enduring. 'He was so important for my career, and I would like to think I was for his to a degree,' says the Englishman. 'Even when I was captain of England in the West Indies and we had all kinds of problems, he would take the time out to come and see me, sit me down and make sure everything was all right. He was also the best player, in my opinion, that has ever lived.'

In trying to rank cricket's greatest legends, Richards is actually one of the hardest to place. His eventual Test batting average of 50.23 is excellent, but still less than other great batsmen of his era such as Greg Chappell, Javed Miandad, Sunil Gavaskar and Allan Border. Yet few can argue Richards' place as one of the game's icons. Bradman, Hobbs and Tendulkar are part of this elite for all their runs, Sobers for his power as a batsman and his unique versatility, Warne because he revived spin bowling, Lillee as the king of fast bowlers, Hadlee for the way he carried New Zealand cricket, Imran and Worrell for their statesmanship as well as their all-round skills. Grace must be there too, for his runs and also for the way he totally dominated the cricket stage in the 19th century. Viv Richards sits with these superstars as much for his 'aura' as anything else. There might not have been a cricketer since WG who had a more distinctive presence on the cricket field *and* was able to follow up with amazing deeds.

On the field, Bradman didn't look like a champion until he sprang into action. Sobers sometimes seemed distant from the game, Hobbs was unpretentious, Warne punkish, Tendulkar is coy, almost mischievous. Sir Vivian Richards always looked great. And he was.

SHANE WARNE
Legend No. 4
Anything is Possible

IN THE 1980s, THERE was genuine concern in cricket circles that spin bowling was dead. Two of the game's finest writers, David Frith and Patrick Murphy, published books devoted to the art and concluded glumly by proposing a number of changes to the laws and attitudes that might initiate a revival. These included deliberately making wickets more suitable for spinners, lengthening the pitch, longer matches, longer boundaries, no second new balls, less lush outfields, limited run-ups, run-ups left uncovered when it rained, wicketkeepers to be made to stand up to the stumps to all bar, say, two of a team's bowlers, different balls that bounce less but spin more …

'As the game becomes less intellectual in its growing obsession with one-day matches, with the consequent shrinkage in the role of the spinner,' wrote Frith in his 1984 book *The Slow Men*, 'those who treasure the art of the slow bowler grasp at any straw.' In *The Spinner's Turn* in 1982 Murphy lamented: 'We cannot wait for the captains to make gestures in their direction, they have to be encouraged to believe that it is in the best interests of the side to encourage spinners. It is clear that spinners must be legislated back into the game …'

IAN WOOLDRIDGE: The first time I saw Warne was down in the nets in Sydney. He must have bowled in the nets for an hour, and what intrigued me was that this was no work for him. This was what he loved doing. He loved spinning the ball.

Meanwhile, in Australia, the former Test leg-spinner Peter Philpott bemoaned the fact that the morale of spinners across the country was at 'an all-time low'.

'It's essential that cricket regains its balance, which it has lost with the current preoccupation with pace,' Philpott said in 1990. 'Is cricket forever condemned to the present war of attrition which so many of us find deadly dull and monotonous?'

No, Peter, it was not. But no rules were changed to buck this trend. Instead, along came a thoroughly modern youth with an earring and dyed blond hair. He was just about punkish by cricket standards, hardly cast in the image of Arthur Mailey, Clarrie Grimmett or Bill O'Reilly. But he could sure rip a leg-break …

BORN ON 13 SEPTEMBER 1969, Shane Warne had been recognised as having sufficient talent to win a place at the Australian Cricket Academy in 1989, on a youth tour to the West Indies in 1990 and on an Australia A tour to Zimbabwe in 1991. But in his home state of Victoria, the first XI was laden with quality pace bowlers — men such as Merv Hughes, Tony Dodemaide, Simon O'Donnell, Paul Reiffel and Damien Fleming — and Warne was so dubious about his future that he seriously contemplated a move to Sydney. He did stay in Melbourne, scraped into the Victorian side for the start of the 1991–92 season, and then, such was the dearth of spin-bowling talent in the country, was suddenly chosen in the Australian team for the third Test against India at the SCG in early January 1992.

BRUCE YARDLEY: He's got the ability to get the ball rotating at such revs. And if he holds the shine away from his hand, as the ball's rotating it curves in and at speed as well. He bowls his leg-breaks pretty fast, so if he's coming over the wicket, the ball is curving in towards leg and looks like it might be missing leg but then it takes the top of off-stump. That is unplayable and that's what he's capable of.

It was a meteoric rise by any standards — let alone a leg-spinner's.

Back in the 1920s, Grimmett had been rejected in Sydney and Melbourne before finally earning his Test debut as a 33-year-old South Australian. In contrast, Warne strode onto the international arena for the first time as a veteran of seven first-class matches and the taker of 26 first-class wickets. The last time he had been available for Victoria, for a Sheffield Shield match at the pace-friendly Gabba in Brisbane, he'd been … 12th man! However, in a match in Hobart just before Christmas, playing for an Australian XI against the West Indians, he took 3–14 and 4–42. Despite the fact five of those seven wickets were tailenders, it was enough to get him a baggy green cap.

Warne's captain in that Australian XI game was the regular Test keeper, Ian Healy, who would become a most trusty accomplice in the years that followed. Ironically, at the time Healy possessed the same sceptical attitude as everyone else when it came to slow bowlers. 'It's funny to think of it now,' he wrote in 2000, 'but before the arrival of Warney we didn't have a high opinion of spinners. Everyone reckoned they were something of a dying breed. I know AB [Allan Border] thought that and I tended to as well. Between the first Test of the 1988–89 summer and the Sri Lanka tour in August-September 1992, I didn't complete one Test stumping. They just didn't happen.'

Warne's Test debut was disappointing. He did not bowl overly badly, but found himself competing on one of the flattest Sydney decks in living memory. He took 1–150, and seemed somewhat out of place, especially in the field, where he was ordinary. But first impressions can be misleading. 'I remember picking up the man-of-the-match award,' recalls India's Ravi Shastri, who hit 206, 'and as I was going into the dressing room there were a few Aussies already in there and I saw Warney pass by. I stopped, and gave him a tap on the shoulder and said, "Young man, you'll bowl a lot worse than this and pick up five or six." And the reason why I said it was the control he showed right through that Test match. The first time I played a shot off the back foot against him was when I was 180 or 190. I pulled him once and cut him once.'

By the end of the series, Warne's Test bowling average was a very unhealthy 228, but Allan Border and Australian coach Bob Simpson decided to persist with him, though they insisted he do something about his weight, which he had been fighting ever since putting on plenty while playing league cricket in England in 1989 and 1990. A leg-spinner of some ability himself back in his heyday, Simpson still believed in slow bowling, but only in slow bowling of the highest class. He had never seen a bowler who spun the ball 'harder' than Warne, and was also encouraged by the tyro spinner's eagerness to learn and ability to learn quickly. In the first Test in Sri Lanka in September 1992, the Australians mounted a brave fightback after falling 291 runs behind on the first innings. In their second innings, everyone reached double figures (Warne, 10kg lighter than on his Test debut and batting at No. 10, made 35) and the Sri Lankans needed 181 to win. They reached 2–127, then stumbled to 7–150, when Border threw Warne the ball. By any account this was a gutsy move, made by a captain not renowned for gambling, for the rookie still had only one Test wicket, for 335 runs. Now he took 3–0 and Australia won by 16 runs.

Back home for the 1992–93 season, the off-spinning all-rounder Greg Matthews was preferred for the first Test of the series against the West Indies but failed to bowl Australia to victory on the final day. Warne came in for the second Test, at the MCG, and responded by taking 7–52 to give Australia a decisive win. Suddenly a hero, especially in Melbourne, Warne had little success in the rest of that series, but was brilliant in three Tests in New Zealand straight after, phenomenally successful on the 1993 Ashes tour, and would not be left out again until 1999.

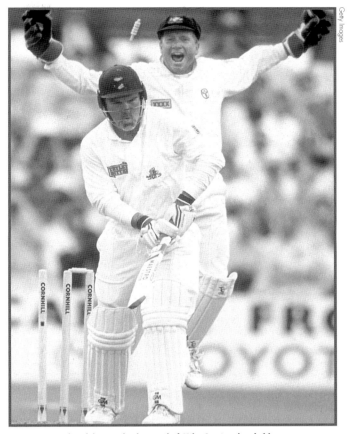

Keeper Ian Healy celebrates the dismissal of Mike Gatting, bowled by Shane Warne's first ball in Test cricket on English soil. Rarely has one delivery made a greater impact in big-time cricket.

single couldn't upset his rhythm. As well, he was a tough aggressive cricketer, with extraordinarily strong hands and fingers, who could bowl all day.

Vital to his success was the fact that in his delivery he was technically magnificent. Back-leg drive was the key to him achieving energy on the ball, and the perfect timing of the shoulder rotation ensured a magnificent follow-through and curvaceous flight. The pivotal role played by that shoulder was amply demonstrated when he hurt it in 1998; without the

THREE THINGS SET WARNE apart from the spinners who came before him. One, he rarely bowled a bad ball. Two, he had a bag of tricks as deep as any magician. For the previous 30 years, most spinners believed they had to work out batsmen by being relentless rather than innovative. Warne brought surprise back into vogue. And three, he was able to change plans effectively in the middle of a game, a spell, even an over. Having to bowl differently to two batsmen never worried him, so a

GREG CHAPPELL: I remember coaching the Australia A team back in the mid-1990s. Shane was the only one of the established Australian Test players who came to the Australia A team and wished the guys well. And he rang up on a couple of occasions and passed messages on to the team via me — because he remembered where he'd come from and he remembered that he was once a young player who'd needed some help. I respect him for that.

joint in perfect working order, he came back to the field. With it, he was able to give the ball that mighty flick out of the hand, which meant the ball drifted and dropped, often savagely.

Through the 1990s, Warne gave the Australian side an edge in that they were suddenly capable of performing on all types of wickets. This was the only failing of the great West Indies teams of the late 1970s and 1980s. With quicks such as Craig McDermott, Merv Hughes and Glenn McGrath, Australia were always competitive on seaming wickets, and Warne gave them an advantage over everyone on the turners. His presence also meant that the Australian attack was beautifully balanced. On a flat wicket he could bowl nice and tight, always at the stumps, and as the wicket deteriorated you could see the opposition starting to sweat, because they knew they'd be facing him on his terms before the match was out.

Opposing batsmen tried all sorts of ways to defeat him. Batting normally might work on a good pitch, but history showed that unless you were very good,

Warne would work you out in the end. The drift he got on his leg-break was often so pronounced that it kept batsmen pinned to the crease — only the most daring danced down the wicket to him. And the bounce he got on his top-spinner made batsmen reluctant to stretch too far forward, for fear of popping a catch to the close-in fieldsmen.

Some batsmen tried to pad him away, working on the theory that if you could survive against the great leg-spinner then runs might come from the other end. But in would hustle the close-in fieldsmen and Warne might change his line to make the batsman use his bat. Others decided to sweep at everything, but the prospect of a top-edged catch to short fine-leg or deep square-leg always loomed. Some batsmen resorted to slogging, but that was never going to last. Ian Healy tells the story of South African tailender Fanie de Villiers, turning around one day before he faced Warne and saying, 'What'll it be today, six or stumped?' It was stumped.

One group that has had some success is the left-handed batsmen, who have an advantage because

Getty Images

England's Alec Stewart is bowled by a classic Warne flipper at the Gabba in Brisbane in 1994–95. Warne would finish with 8–71, his best innings return in Tests.

Warne's wrong 'un isn't as brutally effective as his other deliveries. The lefties can play straight to all but the big-turning leg-breaks, and hit with the spin through and over the legside field. Sri Lanka's Arjuna Ranatunga played Warne as well as anyone, while another leftie, Brian Lara, was superb in the West Indies in 1999, when, admittedly, Warne was below his best. Of the right-handers, Sachin Tendulkar dominated in 1998 in India, but the leg-spinner was struggling with that shoulder injury. In Pakistan in 1994 Salim Malik handled him best of all. The worst, undoubtedly, was South Africa's Daryll Cullinan, who never had a clue.

The thing that makes Warne unique in leg-spinning history is that he was so great so young. Something else that set him apart was his impact on one-day cricket. The conventional wisdom before 1993 was that spinners were too easily hit to be a factor in a 50-over game, but Warne turned that idea on its head when he was given a chance in the one-dayers during the 1993–94 season. In his first four matches he took nine wickets for 87 runs; for the season he took 22 wickets at 13.68 while conceding only 3.34 runs per over. Later, he would play crucial roles in two World Cups, using a cricket brain as alert and clever as any in the game. At the start of the 2001–02 Australian season he had played in 167 one-day internationals and taken 262 wickets (including 13 four-fors), while conceding a little more than four runs an over. Most significantly, few teams now go into a one-day game without at least one slow bowler.

WHAT WERE WARNE'S MOST memorable deliveries? Chief among them must be the famous 'Gatting' ball at Old Trafford in 1993. To set the scene: this was Warne's first delivery in Ashes cricket, critics were dismissive of his potential impact on the slower English pitches, he had not played in the one-day series that preceded the Test, and Mike Gatting was a master of spin, a batsman who had always imperiously bashed hapless slow bowlers from his presence. Then Warne sent down perhaps the finest leg-break ever seen in Test matches, and everything changed. In the commentary box, Richie Benaud, a former great leg-spinner and the finest television cricket commentator of them all, could say no more than, 'He's done it! He's done it!' A stunned buzz enveloped the grand old ground, while back in the

Warne reacts to the Nottingham crowd after Australia had retained the Ashes in 1997.

middle Merv Hughes, who'd been fielding at deep square-leg, asked Healy what had happened. 'Mate, it pitched off and hit off,' the keeper replied, implying it pitched off the wicket and hit the off-stump.

What the ball had actually done was start on an off-stump line, then drift viciously so it pitched around 15 centimetres outside the leg-stump. Then it fizzed back to take the off bail. The way Gatting reacted when he was bowled, as if he'd seen some sort of ghost, built up a sudden mystique that Warne didn't let diminish for the rest of the series. In fact, his spell over English batsmen continues to this day.

In that same series, Warne bowled Graham Gooch around his legs in the fifth Test with a

SUNIL GAVASKAR: He gets this fantastic drift that comes in and which makes it that much more difficult for a batsman to try to charge him in a premeditated fashion. And he's got so much spin, so much turn, that it's very difficult to attack him consistently.

delivery that pitched in footmarks 70 centimetres, maybe more, outside Gooch's leg-stump, but bit back to shatter the stumps. A similar spinning ball cleaned up the West Indian left-hander Shivnarine Chanderpaul at the SCG in 1996–97. Chanderpaul didn't even play a shot at a delivery that out of the hand looked as if it might be a wide, but it was actually a delivery that Warne later called 'the biggest turning leg-break I've bowled to take a wicket'. It landed in the footmarks and snapped back to bowl, via the pads, a good player who had scored 71 runs and been going extremely well.

Warne made up for not having a classic wrong 'un by developing a stunning 'flipper' — a ball squeezed out of the thumb and forefinger, bowled flatter and quicker, that spits through after pitching to trap confused batsmen on the back foot. Two classics knocked over Richie Richardson at the MCG in 1992–93 and England's Alec Stewart at the Gabba two seasons later. The Richardson flipper came during Warne's first great wicket-taking spell in Test cricket, when he took seven wickets on the final day to run through the then world champions. The Stewart one came in the first Test of the series, bringing all the Englishmen's nightmares from 1993 flooding back. Warne took 8–71 in the second innings of that Test (still his best innings figures in Tests) and then a hat-trick in the second Test, at the MCG. There was nothing he could not do.

It was typical of Warne to get a Test hat-trick on the grandest stage — in an Ashes Test in his home town. He had a knack for achieving with a sense of swagger, whether he meant it or not. It seemed, throughout the 1990s and into the 21st century, he was the pivotal figure in Australia's greatest and most dramatic days, and also their most controversial.

Warne's minor involvement in the match-fixing scandal spun into arguably the biggest slur on his career. In many ways, he was unlucky — his crime was not to throw games, but to take some money (a very small amount, it must be stressed, compared to that accepted with alacrity by those later banned) from a bloke who bet on cricket, and in return provide what he saw as harmless information such as pitch conditions and weather updates. When he admitted this to the Australian Cricket Board, he was fined around the same amount he had been given. Astonishingly, in a move that would exacerbate the problem many times over, it was then decided to keep the episode inhouse. When the story did break in 1998, Warne and Mark Waugh, who had also taken money in exchange for providing the same sort of information, were made to look stupid and corrupt. The fact that there was no suggestion that they had ever deliberately played below their best — and that in 1994 they had immediately reported the fact that the Pakistan captain Salim Malik had offered them considerable sums to throw matches — counted, at least as far as many in the media and some fans were concerned, for nothing.

Sadly, Warne has from time to time exhibited personal flaws that have left him less popular than the other great Australian cricketers of the last decade. In 1997, after Australia had retained the Ashes at Trent Bridge — a triumph that Warne was deeply involved in (24 wickets in the series, including a crucial nine in the third Test at Old Trafford) — he stood on the balcony and performed a crass victory dance that looked arrogant even if it wasn't meant to be. In New Zealand in 2000, when he should have been celebrating taking an Australian record 356th Test wicket, he initiated a confrontation with two schoolboys after the lads took Warne's photograph when he didn't want them to. A year earlier he'd accepted a reputed $250,000 in return for using an anti-smoking product for three months, but was seen smoking in a nightclub. And then a newspaper involved him in a 'phone sex' scandal in England in 2000, while he was playing county cricket for Hampshire. By this stage, many parents searching for role models for their children had given up on him, while a disheartened ACB sacked him as vice-captain.

In his defence, Warne has always been a highly-strung fellow, who can get very high *and* very low. His teammates praise him as one of the most generous men on Earth, while conceding that he is a man of contradictions, who seems to like the limelight but also allows it to get him down. Still, he

SACHIN TENDULKAR: When somebody plays well he appreciates that and that's the sign of a great sportsman. I don't need to talk much about Warne because the whole world has seen what he's capable of. He's a great guy, great company, and when it comes to competitiveness he has that in him, which is a great sign.

brought new fans to the game, including the giant sporting goods company Nike, who backed him with a huge contract and a groovy advertising campaign, and at the same time invigorated veteran enthusiasts who happily conceded he was better than Grimmett while refusing to think that Glenn McGrath might be as good as Ray Lindwall. Because Warne was far and away the biggest thing in Australian cricket, he shouldered a lot of the team's media profile, was responsible for much of the team's hype, and also copped most of the media's scrutiny. Thus, he had to face more pressure and exposure than any other Australian player, which was great for his colleagues, not so good for him.

EVERYWHERE HE GOES HE is talked about —shouts or whispers, insults or compliments — so it is little wonder that every now and then he blows up. But rather than receiving understanding in such circumstances, he is quickly condemned. The infamous confrontation with Andrew Hudson in Johannesburg in 1994 was a classic example of this.

The crowd was on Warne's back, and when he finally broke South Africa's second-innings opening partnership, he reacted by charging at Hudson, hurling abuse while his teammates tried to hold him back. It looked ugly, and he was fined by the ICC match referee, a penalty that was later substantially increased by the ACB. Media criticism, especially in Australia, was severe. Warne publicly acknowledged his mistake while suggesting the Board should not have become involved, and then helped bowl Australia to victory in the second Test.

This was an example of a habit of Warne — to attract the wrath of the media, authorities and sections of the public, and then set the record somewhat straight by performing superbly on the field. This has been especially so since early 1998, when he has more than once had to prove that he was not washed up. In India in early '98, Warne was battered by the great Tendulkar. He then had shoulder surgery, and while rehabilitating had to watch NSW leg-spinner Stuart MacGill bowl well in his place. He came back for the fifth Test of the 1998–99 Ashes summer and took two wickets to MacGill's 12. But then, in the World Series limited-overs tournament that followed straight after, regular skipper Steve Waugh was injured, and Warne started

ALLAN BORDER: The two or three years with Warney were the most enjoyable I had as a captain. His coming onto the Australian cricket scene was one of the best things that we've ever experienced.

taking wickets and captained the side with rare skill and flair.

During the West Indies tour that began in February 1999 the Australian selectors tried a two-pronged leg-spin attack of MacGill and Warne. However, after Brian Lara dominated the second and third Tests, Warne was left out of the fourth, a snub that he found hard to accept even though he'd taken only 2–268 in the series. Media reports had he and Waugh at loggerheads. When the wickets didn't come early in the 1999 World Cup in England,

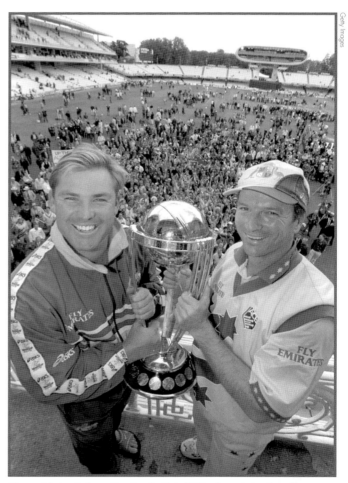

Warne with captain Steve Waugh at Lord's in 1999, after spinning Australia to victory in the World Cup final.

Warne publicly contemplated retirement, but after friends and advisers counselled him, he took stock and came back to earn man-of-the-match awards in the semi-final and final.

In those crucial games, it looked as if he decided, bugger it, I'll let the shoulder rip again. The result was two golden spells, highlighted by a fizzing leg-break that bowled the South African opener Herschelle Gibbs at a crucial time in the semi at Edgbaston. 'It was,' wrote his captain afterwards, 'a delivery not dissimilar to his famous "Gatting" ball from 1993.'

After a reasonable 1999–2000 season, when he played his part in Australia's phenomenal Test and one-day winning streaks and went past Dennis

The great leg-spinner at The Oval in 2001, immediately after becoming the first Australian, sixth bowler and first spinner to take 400 Test wickets.

Lillee as his country's greatest ever Test wicket-taker, Warne missed the 2000–01 home Test series against the West Indies after breaking a finger early in the season. Back for the one-dayers, he did enough to beat MacGill for a place on Australia's tour of India, but had a grossly disappointing Test series, during which India's Harbhajan Singh took a mountain of wickets and new Aussie coach John Buchanan questioned Warne's future. On the final day of the series, when Australia desperately needed him and on a wicket that had yielded 15 wickets to Harbhajan's off-breaks, Warne could do no better than 0–41 from six spiritless overs. Some thought MacGill should have been selected for the 2001 Ashes tour, but Warne was given what amounted to a last chance. He responded, yet again, in style. Thirty-one wickets in the series, including his 400th Test scalp at The Oval, when he took 10 wickets in a Test match for the fifth time, represented another vibrant riposte to his critics. Suddenly, the experts were seeing him as a man capable of taking 600 Test-wickets.

With Warne, anything is possible. He was the sixth bowler, first spinner and first Australian to take 400 Test wickets. By the end of the Australians' series in South Africa in early 2002 he had played in more than 100 Tests and taken more wickets than any bowler bar Courtney Walsh. But more than statistics, his impact and standing in the game should be measured by how the next generation is behaving. Whatever their parents think of him, today's kids are bowling leg-breaks because they want to be like Warney, just as the children of the '70s and '80s bowled fast like Lillee and Thommo. Would Test captains in charge of Saqlain Mushtaq, Muttiah Muralitharan, Anil Kumble, MacGill and Harbhajan have had as much faith in them but for the impact of Warne? Would these spinners have had faith in themselves?

To think that Peter Philpott thought cricket was getting 'deadly dull and monotonous'. With Warney, it's been anything but.

SIR JACK HOBBS
Legend No. 5
The People's Champion

IF WG GRACE WAS the man who developed a batting technique to conquer the new enterprise of first-class cricket, and Don Bradman was the ultimate runscorer, then Sir John Berry Hobbs was a classic bridge between them. Hobbs made his first-class debut in 1905, for a Surrey XI against the Grace-led Gentlemen of England, and played his last Test in the Ashes battle of 1930, Bradman's first great series. In all, he hit 197 first-class centuries (15 in Tests), 98 of them after his 40th birthday, and 61,237 first-class runs, but to reduce his batting to mere statistics dilutes the legend. He became known as 'The Master', simply because he was that little bit more efficient than anyone else.

Across the cricket planet, respect for Jack Hobbs was universal. During his last Test in Sydney, in 1928–29, the patrons on the Hill demanded he walk across and personally farewell them, after the former Australian captain, MA Noble, had made an on-ground presentation of a cheque and an inscribed boomerang, the products of a 'bob for Hobbs' campaign initiated by the Sydney *Sun* newspaper. Stephen Gascoigne, more popularly known as 'Yabba', the Hill's most famous barracker, worked his way down to the picket fence to shake his hand. Wherever he went, friend or foe, Jack Hobbs was the people's champion.

IAN BOTHAM: When I was a kid, Sir Jack Hobbs was the one name from the past that kept on hitting me. To me, he was a legend. He must be one of the all-time great players.

This was so despite the fact that Hobbs was never a character in the manner of Miller or Compton. He wasn't a glorious stylist, like Trumper or Greg Chappell, or brutally powerful like Hammond or Viv Richards. He wasn't ruthless like Bradman, a prodigy like Tendulkar, or an advocate for a cause like Imran Khan. He was Jack Hobbs, no arrogance, wild gestures or hint of rebellion. What you saw was what you got. He came from a battling background, and never forgot it, even after he became a knight of the realm. He was of medium build, athletic, safe, quick and very certain rather than flash in the field. Most importantly, he was the bloke you wanted to bat for your life, determined, shrewd, decent, sure. Everyone, from the young lads

Hobbs (left) with his captain AC MacLaren walk out at Edgbaston to begin England's first innings of the 1909 Ashes series.

selling the scorecards to the wise old members in the pavilion, loved him and respected him, and in different ways identified with him. That was Hobbs' strength, the source of his great appeal. Like a loyal friend, once he had your affection, he never let you down

No one has scored more first-class hundreds or more first-class runs. Yet Hobbs' career first-class batting average is only 50.65, below dozens of batsmen in the game's history, including a number of his contemporaries. Here is a clue about the man. Only 16 of his centuries were double-centuries. Fifty-one of them ended between 100 and 110. Many times, he reputedly sacrificed hundreds because 50 or 60 was enough. His job was to score enough runs to set up victories, not to humble opposing bowlers, hog the limelight or boost his statistics. Like all the great batsmen of first-class cricket's first 50 years, he was at his most valuable on bad wickets, when his team most needed him. 'That was the time you had to earn your living,' he once said. In this way he was like Victor Trumper, Australia's most loved player of the era. Significantly, he averaged six runs more per out in Test cricket than he did in county cricket; Jack Hobbs saved his best for when it mattered most.

'In play, the salient feature of his cricket was that it seemed so unspectacular,' wrote John Arlott. 'His strokes did not seem startling, but inevitable … no violence, no hurry: the stroke rolled away like a well-cued billiard ball. It was only when the watcher perceived that his partner — a Test player of some standing — was in genuine difficulties that the utter perfection of Jack Hobbs' batting was borne in upon him.'

HOBBS WAS BORN IN Cambridge on 16 December 1882. The oldest of 12 children, Jack and his family's circumstances were poor, occasionally dire. As *Wisden* editor Matthew Engel put it in his tribute to Hobbs in the 2000 edition, 'Nothing came easy except the art of batting.' There was no formal cricket coaching, just observing and listening, and his dedication to the game was hampered by obligations to do what he could to help at home. Still, his father was a net bowler and later a groundsman at Jesus College, Cambridge, which gave his son practice and occasional playing opportunities that would otherwise not have come his way, and set up a professional career when his talents were spotted by the great batsman, Tom Hayward (the second man, after Grace and before Hobbs, to score 100 first-class centuries). Hobbs had already been neglected by his native Essex when a trial was arranged at Surrey, where Hayward held sway. Soon a contract was offered, an act that might have kept the 20-year-old Hobbs in the game, for his father had just passed away and the eldest son had responsibilities to his mother, brothers and sisters. Every week, most of Hobbs' cricket wages were sent back home. At one point, Hayward even organised a £10 bonus for the promising young batsman, when he learnt that the family was really struggling. For years after, even when he was the No. 1 batsman in the world, Hobbs held Tom Hayward in awe.

Hobbs scored 18 and 88 in that debut against WG and the Gentlemen, then 28 and 155 against Essex (the county that had rejected him) and was promptly awarded his county cap. His Test debut came in Australia in 1907–08, the second Test of that Ashes series, after he was strangely left out of the XI for the opening encounter. Hobbs suspected the captain, AO Jones, did not rate him highly, and the excellent county batsman, George Gunn, who was in Australia but not officially part of the touring party, was preferred. In the event, Gunn top-scored in both innings of that first Test, but Hobbs came into the side for the final four contests of the series. He began with an innings of 83, but his most notable effort came in Melbourne, when England was caught on a sticky wicket and he made 57 out of 105. Gunn, his opening partner, made 13, but no one else scored more than 8. In his 1935 autobiography, Hobbs called this 'one of the very best innings that I ever played'.

Hobbs faced the Australians again in England in 1909. He was the leading runscorer in first-class cricket that season, but struggled against the tourists, making only 132 runs in the first three Tests, including a first-ball duck, lbw Macartney, in his maiden Test innings in England. He did follow up with an outstanding 62 not out in the second innings, as England won by 10 wickets, but a damaged finger kept him out of the final two Tests.

Straight afterwards, in South Africa, Hobbs established himself as a Test batsman of the highest class. In the first three Tests, his scores were 89 and 35, 53 and 70, and 11 and 93 not out; then, after a double failure in Cape Town, he made his first

century at the top level, an imposing 187 in the final Test. More significantly than these impressive numbers, during the series he successfully countered the famous four-pronged googly-bowling attack of Vogler, Faulkner, Schwarz and White, who were spinning the South Africans to victories in the first, second and fourth Tests. The googly — the delivery that looks like a leg-break out of the hand but is actually an off-break — had been introduced to cricket by England's BJT Bosanquet at the turn of the century, and taken on board by his disciples in South Africa, who found that on their matting wickets the extra bounce the wrist action on the delivery generated made it even more lethal. Tom Hayward was one batsman who never came to terms with the mystery, but Hobbs certainly did. He pushed well forward, bat and pad together, if he could smother the spin, otherwise he went right back on his stumps. Unlike his colleagues, he also had the reflexes and the patience to attack or defend on the back foot if he couldn't read the spin out of the bowler's hand. Thus he became a lone point of resistance. HDG Leveson-Gower, his captain on this tour, said of Hobbs' efforts, 'I have never seen better batting either in England or anywhere else.'

If Hobbs had convinced the experts in England and South Africa of his greatness by 1911, he was still to sway the cynics in Australia. This he did in devastating style in 1911–12, making centuries in the second, third and fourth Tests and a then Ashes record 662 runs in the series. In the fourth Test in Melbourne he and Wilfred Rhodes added 323 for the first wicket in four-and-a-half hours, Hobbs making 178, his partner 179. No pair of Englishmen has ever added more for any wicket in Australia. 'Hobbs by his achievements this tour has proved himself to be the greatest living batsman,' wrote the cricket correspondent from the Melbourne *Argus*.

Hobbs was at the absolute height of his powers in 1914, when he scored 11 centuries and 2697

> **STEVEN LYNCH:** Hobbs is quite unique in cricket in that you never find anyone who has a bad word to say about him. Almost anything you read tells you what a great chap he was, how he was always helping people out. Even Bradman had his detractors, but I've never seen anything rubbishing Hobbs in any way at all. By all accounts he was a bit of a saint.

Getty Images

Hobbs in a relaxed mood in July 1925, having just passed 2000 first-class runs for the season.

runs during the English county season. Earlier in the year he'd scored three half-centuries in five innings as England won in South Africa. But as the county season wound down, the world went to war, meaning that Hobbs lost four of what otherwise must have been his most productive years. He came back in 1919, aged 36, to immediately score another 2594 runs and eight centuries, but he was a different player. Now he went more onto the back foot, deflected more, played with less power, placed greater emphasis on the short single. MA Noble wrote in 1925, after Hobbs had scored 573 runs in the just completed Ashes series, that 'Hobbs, as we know him today, is perhaps a more prolific rungetter than ever, but does not possess the compelling genius that he was

DAVID FRITH: Those who watched Hobbs in the 1920s were told that there had been only one greater batsman. That was the pre-War Jack Hobbs.

a few years ago'. The great batsman himself believed that he was 'twice the player' before the War that he was afterwards.

Between 1919 and 1934 Hobbs scored 35,017 runs and 131 centuries. Before the War he had scored four Test centuries against Australia, afterwards he compiled another eight. Hobbs modestly attributed all this to the fact that the wickets after the War were flatter, the bowlers not as good, the lbw rules more in favour of the batsmen. The truth is that Hobbs understood the art of batting as well as anyone ever has, and was thus able to adapt his game to compensate for his advancing years. In terms of the way he worked out batting and the job of scoring runs, a fair comparison would be today's Steve Waugh.

'I had to think harder bowling at Jack Hobbs than against any other player,' remarked Bill Bowes, Yorkshire's leading pace bowler between the Wars.

'Hobbs could overcome an awkward situation because he knew what to do and had the capacity to do it,' wrote the Australian commentator AG Moyes. 'And he was such a shrewd campaigner that he could trick the bowlers into playing his game for him. Twice, at least, he did this in Test matches on wickets favouring the bowlers — at The Oval in 1926 and at Melbourne in 1929.'

The two innings Moyes refers to are arguably Hobbs' two most celebrated innings in Test matches. Australia had dominated Ashes cricket since the War, winning all five Tests in 1920–21, the first three (of five) in 1921, and four of five in 1924–25. Hobbs scored five centuries in these games, despite not batting in the 1921 rubber because of injury and then a bout of acute appendicitis.

In his autobiography, *10 for 66 And All That*, the Australian leg-spinner Arthur Mailey revealed that Hobbs was so much better a batsman than his teammates in 1920–21 that the Australians gave him 'cheap' singles from just about the first over. 'We all recognised it as a feat to have Hobbs out before lunch and accepted it as putting us on the road to victory,' Mailey wrote. In 1924–25, Hobbs began an extraordinarily reliable Test opening partnership with Herbert Sutcliffe, their first three stands in Ashes Tests bringing 157, 110 and then 283 runs. After that third stand, when the pair batted throughout the third day, the Australians stayed up until 2am, searching for an answer. Herbert Collins, the cagey Australian captain, seriously suggested bowling underarm grubbers on the basis that nothing else had worked. A few hours later, Hobbs missed the first ball of the new day — an overarm Mailey full-toss! — and was bowled.

In 1926, after only 17.2 overs were possible in the first Test, Hobbs and Sutcliffe added 182 for the first wicket at Lord's, then 59 and 156 at Headingley, 58 at Old Trafford, and 53 in the first innings at The Oval. The first four Tests had been drawn, England trailed by 22 runs on the first innings in the fifth Test, and on the third day the great openers found themselves on a dangerous, sticky wicket. The fate of the Ashes depended on them. 'A mistake by either,' wrote Neville Cardus in the *Manchester Guardian*, 'and Australia could hardly have captured less than four wickets before lunch.'

Instead, the pair added 172 for the first wicket. Hobbs, first out, made an even hundred, which Cardus called 'a masterpiece, through and through'. When he reached three figures, the crowd roared out three cheers. 'It was a joy to watch the way

Hobbs adapted his methods to the turf as it changed from docility in the early morning to its later viciousness,' Cardus wrote. Sutcliffe went on to 161, the team to 436 all out, and then Australia were bowled out by Wilfred Rhodes and Harold Larwood for 125. England had regained the Ashes.

At the MCG in the first week of January 1929, England were leading the series 2–0, but had been trapped on a terrible wicket. Set 332 to win, no one gave England any chance, so bad was the sticky pitch. Hobbs remembered the innings in Jack Fingleton's book, *Masters of Cricket*: 'I can recall very well how our friends came to the pavilion to commiserate with us, saying what a pity it was the rain came,' he said. 'We thought so too. We considered we didn't have a chance of getting the runs. That old campaigner Hughie Trumble, then secretary of the Melbourne Cricket Club, told us in all seriousness that 70 would be a good score in our second innings. Well, as you know, we chased 332 and eventually won by three wickets. Our success caused quite a stir at home. I remember that a

Hobbs in 1926, a season in which he played one of his greatest Test innings, a century on a wet wicket against Australia at The Oval.

JACK BANNISTER: Everybody I've spoken to says that never at any time during his career did he ever fall foul of officialdom, of umpires, the opposition. You never heard a bad word. As a gentle man and a gentleman, he was No. 1.

London newspaper cabled out 100 pounds each to Herbert Sutcliffe and myself ...'

Fingleton, a Test opening bat in the 1930s, believed, considering the difficulties the two batsmen faced, that this opening partnership was 'the most outstanding one in Test history'.

Play didn't get underway until 1.22pm, and first Australia had to lose the last two wickets of their second innings. That didn't take any time at all. Quickly, it became apparent, as the sun shone down, that the wicket was drying in patches, so that there were spots from which the ball spat dangerously, while other parts of the pitch behaved more predictably. It was at its most dangerous just before tea, as the Australians, for over after over, operated with a bevy of potential catchers around the bat. But Hobbs and Sutcliffe stood firm, using dead bats when they had to, their pads whenever they could, and, most importantly, their good judgment to not play at the ball at all if they were confident it wouldn't hit the stumps. This game of wits went on for half an hour, an hour, until finally they went in for tea with the score 0–78.

They weren't separated until 5pm. Three years later, South Africa were caught on an MCG sticky and were bowled out for 36 and 45. George Hele, who umpired in both Tests, had no doubt the pitch Hobbs and Sutcliffe conquered in 1928–29 was the more difficult, though he did concede that Australia bowled much better against the South Africans. Hele, arguably Australia's finest ever umpire, wrote in 1974 that Hobbs' effort at the MCG was 'the finest innings I've seen on a wet wicket'. Both Englishmen were hit all over their bodies. Hobbs was once struck on the head, while Bert Oldfield,

DAVID FRITH: 'Hobbs and Sutcliffe' is part of the language now — the Surreyman and the Yorkshireman who didn't need to call. They trusted each other. The ball would leave a bat and off they'd go. It was almost like a sixth sense.

the great Australian wicketkeeper, conceded 15 byes, including two when a ball from the leg-spinner Ron Oxenham pitched on a length and spat over his head. Before this innings, Oldfield had allowed only three byes in the series while England were scoring 1932 runs. Hobbs was finally dismissed for 49, Sutcliffe went on to another century, and England retained the Ashes.

ON THIS AND ALL other tours Hobbs accepted the division that existed between amateurs and professionals. He always saw himself as a role model for other pros, and the amateurs responded with respect and warm friendships. Loyalty mattered, and it went both ways. A downside came in 1932–33, when he was in Australia working as a cricket correspondent, because many Australians were disappointed that Hobbs was not more critical of England's bodyline tactics. His dilemma was that he didn't want to be critical of his county colleague, the England skipper Douglas Jardine. His captains, including his long-time Surrey leader, Percy Fender, and much younger England captains such as Percy Chapman and Bob Wyatt, spoke of the quality of his advice and support. When Arthur Carr, the England skipper, could not field in a Test in 1926 because of illness, Hobbs took over reluctantly, because there was another amateur besides Carr (GTS Stevens, playing in his first Test against Australia) in the side. Hobbs' view was that captaincy was a preserve of the amateurs, and Chapman took over for the final Test, where he leaned heavily on Hobbs for advice. No professional was chosen to lead England until Len Hutton in 1952.

When Hobbs equalled Grace's record of 126 first-class centuries in 1925, he was bemused and astonished by the level of media and public interest. Twenty thousand people went to a day's play of the London derby between Surrey and Middlesex at The Oval, with Hobbs just one hundred behind Grace, but he missed out there, and didn't equal the Great Champion until a game against Somerset at Taunton a few weeks later, in front of a large holiday crowd and plenty of reporters and newsreel camera crews. With the record equalled, everyone went on their way, and a more relaxed Hobbs promptly scored his 127th, to win the game on the last afternoon. This was one of six times Hobbs scored a century in both innings of a first-class match.

In that 1925 county season, Hobbs, aged 42, scored 3024 runs and a then record 16 centuries. And still there were another nine seasons before he finally gave the game away.

Five years after he broke Grace's record for centuries, Hobbs went past WG's record first-class aggregate as well. This was 1930, with Bill Woodfull's Australian team touring, Hobbs' last season in Test cricket. He had volunteered to step down from Test matches before this, to make way for a younger man, but his benevolence was overruled, and consequently he fielded throughout Don Bradman's most prolific series (974 runs, including one triple and two double centuries). 'We kept saying to each succeeding 50 and 100: "Well played, Don," until it became monotonous,' Hobbs recalled wearily.

Hobbs ended his Test career by scoring just 9 at The Oval, and England lost the Ashes, but he remembered the match fondly because of the reception given to him by the crowd and the Australians when he arrived at the crease for his final Test innings. 'It was one of those quick, impulsive scenes which make a man very much in love with cricket and all who play it,' commented Cardus.

'I did not know beforehand that any tribute would be paid to me,' wrote Hobbs in his autobiography, 'although I became a bit suspicious when I approached the middle, because the Australians were all clustered near the wicket, instead of going to their positions in the field. Suddenly Woodfull's voice rang out, "Three cheers for Jack Hobbs!" Off came their green caps, and they gave the cheers in the most cordial way. I could only answer, "Thank you very much, you chaps." Since that day, I have often wished that I had gripped Woodfull's hand. I had the impulse to do so, but I was afraid that the spectators would think that I was "playing up". So I drew back.'

Hobbs finished with 5410 Test runs, at 56.94, from 61 Tests. Of those to play 20 Test innings or more, at 1 March 2002 that average is 11th highest. The only opener with a higher average is Sutcliffe. In England v Australia Tests, Hobbs ranks second only to Bradman in terms of runs scored (3636 at 54.26 in 41 Tests) and most hundreds (12; equal third best are David Gower, Walter Hammond, Greg Chappell and Steve Waugh with nine).

His retirement from first-class cricket finally came in 1934, perhaps hastened by an innings of 79 against Sussex that took him more than four hours and

The Surreyman and the Yorkshireman, Hobbs and Herbert Sutcliffe, who might well have made up the greatest opening batting partnership in cricket history.

ended when he ran himself out. After he returned to the pavilion, he reputedly muttered: 'That's it, I'm finished — I just can't move my feet any more.' After that, he wanted to play one more game for Surrey, his last at The Oval, but was then talked into one more appearance for the county, at Glamorgan, where he made a very inappropriate duck on a wet track. Two more games, one for an England XI against the Australians and finally for the Players against the Gentlemen, and he was done. His last score against the Aussies, caught McCabe bowled Fleetwood-Smith, 38, was only 13 less than his age.

The tributes during that farewell season had been many, and heartfelt. A big crowd at Old Trafford sang *Auld Lang Syne* after seeing him make the last of his 197 first-class centuries. 'I only did it to keep warm,' he modestly claimed. Meanwhile, at The Oval, a decision was made to build a new main entrance to the ground, complete with the 'Hobbs Gates' as a tribute to his services to England and Surrey cricket. The Grace Gates at Lord's, on the

IAN WOOLDRIDGE: He had the reputation for being the most gentle, kindly man. I do remember he had a sports shop in London, and as a kid I went there to buy his book, *How to Play Cricket*. I bought it from him personally, and asked him to autograph it, which he did. When I got home, I thought, you're an idiot, because at the time I entertained thoughts of being a professional. I should have asked for some help with my cricket. So I wrote him a letter, saying I'd met him in his shop, bought the book, and so on. And, you know, he wrote back, a page and a half in his own handwriting, full of good advice. What I didn't know was that he'd also written to Hampshire County Cricket Club, asking them to look out for me. Wasn't that kind? He was a man like that.

other side of the city of London, now had a suitable partner.

Hobbs was proud to be the first professional cricketer to be knighted purely for services to his sport. This honour came in 1953, the year of the new Queen's coronation, although apparently he initially wanted to decline it, for fear his old friends would see him differently. If his batting style can be seen as something of a bridge between old and new, similarly his knighthood demonstrated that the professional cricketer had finally won a sense of parity that did not exist when Hobbs began his career.

In his quiet, principled way, Hobbs proved you don't have to be loud to be heard. Self-taught, pragmatic, calm and adaptable, great on good wickets and bad, against all types of bowling, of all the 'old' legends, Hobbs and WG Grace are the two who would *most definitely* be champions in the hustle and bustle of 21st century cricket. Their understanding of technique and ability to adjust to any conditions would ensure their success. And if Sir Jack Hobbs did somehow re-emerge today, he would bring a sense of style and integrity that the game will always need.

A toast for the master batsman. Hobbs acknowledges the big crowd at Taunton, after scoring the century that equalled WG Grace's record of 126 hundreds in first-class cricket.

Getty Images

DENNIS LILLEE
Legend No. 6
A Captain's Dream

IN EARLY 1971, DENNIS Lillee burst on the Test scene, taking five wickets in his first innings, at a time when the Australian Test team was at its lowest ebb in more than 40 years. As the team surged back to the top of the cricket tree, more than anyone else in the side, Lillee captured the team's hard, brash, give-'em-nothing image. Then, as the game in Australia, on the back of World Series Cricket, moved into the entertainment age, Lillee became its biggest star. Almost to a man, his comrades and rivals put him at the top of the fast-bowling tree. On his retirement in 1984, he left a sport far different from the one he'd joined more than a decade before. And, despite the quiet complaints of some traditionalists, it seemed the game was better for the experience.

Dickie Bird, who has seen half a century of cricket as a first-class cricketer then Test umpire, says simply of Lillee, 'Greatest fast bowler that the world's ever seen.' Ian Botham rates him 'top of my list in the bowling department'. Martin Crowe reckons he was 'as intimidating as any bowler I ever faced'. Lillee became Test cricket's highest wicket-taker having overcome a back injury that cost him 18 months of sport and would have ended 99 of 100 careers, and having also missed two years

IAN CHAPPELL: I've always described Dennis Lillee as being 'a captain's dream and a batsman's nightmare'. As a captain, the greatest compliment I can pay Dennis Lillee is that he never ever asked me for a defensive fielder. If he got hit for four he never said to me, 'Can I have a fieldsman out there, can I have a man down at third man?' If anything, he was more likely to say, 'Put another bloke in at bat pad.' I mean, I've been criticised as a captain for overbowling Dennis Lillee. My answer is: have you ever tried to take a bone off a doberman? That was what it was like trying to get the ball off Dennis Lillee.

of Test cricket because of WSC. In doing so, he evolved from an explosive firebrand to become the craftiest fast-medium bowler and most professional cricketer of his generation, and the measuring stick for those outstanding Australian pacemen who followed his path, such as Geoff Lawson, Craig McDermott, Merv Hughes, Glenn McGrath and Jason Gillespie.

Born on 18 July 1949, he had joined the Perth grade club at age 15. All he wanted to do was bowl fast, very fast, which he did, deliveries spraying in the general direction of the stumps after a ridiculously long run-up. The sight of the famous West Indian, Wes Hall, bowling nasty at the WACA in late 1960 remained an inspiration. Fortunately, the coaches at Perth saw through the rawness, and discovered a likeable, talented young bloke who wanted to learn and was keen to work.

Lillee's initial first-class wicket was the veteran Queenslander Sam Trimble, caught at short-leg. The second was Keith Dudgeon, caught by a rookie WA keeper, 21-year-old Rod Marsh. This, truly, was the start of a beautiful friendship. A little more than 15 years later, in the final Australia-Pakistan Test of 1983–84, Abdul Qadir was caught Marsh bowled Lillee, the 238th and final time this keeper–bowler dismissal occurred in first-class or World Series cricket.

Lillee finished that maiden season with 32 wickets at 22.03, equal third on the first-class wicket-taking list and sixth on the averages. He toured New Zealand with an Australian second XI. The following year he was in the Test side, for the sixth Ashes Test (of seven in the series) as the selectors searched for a bowling attack of Test class. No less than nine Australians made their Test debut that summer, six of them specialist bowlers. Of those six, only Lillee would ever have a significant impact on the international game.

His approach to the wicket remained long and exuberant, arms everywhere, and cricket scribes invariably used 'tearaway' as their first adjective

when describing him, but he had the ability to take five English wickets, for 84, in his first innings. 'Immediately one had to be impressed by his bowling,' recalls Bob Willis. 'I remember John Hampshire was playing for England. Eight-ball overs in those days, and John Hampshire played and missed at five in a row from Dennis bowling from the city end. We knew that a special talent had arrived on the scene.'

After the series ended, Lillee walked up to Keith Miller, to ask for Ray Lindwall's address. 'He might be able to teach me how to bowl,' the unassuming young quick explained to the great all-rounder.

It was not until the following season that Lillee established himself as a genuine force in international cricket. He did so in sudden, devastating style, against a 'Rest of the World' team that had come to Australia after a scheduled series against South Africa had been cancelled. After a rain-interrupted draw in Brisbane (Lillee 1–73 and 2–38), the two teams moved to the WACA in Perth, for the second unofficial 'Test'. The Australians were all out for 349, minutes before stumps on the opening day, and then Lillee, in front of his home fans, produced a spell of fast bowling that had not been seen since the days of Tyson, Lindwall or Larwood, perhaps ever. In 57 deliveries Lillee took 8–29 — the last six wickets in a spell of 31 balls for no runs — and totally demoralised his high-class opponents with frightening bounce and sheer speed.

'Even at that stage, you saw that he had so much intelligence,' remembers Gavaskar. 'He varied his pace, he didn't try to bounce you out, he realised very quickly that it was a fast pitch, he pitched the ball up to you, he didn't try to bang the ball in short because every time he did that it would sail over the wicketkeeper's head. So he pitched the ball up and he got batsmen like Garfield Sobers, Clive Lloyd and Rohan Kanhai into all kinds of trouble.'

Sir Garfield Sobers has a special memory of that day. 'Dennis really destroyed us,' he explains. 'I remember as I went into bat, Rodney Marsh was standing something like 20 yards back, and I looked at Rodney and I said to him, "What are you doing back there?"

'And he said, "You wait, you'll find out."

'And the first ball that Dennis bowled to me was a short-pitched ball. I'd never seen anything like it.'

Soon after, Lillee, now with Zapata moustache and long, flowing hair, went to England as the most experienced pace bowler in the Australian side. He had played two official Tests, the other three quicks in the squad — Bob Massie, Dave Colley and Jeff Hammond — had played none. Ian Chappell, the captain, had led Australia in just one Test. Yet Lillee and Massie, shrewdly if relentlessly marshalled by Chappell, became the talking point of the summer. In 1971, Lillee had played, with some though not great success, for Haslingden in the Lancashire League, but had clearly learnt about English conditions. For Australia a season later, he took 31 wickets in the series, at that time the most ever by an Australian in an Ashes series in England, and twice took three wickets in four balls. At The Oval he took 10–181, but even at Lord's, where Massie took 16 wickets and Lillee the other four, he was a key player.

'After the second Test match,' recalls Australia's then vice-captain Keith Stackpole, 'when Bob Massie took those 16 wickets, John Inverarity [the third selector on the tour] said, "We've unearthed a great bowler here." And I remember saying at the selection meeting, "Well, we may have, but I reckon there's going to be an even better bowler up the other end in Dennis Lillee." And that proved to be the case. He was certainly the best fast bowler that I ever played with or against.'

Lillee was measured during the series as walking back 44 paces to the top of his run. 'His run-up is in effect a sprint in which he positively races as fast as he can,' wrote John Arlott, 'so fast that his coordinated, flowing delivery action comes almost as a surprise. Like Tyson and Wesley Hall, he makes crowds gasp when they first see him bowl; that is the measure of real speed in a bowler.'

Back in Australia for a three-Test series against Pakistan, Lillee's impact was restricted by a worrying back complaint, but he came out in the final Test, in Sydney, to bravely send down 23 eight-ball overs and help Max Walker win a Test that had seemed lost. Walker took 6–15 and Lillee 3–68 as Pakistan crashed for 106 chasing 158. Ian Chappell

A mode of dismissal batsmen the world over would need to get used to. Alan Knott, caught Marsh bowled Lillee, at The Oval in 1972.

has fond memories of Lillee volunteering to bowl, despite his injury, and also the impact the first wicket of that innings — Nasim-ul-Ghani, bowled Lillee, 6 — had on the visitors' dressing room. Though the delivery was really only medium pace, a stump was broken clean through in the process. Chappell is convinced it was just a weak piece of timber, but the sight of the stump being taken from the ground in pieces after a Lillee 'thunderbolt' was enough to shatter the Pakistanis. This new-look

TONY COZIER: He first came to the West Indies in '73, when he was an out-and-out fast bowler. He only played one test match and his back went. When he came back, perhaps he wasn't as fast as he was in '73, but he was a much better bowler. He swung the ball away, he cut it back in, he could do almost anything with a ball. I'm sure that if you ask the West Indians of that era, and all West Indians who saw him, they'd say that he was the best they've seen.

Australian team was taking shape; that win at the SCG was the fourth in a row. Next stop, the West Indies.

Through the 1960s, the Caribbean had become renowned for its fast bowlers, most notably Wes Hall and Charlie Griffith. Consequently, the arrival of the new pace king, Lillee, was enthusiastically anticipated. In this regard, the series evolved into a giant anti-climax, because Lillee was at first

The classic action. Lillee at Lord's during the second Test of 1981.

restricted and ultimately thwarted by his back injury. He did play in the opening Test (0–112 and 0–20), then bowled in the first innings of the following tour game, but after that did not bowl again on tour. Still, the team resurgence continued; Australia won the series 2–0.

Lillee told later of the pain and self-doubt he felt during that tour, as some questioned the extent of his injury. It wasn't until he saw the noted sports medicine expert and former professional cricketer Dr Rudi Webster in Barbados that it was recognised that the fast man had three fractures in his lumbar vertebrae. 'You beauty, I knew there was something there,' Lillee is reputed to have exclaimed when he saw the X-rays. 'Perhaps the bastards will believe me now.' But even then, after a contrary opinion was found, Lillee was forced to bowl with the aid of painkillers in the nets at Trinidad. That ill-advised session led to a fourth fracture. Lillee would be out of the game for a year and a half.

Some assumed he was gone for good, but these cynics had severely underestimated their man. The story of Lillee's long battle back to full fitness is one of the most inspiring in cricket's history. First, he was required to endure an awkward and frustrating six weeks with his back encased in a plaster cast from his buttocks to his chest. Then, supported by Dr Frank Pyke and others at the physical education department at the University of Western Australia, Lillee put himself through a strength-building and fitness program that became something of a blueprint for the future preparations of young pace bowlers and the rehabilitation of injured quicks. At the same time, he set about understanding the mechanics of his trade, and modifying his run-up and delivery to limit as best as possible the chances of his back failing again. These learning processes would continue for the rest of his career, and beyond.

In the 1970–71 Ashes series, the Australian fans had often made their point about the slow play by aiming derisive slow handclaps at the players using empty beer cans. Four years later, there was no need for such protests. Doug Walters, who scored a century in a session in Perth, had the Sydney Hill unofficially named after him. The new fast man, Jeff Thomson, slung them down even quicker than Lillee and made the Poms look like old fools. There were the Chappells, Marsh ... and Lillee, to whom the fans across the country devoted their most

Lillee is introduced to the Queen at Lord's in 1981. The other Australians are (left to right) Geoff Lawson, captain Kim Hughes, Rodney Hogg, Graeme Wood, Ray Bright, Allan Border and Graham Yallop. In the left foreground, with his back to the camera, is the England captain Ian Botham.

fervent support. Only in Sydney, where Dougie was king, did Lillee take second place, but even so no fans took up the chant 'LILLEE … LILLEE … LILLEE' with more gusto than the Hillites.

Lillee took 25 wickets for the series, good at any time, but remarkable given what he had been through. Most observers thought he got quicker as the series went on; no doubt, he was restoring confidence in his back throughout the summer. Soon after Australia regained the Ashes, they were at Lord's playing the West Indies in the first World Cup final. This was a thrilling encounter, televised live back to Australia in full colour (colour television having been introduced to the country the previous year). Lillee was belted as much as anyone by Clive Lloyd, who made a majestic 102, but he and Thomson then became involved in a dramatic last-wicket stand that almost won the day. Australians like their heroes to never say die. Earlier, Lillee had taken 5–34 against Pakistan, becoming the first bowler to take five wickets in a one-day international and the first Australian to win a player-of-the-match award in a World Cup encounter. Afterwards, Australia stayed in England to win another Ashes series, with Lillee the leading wicket-taker (21 wickets) and the maker of a swashbuckling 73 not out, including three sixes, in the second Test at Lord's. This was the first first-class half-century of his life.

When he returned after his back injury, the reckless charge-in to the bowling crease had been replaced by a much smoother run-up. Max Walker, first change through the 1974–75 Ashes series, compares Lillee's now classic run-up and delivery with Thommo's slinging style: 'Dennis had that

> **CLIVE LLOYD:** The thing that was best about Dennis was that — if he had the new ball or the old ball, if it was half eleven or it was 5.30 — he was still running in, trying different things. He never gave up. If things were in his favour, he tried even harder. He was one of the greatest bowlers, if not the greatest, I've known.

gathering momentum, then the rock back and side-on position, and then he let it go, whereas Jeff Thomson just picked up the ball, went out and bowled like a gorilla at a million miles an hour. It was just awesome, the contrast between the two physiques and the two approaches.'

Alongside Lillee's superb action and his many wickets was an on-field manner that was brash, ebullient but sometimes boorish. Lillee saw no harm in trying to rile or intimidate the opposition, with words and actions, but sometimes appeared to extend this approach to umpires, too. He stated flatly that he aimed bouncers at batsmen, hoping to frighten them. 'When you are out in the middle,' he told journalist Keith Butler in 1976, 'you have to hate the opposition player. There's no doubt about that, but what I mean by hate is not to hate him personally — but to hate what he represents. You have to regard him as someone who is trying to steal something from you.' However, Lillee never bore grudges, and while occasionally during his great career one felt that his on-field rage might have damaged his public image, it never got the better of his bowling.

England's Paul Allott tells of meeting Lillee during his own debut Test, at Old Trafford in 1981: 'He was a good bloke off the field, he really was. Very kind to me actually, he made a point of coming up and saying, "Well bowled and well done, and congratulations on making your debut." Completely unexpected. I didn't think he'd be like that off the field.'

Back to 1975–76, where the Australia-West Indies series was advertised as a heavyweight battle of the fast men, between Lillee and Thomson in one corner and Andy Roberts and Michael Holding in the other. The pace was hot throughout, but the result was a no contest, Australia winning 5–1, with Lillee taking 27 wickets in five Tests, including his 100th Test wicket. The following season was one of his finest, featuring 47 wickets in six Tests, including

11 in the Centenary Test against England at the MCG, an occasion which developed into a major personal triumph. Exhausted after a long international season, in which he had already bowled over 1700 deliveries, Lillee was called to the front once more after Australia was bowled out for only 138 on the opening day. He responded by taking 6–26 from 13.3 overs, as England capitulated to 95, and then toiled through another 34.4 overs, taking 5–139 to prevent England achieving an unlikely victory on the final afternoon. Bob Willis thought this was Lillee's finest hour. At game's end, the Aussie champion was chaired from the field. Soon after, he announced his body desperately needed a rest and that he would not be available for the 1977 Ashes tour.

On the final day, when the Queen was introduced to the teams on the field, Lillee marked the occasion by producing a pen and paper and asking for an autograph. He was knocked back there, but did receive a signed photograph from Buckingham Palace soon afterwards. Away from the international scene, Lillee produced an extraordinary performance in a Gillette Cup one-day semi-final against Queensland at the WACA. Western Australia were bowled out for just 77, but still won by 15 runs, with Lillee taking 4–21 from 7.3 overs, including Viv Richards for a first-over duck and Greg Chappell for 9. Rod Marsh, the captain, had asked his men to 'put on a show' for the disappointed local crowd. 'Put on a show!' roared an indignant Lillee. 'C'mon, let's get 'em. We CAN do this!'

Perhaps the true measure of Lillee's greatness as a bowler is that he was able to not only sustain his career beyond his fastest years, but in fact become even more effective. In World Series Cricket, 1977–79, Lillee was supreme among a plethora of great pacemen — Roberts, Holding, Garner, Procter, Snow, Imran Khan, et al. He took 67 wickets in the SuperTests, another 54 in the one-day internationals, all the time operating at an intensity

GREG CHAPPELL: I remember my last game for Queensland, my last first-class game. It was the Sheffield Shield final in March 1984 against Western Australia in Perth and I got 84 in the first innings. I got out caught in the slips off Dennis Lillee, trying to cut one. It was the first ball he'd ever bowled that I could have played a cut shot to and I got so excited I tried to hit it as hard as I could and finished up getting a thick edge. He bowled so few bad balls that he just wore you down; it was like Chinese water torture batting against Dennis. He was most dangerous on wickets that suited batsmen, because he wasn't going to give you runs, he wasn't going to let you win. He made himself into the greatest fast bowler I've ever seen.

that gradually won over the cynics who originally thought WSC was not fair dinkum.

At the MCG in 1979–80, the season after traditional cricket and WSC made up, Lillee destroyed England on a slow pitch that reduced other fast bowlers to bystanders. Cutting his run, he relied on changes of pace and a collection of leg- and off-cutters, and took 11–138 for the match. 'We're talking about a flat batting wicket, one of those wickets that's not that easy to score runs on but difficult to take wickets on,' recalls Allan Border. 'Dennis was able to produce incredible spells; instead of bowling what I call seam-up, traditional fast bowling, where you hit the seam and move it this way and that way, he started to work on the delivery where he ripped his hand across the seam. He had this incredible ability to do that and still maintain his accuracy.'

Less impressive was Lillee's attempt to promote a new aluminium bat during the first Test of that same series, at the WACA Ground in Perth. After Lillee clanged the first ball away, England captain Mike Brearley complained to the umpires, who ruled that because the bat might damage the ball, it would have to be swapped for a traditional willow. Lillee argued, ponced about, and then hurled the offending implement away. He got his publicity, but at what cost?

Lillee took 35 wickets in that 1979–80 season, another 37 in 1980–81 (against New Zealand and India), 39 in England in 1981 and then 31 back in Australia in 1981–82. Through this time, he established a litany of records. At the MCG in early 1981 he dismissed Sunil Gavaskar to break Richie Benaud's then Australian wicket-taking record. A few months later he passed Hugh Trumble to become the leading wicket-taker in Ashes history. In the final Test at The Oval he took 11 wickets, becoming the only Australian since the 'Demon' Fred Spofforth to take 10 wickets in an Ashes Test four times. In December, against Pakistan, he took his 300th Test wicket, the third bowler to do so, and then his 310th, the West Indies' Larry Gomes caught by Greg Chappell at the MCG, to break Lance Gibbs' world record.

Lillee took 10 wickets in that Melbourne Test against the Windies, including 7–83 in the first innings, his best innings analysis in Tests. The most thrilling moment was his dismissal of Viv Richards. It was the first day, and the crowd was

> **SIR RICHARD HADLEE:** The thing that I admired greatly about Dennis was the fact that he was big and strong and aggressive, had confidence, marvellous skills, wonderful bowling technique; he intimidated the batsmen with a bit of chatter from time to time, a bit of gamesmanship. And he got you out. What a tremendous role model he has been for pace bowlers.

already in a vibrant mood following a dynamic unconquered 100 by Kim Hughes out of 191 all out, after Australia had collapsed to 4–26. The Windies had 35 minutes to bat, and Lillee was inspired. Terry Alderman dismissed Faoud Bacchus, before the great fast man had Desmond Haynes caught at second slip, nightwatchman Colin Croft lbw and finally, dramatically, Richards bowled off the inside edge from the final ball of the day. Half an hour later, thousands were still at

Lillee argues with England captain Mike Brearley in Perth in late 1979, while the subject of the dispute, an aluminium bat, remains in the great fast bowler's right hand.

the ground, chanting and cheering, still caught in the moment and only half-believing what they had seen.

But amid these famous days were more unfortunate episodes. Whether he enjoyed the role of villain is not clear, but he often seemed happy to audition for it. At Headingley in 1981, the Test that Ian Botham turned so completely around that England won after being forced to follow on, Lillee and Rod Marsh admitted they'd backed the Poms at 500–1 when England were furthest behind. There was no suggestion that either player had gone slow, but it still looked bad. Then in November at the WACA, Lillee responded to Pakistan's Javed Miandad, who'd bumped him as he completed a single, by kicking him gently in the leg. Miandad reacted by lifting his bat high above his head, as if he was about to launch a physical assault, and umpire Tony Crafter jumped between the pair. There was fault on both sides, and Lillee was subsequently fined and suspended for two World Series Cup one-dayers.

Lillee retired after the 1983–84 Australian season. He had claimed 20 more Test victims against Pakistan that summer, including a wicket with his last delivery in international cricket, and then captained Western Australia to victory in the Sheffield Shield final, against a Queensland team skippered by his old mate, Jeff Thomson. Lillee finished with 355 Test wickets (coincidentally, Rod Marsh, who also retired from Test cricket after that

Pakistan match in Sydney, completed 355 Test dismissals), which remained the Australian record until Shane Warne went past him in New Zealand in 2000. Lillee was the first Australian to take 100 one-day international wickets. Typically, controversy dogged the great man until the end, as he was suspended for two Shield games late in the season, after getting into an argument with the umpires at the Gabba over a drinks break in a rain-interrupted session of play.

Ever the athlete, he returned briefly to first-class cricket in 1987–88, with Tasmania — where he was fined $750 after causing damage to a Launceston dressing room during a quiet drink with Queensland's Ian Botham — and then in 1988, with Northamptonshire. Finally, he called it quits for good, 882 first-class wickets after he'd started. In the years since, he has stayed largely out of the spotlight, preferring to devote his cricket time to coaching young fast bowlers, in Australia and overseas. His advice has been available to potential top-liners, too. Bob Simpson, after his 10-year spell as Australian coach ended in 1996, recalled that Lillee had been given an open invitation to help out and had often made a significant contribution.

So what set him apart? Yes, he had natural talent, competitiveness, great courage and an iron will. But crucially, and surprisingly for a cricketer who often attracted headlines for the wrong reasons, the key to him was that he was a genuinely humble man. He discovered early, and never forgot, that there was always more to learn. After his back injury, the fight for peak fitness became a priority for him. He always strove for excellence, never stopped trying to be even better than what he was, and applied a level of professionalism to his cricket that was ahead of its time. 'When I was younger,' Lillee told Rudi Webster for the 1984 book *Winning Ways*, 'I used to idolise a few cricketers. They were like little gods to me. After I broke the world record, I realised that I had more wickets than any of them and got them at a better strike rate. I then started to say, "I'm not great, why did I think that these people were so great? Why do the press and the fans regard them as immortals? I am certainly not an immortal." Don't get me wrong, I am not running down the other guys.

'What I am saying is that if you have ability and you work hard and use your mind properly, you can do it too.'

IAN BOTHAM: I remember we were in Perth, on a quick, bouncy, green wicket. I went out to bat and Dennis came steaming in, and the first ball, I played and missed. And Dennis' gold medallions were swinging here, sweat there, he kicked the ground and back to his mark he went …

And this went on for three, four deliveries and each time I played and missed he got further down the wicket, so he was getting nearer to me. The fifth delivery came whistling through and I played and missed again. By now, the last ball of the over, he's standing right in front of me. The medallion's still swinging, the sweat's still pouring, and this time he flicked his sweat straight down the front of my shirt. And he just looked at me and said, 'Beefy, do me a favour, mate. You hold the bloody bat still and I'll aim at it.'

SACHIN TENDULKAR
Legend No. 7
The Little Maestro

ONE OF THE MOST popular exercises among cricket fans in the final few seasons of the 20th century was to try to nominate the best batsman in the world. By general consensus, there were three contenders: the West Indies' Brian Lara, Australia's Steve Waugh and Sachin Tendulkar of India. By even greater consensus, there was one winner: Tendulkar.

The adulation he receives in his homeland is unprecedented in cricket. Not even Bradman had to cope with the frenzied support that Tendulkar receives, or the stark silence he hears when he walks off after a rare failure. He has wonderful style on the field, humility off it, is intelligent and good looking, has fulfilled all expectations (despite their excesses) and through his runs and persona has rewarded his supporters much more often than not. Not only is he the best batsman in the world, he also appears to be a thoroughly decent person. Boys yearn to be like him, mothers would love him to be their own, men who've seen the champions of the past have no problem conceding that he is better than almost all who came before.

He was *always* going to be a champion. 'We have a young batsman in Bombay called Sachin Tendulkar,' boasted Ravi Shastri in 1988, 'who is sent from upstairs to play the game. He is only 15,

> **SACHIN TENDULKAR:** Back in 1983 I was just 10 years old and I saw India lifting the World Cup and that really inspired me. Though at that age I didn't understand much about cricket; I was just jumping around with my friends because we'd won the World Cup. That was a big morale boost for me, and I thought, yeah, one day I want to be there as well.

a right-hand bat, five foot four inches tall, but I tell you, he's going to be a great player.'

No one who saw Bradman bat for Bowral when he was 15 would have been as confident of the young Don's future greatness.

Nothing Tendulkar has done in the years since 1988 suggests that Shastri overrated him. Indeed, eight years later, during an interview with the Australian television journalist Ray Martin, Sir Donald Bradman said of him: 'I asked my wife to come look at him. I never saw myself play, but I feel that this fellow is playing much the same as I used to play, and she looked at him on the television and said yes, there is a similarity between the two. To me, it's his compactness, his technique, his stroke production, it all seemed to gel as far as I was concerned.'

There can be no higher praise.

THE ATMOSPHERE TENDULKAR GENERATES when he is carving up opposition attacks at home can be quite awesome. Examples of the extent of the hero worship are everywhere, and not just in the huge billboards that feature his product endorsements. Security guards travel with him wherever he goes, in India and beyond. During the lead-up to the 1999 World Cup, Sachin's back injury was the talk of the nation. Newspapers carried prominent daily reports on his progress, pushing news of the upcoming election off the front pages.

> **DICKIE BIRD:** I think Tendulkar is the best player in the world today, without a shadow of doubt. Another small man, you see, like Bradman, but his footwork is out of this world. He has so much time in which to play the ball. And again, as I've said about all the greats, tremendous balance. There's a lot to be said for that.

Fans were instructed to pray for his recovery, and financial experts pondered just how much the companies he was associated with might suffer on the stock exchange if he had to miss out. Then, when he announced he would play, the celebrations were such it seemed the Cup was already won.

Earlier in that year, after his run out in a Test against Pakistan set off a riot that caused play to be suspended, he had to walk round the boundary to quieten his fans. The joy and satisfaction he brings to so many Indians' lives, especially those from his hometown, is extraordinary.

To the man himself, this support is a delight rather than a grind. 'It's just a little difficult to move around freely,' he concedes. 'You don't have your privacy but that's the price one has to pay. But looking at the other side of the coin, I feel the love and the good wishes, when I go on the ground. To have 100,000 people cheering for you, praying for your success, it does help and it means a lot to me.'

And then he adds, 'It is a special thing, always, to play in India.'

When Mike Denness, while working as a match referee in South Africa in November 2001, had the audacity to doubt the absolute integrity of their champion, a crisis was triggered that for a brief period threatened to split the cricket world. In fact, Denness found fault in six Indian players, but it was his action against Tendulkar that did the damage. Tendulkar had cleaned out the seam of the ball without gaining the permission of the umpires (he said later he didn't realise that he needed to), but it was hardly a hanging offence, and across India, indeed in the minds of almost all cricket fans, it was ridiculous that Tendulkar's spotless record was tarnished.

Shane Warne is just one of a large group who consider Tendulkar the best batsman they've seen. 'He judges the length much quicker than anyone else,' the great leg-spinner said in early 2002. This expertise is a gift, of course, that many said separated Bradman from the mortals. 'He is, simply, the second greatest batsman of all time,' reckons Martin Crowe. 'A wonderful cricketer,' says Clive Lloyd. 'He loves playing, he loves the game and he represents his people, his team and the game itself really well.'

'He's definitely the best player that I've seen,' says the Indian team coach John Wright. 'He has a genius about him, he can play amazing shots and manufacture shots. And he has a great presence — as a cricketer and as a person.'

While it is easy to focus on his batting, Tendulkar is also capable of significant contributions with the ball, usually bowling leg-breaks and wrong 'uns and always trying to get a wicket. An example of his prowess came in early 2001, in Kolkota, when he came on after tea on the final day and dismissed Matthew Hayden, Adam Gilchrist and Shane Warne as India won perhaps their greatest ever Test win, a victory gained after they had been forced to follow on. Eight years earlier, in a one-day international at the same venue, Tendulkar bowled the final over (after Kapil Dev had declined the opportunity) and prevented South Africa scoring the six runs they needed to win.

S ACHIN TENDULKAR WAS BORN on 24 April 1973, and began his first-class career in style just 15 years later by scoring 100 not out on his Mumbai debut. He went on to become the first batsman to make a hundred on debut in all three of the domestic competitions, the Ranji Trophy (that unbeaten 100), the Duleep Trophy (159 for West Zone v East Zone at Guwahati, 1990–91) and the Irani Trophy (103 not out for Rest of India v Delhi at Bombay, 1989–90). Whether he is the youngest ever to score a first-class hundred is open to conjecture, as some young prodigies' birth certificates are not as authentic as his; many record books do give him that honour.

Before that first-class debut, when he was 14, he had enjoyed an extraordinary run of scoring in school cricket, where he made 27 not out, 125, 207 not out, 346 not out and finally 329 not out in successive innings (an average of 1034!). In that final knock, playing for Shardashram Vidyamandir School against St Xavier's High School at Bombay in February 1988, he shared an unbroken partnership of 664 with his friend and future India teammate Vinod Kambli, who scored 349 not out. St Xavier's attack included the future Test bowler Sairaj Bahutule, who took 0–182. *Wisden* suggests this is the highest partnership ever recorded.

Even more astonishing, when he made that 329 not out he was actually playing in two games at once! While he scored that triple century his other team was fielding one man short. Then, he changed

SUNIL GAVASKAR: Tendulkar is close to being the perfect batsman. His backlift is straight, his balance is unbelievable. He can play off either foot, he can play on either side and, again, he has that ability that separates the men from the boys — the ability to hit the good ball for boundaries or sixes.

grounds, left his first team with 10 fieldsmen, and scored 178 not out.

Tendulkar, all of 16 years and 205 days old, made his Test debut on 15 November 1989, the third youngest Test cricketer in history, in the most testing of circumstances, against neighbours Pakistan at the National Stadium in Karachi. This was Kapil Dev's 100th Test. Pakistan were led by the great Imran Khan, who was part of an attack that included Wasim Akram, Abdul Qadir and a young fast bowler also making his first Test appearance, Waqar Younis. In at 4–41 after Pakistan had been bowled out for 409 (Imran 109 not out), Tendulkar

Getty Images

Tendulkar, all of 16 years old, during his first Test series, in Pakistan in late 1989.

and Mohammad Azharuddin added 32 before Waqar bowled his fellow debutant.

'I was terribly nervous,' Tendulkar recalls. 'I didn't know what was happening around me. I thought for a sec that it was a school game going on and I batted as one would bat in a school game. I felt this was the first and the last Test match of my career.'

Maninder Singh saw things differently: 'The day Sachin got into the Indian team he started batting in the nets and looked so good that everybody knew that this fellow was going to go very, very far. It never looked as if he had just come into the Indian team for the first time.'

A Test later, Tendulkar became the youngest person to score a Test half-century (lbw Imran 59), and the youngest to share in a Test century

Tendulkar at Old Trafford in 1990, after scoring his maiden Test century.

partnership (143 for the fifth wicket with Sanjay Manjrekar), the start of a succession of 'youngest ever' Test records that included youngest to 1000, 2000, 3000, 4000, 5000, 6000 and 7000 runs, and youngest to score a Test century in England and Australia. In making 119 not out at Old Trafford in 1990, when 17 years 112 days, he narrowly missed out on being the youngest to score a Test century (Mushtaq Mohammed made 101 for Pakistan against India in Delhi in 1960–61, when aged 17 years 82 days).

Tendulkar's maiden Test hundred was hardly an easy one. India had been set 408 to win, and Tendulkar was in at 4–109, which quickly became 5–127, then 6–183 before the tea interval. But with Manoj Prabakhar, Tendulkar saw out the day, reaching his century in the final hour and finishing on 119 not out as the team total reached 6–343. His first Test hundred in Australia, made 18 months later at the Sydney Cricket Ground, is remembered by all who saw it for the maturity he showed, the quality of his strokeplay, and the way he always found the gap in the field. A month later, batting ahead of his more experienced teammates Vengsarkar and Azharuddin at No. 4 in the fifth Test (he'd gone in at No. 6 in Sydney), Tendulkar made 114 from 161 balls out of a total of 272 on the bouncy WACA pitch, against an attack led by Merv Hughes and Craig McDermott. 'I still think that's the best Test innings I've played,' Tendulkar says today.

'I remember him playing these back-foot cover drives at regular intervals while the rest of the batsmen were just struggling to keep their wickets intact,' declares Manjrekar. 'This boy, this young man, was scoring runs briskly and without a problem …'

In 1992, Tendulkar became Yorkshire's first overseas player, but the move was only moderately successful, though he went past 1000 first-class runs for the season. 'I never got going,' he said afterwards, refusing to deflect responsibility. 'Perhaps there was more pressure than I'd first thought. I received a fabulous reception each time I came out to bat and I respect the people of Yorkshire for that. The guys in the dressing room were fantastic, the whole thing was good for my learning curve.'

With all this experience behind him before his 20th birthday, he blasted through the 1990s, scoring hundred after hundred. By the end of April 2002, he had 60 international centuries — 29 in Tests and 31 in one-day internationals — 26 of them made at home, 34 away.

WHILE TENDULKAR'S TEST RECORD is superb, it is his one-day statistics that are quite magnificent. The turning point came in March 1994, in a one-day international at Eden Park in Auckland. New Zealand could only set India 146 to win. The wicket, however, was seaming, Indian opener Navjot Sidhu had a stiff neck, and no one seemed keen to take his place at the top of the order. So Tendulkar volunteered — 'Let's give it a try, I'm pretty sure it's going to work,' he said to the tour selectors — and blasted 82 runs from 49 balls, including 15 fours and two sixes. He's been opening Indian one-day innings ever since.

He scored his first one-day century against Australia in Colombo in a Singer Cup match in September 1994. It was his 78th one-day international. Four years and 120 one-dayers later, he hit his 18th against Zimbabwe at Bulawayo, breaking Desmond Haynes' record. Another two years, and he overtook Mohammad Azharuddin as the leading runscorer in the one-day game, doing so in 81 matches and 62 innings less than it had taken his former India colleague. By March 2002, he had passed 11,000 runs, and in a unique double had more than 100 wickets to go with it.

In July 2001, in an interview with the cricket website *cricinfo.com*, Tendulkar nominated his best one-day innings. His favourites were consecutive knocks made in Sharjah against Australia in 1998, the first of which was a phenomenal effort where he had to conquer not just Shane Warne but Mother Nature as well. The cricket ground at Sharjah is beautifully grassed, but it is built on sand and surrounded by desert, and not long after Tendulkar began dismantling the Aussie attack a fierce sandstorm speared in. The players were obliged to lie on the turf, or crouch with their backs to the gale. Eventually, the storm abated, and Tendulkar resumed his assault as if the delay had been no more than a drinks break. He

This was one of the little maestro's most emotional innings, a century against Kenya in the 1999 World Cup that he dedicated to the memory of his father, who had died just before the start of the tournament.

finished with 143 from 131 deliveries. In the final, on his 25th birthday, he hit 134 from 131 balls, as India successfully chased 273 to win the tournament.

Tendulkar's other three favourites were his 104 on a bad wicket against Zimbabwe at Benoni in the 1996–97 Triangular series, his highest score, 186, against New Zealand at Hyderabad in 1999 — 'It never seemed that I would get out on that particular day. Whatever I tried came off.' — and 140 against Kenya at Bristol during the 1999 World Cup, an innings he dedicated to his father, who had died a few days before.

TWO YEARS AFTER HE made his first one-day century, Tendulkar scored his ninth century in ODIs in his first match as India's captain, against Sri Lanka in Colombo. Back home, Tendulkar commenced his Test captaincy career with an emphatic victory over Australia, and then a series win over South Africa. In between, he led India to victory in the Titan Cup one-day competition against Australia and South Africa, successes that had his legion of fans believing that his golden touch extended to generalship as well. But it was not to be. The one weakness on Tendulkar's cricket résumé is his record as an international captain. It appears he cannot motivate or gel a disparate group, and worse still the responsibility of leadership has acted as a bridle on his runscoring.

After those initial successes in 1996, Tendulkar's team failed awfully on tours to South Africa and the West Indies, losing Test and one-day series comprehensively. His captaincy was criticised, and a slump in his batting form — just one century in 22 Test innings — quickly had many questioning his future as captain. He was back among the runs when India played Sri Lanka home and away, but all six Tests were drawn and India couldn't fashion a victory in one-day carnivals in Sri Lanka and Sharjah. After that, Azharuddin was appointed captain for the 1998 home series against Australia.

Between March 1998 and July 1999, Tendulkar enjoyed another remarkable period of rungetting that included 10 ODI centuries and five Test centuries. But when the decision was made to sack Azharuddin after India's ordinary World Cup, the selectors found themselves with no alternative but to press Tendulkar into taking the job again. Initially, things worked out well, as India defeated New Zealand in Tests and one-dayers at home, with the captain starting his new reign with a century and then scoring his first double century in Tests. However, against the all-conquering Australians in Australia, India were overwhelmed. Steve Waugh's

men seemed to specifically target him, and though he still managed a glorious hundred in the second Test, in Melbourne, by tour's end he did not seem to be coping with the pressure he and his team were under. 'By series end,' Waugh wrote, 'he was reduced to the same level as we mere mortals.'

Tendulkar announced he was taking 'moral responsibility' for the losses and would stand down, but there was still no one to take over and he was asked to stay on for a two-Test series against South Africa. 'He was miserable,' says Manjrekar. 'Some of the guys in the team told me that he was not the Tendulkar of old when he was leading; he was not having fun any more because the pressure was getting to him.' When both these Tests were lost, Tendulkar was able, finally and perhaps forever, to hand back the captain's armband. He vowed never to take on the leadership again.

This seems to be a case of a captain lost, but a batsman gained. As captain he won just four of 25 Tests and 22 of 68 one-day internationals. By comparison, of his first 31 one-day international centuries, 24 came in matches India went on to win. In Tests, his batting average in Tests India have won (62.96 in 25 matches to March 2002) is more than 21 runs-per-innings higher than it is in Tests lost (41.80 in 26 defeats). And whatever his failings as a leader, he has remained remarkably sellable, making more money from endorsements than any other cricketer in history by backing products as diversified as toothpaste, sportswear, electronics, soft drink, tyres, credit cards and watches.

TENDULKAR DID NOT SCORE a double century in Test cricket until his 71st Test, against New Zealand in Ahmedabad in October–November 1999, having already scored 20 single centuries. Incredibly, it was only in the previous year that he had made his maiden first-class double ton. It was as if, after scoring so many runs in the previous decade, he developed an even greater appetite for runs. In the one-day tournament that followed that big innings against the Kiwis, he smashed an unconquered 186 from 150 balls at Hyderabad, just eight runs short of Saeed Anwar's world record score.

To try to identify Tendulkar's greatest Test innings is difficult, simply because there have been so many that are special. Here we will focus on two.

The first came in 1998, when the Australians came to India and much was made of Tendulkar's confrontation with Warne. In the end, it was no contest. However, though he never used it as an excuse, Warne was definitely hindered by a shoulder injury that required surgery soon after. Tendulkar started with a double century for Mumbai against the tourists, fell cheaply on the opening day of the series, but then launched a fantastic assault in the second innings.

India were two wickets down and led by 44 runs; the sense of occasion was extraordinary. The ball was turning out of the footmarks and Warne had dismissed him in the first innings. Now, the great leg-spinner specifically changed the line of his attack and Tendulkar, who'd been practising assiduously length on a specially worn wicket in the nets, went on the attack.

The former Australian captain, now commentator, Ian Chappell was at the Chepauk Stadium in Chennai when the pair came face to face for the second time in the match. 'I will never forget for as long as I live the moment when Shane Warne came around the wicket for the first time and Tendulkar deposited him over the mid-wicket boundary.'

He finished 155 not out, from 191 balls. In the second Test he scored 79, in the third 177 and 31, as India ended the Australians' run of nine straight series wins.

His second great innings came in early 1999, when India and Pakistan met on Indian soil in a Test series for the first time in 12 years, and for the first time since Tendulkar's debut Test series. From the jump there was controversy, as the opening Test had to be transferred from Delhi to Chennai after extremists vandalised the pitch. Tendulkar was dismissed for a duck early on day two by off-spinner Saqlain Mushtaq, which left all India stunned and alarmed, even though their team was able to glean a first-innings lead of 16. That turned into a target of 271, a run chase which produced some of cricket's most dramatic scenes, amplified many times over by the noise then deathly quiet of the 50,000 crowd and also, of course, by the immense national pride or hurt that hinged on the result. India crashed to 2–6, then 5–82, but with Sachin still there and scoring most of the runs. The London *Daily Telegraph's* correspondent, Peter Deeley, described Saqlain's off-breaks as 'spitting' from the pitch, but the wicketkeeper, Nayan

Mongia, stayed while 136 were added for the sixth wicket.

Tendulkar was past his hundred, but clearly suffering from back spasms. Still, he edged his country to within sight of a famous victory, until with just 17 runs needed and four wickets in hand, he hit a catch to Wasim Akram. Incredibly, the final three wickets fell for just four more runs and it was the Pakistanis who celebrated a great triumph, while Sachin was too exhausted to come out for the presentations.

He had batted for 405 minutes, ultra slow by his standards, but proof of the dedicated concentration he brought to the task. 'I have long said that Tendulkar is the best batsman in the world,' Wasim said immediately afterwards, 'and today we saw one of the best innings I have ever seen played.'

IN SPORTS IN WHICH performances can be precisely measured, such as track and field and swimming, the modern athlete holds all the world

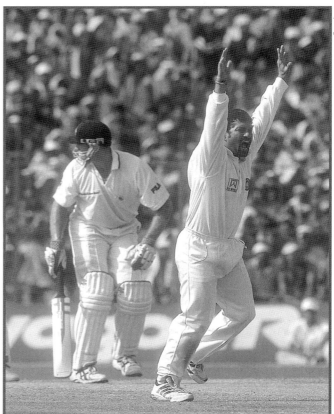

It is impossible to keep him out of the game. Australia's Matthew Hayden is lbw to Tendulkar at Calcutta in 2001, as India moves towards the 'impossible' victory on the final day of the second Test.

The look on England keeper James Foster's face captures the magic of this moment. Foster's gloves indicate the ball has pitched wide of the leg-stump, but Tendulkar has still driven it over cover.

records. Of course, it is not that simple in cricket, but still a case must be able to be put that the greatest batsmen and bowlers of the modern era might be superior to their predecessors. Without doubt, the players of the 21st century find themselves under greater media scrutiny, are asked to perform at their finest on more occasions, are asked to travel more kilometres to ply their trade. On this basis, it can be argued that Tendulkar, while probably not as good as the freakish Bradman, is a greater batsman than any other champion in the game's history.

And most stunningly of all, it is very likely that the best is yet to come. Of the top 15 ranked batsmen in the world at 1 March 2002, Tendulkar was the fourth

youngest, older only than South Africa's Jacques Kallis, Pakistan's Yousuf Youhana and Sri Lanka's Mahela Jayawardene, and almost eight years younger than the oldest of the 15, Steve Waugh. And in the past five years, his batting average has risen consistently. In January 1998, that average was just below 52. Twelve months later it was up closer to 55, slightly over 56 after the series in Australia in 1999–2000, and up to 57.28 in January 2001. By midway through the series in the West Indies in April–May 2002, his Test average was 58.72, within sight of Graeme Pollock's 60.97, the second highest of all Test batsmen to have played 20 innings.

'I think there is always room for improvement,' Tendulkar says modestly. Although it is not his intention, he is sending out an ominous message for the world's bowlers. 'One is never satisfied with what you've achieved in life, you want to try and get more out of it, and that's the same with me.

'I want to try to score as many runs as possible, try to be as solid as possible and try to play good cricket.'

GARY KIRSTEN: He once got 40 in a one-day game at Kingsmead in about 20 balls, which featured some of the hardest hitting I've ever seen. Then he went for a drive and hit the ball as hard as I've ever seen it hit, but Jonty Rhodes took a brilliant catch. That was a scary innings.

IMRAN KHAN
Legend No. 8
Lion of Pakistan

YOU KNOW YOU'RE A good player when you announce you're retiring, but the leader of your country won't let you. So it was with Imran Khan at the start of 1988. He had hoped to bid farewell in grand style, with a victory in the World Cup held on the Indian sub-continent in late 1987, but a stunning loss to Australia in a semi-final in Lahore put paid to that. Still, in Imran's eyes at least, the end was near.

'I had always promised myself that I would leave cricket when I was still at the peak of my form and still enjoying the game,' he explained. However, the head of Pakistan's government, General Zia remarked that while Imran's retirement might have been a good thing for Imran, it was not a good thing for Pakistan. 'Sometimes,' he said, 'one has to rise above the self.'

Fortunately for the General, the team and the country, nagging at Imran was the realisation that he was leaving the game without beating the mighty West Indies, who Pakistan were due to visit in 1988. No away team had won a series in the Caribbean since 1973, or a Test since 1978. Most had been trashed. The last team to venture to the Windies had been England, who were destroyed five Tests to nil.

'All my career I have taken risks,' Imran concluded. 'How could I forgo a chance of beating the West Indies on their home ground? To do so would result in Pakistan's being recognised for the first time as the best team in the world. I would never forgive myself in years to come if I thought that being scared to lose had made me miss such a unique opportunity ...'

So Imran came back, and although he wouldn't win the victory over the Windies he craved, he did, ironically, get to retire from the game after a famous World Cup triumph. That would come in Melbourne in 1992, by which time he had achieved a level of fame and esteem unmatched by any other Pakistani cricketer, before or since. As classy all-rounder, shrewd captain and brave promoter of all things good about his country, Imran changed the way we perceive Pakistani cricket, bringing a new respect for his national team in the same way Sir Frank Worrell changed the status of the West Indies earlier in the 20th century. Whenever the history of the game in Pakistan is studied, Imran Khan will be recognised as its most significant force.

IMRAN FIRST ESTABLISHED HIMSELF as a cricketer in the mid-1970s, in a side that contained fine players such as Mushtaq Mohammed, Asif Iqbal, Majid Khan and Zaheer Abbas but which rarely won. At this time Pakistan's batting was recognised for its style, but often also for its frailty. The bowling attack was mediocre. To this mix Imran brought shrewd pace bowling, genuine batting skill and an ability to sustain excellence under pressure. Further, when he became captain of Pakistan for the tour of England in 1982, he brought a focus to the way the team prepared and played. As the team's unequivocal commander-in-chief, Imran provided runs, wickets, calm, example and inspiration, and also took full responsibility for the development of Pakistan's next generation of stars, such as Wasim Akram, Waqar Younis, Salim Malik, Inzamam-ul-Haq and Saeed Anwar.

'Imran changed the attitude of Pakistan cricket because of his own attitude towards cricket,' insists Wasim Akram. 'He was so positive about it, he was so passionate about it. He wanted to win badly ...'

This said, it must be stressed that it is not just for his leadership that Imran is so highly ranked among *ESPN's Legends of Cricket*. As a fast bowler, he was one of the very greatest, as an all-rounder, superb. For a brief period, through 1982–83, before he was hobbled by a serious leg injury, his bowling returns were astonishing — in nine home Tests, three against Australia and six against India, he took 53 wickets. That he did so on wickets that traditionally offer little to pacemen, and considering that he was also required to captain his team and score runs too, it could be argued that this was the greatest fast-bowling performance over a season in cricket history. During the India series, he took 11–79 in Karachi, including a spell of 5–3 from 25 balls. A Test later, in Faisalabad, a known graveyard for quick bowlers, he took 11 wickets again, as well as scoring a century which included 21 runs from one Kapil Dev over. In the fourth Test, on a pitch so docile that he was able to declare at 3–581 (Kapil Dev 0–111), he then took 6–35 and 2–45 as Pakistan won by an innings and 119 runs.

'I was then at my peak as a fast bowler,' he recalled in 1988. 'All the hard work I had put in was paying off. I felt I had never been so fit in my life, and knew that I could sustain long spells of consistently hostile bowling.'

His bowling run-up started slowly, leaning forward, gathering momentum, until he leapt at the bowling crease. 'Imran running into bowl is a sight for gods,' gushed Sunil Gavaskar in 1984. At his peak Imran could swing the ball both ways and fire in a lethal bouncer, which he was never afraid to use. Most significantly, he pioneered the concept of 'reverse' swing, the ability to get the old ball to bend, sometimes prodigiously.

As a batsman, he was stylish and hard-hitting. Though he delighted in improvising and smashing the bowling in the latter overs of a one-day innings, he actually possessed a sound and orthodox defensive technique, on which some of his most important knocks were based. 'Not too many people really noticed, but he had the most perfect technique for a batsman,' says Sanjay Manjrekar. 'He worked hard at it and I think he had one of the straightest bats in the game.' His Test career batting average of

37.69, coming as it did on top of all his overs and all his wickets, is testimony to his batting skill.

From the late 1970s to the early 1990s, cricket celebrated the feats of four great all-rounders: Imran, Ian Botham, Kapil Dev and Richard Hadlee. All four achieved the double of 3000 Test runs and 300 Test wickets. All four were dominating figures, who stamped their personalities on the teams and matches they were a part of. Although statistics tell only part of the story — the figures of all four are awesome — it should be noted that Imran has the highest Test batting average of this elite group, and the second-best Test bowling average, marginally behind Hadlee.

IMRAN'S PARENTS CAME FROM Pathan land-owning tribes in what became Pakistan after the Partition in 1947. As he explained in his 1988 autobiography *All Round View* of his upbringing and that of his brothers and sisters, 'Independence is a hallmark of the entire Pathan race, and both my parents drummed into us that we should not be dominated by anyone.' He was born on 25 November 1952, into a family with a strong cricket tradition, and studied at Atchison College, Lahore's finest school. Eight of his cousins played first-class cricket, including Javed Burki and Majid Khan, both of whom studied at Oxford University and led Pakistan in cricket.

Imran was first picked to play for Lahore when aged 16, as an opening batsman and bowler, and for Pakistan for the 1971 tour of England at 18, despite the fact that he was so raw that he had not even settled on a standard run-up. In the next five years he studied at Worcester Royal Grammar School and then Oxford, which meant he missed Test and first-class matches that would have helped his cricket education, but as ample compensation did learn to think logically, which helped him analyse his game and the sport in general. It was late 1976 before he emerged as a genuine Test player — first in a home series against New Zealand, when he took four wickets in one innings and scored his first Test 50; and then in Australia immediately after, where he produced a glorious performance that announced to the world that Pakistan had finally produced a fast man of high class.

Imran had little impact on the first Test of this series, or on the first innings of the second Test, in

England's Derek Randall is bowled by Imran at Edgbaston in 1982. This was Imran's first Test as Pakistan captain.

Melbourne. However, in the second innings at the MCG he bowled with great fire, producing a wonderful off-cutter to bowl first Test century-maker Doug Walters, hitting Rod Marsh on the head as he was late on a hook shot, and finishing with 5–122. Imran candidly put his success down to forgetting about line and length and simply charging in. A week later, in Sydney, he was the star of the show, taking 12–165 (6–102 and 6–63), the best figures ever by a Pakistani bowler in Australia. At one stage on the third day he bowled 19 eight-ball overs in a row, and in Australian captain Greg Chappell's view 'equalled the pace of Dennis Lillee in his more torrid spells'. A few months later, when

WASIM AKRAM: Ability to swing — he was master of it. New ball — he was master of it. Yorkers — he used to bowl brilliant yorkers in one-day cricket. A totally committed cricketer.

Getty Images

Few cricketers have had as much charisma, or been so able to influence teammates and matches with personality as well as cricket ability.

Kerry Packer was scouting the world looking for the best players in the game to join his rebel cricket, Imran's name was high on his wish list.

Before World Series Cricket, Pakistan went to the Caribbean, for an absorbing battle that went all the way to the final Test, which the West Indies won to take the rubber 2–1. Imran's battles with the Windies pacemen — Andy Roberts, Colin Croft and Joel Garner — was a feature of the series … he bounced them and they bounced him back. In doing so, Pakistan's new spearhead demonstrated that he at least would not be backing down against anyone. He finished the series with 25 wickets.

For the 1977 county season, he moved to Sussex, which meant he had to serve a three-month ban, but which also gave him an opportunity to work on an outswinger to go with his natural inswinger. In World Series Cricket he was able to watch all the great bowlers at once, and learn from masters such as John Snow and Mike Procter, who helped him with his run-up, and, of course, all the West Indians. Through this time, he proved himself a genuine student of the game; however, when Pakistan lost a series to India in 1979–80, Imran was heavily criticised by sections of his home media who compared his efforts unfavourably with those of India's new star, Kapil Dev. The fact that Imran was injured during the series but fought back to claim nine wickets in the final Test was apparently irrelevant. But now his resilient spirit and confidence came to the fore, and against the West Indies in Lahore in November 1980 he celebrated his 28th birthday by scoring his first Test century and becoming the second Pakistani (after Intikhab Alam) to complete the 1000 runs/100 wickets Test double. The hundred, 123 against Malcolm Marshall, Garner, Croft and Sylvester Clarke, was made after coming to the wicket at 5–95. During a three-Test series in Australia in 1981–82, he took his 140th wicket to become Pakistan's leading wicket-taker in Tests. And then against Sri Lanka, after missing the first two Tests of the series as part of a player protest over Javed Miandad's captaincy, he returned to take 14–116 (8–58 and 6–58) in the final Test, in Lahore, which remains the best match analysis by a Pakistan bowler in Test history.

As a player, he was now established as a leading light of the sport. In England in 1982, Imran was a revelation … as a captain! By series end, supporters' banners around the ground and newspaper headlines proclaimed him the 'Lion of Pakistan'. Yet he had been something of a compromise candidate for the leadership, after internal squabbling precluded the re-appointment of Javed or Javed's replacement by more senior men such as Zaheer Abbas or Majid Khan. This was the first time Imran had captained a cricket side since his Oxford days, but he responded quickly, taking greater responsibility with his batting and having the

SIR RICHARD HADLEE: Imran was the one I rated very highly. Penetrative new-ball bowler, as a batsman he could bat high in the order and play a very subdued innings or if necessary take the attack to the bowler and change the course of the match. And, of course, he fielded OK and he was a captain. He was more consistent, I believe, than the rest of us.

courage to back his judgment — and to ignore family ties — when he made the decision to leave cousin Majid out of the first Test. Like another successful bowling captain before him, Richie Benaud, Imran was not afraid to acknowledge that he was one of his team's best bowlers, and accordingly gave himself long spells. And he impressed with his strategies, and his willingness to go against the norm: at Lord's, for instance, he introduced opening bat and part-time medium-pacer Mudassar Nazar to bowl a match-wining spell and refused to take the second new ball just because it was available. Mudassar was going well with the old one, so why change it? In his first Test innings as a bowling captain he took seven English wickets and finished with 21 for the three-match series, as England won narrowly, two Tests to one. The series had been lost, but there were strong indicators that the Pakistani team now had some steel in its spine.

This view was confirmed in home series against Australia (a 3–0 cleansweep) and India (3–0 in six Tests), when Imran made his claim for fast-bowling greatness and comprehensively outpointed Kapil Dev in the process. Astonishingly, he performed so heroically despite a worsening shin complaint. For a long time, doctors believed it was a deep-seated bruise and Imran bowled through the pain, but later it was confirmed that in fact he had a severe stress fracture in the shin. Refusing to surrender totally to the injury, he played in the 1983 World Cup (Pakistan reached the semi-finals) as a captain/batsman, missed a dreary three-Test series in India, and then endured a frustrating time in Australia, when he avoided the first three Tests as his shin refused to improve, played with some personal success in the fourth and fifth Tests, but then had little impact on the one-day series that followed. As is the way in Pakistan, the critics — including some senior teammates — were suddenly out in force, and Imran relinquished the captaincy to concentrate on getting his leg right.

Season 1984–85 was a highly significant one for Imran: his mother fought but lost a battle with cancer, while Imran took the first tentative steps back onto the cricket field. In Australia, despite making flying visits to and from Lahore, he played a key role in NSW's win in the Sheffield Shield and McDonald's Cup one-day competition, and performed well, purely as a player, as Pakistan reached the final of the one-day World Championship of Cricket. A classic Imran moment came in the Shield final against

Queensland at the SCG, when, from the top of his bowling run-up, he instructed the solitary slip fieldsman, John Dyson, to move to about third slip, leaving a pronounced gap between Dyson and wicketkeeper Steve Rixon. Imran then somehow induced a well-set Allan Border to immediately slash a catch straight to Dyson. This was superb theatre; it was as if he'd cast a spell over the great batsman. Afterwards in Sharjah, Imran bowled what he considered to be his finest spell in one-day internationals: 6–14 from 10 overs against India. In October '85 he played his first Test for nearly two years, and by February 1986 was captain again, for a three-Test series in Sri Lanka.

As we have said, Pakistan's clashes with the West Indies provided the fiercest, most competitive

Imran hooking the West Indies fast men at Lahore in 1980, during his first Test century.

confrontations of the decade. In 1986–87, a three-Test series finished even, after Pakistan won the first Test decisively, but lost the second by an innings. The young batsman, Salim Malik, showed great courage in batting with a broken arm, and Imran inspired superb performances from leg-spinner Abdul Qadir, who had struggled under earlier captains, and from 20-year-old Wasim Akram. Imran was never afraid to back his own judgment of a young player, and often infuriated the Pakistan Board of Control by his insistence on having a say in team selections. However, invariably, his view was more prescient than that of the selectors.

Sanjay Manjrekar identifies Imran's ability to relate to all Pakistani cricketers as being vital. 'He could talk the language with the newcomers who couldn't speak too much English, who were overawed,' the former Indian batsman explains. 'He could make them feel at home *and* he could also handle the stars in the Pakistan team. I think that's where he was unique and [it's] one of the reasons why he was so successful.'

'He was Pakistan's greatest captain, there is no doubt about it,' says Ravi Shastri. 'His ability to motivate youngsters was quite amazing. He passed on the art of fast bowling — he was always talking to the likes of Wasim or Waqar. When today you see the aggressive and positive attitude of the young Pakistani bowlers, you have got to thank Imran Khan for that.'

In England in 1987, Pakistan won the five-Test series 1–0. Imran took his 300th wicket in the third Test, in which he took 10–77 (3–37 and 7–40), and then scored a century at The Oval, as Pakistan ran up a first innings total of 708. He caused a storm when he became involved in an on-field spat with umpire David Constant, but Imran was never shy to make his displeasure with umpires known. If an official was struggling, why not say so? Imran,

ahead of his time, led the push for neutral umpires to be used in all Test matches. When this was initially denied, he remarked with some exasperation that teams could hardly then complain about perceived hometown bias.

THE WEST INDIES–PAKISTAN confrontation in 1988 evolved into the best Test series since 'Botham's Ashes' in 1981. It remains a shame that this battle was only played out over three matches. The teams were led by two giants of the game — Imran and Viv Richards — and featured champions such as Malcolm Marshall, Wasim Akram, Gordon Greenidge, Javed Miandad, Courtney Walsh and Abdul Qadir. Curtly Ambrose made his debut in the first Test, Richie Richardson went past 2000 Test runs in the second, but for a while the Pakistanis were in charge, as they won the first Test by nine wickets and were in front in the second Test until Richards and Jeffrey Dujon scored second-innings hundreds. Pakistan, set 372, made a brave attempt at the target, but the game ended with No. 11 Abdul Qadir keeping out the last over from Richards. In the third Test, the Windies snuck home by two wickets after Winston Benjamin and Dujon added an unbeaten 61 for the ninth wicket on the final day.

Pakistan would finish level again with the West Indies at home in 1990–91. In the meantime, Imran would lead Pakistan to drawn series with India, but lose in Australia (Imran, though, was named International Cricketer of the Year), before ending his Test career with a victory over Sri Lanka. Then came Pakistan's famous triumph in the 1992 World Cup in Australia, when the team started slowly, seemed to be out of contention, but came back to win a stirring victory over New Zealand in the semi-final and then beat England in the final. Imran's contribution to that win over the Englishmen was critical. First he came to the wicket with the innings teetering at 2–24, but refused to panic, reconstructing the innings with Javed Miandad. The 100 was not reached until the 31st over, and the pair weren't separated until the score was 169 (Imran 72, Javed 58), but by then a platform had been built and Inzamam-ul-Haq and Wasim Akram slammed the total all the way to 6–249. In the field, Imran brought Mushtaq Ahmed on first change and was rewarded when the little

SANJAY MANJREKAR: Imran Khan is so special to me. As far as I am concerned he is God to me. If I was reborn and given the choice of who I wanted to be, I would want to be Imran Khan because I just love everything about the man — his appearance to start with, then the fact that he is a guy who worked hard at his cricket. He wasn't natural, like Tendulkar or Lara, he worked really hard and became a great cricketer.

Imran swings England's Richard Illingworth away as he and Javed Miandad launch their counter-attack during the afternoon of the 1992 World Cup final.

leg-spinner trapped the dangerous Graeme Hick lbw with a wonderful wrong 'un. Later, with the game in the balance, Imran asked Wasim to just bowl flat out at Allan Lamb, and his fast man responded with the delivery of the tournament, knocking Lamb over for 31. Imran himself bowled only 6.2 overs, but he took the final wicket, a crowning moment of the game and his career.

'The World Cup victory here in Australia was the culmination of Imran's ability to give his players the courage to play their game,' says Greg Chappell. 'Wasim Akram's performance in the final was an example of Imran's ability to get the best out of his players and to encourage them to play their way, to do it their way and to be natural in what they did.'

Around this time, Imran came face to face with the problem of match-fixing. In the inquiries that cast such a pall over the game in the late 1990s, Imran said he believed that some of his players had taken money to throw unimportant one-day matches, though he himself had never been offered such an inducement. He told of one extraordinary situation in Sharjah, where he learnt that some players were on good money to lose. His solution was to put all the prizemoney the team had earned to that point on Pakistan to win, which solved the problem, at least in the short term. Imran also suggested that match-fixing had been a problem since the 1970s, and criticised cricket officials for their intransigence over the issue.

Away from cricket, the experience of seeing his beloved mother, Shaukat Khanum, suffer and then die of cancer in 1984 had a deep impact. He was appalled by the lack of medical facilities in Pakistan and set his sights on trying to alleviate this problem. That his mother's suffering occurred during a period of Imran's career when he was recovering from a shin injury that some doctors had said would end his career only exacerbated his feelings. Life is short. He committed himself to raising enough funds to construct and equip a cancer hospital in Lahore.

Although the Government of Pakistan donated land on the outskirts of Lahore on which the hospital would be built, it quickly became apparent that for

IAN WOOLDRIDGE: I believe he was the last of the really great amateurs, in that — yes, he got money from the game — but he lived his own life. He was an aristocrat in attitude and an amateur in attitude, but a helluva professional in performance. He was in control, always in control.

the hospital to be viable long-term much more than the originally projected £5 million was needed. Fortunately, the World Cup victory in 1992 provided a huge boost to Imran's dream project. It had taken more than two years to raise the first £1.5 million; in the six weeks immediately after the World Cup that figure was doubled. Finally, the Shaukat Khanum Cancer Hospital opened, in December 1994. Today the hospital runs without any assistance or aid from government and with Imran its largest backer.

As he fought to raise funds for the hospital, Imran became something of a spokesperson for the underprivileged and ill-educated in his country.

Gradually he also became involved in the political process, to the point that in 1997 he found himself campaigning for office. But his inexperience, and inability to counter the establishment's power base, saw him struggle in the final ballot. Imran lamented a poor voter turnout and the fact that he had not had sufficient time to prepare properly for the election (he had only decided to run four months before), but took comfort from the fact that he had emerged from the battle with his credibility intact.

'It's more important to try to do something for the scores of poor people of my country,' he said as he contemplated his future. 'In a country where half a million die every year only for drinking polluted water, it is more necessary for us to do something for them. I don't need to use politics as a way of making money. As a citizen of my beloved country, I have some moral duties, which I don't want to escape. That's why, in spite of being defeated regularly in elections, I am not leaving the field. It's tough, but then I love challenging tasks.'

His magnificent cricket career is proof of that.

Pakistan have just won the 1992 World Cup.

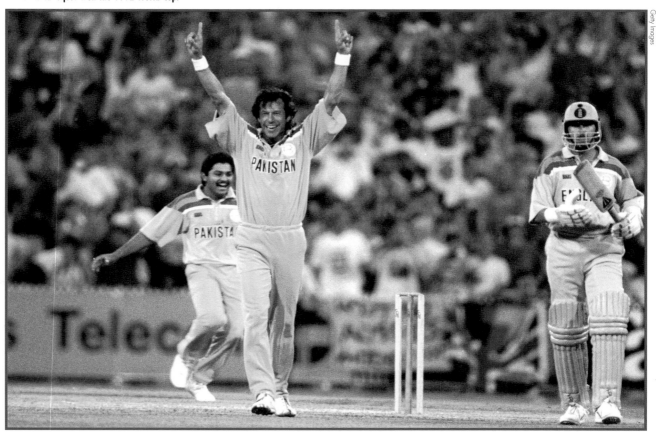

Getty Images

WALLY HAMMOND
Legend No. 9
A Galleon in Full Sail

*I*N 1968, THE VETERAN cricket writer RS Whitington arranged a lunch with the great Australian opener Arthur Morris. He wanted to discuss with Morris a comment that Sir Donald Bradman had made the previous day — that the West Indian, Garry Sobers, was 'unquestionably' the greatest all-rounder of all-time. On the way to his lunch he stopped in at the sports store of another former champion, the gallant batsman of the 1930s, Stan McCabe.

Before the journalist could say anything, McCabe greeted him with, 'Did you see what Don said in the paper this morning?'

'Yes,' replied Whitington, 'I'm on my way to talk to Arthur Morris about it now. Do you think he's forgotten Keith Miller?'

'I fancy Don's forgotten Keith *and* Wally Hammond,' McCabe said firmly.

When Whitington expressed surprise at this ranking of Hammond in the same company as Miller and Sobers, McCabe said flatly, 'Wally was the greatest cricketer I ever played against.'

Lord Cowdrey once said: 'If Hobbs was the master craftsman, Bradman the greatest runmaker, Walter Reginald Hammond was, for me, as a schoolboy, everything that a cricketer should be.'

The old pros at Yorkshire used to tell the young Len Hutton that Wally Hammond was the most thrilling batsman in the country. In Australia, Alan Davidson as a boy would practise the cover drive in front of a wardrobe mirror, trying to imitate Hammond in a famous photograph — head over the ball, front foot to the pitch, follow-through grand, silk handkerchief peeking out of the trouser pocket, Bert Oldfield low behind the stumps, almost as beautifully balanced as the batsman.

'That photograph had the greatest impact on me,' Davidson remembers. 'Later on, I could always drive the ball through the offside, that was easily my best shot. I owe WR Hammond quite a bit.'

Hammond was one of the heaviest runmakers in cricket history, scorer of 22 Test and 167 first-class centuries, four first-class triple centuries, 36 double centuries, first man to score 6000 and then 7000 Test runs, one of only two men to score 900 runs in one Test series. Yet because his career ran roughly parallel to that of Don Bradman, many of his grandest achievements were immediately overshadowed by the unique runscoring power of The Don. Only Bradman has scored more first-class double centuries (37 to 36) or first-class triple centuries (six to four) than Hammond. When Hammond scored a record 905 runs in one series in 1928–29, Bradman responded by amassing 974 runs in 1930. Hammond was the first to score double centuries in successive Tests; in the following series Bradman scored a triple century followed by a double. When Hammond scored an unbeaten double century in the second Ashes Test of 1936–37, and England led the series 2–0, Bradman responded with 270, 212 and 169 in the last three Tests and Australia escaped. Bradman only took two wickets in Test cricket, but one of them was Hammond.

For five years Hammond held the record for the highest score in Tests, going past Bradman's 334 when he made 336 not out against New Zealand in 1933. Len Hutton, of course, went to 364 in 1938 (then Sobers made 365 not out and Brian Lara 375), in a Test in which Hammond, as captain against Bradman's Australia, let his men bat on until they reached 7–903 — or more significantly, until Bradman was carried off with a suspected fractured ankle, which meant the Australian captain wouldn't be making 366 in reply.

It may be hard to forget Bradman when looking at Hammond's career, but to appropriately judge the Englishman's place in cricket's pantheon that is what must be done. On the field, at least, Wally Hammond was supremely confident, like Viv Richards of a later generation, a batsman with a bearing that made bowlers seem somehow more of a hindrance than a threat. He dismissed from his presence the best bowlers could offer. 'Whenever I saw him bat, I felt sorry for the ball,' Len Hutton once commented. Hammond was not a stylist like Victor Trumper or Barry Richards, but his method incorporated everything the textbook had to offer. He was not so much graceful as ruthlessly natural. The front foot was never far from the bat when he played forward, and when he went back he kept his head still and over the ball. Whether batting, bowling or taking lightning catches in the slips cordon, everything seemed in the right place. Many reckoned him to be the greatest offside player of them all.

Off the field, he was an aloof individual, often a lonely man, whose life had an element of tragedy to it. On it, he usually carried a cool superiority that led to 167 hundreds, over 50,000 runs, 732 wickets and 819 catches in his first-class career. And to think that a mixture of illness, war and autocratic cricket officials stole seven full seasons from him. Some saw him as a form of cricket royalty. The London *Times* correspondent Geoffrey Green once wrote, 'My fondest memories of cricket are of Frank Woolley driving lyrically through extra-cover, and of Walter Hammond striding down the pavilion steps at Lord's like a stately white galleon in full sail.'

HAMMOND WAS BORN IN 1903 in Dover, spent some of his early years in Malta, lost his father in World War I, and then, after officials at Kent complained, was cruelly forced by the administration at Lord's to serve a two-year 'qualification' before being allowed to perform full-time as a professional for Gloucestershire. In the meantime, he played occasionally on the wing for Bristol Rovers. In the 10 first-class cricket matches he did play between 1920 and 1922, Hammond scored

ARTHUR MORRIS: O'Reilly and the others thought he was a really great, great player, particularly strong on the offside. He certainly scored a lot of runs against Australia, against great bowlers such as O'Reilly and Grimmett.

Hammond plays Grimmett at Leeds in 1930. He made 113, but earlier in the match Bradman had scored 334.

just 117 runs at an average of 7.80. Over the next three years, he was a reasonable county cricketer, averaging in the low thirties and scoring six centuries.

The sixth of those centuries was a watershed. On 19 August 1925, against a Lancashire attack that included the great Australian fast man, Ted McDonald, Hammond batted for five-and-a-half hours for 250 not out, after coming to the wicket at 2–20. Suddenly, with England having been thrashed in each of the three Ashes series that had taken place since the War, he was in contention for a Test place. The men selecting an MCC team for a non-Test winter tour of the West Indies sent him an invitation.

Cricket-wise, this Caribbean tour was a real success for Hammond, who topped the batting averages and finished second in the bowling averages. Unfortunately he contracted a serious illness — blamed publicly at the time on an errant mosquito but in actual fact a form of syphilis — and missed the entire 1926 season. For a while, as

the virus took hold, it seemed he may not survive, and he was the subject of much gossip and rumour while he was absent. David Foot, in his superb study of Hammond's life, *The Reasons Why*, examines in depth the full ramifications, to the young man's health and character, of the illness and its treatment. For the rest of his life, whatever the outward facade, Hammond lacked confidence everywhere but at the batting crease. When he returned to county cricket in 1927 he was tougher, if more reserved, even bitter. And a great batsman. It was as if he appreciated every run.

In that 1927 season, he scored 1000 runs in May, 2969 runs and 12 hundreds for the first-class season, and was chosen for the MCC team to tour South Africa. There he took 0–21 and 5–36 and scored 51 on his Test debut, made two further half-centuries and opened the bowling during the series, and then came home to score two more fifties against the West Indies. With that, he was on the boat for an Ashes tour down under, having scored 432 runs in eight Tests, at 39.27. Cricket fans in

Australia, worried that their team was in serious decline and aware that the English batting line-up looked a strong one, could still not have known what was about to hit them.

Hammond approached the series with a burning desire to be successful. He knew that Tests in Australia were played to a finish, regardless of how long that took, which would give him ample opportunity to succeed, so long as he was patient. A century in Adelaide and a double century in Sydney in the lead-up to the first Test proved that he was suited to the true, hard wickets. And then a double failure in the opening encounter of the series, as England won by a colossal 675 runs, further toughened his resolve. He knew he was good enough for this Test-match cricket. Now, all he had to do was prove it.

His solution was simple. Eliminate risk. Hammond, as Steve Waugh was to do 60 years later, decided to no longer play the hook and pull shots. Until he was completely — and he meant completely — set, he wouldn't square cut either, while early on he would aim to play very straight, hitting only in the arc between mid-on and mid-off.

AG Moyes saw Hammond bat in Adelaide before the Tests, and wrote, 'he nonchalantly lifted the ball over the head of mid-off for four, a stroke I thought had gone the way of top-hats, moustaches and the five-ball over. He was a carefree, brilliant stroke player that day, the Hammond he wished to be. In the Tests we saw the Hammond of necessity, still an accomplished player, but not so thrilling to watch.' Whatever the aesthetics, the results were prodigious: 251 in Sydney, 200 and 32 run out in Melbourne, 119 not out and 177 in Adelaide, and finally, with the series well and truly won, 38 and 16 in Melbourne.

Never has a Test batsman seemed less likely to be dismissed than Hammond in those middle three Tests. Bradman made his Test debut in that series, scoring centuries in the third and fifth Tests (and being dropped to 12th man in the second). Of Hammond's batting, he said in 1988, 'probably the best I'd seen to that time, Walter was then at his peak'. The Australian umpire, George Hele, had a close-up view of the action, and commented, 'His strokes to the offside have never been equalled, let alone excelled, by an English batsman in my presence.'

'Instead of hooking,' said Jack Hobbs, 'he steps back towards his stumps and forces the ball to mid-off or extra cover.'

BY TOUR'S END, HAMMOND was recognised as the greatest batsman in the world. He kept that title for all of a year and a half. By midway through the 1930 Australian tour of England, Bradman was No. 1, establishing the theme that continued through the decade. The result, it seems, was a further hardening of Hammond's cricket soul. When England batted and batted and batted at The Oval in 1938, and Hutton made his 364, the young Yorkshireman remembers Hammond, now captain, appearing on the dressing room balcony during his marathon, to implore him to keep his head down. Earlier in that series, the 20-year-old Denis Compton threw his wicket away after making a debut Ashes hundred and was met by an unimpressed Hammond, who growled, 'Don't ever do that to me again. You will remember, I hope, that when you play against Australia and you make a hundred you take fresh guard, start again, and rub it in.'

Eight years later, on the opening morning of the first Ashes Test after World War II, Bradman was given not out on a catch to second slip when most (but certainly not all) observers thought he was out. At the end of the over, Hammond walked up to his rival leader and reputedly snapped, with the odd adjective thrown in, 'A fine way to start a series.' Bradman, who had scored 28 at the time, went on to 187. 'It is difficult to find evidence,' wrote one of Bradman's finest biographers Charles Williams, 'of the two captains greeting each other with anything but hostility for the rest of the series.' The Australian captain, though, recalled Hammond saying, perhaps for public consumption, 'I thought it was a catch, but the umpire may have been right and I may have been wrong.'

If Bradman had an edge over Hammond, no one else did. Even the great Australian bowler of the 1930s, Bill O'Reilly, often struggled to contain him. 'I knew all the time that I couldn't afford to give him any licence,' O'Reilly once said. 'He'd be into

Hammond tosses and Bradman prepares to call at The Oval in 1938. England would bat, and bat and bat, all the way to 7–903 before declaring, while the Australian captain would not bat at all, after damaging his ankle while having a bowl.

you like a sailfish if you did. Wally was easily the best-equipped English strokeplayer I bowled against. Bowl him a loose ball and it was four.'

Then he added, 'He was a moody bloke, but a very good bloke deep down.'

Rarely did Hammond drop his guard, though there were moments, such as when he decided to end the 1932–33 bodyline series with a six. Philip Lee was promptly lofted into the crowd beyond the long-off boundary. That happened in Sydney, where Hammond was almost inevitably successful, scoring four hundreds in Test matches (251 in 1928–29, 112 and 101 in 1932–33, 231 not out in 1936–37) and averaged 256.67 in Tests before the War.

Further, Hammond could be cutting in his criticism of teammates, but sensitive when the torch, however gently, was turned on him. One young Gloucestershire player had the temerity to ask him why he wasn't selected for a match in the 1930s. 'You're not a very good player, are you?' was his captain's reply. When Hammond dropped a slip

catch in a Test during the bodyline series, he didn't exactly apologise, instead saying to the disappointed bowler, Gubby Allen, 'Suppose you thought I was going to catch it.' Underlining Hammond's enormous reputation as a slip fieldsman, that miss gained great prominence in match reports. Once, while playing for Gloucestershire, he took a colleague who had just bowled his side to a victory back out to the middle and played him with the edge of his bat, to prove that when he said the poor teammate wasn't much of a bowler he was right. After Hammond's death, Allen commented, 'I was fond of Wally, and perhaps I was lucky enough always to see the better side of him.' EW Swanton

> **DAVID FRITH:** Wally Hammond may well have been the greatest — and this is using the word very carefully — the greatest cricketer that England has ever produced. He was certainly a better bowler than WG …

Getty Images

Hammond at The Oval in 1936, slamming a double century against India.

called Hammond 'the least expansive of men'. A number of his contemporaries just didn't like him.

He was often very reticent about having a bowl, which some thought was a deliberate — and in many ways sensible — strategy to extend his batting career. Yet there were times when he did things that only the very best all-rounders can do. Never were his bowling skills more boldly on show than at Cheltenham in 1928, when he took 9–23 and 6–105 against Worcestershire, a game in which he also top-scored with 80 in Gloucestershire's only innings. In the previous match against Surrey he'd top-scored in both innings, with 139 and 143 (next best was 56 in the first dig, 45 in the second), and dismissed Jack

IAN CHAPPELL: He took 83 Test wickets, so he must have been a useful seam bowler. And he was also the first guy to take 100 Test catches, so he must have been a very, very good slip fielder. All adds up to make Wally Hammond a damn good cricketer.

Hobbs. All up, three top scores, 362 runs and 16 wickets … in six days, one of which was a rest day!

While many questioned Hammond's magnanimity, few doubted his courage. In the third Test of 1936–37, at the MCG, he somehow played an innings of 32 on a dangerous pitch on which 13 wickets fell for 98 runs during the day. In doing so, he might have cost England the Ashes. By making the diabolical track seem playable, Hammond fooled his captain, Gubby Allen, into delaying his declaration. But after Hammond was dismissed to make it 4–68, England lost 5–8 even though Bradman had instructed his bowlers not to get anyone out, and Australia was able to escape with only one wicket lost before stumps. The next day, Bradman made 270, Jack Fingleton 136, and the momentum of the series was reversed. Had the Australians been put back in even half an hour earlier, immediately after Hammond was dismissed, the story might have been very different.

Just 32 runs, but this was Hammond's greatest innings. Denzil Batchelor, working for the English papers, wrote, 'He actually contrived to defy destiny by playing an occasional forcing shot. He drove Sievers to the boundary so vigorously that even on that dead outfield the eye could not follow the flash of the speeding ball …'

Neville Cardus, seeing a Melbourne sticky for the first time, was enthralled. One ball from O'Reilly 'rose straight from a good length to Hammond's cap', he wrote in his book, *Australian Summer*. 'I was lost in amazement and admiration of the way Hammond continued in the gyrating circumstances to maintain something of his own poise and reasonableness. He was like a cool, cultivated surveyor applying a spirit level in a volcanic region.'

Cardus described the bruises of the Yorkshireman Maurice Leyland, who scored 17 and added 42 for the third wicket with Hammond, as 'spectacular', while arguing that Hammond had revealed himself as 'the world's greatest batsman, fair weather and foul'. He had not been dismissed, he wrote grandly, rather 'dethroned'.

Ten years later, Hammond, now 43, played a similar innings on a gluepot in Brisbane. England's outstanding post-war opening bowler, Alec Bedser, said of that knock, against Keith Miller, Ray Lindwall and Ernie Toshack: 'When it was short, he stood aside and let it go. If pitched up, he let fly, playing straight past the bowler to eliminate risk. He hit cleanly and sensibly and in the circumstances, it was the best bad-wicket innings I've seen.'

IN THE ENGLISH WINTER before the 1938 Ashes series, there had been much press speculation as to who would be the England captain, with most considering the selectors were faced with a choice between Gubby Allen and Walter Robins. Suddenly everything changed when it was announced that Hammond had been offered a business position that would allow him to play as an amateur. Overnight he became the leading candidate. The men at Lord's named Hammond as skipper of an England XI to face a 'Rest' side to be led by Allen. But Allen, upset at the snub, cried off with an injury and the way was clear for Hammond to assume the Test captaincy.

It must be said that Hammond was not an overly popular captain, at county or Test level, even if he scored five hundreds in his first 12 Tests as skipper (including three in South Africa in 1938–39). He did lead his country to series wins against South Africa, the West Indies and India, and drew the Ashes series in England in 1938 and the 'Victory' series in 1945. Denis Compton thought him 'too non-committal, and exceedingly difficult to talk to, particularly for a young player'. More than one player went as far as to call him the worst captain

they ever played under. Some in the cricket aristocracy never forget that he was in essence a pro in amateur's clothing. Bob Wyatt, captain of England in 1934, reckoned he was 'a bit out of his depth socially'. On the other hand, Cyril Washbrook, who opened with Hutton throughout the 1946–47 Ashes series, thought Hammond 'would have been a great captain of a great side'.

The squad that went to Australia after the War was hardly that, and things fell apart on the skipper. As the tour went painfully on, Hammond retreated into his privacy so much that he preferred to travel away from the team; his mind in turmoil as he battled fibrositis, a lack of penetrative bowlers and the stress of his divorce from his first wife. Perhaps most difficult of all, he fretted over his wife-to-be, a South African woman who yearned to be home in Durban rather than left behind in an England depressingly austere after the war. Exacerbating his problems, though he'd often been in devastating form in 1945 and 1946, now the runs from his own bat dried up. And without runs he was without inspiration. Those young fans who saw Hammond for the first time on that tour — except for the lucky few who witnessed his brave knock in Brisbane — could hardly have believed what their fathers told them about what a superb batsman he once was.

Some saw his struggles in this series, in which he was confronted with the pace of Lindwall and

JACK BANNISTER: In 1964–65, my former county captain, MJK Smith, led England to South Africa under the managership of Donald Carr. Broadcasting for the BBC was Brian Johnston. In Durban, where Wally then lived, Brian spotted him standing in a very lonely and detached way at the back of a net. He went up to him and said, 'You wouldn't remember me, Mr Hammond. Back in 1948 I did a radio interview with you in London.' And Wally said, 'Well, I do, yes.'

Brian said, 'What about this England side?' And for 10 minutes they had a very animated conversation about Barrington, Boycott, Dexter, Smith, all these players. And then Brian said, 'Well, have you spoken to the players on this tour?' Wally said, 'No, I don't like to. I don't want to push myself.' This is one of the all-time greats!

And Brian Johnston said, 'If I can arrange it, would you like to go into the dressing room?'

And Wally said, 'Yes.'

So Brian went to Donald Carr and arranged it. And Wally went in and for half an hour people like Ken Barrington and MJK and Fred Titmus and David Allen, they sat in absolute awe as this god from the past talked to them at a level that they understood. They worshipped him so much.

He was in failing health then, he'd had a car accident. They didn't know that he was going to die within months, but they all clubbed together to pay for an airfare to fly him into Port Elizabeth for the final Test match. And that was a mark of the esteem and admiration of another generation for the great man.

Miller, as evidence that he while he was brave, he was not proficient against very fast bowling. As further proof they pointed back to a Test against the West Indies in 1933, when Learie Constantine was said to have ruffled him by sending him down a Caribbean version of bodyline. 'If that's what Test cricket is coming to,' Hammond is reputed to have said, 'then I'm getting out of it.'

But these critics had forgotten his batting against McDonald in 1925, when he made that unconquered 250, and also another innings against Lancashire two years later, when he made 187 in three hours, having driven the first five balls the Australian bowled to him for four. They also forgot Hammond's imperious 240 at Lord's in 1938, made after the Australian fast man Ernie McCormick had reduced England on a green pitch to 3–31. 'As he came back to the pavilion,' recalled Cardus, 'the whole of the vast crowd at Lord's stood up to him.' And they forget innings in county cricket, when he not only stood up to fast men such as Larwood,

Hammond batting in the 'Victory Tests' that were staged after the War in Europe ended in 1945.

Voce and Ken Farnes, he clouted them. Perhaps occasionally he lost the taste for such battles, but until the very end he never lost the ability to win them.

Following the 1946–47 Australian tour, Hammond turned from cricket to selling tyres (augmenting his income by writing on the game) and then left England, with his wife, to live in South Africa. Sadly, bad luck followed him — a business partnership failed, elsewhere work was difficult, and in 1960 he was involved in an awful car crash; he suffered a fractured skull, his legs were trapped under the dashboard. Doctors reckoned only a man as tough and fit as he could have survived, but he never really recovered and died in 1965, aged 62.

Hammond's Test aggregate of 7249 runs remained a record until Colin Cowdrey went past him in November 1970, and was still the highest for those to have played fewer than 150 innings until Sachin Tendulkar outdid him in 2002. Cowdrey had also joined Hammond as the leading English maker of Test centuries when he scored his 22nd hundred, a feat later matched by Geoff Boycott but still to be beaten by an Englishman. Across all countries, of those batsmen to have played in 50 Tests, only Bradman, Sutcliffe, Tendulkar and Barrington have a higher Test batting average. Hammond's 336 not out in Auckland in 1933 remains the fastest triple century made in Test matches (288 minutes, including the third hundred in 48 minutes). The 10 sixes he hit in that innings was a Test record until Wasim Akram slammed 12 for Pakistan against Zimbabwe in 1996–97.

Stan McCabe clearly had every right to rate him so highly. Hammond was as gifted a batsman as England has ever produced, though he was never as influential as Grace nor as loved or technically perfect as Hobbs. Where he matched these two legends, and stands above all the English batsmen who followed, even Len Hutton, was the way he dominated the batting orders he was a part of. He was always the key wicket, always the one who set the tempo. 'From the moment he walked from the pavilion to begin his innings he looked the master,' wrote Hutton of Hammond in 1956. 'The moment he faced up to bowling that had held difficulties for the other batsmen, that bowling appeared to lose its venom …

'Hammond made batting appear ridiculously easy, and it never is that.'

SUNIL GAVASKAR
Legend No. 10
Always in Position

ADHAV MANTRI WAS AN opening batsman and wicketkeeper from Bombay, good enough to play four Tests for India in the early 1950s and tour England in 1952. Fourteen years later, Mantri was on the selection committee that chose the Bombay sides for the Ranji Trophy matches.

Which presented something of a problem for him. Among the potential candidates for a place in that Bombay side was a teenage opening batsman who had recently been named India's 'Best Schoolboy Cricketer of the Year'. After this youngster made a century against the touring London Schoolboys, having already made scores of 246 not out, 222 and 85 during his final school year, the clamour for his selection at the first-class level grew louder. But Madhav Mantri was hesitant. The schoolboy was his nephew, and he didn't want to be accused of nepotism.

Mantri's nephew's name was Sunil Gavaskar. Born on 10 July 1949 in Bombay, Sunil, or 'Sunny' as he became widely known, made his maiden first-class appearance for the Vazir Sultan Colts XI against an XI from Dungapar in 1966–67, but remained on the periphery of Bombay's Ranji Trophy squad for the next two years. When he finally made his Ranji debut, against Mysore, he was

SUNIL GAVASKAR: My early heroes were ML Jaisimha from Hyderabad in India, then the West Indies' Conrad Hunte. I watched a lot of his batting. I wanted to bat like him; he had the straightest of backlifts and he had such terrific balance. Then the heroes kept on changing, according to the teams that came to India, so if it was the Australian team that came in 1959–60, Norman O'Neill was my hero; in 1960, when Pakistan came, Hanif Mohammad was my hero. I admired their cricket, I loved to watch them play.

out fifth ball, for 0, and returned to the pavilion to whispers that he indeed owed his place to his uncle's influence. Those jeers stayed with him — and, one presumes, with Mantri — until his second game, against Rajasthan, when he scored 114. A century in each of his next two games followed, and suddenly Gavaskar was the bright new hope for the national team's 1970–71 tour of the West Indies.

In the 16 seasons that followed, young Sunny evolved into the most consistently productive batsman in the international game. Just 163cm (5ft 4in) short, he became a Test opener who could bat for nearly 12 hours for 172 (against England in Bangalore in 1981) but also score a hundred from 94

Gavaskar in England in 1971, trying to justify the huge reputation he'd earned after scoring 774 runs in his debut series against the West Indies earlier in the year.

balls (against the West Indies in Delhi in 1983). There was no shot that he could not play (though some, deemed too risky, were often left in the locker), no situation too desperate, no style of bowling, fast or slow, too difficult. When Gavaskar retired from big-time cricket in 1987, he held a plethora of records, including most Tests (125), most innings (214), most runs (10,122), most hundreds (34), most scores of 50 or more (79), most hundred partnerships (58). All his Test centuries were made in an era dominated by superb, often intimidating opening bowlers. Consider the quicks he confronted: Andy Roberts, Michael Holding, Joel Garner, Courtney Walsh, Malcolm Marshall, Sylvester Clarke, Wayne Daniel, Dennis Lillee, Jeff Thomson, Rodney Hogg, Len Pascoe, Craig McDermott, Imran Khan, Wasim Akram, Richard Hadlee, John Snow, Ian Botham and Bob Willis.

'What Tendulkar is today to this generation, Gavaskar was to our generation,' says a proud Sanjay Manjrekar. 'He was the role model, the ideal cricketer to idolise. He concentrated on being a good batsman against the quickest bowlers. He was a master at choosing the right ball to hit; he could wait for days for the loose ball to come. Tremendous patience, temperament, technique and all in a beautiful package.'

AFTER A LATE START, caused by an infected fingernail that kept him out of the opening Test, Gavaskar was phenomenal during that 1970–71 tour of the Caribbean, producing the most prolific debut series by a batsman in Test history. In the second Test, at Port-of-Spain, he scored 65 and 67 not out, and hit the runs that gave India their first-ever win over the Windies. Two weeks later, in Georgetown, Gavaskar scored his maiden Test hundred, 116, and an unbeaten 64, and then came innings of 1 and 117 not out in Bridgetown. Amazingly, he was only getting his eye in. Back in Port-of-Spain, despite a nagging toothache he made 124 and 220, becoming the second man (after Australia's Doug Walters) to score a double century and a century in the same Test. He also became the first Indian to make four centuries in one Test series, the second Indian to score a century in each innings of the same Test (after Vijay Hazare) and the third Indian to score centuries in three consecutive Test innings (after Hazare and Polly Umrigar). Throughout the series, West Indies captain, the great Garry Sobers, kept touching him on the shoulder, wanting some of his magic and his luck. Gavaskar's aggregate for the series of 774 (average 154.80) remains the world record for a batsman in his maiden Test series. No Indian had ever scored 700 runs in a series before. For the first time, India had won a series against the West Indies.

Gavaskar returned home a conquering hero. Waiting for him in Bombay, Madhav Mantri must have chuckled as he thought about the days his nephew had visited his home to stare at and absorb the trophies, caps, sweaters and cricket memorabilia his uncle had won. Madhav might have reminisced about how young Sunny had reputedly used a cricket scoreboard to teach himself to count, about the mock cricket Tests he had played with Madhav's sister and her son. He must have thought about those cynical chuckles, the jeers and the taunts he, as a selector, had worn that day when Sunny was out for a duck …

Gavaskar's arrival in England in 1971 generated much interest, given his colossal feats in the Caribbean, but he could make only two half-centuries in the three-Test series. He made the most headlines as the innocent victim in a controversial moment, when the fiery John Snow knocked him over as the batsmen dashed through for a single. In truth, there was little to the affair: the collision was hardly deliberate, but Snow was suspended and Gavaskar was unfairly perceived by some as being a little man in a big man's world. This rating was not tempered in England until 1974, when he made 101 and 58 in the first Test of a new series, at Old Trafford.

In 1975, Gavaskar played perhaps his weirdest knock, batting throughout India's first innings in the inaugural one-day World Cup, 60 overs in all, to score a miserable 36 not out. Confused and angry Indians ran onto Lord's to remonstrate with him. Afterwards, India's embarrassed manager, GS Ramchand, commented sadly, 'I do not personally agree with his [Gavaskar's] tactics. But he felt that against such a big English total [the home team had made 4–334 from their 60 overs] he would get in some batting practice on a good wicket against a good attack.'

Gavaskar led India in a Test for the first time in January 1976, against New Zealand in Auckland, when regular captain Bishen Bedi was sidelined with a leg injury, and he marked the occasion by scoring 116 and 35 not out in an eight-wicket victory. Two months later, he scored centuries at Port-of-Spain in the second and third Tests of a series against the West Indies, his third and fourth hundreds at the ground. In that third Test, India were set 403 to win, and scored 4–406 (Gavaskar 102, Gundappa Viswanath 112, Mohinder Amarnath 85), still the highest total ever made in Tests to win a match. Such was the Indians' dominance of the West Indies spinners on what was supposed to be a turning track, Windies captain Clive Lloyd reputedly swore to rely on pace and pace alone to win future Test matches.

Strangely, it wasn't until November 1976 that Gavaskar scored a Test century in India. Eight Tests were played in India that season — three against New Zealand, then five against England — and Gavaskar hit hundreds in the first and last of them. The century against the Kiwis, at the Wankhede Stadium in Bombay, boosted his 'hero' status in his hometown. In Delhi, he was mobbed when he reached 1000 runs for the calendar year, the first Indian to do so.

In Australia in 1977–78, Gavaskar scored second-innings centuries in the first three Tests. In a season when the 'rebel' World Series Cricket was supposed to be showcasing all the game's finest talent, Gavaskar was one of the brightest lights in the traditional game. In the following October, India were in

TONY COZIER: In 1971 he came to the West Indies. After that series, when he completely got on top of the West Indies bowling, they composed a calypso. You compose calypsos about West Indian heroes and great West Indian cricketers, not about someone from overseas, so that was a great honour for him — the Calypso Gavaskar, the Little Master. Whenever the West Indies played against him he seemed to relish the challenge. He was so difficult to dislodge, with a tremendous technique and tremendous concentration to keep on going against fast bowling that was coming at him all the time.

Gavaskar sweeps at The Oval in 1979, during his superb double century that almost won India a famous victory.

Pakistan for the first Tests between the two nations for 17 years, and for the first time Gavaskar faced the bowling of Imran Khan in a Test. 'The most compact batsman I've ever bowled to,' was Imran's assessment, 'a masterful batsman with a great temperament.' Imran had just returned from a season of WSC, which made his rating particularly telling. Gavaskar scored 89 in the first Test — where he also provoked a strong protest from the umpires, who objected to his reaction to Mohinder Amarnath being warned for running on the pitch — 97 in the second, and 111 and 137 in the third, but even this couldn't prevent Pakistan achieving a 2–0 series victory. In scoring those runs in the third Test, he became the first Indian to score a century in both innings of a Test twice, and passed Umrigar to become his country's leading rungetter in Test cricket.

Such is the nature of Gavaskar's career, and the fact he was constantly reaching landmarks never achieved by his Indian predecessors, it is difficult to avoid simply recounting record after record. Two weeks after that Pakistan series concluded, India were involved in another home Test series, against the West Indies, and Gavaskar's statistical march continued. In the first Test, amid wild celebrations, he scored 205 in Bombay, becoming the first Indian to reach 200 in a home Test against the Windies. In the third Test, he became the first man to score hundreds in both innings of a Test three times, and the first Indian to score 4000 Test runs. For the second time in his Test career, he scored four centuries in one Test series.

On to England, where he scored four half-centuries in the first three Tests. However, it wasn't until the fourth and final Test that he finally convinced Englishmen of his class. At the start of the series' last day, India were 0–76, needing 438 to win the Test. And win they so nearly did, thanks to a magnificent 221 by Gavaskar, which took his side to within sight of what would have been a remarkable victory. 'It was one of the greatest innings that he's played,' reckons Manjrekar. 'Vintage Gavaskar, playing swing bowling to perfection, taking his time initially and then opening up. Nothing in the air, everything copybook. I remember being stunned by the greatness of the man.'

With 20 overs to go, India needed 110, with nine wickets in hand, but Ian Botham revived the English attack, and after Gavaskar was fourth out, with 49 still wanted in 7.4 overs, the run chase petered out. Still, with three balls left, all four results were still possible, and the gripping Test ended with India eight wickets down and nine runs short. At season's end, *Wisden* named Gavaskar as one of its five cricketers of the year, an assessment based to a large degree on just one fantastic innings.

WHAT WAS GAVASKAR'S SECRET against the quick stuff? He surely needed an edge, because, as Ravi Shastri explains, 'When Sunny was playing for India, the fastest bowler he faced in the nets was bowling at 70, 80 miles an hour. And that was Kapil Dev, who hardly ever bowled in the nets, maximum of eight or 10 deliveries.'

Gavaskar credits an innovative practice routine. 'What I used to do to practise against the quicker bowlers,' he explains, 'was ask the Mumbai [Bombay] net bowlers to bowl from, say, about 18 yards instead of the regulation 22 yards. Otherwise I had somebody bowling at me in the nets from about 16 yards, just standing and bowling, not running up and bowling. Occasionally I had them bowl on concrete as well, where there was a bit more bounce in it — that's the way I tried to practise against the quicker bowlers. It wasn't always enough, but at least it got the reflexes into some sort of motion.'

That might have been part of it, but not all. 'He played straight, that was the important thing about Sunil Gavaskar,' says Michael Holding. 'He had a perfect technique. He would not want to hook, he hardly every hooked, especially early in his innings. Not one to cut too much either, especially early in his innings. All great batsmen have good eyes, they pick up the line and the length of the ball that quickly. But his technique was the important thing.'

A rock-solid technique, and balance, too. 'I enjoyed watching fellow opening batsmen and he was the one I enjoyed the most,' remembers New Zealand's John Wright. 'He was a beautiful player of fast bowling and his record against the West Indies is testament to that. He was so well balanced and because of that, not only was he in the correct position to play his shots, but he was also in the

IAN BOTHAM: I played with him at Somerset for a year, and played a lot of Test cricket against him. Thoroughly enjoyed his company — a very generous, very warm person, and a magnificent player. Low sense of gravity, he had great balance. He was a great timer of the ball, could work it either side of the wicket. He had everything.

correct position to leave a ball. Against top fast bowling that's one of the skills that you really need. I thought he was the complete opener.'

While the runs and respect Gavaskar gave Indian cricket were usually grandly applauded, it must be said that there were times when the adulation was muted. In 1978, he was criticised for *thinking* about going to World Series Cricket, when India had made clear its disappointment at cricket's great split, and though he didn't do so he still lost the Test captaincy. Many summers later, he, along with Kapil Dev, was fined by Indian cricket officials for wearing a personal sponsor's logo too prominently. Some claimed he was

A wave to the crowd after The Oval Test in 1979. The stump came from Ian Botham, who souvenired it for Gavaskar at the match's conclusion.

money hungry. Yet he never missed a game for India in a run of 106 Tests, no one ever questioned his courage, and only the ultra-cynical (of which there were a few) doubted his commitment. Today, in an era when Sachin Tendulkar can make millions of dollars from just one endorsement, it is apparent that Gavaskar was simply more aware than were most of his Indian contemporaries of the commercial world in which he was a part.

Adding further pressure was the fact that many fans and observers set Gavaskar's standards ridiculously high, then criticised him, sometimes passionately, when he failed to meet them. On that famous day at The Oval, when Gavaskar made his 221 but was out, exhausted, on the threshold of victory, a few hard markers seemed more concerned that his dismissal had cost India a win, rather than celebrating the fact that he had played one of cricket's finest hands. Absurdly, they argued that he did not want to win, as if that might have vindicated the decision to replace him as captain. Such snide criticisms were simply a reflection of Indian cricket politics, and the simple fact that provincial biases in Indian do run deep.

Back as skipper in late 1979, he led India to home series wins over Australia (2–0 in six Tests) and then Pakistan (2–0 in six). That win over the Pakistanis was India's first against their neighbours since 1952–53, and during the rubber, Gavaskar made his 23rd Test century. This put him third on the all-time list, behind Sir Donald Bradman and Sir Garfield Sobers. No other Indian had made more than 12.

BETWEEN DECEMBER 1978 AND the first week of February 1980, Gavaskar was on display in 22 Tests, plus the 1979 World Cup. In that time he scored 2301 runs, including eight centuries. Then came a season with Somerset in county cricket. Little wonder that he lost form in Australia soon afterwards, appearing tired and irritable. This culminated with his awful demonstration in Melbourne, when, after being given out lbw when clearly he shouldn't have been, he stormed off the field, taking his opening partner, Chetan Chauhan with him. It seemed he wanted to forfeit the Test, in protest at the lamentable Australian umpiring, but wiser heads, in the form of Indian management, met him at the gate and pointed Chauhan back out towards the middle. India recovered to win that Test, but in the following three years, Test victories for Gavaskar and his team were desperately hard to find.

Such a run inevitably tested the patience of India's cricket faithful, most notably at the Eden Gardens in Calcutta, where the applause for Gavaskar was never quite as loud or as heartfelt as it was elsewhere. Against the West Indies in 1983, six months after India had sensationally won the World Cup at Lord's, huge crowds turned up, only to see the home team humiliated by an innings and 46 runs. This was India's third heavy defeat against the Windies in five Tests. The World Cup win, it seemed, had been a mirage. India had won just one of its last 32 Tests, none of its last 28. Angry spectators confronted armed police after hurling fruit, stones and bottles onto the ground and attacking the team bus. Gavaskar, who made a first-ball duck and 20, was the focus of the rage.

Twelve months later, he led India in another Test in Calcutta, this time against England, but again the mood was furious. Responding to the continuation of the depressing losing run, Kapil Dev had been dropped, then India crawled to 7 declared for 437 from 203 overs. 'Gavaskar down! Gavaskar out!' chanted the crowd, who blamed him for everything.

RAVI SHASTRI: I think his best shot was the straight drive down the ground to the fast bowlers. He got into such great position. He would go back and across against the quickest and then just wait for them to pitch the ball up, and he would offer the full face of the blade and just punch it down the ground between mid-on and the bowler. It was an outstanding shot. He played it against all the great fast bowlers.

I remember one shot that stands out. He was 49 in Guyana and Malcolm Marshall was bowling round the wicket and bowling as quick as he ever did in his career. Malcolm hit Sunny straight in the forehead and the ball rebounded straight back to the bowler, so it was clear that Sunny took the whole impact.

The whole dressing room was up watching, to see what was going to happen next. Would it be another bouncer? Would it be pitched up? It was an attempted yorker, and Sunny was in position and he banged it down the ground to reach his half-century. He went on to 147 not out.

Rumour has it that the local police chief had to ask Gavaskar to declare, to keep the peace. When the Indian captain led his team out to field after the declaration, he was pelted with fruit. Later, Gavaskar vowed never to play at Eden Gardens again. When Test cricket next came to Calcutta, in February 1987, Gavaskar, true to his word, pulled out, breaking his run of consecutive Test appearances.

He was a cautious captain, and could be a stubborn man, but through this testing time he remained a great batsman. That he kept scoring runs reflected the fact that he was a master at focusing purely on the challenge immediately ahead. During the 1983 series against the West Indies, Gavaskar made his 29th and 30th Test centuries, the ones that took him level, then past, Sir Donald Bradman's previous record, and they were two of his finest. No. 29 came in Delhi in the second Test, and was compiled from just 94 balls. The Windies, at the very height of their considerable powers, had won the first Test by an innings, during which Gavaskar had had his bat sensationally knocked out of his grasp by Malcolm Marshall. He saw it as his duty to reinvent himself, betray his preference for a cautious opening, and inspire a counterattack. Which he surely did, starting with two electric hook shots off Marshall, for four and six.

'What a great innings that was,' remembers Maninder Singh. 'He had decided the previous night that he was not going to duck any more, he was not going to sway away any more, he was just going to play all his shots. And he just hooked everybody — Michael Holding, Malcolm Marshall — with so much ease.'

His first 50 came from just 37 deliveries, and during the innings he scored his 8000th Test run. On day two, the Indian Prime Minister, Mrs Indira Gandhi, came to the ground to personally offer congratulations. But six weeks later the Calcutta crowd was condemning him.

The 30th hundred came in Madras in the final Test of that series, just a fortnight after Calcutta. This time batting at No. 4 (but in before a run was scored), Gavaskar broke Bradman's record with style, compiling 236 not out, then the highest Test score ever made by an Indian (since beaten by VVS Laxman against Australia in 2001). It was his 13th hundred and third double century against the West Indies.

Again Maninder Singh: 'Before he went into bat I was sitting beside him and he told me, "Today's the day that I have to show my mettle, I'll have to

Gavaskar in an aggressive mood against the West Indies at Delhi in 1983, during his 29th Test century, which brought him level with Sir Donald Bradman's record for most hundreds in Tests.

concentrate harder." I just kept sitting there, amazed that this man had planned what he was going to do and then went and achieved it. That was his greatness, that was his quality.'

DURING THE LAST THREE years of Gavaskar's career he could not avoid extending records he'd already established. Having gone past Geoffrey Boycott's Test runscoring record (8114 runs) at Ahmedabad in November 1983, he continued on towards 10,000, a mark he reached

TIM DE LISLE: If you were picking a team to play the great West Indian sides of the '70s and '80s, the first player you would pick would be Sunil Gavaskar. Quite a lot of the batsmen of that era wilted against the formidable pace attack of the West Indians, but Gavaskar just got better.

Getty Images

A cover drive against Zimbabwe during the 1987 World Cup, his farewell from international cricket.

in his 124th Test, against Pakistan at (again) Ahmedabad in March 1987. In the process, he became the first batsman to play 200 Test innings, the fourth man to play 100 Tests (and the first to play 115), the first Indian fieldsman to take 100 catches and the first man to play 100 consecutive Tests. That 100th straight Test was the Tied Test in Madras, against Australia in 1986. Set 348 to win on the last day, Gavaskar's 90 gave India a chance, setting the scene for a dramatic final hour which ended with India's final wicket falling off the second-last possible delivery. He also led India to an unexpected victory in the World Championship of Cricket in Australia in 1985, a one-day international tournament featuring all the Test-playing nations, winning plaudits for the clever way he used the spinners throughout the competition, especially the young leg-spinner Laxman Siviramakrishnan. Two weeks after, in Sharjah, Gavaskar was named 'Man of the Series' in the inaugural 'Rothmans Four Nations Trophy', which India won by beating Australia in the final.

Gavaskar's final first-class match was at Lord's in

August 1987, when he scored 188 (his only century at the ground) and 0 for a Rest of the World XI against the MCC. From there it was back home to India, for the fourth World Cup, his farewell. Before the tournament, he, along with nine of his colleagues, refused for a period to sign a playing contract that restricted his right to service personal sponsorships. That dispute resolved, in India's first game, against Australia, he scored a quickfire 37, including a backfoot drive off Craig McDermott which English journalist Henry Blofeld called 'the stroke of the year'. Against New Zealand, he slammed 103 not out from 88 balls, his only one-day international century, an explosive knock that came six days after Kapil Dev had publicly censured him for batting too slowly against Zimbabwe.

That century, and the speed at which it was scored, secured India a semi-final place in Bombay, against England, with Australia sent off to Lahore to face Pakistan. Everyone expected an India-Pakistan final, but it was not to be, with both semis resulting in stunning upsets. So Gavaskar ended his career in big-time cricket where it all began, in the city of his birth. Sadly, there was no romantic personal farewell, as he was bowled off his pads by de Freitas in India's third over.

Thus, the career that started with a duck in his debut Ranji Trophy appearance ended with an innings of 4, and the whole of Bombay now shared the same disappointment that Sunil and his uncle had felt on his ill-fated debut back in 1969. His supporters were left to reflect on one of the game's great careers. Greater still is his overall contribution to the history of Indian cricket.

Sunil Gavaskar evolved into a resolute man and cricketer, aware of his few limitations, his enormous skill, his place in the game and the rewards on offer. His single-minded approach was reflected in his polished technique, his consistency and all his runs, things that were not typical of Indian cricket in pre-Gavaskar times. He changed how the cricket world, within and beyond his homeland, perceived Indian cricket, and though he might not have been universally loved across all India, he inspired so many more than the few he annoyed. His legacy is that he increased immeasurably the regard the cricket world has for Indian batsmanship, and paved the way for countrymen such as Mohammad Azharuddin, Sachin Tendulkar, Rahul Dravid and VVS Laxman, the stars of the 1990s and beyond.

IAN BOTHAM
Legend No. 11
Last Action Hero

IAN BOTHAM, AGED 21, took five Australian wickets on his first day of Test cricket. His first wicket was no one special, just Greg Chappell, the Australian captain, the finest Australian batsman of his generation. The year was 1977, and Botham was a new but very confident addition to an English XI that had not beaten Australia in an Ashes series in six years. The previous season, England had been humbled by the West Indies. Now, under the shrewd captaincy of Mike Brearley, they were suddenly on top. The precocious and prodigiously talented Botham very quickly became the face of this resurgence.

Four years later, Botham dominated an Ashes series in a way no one has ever done before or since. Not even Bradman in 1930 was more pre-eminent. At Headingley and Old Trafford, Botham smashed extraordinary centuries — the first to retrieve a position so dire that the bookmakers had offered odds of 500–1 about an English victory, the second to emphatically confirm a series triumph that just a few weeks before had seemed so unlikely. In between, at Edgbaston, he took five wickets for one run in a spell of 28 balls, precipitating a dramatic Australian collapse just when it seemed the Aussies had the Test in their keeping.

Throughout, he carried the entire nation's hopes on his shoulders. Of his magical spell at Edgbaston, Botham remembers, 'I think the crowd got the majority of those wickets for me, because the atmosphere intimidated the batsmen. I don't care what they say, you could see it, you could see it in their eyes. You run in and the crowd, and this noise, it just built up. I imagine it was like a Roman amphitheatre, the gladiators, it was very, very intimidating for the players out there, if you were on the receiving end.'

Old Trafford was little different. The stats give ample evidence of what Botham achieved during that momentous innings — he went from 50 to 100 in 28 minutes, off 26 balls. In all, he hit six sixes and 13 fours. Having scored only five runs, all singles, from his first 33 balls, he then smashed 113 from 69. 'It was an attack, wrote *Wisden*, 'which, for its ferocious yet effortless power and dazzling cleanness of stroke, can surely never have been bettered in a Test match, even by the legendary Jessop.' Throughout, the Manchester crowd was in pandemonium, as if United were slaughtering Liverpool in a Cup Final. The bowlers, including Dennis Lillee and Terry Alderman (who between them would take 81 wickets in the series), were unable to stem the flow; instead the highly-charged atmosphere seemed to have them feeding Botham's considerable strengths. Three times, Lillee was hooked high into the stands beyond fine-leg. 'To take on the man I think is the best bowler of all-time and win comprehensively was a nice feeling,' says Botham of his clash with the great Lillee.

From this day on, the series was known as 'Botham's Ashes'.

BOB WILLIS: He was out in Melbourne in 1977, during the Centenary Test Match, on an Esso Scholarship. He was meant to be helping out in the dressing rooms. Benson & Hedges, the sponsor of the Centenary Test, had 500 bats no less that we had to sign during the game and his job, with Graham Stevenson, the former Yorkshire bowler, was to get us lot to sign these bats.

Well, you'd come into the dressing room in the morning and Ian would be curled up in the corner asleep, having been out all night on the turps. So we knew what we were letting ourselves in for when he finally made the England side in 1977.

IAN BOTHAM WAS BORN in Cheshire on 24 November 1955, but his family moved to Yeovil, in Yorkshire, when he was three. He would have made a very proud and belligerent Yorkshire cricketer, but the county's then stringent qualification rules meant that anyone born outside the county had to go elsewhere. So elsewhere the young Botham went, to Somerset, for whom he produced his extraordinary performance in a 1974 Benson & Hedges Cup quarter-final against Hampshire. Leading the Hampshire attack that day was the fearsome West Indian fast bowler, Andy Roberts, and when Somerset, chasing 183, were reduced to 8–113, the cause seemed lost.

Botham came in at No. 9, and almost immediately, confronting Roberts, was struck a frightening blow to the mouth. Doctors and concerned teammates suggested the 18-year-old leave the field, but stubbornly — and a bit stupidly he admitted later — Botham stayed, despite the blood and the smashed teeth, to overcome Roberts, make 45 not out, win the game and start the legend. From not too long after until the early '90s he was a central figure in English cricket, controversial, flamboyant, sometimes frustrating but usually successful. In an era when the game moved dramatically, to some degree kicking and screaming, into a world of glamour and entertainment, Ian Botham was English cricket's box office star. In the years since his retirement, England have searched forlornly for an all-rounder to fill his considerable boots.

Botham was a unique cricket force, a big, muscular cricketer, nicknamed at different times 'Both', 'Beefy' or 'Guy the Gorilla', athletically gifted enough to play first-team football for the English club side Scunthorpe United. From day one, he loved to hit the cricket ball (and, one imagines, football opponents) hard, but he was also a technically correct batsman. 'He has a superb defensive technique,' long-time Somerset teammate, Peter Roebuck, once wrote, 'when he cares to use it.'

Imran Khan rated Botham 'easily' the hardest hitter of the ball he bowled to during his career. The Englishman stood tall at the crease, bat aloft, waiting impatiently for the ball to hit for four. However, he rarely slogged; rather, he hit through the line or saw the short ball early, balance right, eye on the ball and head still, always willing to go over the top or hit on the up. As a bowler, at least until a back injury caught up with him, he surged in from

MIKE PROCTER: Beefy's almost a 'non-English' player, because he was such an attacking player. English players are brought up to defend first and attack second. But Ian Botham is a guy who believes in attacking — he bowled like that and he batted like that.

a fairly short run. Again, he was technically excellent, which gave him the gift of being able to swing the ball both ways, and his pace varied from medium pace to surprisingly quick. Few bowlers have got as many wickets with bad balls, but such successes were usually a result of his energy, his wide variety of deliveries, and that rare bowler's nous of being able to send down what was needed at exactly the right time. As a fieldsman he was brave, agile and sure-handed; England has not had a better slips fieldsman in the last 30 years.

Bob Willis wrote in 1981 that there were only four great English players in the 1970s — Geoff Boycott, Alan Knott, Derek Underwood and Botham. To show such high regard for Botham is in one way surprising, given that he did not make his international debut until so late in the decade. But in his first three seasons of Test cricket, Botham had emerged as a young man capable of extraordinary performances with both bat and ball. That he did so at a time when the sport was responding to the marketing impulses of Kerry Packer's World Series Cricket accentuated his appeal, and he became a hero to a new generation of cricket fans, while thrilling but sometimes frustrating the students of the game.

His first Test century came on a bowler's wicket in New Zealand in early 1978, part of a sensational all-round performance that also featured eight wickets, three catches and a quickfire 30 in England's second innings that left enough time for the Kiwis to be bowled out on the final afternoon. Folklore has it that he also deliberately ran Boycott out in that second innings, and then, colourfully and straight to the point, explained he'd done so because the veteran opener wasn't scoring fast enough. Back in England, against Pakistan, he scored a century at Edgbaston and then another at Lord's, where he also took 8–34 in one innings, a Test record at the ground. Later in that season, he took 24 wickets in three Tests against New Zealand, including 11 at Lord's, before going to Australia, where he became the first Englishman to score more than 275 runs and take more than 20 wickets in one Ashes series. In 1979, aged 23, he became the seventh Englishman to achieve the 1000 runs/100 wickets Test double, in 21 matches. This was 12 Tests quicker than any other Englishman had taken to reach this landmark, and two Tests faster than anyone at all.

The man Botham dismissed to reach 100 Test wickets was Sunil Gavaskar. Two Tests later, at The Oval, Botham approached Gavaskar during India's second innings, when the tourists needed a record-breaking 438 to win, and explained that he had dreamt that Gavaskar would score a double century. Now, Botham continued, it would be his job to make sure that dream did not come true. But Gavaskar was superb, and went on to 221 as India finished just nine runs short, with two wickets in

Botham, not yet 19 years old, swings freely for Somerset against Kent in August 1974.

DAVID GOWER: The great thing was simply that he believed he could win a game almost single-handedly at virtually any time. Any team meeting you care to mention and he would say, 'This is a waste of time, let's just go and beat them tomorrow.' He'd say, 'What are we talking about this for?' And he'd be thumping the table, he'd be all enthusiasm. I suppose of all the players I've played with over the years he's the one who could actually back it up with his deeds on the field.

hand. As the crowd invaded the field at the end, Botham souvenired a couple of stumps at the end. But not for himself, for Gavaskar.

By the start of the 1980 English season, Botham had a higher profile in England than any other sportsperson, even Kevin Keegan, the nation's football captain. He had scored Test hundreds, six in all, in England, Australia, New Zealand and India, and taken five wickets in a Test innings 14 times, 10 wickets in a Test three times. Best of all, in

the one-off Test staged in India in March 1980 to celebrate the Golden Jubilee of the Board of Control for Cricket in India, he had produced an all-round performance unprecedented in the history of Test cricket. 'There was hardly a session when he did not bring his influence to bear,' wrote *Wisden*. Mike Brearley's successful tenure as England captain was coming to an end, and Botham marked his commander's departure by scoring 114, after England had collapsed to 5–58, and taking 13–106 for the match. Botham won the Test by 10 wickets.

His single-minded approach was perhaps best epitomised by his effort in Sydney in early 1979, when, fighting a headache and with defence the order of the day, he batted an hour and a half for six. Brearley wondered whether natural aggression might have been a better way, but Botham settled on a plan and stuck to it. For the rest of the series, however, he was more likely to be caught on the boundary. His gambler's luck was illustrated by his dismissal of Graeme Wood at the Melbourne

Botham enjoying himself at Headingley in 1981, during one of cricket's most extraordinary fightbacks.

Cricket Ground earlier in the same series. Wood, who'd made a hundred in the first innings, was bowled by an ultra-slow Botham 'donkey drop' in the second. Nothing, it seemed, was too ludicrous that it might not work.

The English authorities bucked their conservative image and made Botham captain for the 1980 home series against a mighty West Indies side, but the bold move did not prove successful, for although England stayed competitive throughout the series, losing just one Test of five, Botham's own form tailed off. A rain-ruined Centenary Test against Australia at Lord's proved no different and then in the West Indies, England were beaten comfortably. In 10 Tests under Botham, England had no victories, and the new captain had scored just 242 runs and taken 29 wickets.

'I think in a way, his self-belief that he could win under any circumstances hampered his captaincy,' reckons David Gower, 'because it's not easy to transmit that to 10 other players, some of whom, inevitably, being more mortal, as it were, than him, would have the odd little bit of doubt there. I think as a captain, he would look back now and say he needed to do more than he did. There was this feeling pre-game — let's just go and do it, lads — and you need more than that as captain, you need to understand the needs of individual players. At that stage of his career, the captaincy wasn't quite what he needed.'

Few cricketers, or people, could have been made up of more contradictions than Botham. A self-avowed political conservative, advocate of self-help, and ardent monarchist, he was also a strident team man and remains among the first to climb aboard a worthwhile cause. His marathon walks for charity did as much good for his reputation as the front-page stories about smoking pot did damage. He wore his rebellious streak like a badge, but he was also clearly a sportsman, ever-willing to acknowledge good umpires and gallant opponents and ever-eager to share some beers and some camaraderie after play. He craved privacy, appeared street-wise, yet many a headline was inspired by his own boisterousness and his rare ability to too often find himself at the scene of the crime. He developed a severe mistrust about sections of the media, yet still contributed exclusive columns for the tabloids.

The first two Ashes Tests of 1981 were a personal disaster. England lost the first Test and drew the

The end of the fourth Ashes Test of 1981 at Edgbaston. Terry Alderman is bowled, Botham completes a spell of 5–1 from 28 balls, and England have a second straight improbable victory.

second, appearing dispirited and ordinary. Botham was out for nought in both innings in the second Test, at Lord's, and returned to the pavilion to total, embarrassing silence. That within weeks, excited cricket patriots were joyfully chanting his name was stark evidence that this was an extraordinary series. And an extraordinary cricketer.

Botham resigned the captaincy after the Lord's Test, hours before the selectors were going to sack him. Brearley returned, and the two teams went to Leeds, where Australia made 9–401 (declared; Botham 6–95) and England replied with 174 (Botham 50). Kim Hughes, the Australian captain,

> **KEITH STACKPOLE:** He didn't mind buying wickets, not like a lot of English bowlers who bowled line and length. Botham used to come in and try things. He'd bounce guys and get hit for four, he didn't mind that, so long as he set up someone. He always had a plan.

> **CLIVE LLOYD:** I really think he had a bit of West Indian blood in him, the way he played. When he had a ball in his hand, he was doing something all the time. When he went out to bat he played like he wanted to play, and not the way the coach might want or the captain might tell him to. He enjoyed his cricket and gave England great service. And he gave cricket in general a boost.

quickly enforced the follow-on, and Lillee and Alderman reduced England to 7–135. At this point, Botham was joined by Graeme Dilley, whose career Test batting average at that point was a little less than 16. Only once had a team won a Test after following on. Some members of the England team rang to book out of their hotel. Brearley rehearsed his loser's speech for the post-Test interview.

Early on, Botham was (for him) discreet, scoring just 39 in the hour and a half before tea. If anything, Dilley was the more aggressive. But in the final session Botham was awesome, turning the Test on its head as a Test had never been somersaulted before. Lillee, Alderman and Geoff Lawson were suddenly medium-pacers, benign ones at that. At tea, the score was 7–178. Forty-four minutes later, it was 8–252, Dilley out for 56, Botham in complete control. In effect, England were 8–25.

New batsman Chris Old stayed while Botham went to his hundred off 87 balls, in 155 minutes with 19 fours and a six. No Englishman had ever scored a century and taken six wickets in an innings during the same Ashes Test. The second 50, from 51 to 103, had taken 44 minutes and 30 balls, and included, astonishingly, 11 fours and a six. In the last 30 minutes, after Old was dismissed, Botham shielded last-man-in Willis from the strike so well, that Willis faced only five deliveries, while another 31 runs were added. At the close, England were 9–351, a lead of 124, Botham 144 not out. The man who had stumbled off at Lord's in courtroom silence two weeks earlier now ran off to wild acclaim. It was as if the previous 12 months had not happened.

The next day, Botham added five more before Willis was out, and then Willis (8–43) came out and bowled Australia out for 111. A famous victory, the first Act in a very famous series.

IN INDIA IN 1981–82, Botham became just the third all-rounder to complete the 2000 Test runs/200 Test wickets double. Again against India, this time at The Oval, in 1982, he made his highest Test score, 208, during which he managed to break some tiles on the Pavilion roof. He scored hundreds, home and away, against New Zealand in 1983 and 1984, plus five wickets in an innings in the latter match. Against Sri Lanka at Lord's in 1984, he took 6–90. Meanwhile, in international one-day cricket, he produced cameos without ever becoming the dominant figure his all-round gifts suggested he should have been. In fact, he never scored a one-day international century and never took five wickets in a one-day international innings. In county cricket, he stayed at Somerset until an acrimonious split in 1986, over the sacking of his great friend and comrade Viv Richards, then played for Worcestershire (1987 to 1991) and Durham (1992 and 1993).

After 1981, Botham's struggles with a nagging back injury that had first emerged in 1980 clearly impacted on his cricket. When he came out to Australia in 1982–83, he was overweight, and his impact diminished, though one sensed he was still, with Gower, the wicket the Australians craved most. He did conjure one magic moment, dismissing Aussie No. 11 Jeff Thomson in Melbourne when just three runs were needed, to give England their only Test victory of the summer. At home in 1985 he was dominant once more, taking 31 wickets, and then in Brisbane in November 1986 he played another phenomenal innings, slaughtering an inexperienced Aussie bowling line-up while slamming 138. It was his final Test century.

'That's one of the best innings I saw him play,' says Allan Border. 'We were in a situation where we had England in a little bit of trouble when Ian turned up at the crease. Typical of him, he summed up the situation pretty quickly and decided, right, I'll take the attack to the Aussies, and we'll see what happens. One minute we had a real sniff, good decision to send them in, we've got England in a bit of strife … an hour and a half later, we're deflated, he's taken the wind right out of our sails with extraordinary batting.'

A few months earlier, against New Zealand at The Oval, Botham had scored a Test fifty off just 32 balls, during which he took a liking to the right-arm fast-medium Derek Stirling, hitting 24 from one over (4-6-4-6-0-4). These occasions came often enough to preserve his image; so too did his brushes with cricket officialdom and the law.

In 1984, he was fined by the Test and County Cricket Board for suggesting Pakistan was a good place to send your mother-in-law. A month later, he sued an English Sunday paper after it was alleged that he had possessed and used prohibited drugs on a tour of New Zealand. At around the same time, Botham was in court defending a speeding charge. On the field that English summer he captained Somerset with little success (for the first time in four seasons, the county did not win a trophy) and was part of the England Test side that was swept by the West Indies. However, he did pass the 4000 Test runs and 300 Test wicket milestones, and at Lord's he took 8–103 in the Windies' first innings. 'A real reminder of his old self,' wrote *Wisden*. After the Windies series, having played 73 Tests in seven years, he declared himself unavailable for England's tour of India. Then on New Year's Eve, after a police search prompted by the discovery of some cannabis in a trouser pocket at the dry cleaner's, he was charged with drug possession and copped a small fine.

In October 1985, he took off on a 1500km walk from John O'Groats in the very north of Scotland to Land's End on the southern English coast, raising £880,000 for the Leukaemia Research Fund. Botham's backing for research into the disease had actually been prompted years earlier, back in his first season of Test cricket, when while being treated for a broken foot, he came into contact with young leukaemia sufferers. The walk was a culmination of a decade of typically totally-committed support, and a precursor of further acts of great charity. From Land's End, he headed to the Caribbean, where England was 'blackwashed' again and Botham scored just 168 runs and took 11 wickets in five Tests. And during the gap between the fourth and fifth Tests, a sensational story was published describing a 'Botham cocaine and sex scandal' that allegedly involved, among other things, an ex-Miss Barbados and a broken bed. Botham later commented that it would have been hard for this story to be true, as he was actually with his father-in-law at the time.

'There was a tabloid war going on,' Botham recalls. 'Obviously, there was a period where editors perhaps didn't worry quite so much whether it was true or not.' But in early 1986, after protracted legal negotiations, Botham confirmed that he had

DEAN JONES: What a bloke to have around you. I know he's had a couple of bad spots with the media here and there, and done a few funny things, but the best thing I could say about Ian Botham is that he's good enough to be Australian.

occasionally used cannabis, for which he was promptly fined and suspended by cricket authorities until the end of that July. In Australia, for a season of Sheffield Shield cricket with Queensland in 1987–88, he was the dominant figure as his new team surged to the top of the table. But then things went awry, as Botham was in trouble for damaging a dressing room in Tasmania (after a few drinks with DK Lillee), and then for assaulting a passenger on a flight from Brisbane to Perth. Queensland lost the final to Western Australia, and his contract for the following season was cancelled.

'He likes going out, he's a social animal, a party animal, in fact none of us can keep up with him if

Botham traps New Zealand captain Jeff Crowe lbw at The Oval in 1986, to break DK Lillee's record for most wickets in Tests.

he's in the mood,' says David Gower. 'For years now, we've tried to share it around. If someone goes out with him on a Monday night, it's someone else's turn on a Tuesday night, and woe betide anyone who goes out with him on a weekend. But throughout his career you'll find that he worked hard and played hard.'

Michael Holding echoes these sentiments: 'Beefy just lives every day for the day. When Beefy goes out for dinner you would think it's the last time he's going to have dinner. He goes out, he enjoys himself, has a few bottles of wine, has a nice lovely meal. He just goes out and tries to get the best out of every day. He's not thinking, let me hold back a bit, tomorrow is another day, he just tries to enjoy every day. That's the way I think you have got to live, it's a great way to live.'

ON 4 AUGUST 1986, Botham celebrated his return from the suspension by bashing Worcestershire for 104 not out from 66 balls. Soon after, he made a record 175 not out, including 13 sixes, against Northants in a John Player League match. Back in the Test side, he took a wicket almost immediately to go equal with Lillee as Test cricket's greatest wicket-taker. That was an outswinger, then an inswinger had the Kiwi batsman Jeff Crowe lbw. It was glory days again.

Botham played a full Test series at home against Pakistan in 1987, batting almost the entire final day of the fifth Test, at The Oval, to force a draw, but after that just eight more Tests until his final appearance, against Pakistan at Lord's in 1992. At one point, he was rushed back into the England team for the Ashes Tests of 1989, despite having played little because of injury, in the hope that he would once again bodyslam the Australians. He had always seemed to reserve his finest for the oldest enemy. This time, it was not to be.

Botham retired from first-class cricket in 1993, his final match being for Durham against, appropriately, the touring Australians. Steve Waugh recorded his unusual farewell this way: 'With steady rain falling and both teams assuming the game would be called, Beefy Botham emptied the contents of a couple of bottles of sauvignon blanc, in recognition of the end of his career. But the celebrations were halted by the unwelcome news that rain had stopped falling and play would begin in 15 minutes … I made my way to the middle with 20 minutes left and the game having deteriorated to the state where Botham was wicketkeeping without pads or gloves.'

It was a long, long way from Trent Bridge in 1977, Bombay in 1980, Headingley, Edgbaston or Old Trafford in 1981. No cricket legend has ever had such an unlikely or unconventional end to his career, but it was so typical of the man to do things differently. 'He was someone who could do all he did on the field and do everything that he did off the field as well,' says David Gower of Botham's unique cricket experience. 'The way that man has lived life, he is the genuine all-rounder.'

Getty Images

Botham hooks during his last great innings against Australia — a century at the Gabba he rates as one of his most important — as England take the initiative early in the 1986–87 series.

SIR RICHARD HADLEE
Legend No. 12
The Quintessential Pro

SIR RICHARD HADLEE ENJOYED one of the finest careers in cricket history, and most certainly the greatest in New Zealand's cricket history. Today, he stands as far above all other New Zealand bowlers as Sir Donald Bradman does above all batsmen, perhaps further. He took 431 Test wickets, more than double the number taken by any other Kiwi bowler, at an average (22.30) more than four runs better than any other Kiwi with 100 Test wickets. Add to that 3124 Test runs, sixth highest among all New Zealanders, plus 158 one-day international wickets and 1751 one-day runs. A spin bowler could not have been *this* good for so long. And he did all this without an accomplished accomplice to share the load, soften up the opposition, stop frantic batsmen escaping to the other end. 'What he and his team would have done,' reflects Ian Healy, 'to have had bowlers at the other end to support and maintain the pressure on batsmen he was constantly generating.'

He was born on 3 July 1951 in Christchurch, into a most distinguished cricket family, the son of one of New Zealand's finest players, Walter Hadlee, and younger brother of Barry and Dayle, who both went on to represent their country in cricket (all three played together in the 1975 World Cup).

IAN SMITH: He demanded a lot of himself, and he demanded high standards from his teammates. Through it all he was one of the wisest bowlers. He looked at conditions and used them well on most occasions.

As a cricketer Richard became more earnest and immaculately professional than Bothamly bumptious, without the trademark fury or histrionics of a Lillee, the flair of an Imran Khan, the height of a Garner or Ambrose, the lightning pace of a Marshall, the unique action of a Thomson. What he did bring to his profession was as complete and comprehensive an approach as is possible. Whenever he performed, you knew that if he did not succeed it would not be for lack of preparation and concentration. He sought any advantage, and got everything out of his bowling talent that he possibly could.

'He did everything he could to achieve his goals,' says John Wright. 'His preparation was meticulous. For a particular batsman, he could adjust his line and length. For a particular pitch condition, he could adjust immediately. He had tremendous control. And when he wanted to, he had the pace.'

Getty Images

Hadlee in England in 1978. More than a decade of supreme excellence is in front of him.

This, of course, is an accomplished teammate looking back on a long career. Back in the early 1970s, after Hadlee had made his first-class debut for Canterbury, few could have believed — even though he marked his maiden appearance with a hat-trick — that his life would work out the way it did. Here we will travel through 18 years in Tests, using particular matches as benchmarks, to see how this unique sportsman built his reputation …

Test debut, New Zealand v Pakistan, first Test, Wellington, 2–5 February 1973

Earlier in this season, Hadlee had made his debut for the New Zealand national side, in the Australian domestic one-day competition, the Gillette Cup, in which the Kiwi national side played between 1969 and 1975. He began his Test career by taking 2–84 and 0–28, bowling the first over, and scoring 46, batting at No. 8. His first victim was Asif Iqbal, then Pakistan's most dynamic batsman, caught and bowled. Hadlee remembers that his first delivery at this level was a full toss that was hit for four, and that it took quite a while before he had that initial Test wicket.

For the following three years, Hadlee struggled at the highest level. For the second Test of that Pakistan series, he was dropped and brother Dayle recalled to bowl the first over. The brothers first played together in a Test in the first Test of the 1973 England tour, Richard's only Test of the tour (he took 0–64 and 1–79 and scored 0 and 4 not out batting at No. 10). In fact, he remained on the periphery of the Test side until 1976, despite the occasional good performance — such as in Sydney in early 1974, when he took six wickets in the match, including Keith Stackpole (twice) and Ian Chappell. In the Tests either side of this match, his bowling figures were 0–104 and 1–102 as Australia won both matches by an innings.

New Zealand v India, third Test, Wellington, 13–17 February 1976

Hadlee was left out of the New Zealand side for the first Test of this series and, opening the bowling in the second, returned the ordinary figures of 0–75 (from 12 eight-ball overs) and 1–64. Not surprisingly, his selection in the third Test was far from assured. In fact, he didn't think he would be playing, but the selectors opted for a four-pronged pace attack and Hadlee bowled second change, taking four confidence-boosting wickets in the first innings. In the second, again bowling second change, he was, in his own words, 'able to have a bit of a blitz' and snared 7–23, at that time a New Zealand record. In a comment that revealed something of the perfectionism that would come to mark his cricket life, he admitted that he was not entirely satisfied because at times he had been 'decidedly inaccurate'.

This was New Zealand's ninth Test victory, in their 119th match, and their first by an innings. Hadlee's match figures of 11–58 were also a New Zealand Test record (and remained so until Hadlee himself improved on them in 1985–86). The match was a watershed not just for him but for his country. When he next bowled in a Test, he was opening the attack, in Lahore in October 1976, and he responded by taking 5–121. In the third Test, in Karachi, he scored 87, his first Test half-century, and with wicketkeeper Warren Lees added 186 for the seventh wicket. After three Tests in India, Hadlee returned home having, in the upbeat words of his captain Glenn Turner, 'come of age'.

Against Australia at home in 1977, Hadlee had little success with the ball, despite being portrayed as being his team's answer to Lillee. While the great Australian took 15 wickets in the two Tests, Hadlee took only six, but he did contribute a stirring knock of 81 on the final day of the series, after New Zealand had crashed to 5–31. He batted for 145 minutes, and hit 10 fours and one spectacular six — a straight drive, of all things, off Lillee. Australia still won the match by 10 wickets, but the importance of the innings should not be underestimated. New Zealand did not go down lamely. Instead, they had a player brave and skilful enough to stand up to the Australians, to Lillee, for themselves.

For the past three seasons, Kiwi cricket fans had gazed longingly across the Tasman to see their Australian counterparts roar on their champions, chanting out support for Lillee and Thommo, Dougie Walters and Rodney Marsh. Now, for the first time, they did the same thing for one of their own.

'The crowd's reaction when Richard bowled three fast overs on the second afternoon was unreal,' Hadlee's new-ball partner Ewen Chatfield remembered in his autobiography. 'The new ball was taken at 5.15pm and the crowd began chanting,

> **IAN BOTHAM:** I can certainly speak for myself. I'm pretty sure I can speak for the other guys. The first scores I'd look at, if Pakistan were playing, were to check what's Imran done. If India were playing: what's Kapil done? What's 'Paddles' [Hadlee] done down in New Zealand? I would always look at those. And I'm sure they did the same with me.

"Had-lee, Had-lee!" Marsh was lbw in Hadlee's first over and the crowd was delirious with joy. Then Gary Gilmour, who had scored a century in backing up Walters in Christchurch [in the first Test of this series], played and missed at the next two balls. Richard rose to the occasion and bowled as fast as he ever had. Between his overs, Walters mistimed a hook off me and Richard raced in to take a sprawling catch in front of the raving terrace supporters, who then went into more of an uproar …'

Hadlee concedes that in these early days he often played the role of the young tearaway. 'It wasn't until I went to England in 1978 to play county cricket that I really honed my skills, my routines, my discipline, the fact of professionalism, my fitness,' he says today. 'I had to look at my technique, had to look at my mental toughness. If it meant changing my personality and at times being a little bit aloof, being single-minded or determined, even calculating, so be it. At the end of the day, you're representing your country. There's a job to be done out there, and with a great deal of pride and satisfaction. I made a number of sacrifices and if I was criticised for that, well, so be it. That to me was instrumental in some of the successes I was able to enjoy.'

Before he began his county career with Nottinghamshire, Hadlee took 10–100 in Wellington as New Zealand defeated England in a Test match for the first time, at the 48th attempt. It

> **MARTIN CROWE:** There is no doubt that Richard Hadlee was at his best when he was up against New Zealand's greatest rival in Australia, particularly on their own turf in front of their hostile crowds. In doing so, he was able to lift his teammates — as he did throughout his career — to ensure that in New Zealand cricket history, the 1980s will go down as the greatest era.

Hadlee at Lord's in 1986. Six months earlier he'd destroyed Australia in Australia; now he took 19 wickets in three Tests as the Kiwis won a series in England for the first time.

was an astonishing victory, Hadlee taking 6–26 as England, chasing 137, were bowled out for 64, and afterwards the local fans celebrated by singing 'For They Are Jolly Good Fellows!' and gave a hearty three cheers. The Test also instigated something of a 'feud' between Hadlee and the exciting young English all-rounder Ian Botham, which continued throughout this series and the subsequent three Tests in England in 1978. Both men bounced each other liberally, but Botham decisively had the better of the exchanges.

Hadlee did take 13 wickets in the three Tests in England, but never Botham's. In county cricket, he was disappointing, often injured, for three seasons

DEAN JONES: He is what I call the 'Geoff Boycott' of bowling. He used to meticulously work out, day in day out, 'I'm going get five wickets today, I'm going to bowl at the right times ...' He was the complete professional.

until 1981, when he took advantage of a summer of peak fitness to become the only bowler to take 100 wickets in the season and to lead Notts to the county championship for the first time since 1929. Significantly, he used a shortened run-up, cut from 23 paces to 15 ...

New Zealand v West Indies, first Test, Dunedin, 8–13 February 1980
In February 1979, against Pakistan in Napier, Hadlee took his 100th Test wicket, the fourth New Zealander to do so, in his 25th Test. Against the West Indies in Dunedin, he was magnificent, fighting an ankle injury to take 5–34 and 6–68 and score 51 and a critical 17 (out of a fourth-innings total of 9–104) in a famous — for the Kiwis! — and very controversial match. In the second Test, he scored his 1000th Test run during his first Test century (103). From this series on, specifically from that first Test, he was recognised as an outstanding Test cricketer, without doubt a member of the game's elite, as he took off on an unrelenting pursuit of Test wickets that would not end until he retired a decade later.

This status was confirmed in Australia in 1980–81, when the media seemed to hand him the mantle of 'villain' in a tempestuous season that culminated in the infamous 'underarm' one-day international. Throughout, Hadlee was booed by the Australian crowds, but (and because) he rivalled Lillee and Greg Chappell as the cricketer of the summer. In the Tests he took 19 wickets (Lillee managed 16) despite not getting even one lbw decision.

Whenever he is asked who was his greatest role model, Hadlee always nominates Lillee. 'He was the epitome of what fast bowling was all about,' he explains. 'He was big, strong, fit, confident, aggressive, had marvellous skills, great technique, he intimidated the batsmen with sheer presence and, of course, he got you out!'

Hadlee's decision to retain the shortened run-up he'd used so successfully at Nottingham was strongly criticised back home. 'I was carrying niggling injuries with ankles and so on,' Hadlee explains, 'and the last game of the [1980] season was Notts playing Lancashire, a Sunday league match, and I got 6–12 off the short Sunday league run-up, which was 15 paces. So with that, I went back to New Zealand and started bowling off a short run, even in Test cricket. Some of our writers were very severe on me, and some of the players were very severe and critical. They felt that I was taking shortcuts and not putting in the effort, because the perception was that if you're a fast bowler, you've got to run in off 25, 30 paces and look as if you're bowling fast …'

Hadlee's view is that the abbreviated run-up made him more 'clinically efficient', and history supports that view. Anything lost in pace was amply compensated for by an extraordinary control and a broader range of deliveries. His stock delivery was the leg-cutter, but whenever he needed, he could nip one back the other way, usually after delivering the ball from a little wider on the bowling crease. He could swing the ball both ways, always late. His slower ball usually swung into the batsmen. And he had a quicker bouncer, which always seemed to be bowled when the batsman least expected it. The stodgy Chris Tavare, struck in the mouth at The Oval in 1983, was just one example of a batsman stunned by a Hadlee riser.

Hadlee went past 200 Test wickets in the 1983 series in England (the fourth fastest, in terms of Tests played, to do so), and then raced to 250 in nine matches. During this run he produced a superb all-round effort against England in Christchurch, top-scoring with 99 from 81 balls and then taking 3–16 and 5–28 as New Zealand won the second Test by an innings and 132 runs. He also dominated the Kiwis' first series in Sri Lanka, where he took 23 wickets for 230 runs in the three Tests. New Zealand won both these rubbers, giving them not just their first-ever series win over England (at the 21st attempt), but also their first-ever consecutive series victories.

If Hadlee had not made New Zealand a world cricket power, he had certainly made them ultra-competitive.

New Zealand v Australia, first Test, Brisbane, 8–12 November 1985

For Hadlee, this was 'the most perfect Test match New Zealand have played in'. His contribution to this New Zealand victory at the Gabba was immense — 9–52 and 6–71, and an innings of 54 — but in fact his performance went beyond statistics, for this might have been the finest, at the very least the most controlled, pace bowling performance in cricket history. He himself says of his nine-for: 'I moved it around all over the place with complete control.'

> **SIR RICHARD HADLEE:** I had four key words that went through my mind when I was bowling. One was 'rhythm', another was 'off-stump', another was 'desire' and the other one was 'Lillee'. 'Off-stump' was the target area where I was trying to get that ball. 'Rhythm', because I had to be relaxed — if the body was stiff and tense it wasn't going to perform and function. I had to have this rhythm, to be loose and relaxed. 'Desire', because the batsman's a problem, he's an obstacle, he's got to be removed. And, of course, Dennis Lillee was the role model, the inspiration, particularly when things got tough. What would Dennis do? He wouldn't give up, a 100-per-cent man.

Especially in that first innings, it seemed as if Hadlee could place the ball wherever he wanted; each ball had a purpose, a wicket seemed likely with every delivery. While it must be conceded that he

Hadlee the batsman, a dangerous hitter who did enough during his career to suggest that had he really put his mind to it, he could have been a Test-class batsman. He once went to 151 not out in a Test match, the highest of his two centuries at that level, and scored over 3000 Test-match runs.

Getty Images

Hadlee breaks Ian Botham's world record by taking his 384th Test wicket, in Bangalore in November 1988.

was facing a mediocre — Allan Border apart — Australian side, it should also be remembered that this was a good batting wicket, on which four batsmen would score centuries and New Zealand, when they batted, reached 7 (declared) for 553.

For the next two years, Hadlee's wicket-taking was prodigious. In all, he took 33 wickets in that 1985–86 series in Australia, as New Zealand won a series against their neighbours for the first time, then took another 16 as they repeated the feat at home. In the

WASIM AKRAM: Richard Hadlee is definitely one of the top four all-rounders in the world that I've ever seen. His line and length were immaculate. He used to bowl away swingers perfectly, with good pace. And when he shortened his run-up, his pace was still there. A great cricketer, it was great to know him. I really enjoyed playing with him and playing against him.

first Test, at Wellington, he had Border lbw, his 300th wicket, while at Christchurch he took 7–116, the 25th time he'd taken five wickets in a Test innings. By bowling Wayne Phillips in the second innings of that second Test he completed 100 Test wickets against Australia. Then, on his fourth England tour, he took another 19 wickets (no other bowler on either side took even 10), including 10–140 at Nottingham, the seventh time he'd taken 10 wickets in a Test match and the 27th five-for of his Test career. Both these achievements were world records (the former shared with SF Barnes, Clarrie Grimmett and Lillee, the latter beating Botham). More importantly, New Zealand won a series in England for the first time.

Hadlee recognises his role in New Zealand's successes through this decade. 'We didn't play for money in the '70s; we played for the honour, the pride, the passion, all these common terms that are so important,' he explains. 'As time went on, I became a professional and I changed as a person. But at the same time, there are only two or three professionals in that [New Zealand team] environment. To convince the amateur players to change their philosophies and their approach to training and planning and preparation, to what it was all about, there was some reluctance it would be fair to say. But in time, there was a turnaround, and we enjoyed some wonderful successes in the '80s. It is fair to say that we were a professional side, not necessarily monetary-wise, but in the way that we planned and prepared.'

Botham had gone past Lillee as Test cricket's leading wicket-taker in the final Test of the series against New Zealand, and now Hadlee set out to reel him in. He took his 350th wicket against the West Indies in Christchurch in March 1987, and then in Australia was in stirring form as he single-handedly took on an improving Australian batting line-up.

Every match brought new landmarks. In the first Test, he went past Lillee's total of 355 Test wickets. In the second, he became the first man to take 30 five-fors in Tests, and in the third he bowled 75 overs to take 10 wickets for the match (5–109 and 5–67) and almost won the day. He also equalled Botham's world record of 373 Test wickets. On the final afternoon, he bowled unchanged from 5.15pm to 6.49pm, but could not break the final Australian partnership. 'I had to bowl the last over at Mike Whitney and he kept me out,' he remembers ruefully. 'But I had to dig so deep that it took me three days to recover. Normally I am fine the following day ...'

For Whitney, one of cricket's most natural No. 11s, overcoming Hadlee in such dramatic circumstances was the highlight of his career. To him, the great New Zealander was the 'quintessential pro'. A photograph of the pair, taken immediately after the last delivery, with Whitney trying to contain his excitement and Hadlee offering an exhausted but good-natured congratulatory pat on the helmet, and with the penned message, 'To Whit, well batted, regards, Richard Hadlee', a feature, remains one of the Australian bowler's most treasured possessions.

New Zealand's next Test was against England in Christchurch, Hadlee's home ground, and seemed to represent the perfect stage for him to break the record. Preparations were made for a grand celebration, but fate took a hand. Having bowled 18 overs without reward, he tore a calf muscle and was forced to miss the rest of the series.

New Zealand v India, first Test, Bangalore, 12–17 November 1988

The record finally came 318 days after Hadlee had equalled Botham's mark, when he bowled Kris Srikkanth, the first of 18 wickets he took in the series. In Bombay, he took 10–88 for the match as New Zealand won a Test in India for only the second time.

Because New Zealand played few Tests through 1989, it wasn't until February 1990 that Hadlee became the first man to 400 Test wickets, in his 80th Test. He did so by dismissing Sanjay Manjrekar in Christchurch, some compensation for the locals who had missed seeing him break Botham's record. A Test later, he dismissed WV Raman with the first ball of the match, becoming only the second man (after England's Geoff Arnold) to achieve this feat twice. It was as if no record was beyond him. In the third Test he took only two wickets, but scored 87 with the bat.

There is little doubt that Hadlee had the batting talent to score many more runs than he finally did in Test cricket. On occasions he seemed more intent on hitting than batting, but at other times, such as in England in 1983, when he scored a half-century in three of the four Tests, or in Sri Lanka in April 1987, when he hit his highest Test score, 151 not out, he showed he was capable of scoring Test-quality runs. In 1984, he did the double of 1000 runs and 100 wickets in county cricket, one of only two men (Franklyn Stephenson in 1988 being the other) to do so since 1967. Certainly, he has done enough to be classed as a genuine all-rounder.

> **JOHN WRIGHT:** All of us from that era feel that we were lucky and fortunate to play with him. He won games for New Zealand, many games. He was hugely competitive and very, very motivated to achieve the high goals that he set himself.

'Hadlee could be dangerous with the bat,' reckons Ian Botham, 'but he didn't score as many runs as I think he should have done. Having said that, he was carrying the bowling for New Zealand, which wasn't a strong side, so something had to suffer.'

In a one-off Test against Australia, his final Test on home soil, Hadlee scored his 3000th Test-match run. He also took five wickets in an innings for the 100th time in first-class cricket and the 35th time in Tests, as New Zealand won decisively by nine wickets. This result meant that in the decade of cricket, 1980–81 to 1989–90, the two countries had five victories each, from 17 Tests. Before 1980, Australia won five Tests to the Kiwis' one; in the 12 years since 1990, the record is Australia eight victories, New Zealand one.

Getty Images

Hadlee in a contemplative mood at the start of his final Test tour, to England in 1990.

New Zealand v England, second Test, Lord's,
21–25 June 1990

Nine days before this Test began, the Queen's birthday honours were announced, and among those honoured was Sir Richard Hadlee. At Lord's he became the third knight to play Test cricket after receiving his title, although the others, Sir Timothy O'Brien and Sir Vijaya Vizianagram, were not honoured for their services to cricket.

To Sir Richard, the knighthood is the 'ultimate accolade', and he celebrated at Lord's by slamming a belligerent 86 from just 84 balls. A fortnight later, in the 86th and last Test match of his career, he took another eight wickets, including 5–53 in England's second innings (the 36th five-for of his career). And he was excellent to the very end, taking two wickets in his final over in Test cricket, one of them, Devon Malcolm, his 431st Test wicket, with his very last ball. He remained the leading Test wicket-taker until February 1994, when Kapil Dev took over.

Kapil and Sir Richard were half of the quartet of great all-rounders who thrilled cricket fans through the 1980s, Ian Botham and Imran Khan being the others. 'Whenever we had a confrontation, playing against each other in a one-on-one situation, for all of us, the will and desire to outdo your opponent became that much greater,' says Sir Richard. 'We had some fierce contests.'

Trying to rate one higher than the others is difficult, though, of course, that is one of the aims of *ESPN's Legends of Cricket* series. It is fair to say that if the four were in the one team, Hadlee would be the lowest in the batting order. Who would bowl the first over would pose a glorious dilemma for the captain. Perhaps it would be the Imran of 1982, or the Botham of 1978, or the Kapil of 1980–81. If it was to be Sir Richard Hadlee, it could be the Hadlee of any year from 1980 to 1990, for he was proud, dangerous and productive right through that era. That is what set him apart. No great pace bowler, not even his hero Dennis Lillee, has been so magnificent for so long.

Graham Gooch is bowled at Lord's in 1990, most likely the first instance of a cricketing knight knocking out the off-stump of an opposing captain. Sir Richard's knighthood had been announced nine days before the Test began.

Getty Images

KEITH MILLER
Legend No. 13
Cricket's Errol Flynn

So MANY OF THE *Legends of Cricket* were renowned for their dedication, their hunger, their singled-minded sense of purpose to the game. Almost to a man, these champions dedicated themselves to excellence, and they all succeeded admirably.

Keith Miller was different. Yes, he was successful: as an all-round cricketer he has had few equals, and perhaps only Sir Garfield Sobers in cricket history has clearly surpassed him. But Miller, when it came to cricket, could never be described as 'single-minded'. He was an instinctive, unpredictable genius, and an entertainer who, as another fine Australian all-rounder, Alan Davidson, puts it, 'was the Errol Flynn of cricket, he just loved adventure'.

Miller is a man who enjoyed the spoils of high society while remaining charitable, conscious of his roots and aware of the expectations and hopes of the working man. He delighted in the unexpected, hated being bored and was keen to explore different ways to win, always believing that it was far from the end of the world if you happened to lose.

To a degree, the sobriety and seriousness of Test cricket restrained him, and many of his most exciting and flamboyant cricket escapades occurred away from the Test arena. Even so, he became, in his way, almost as big a hero as Bradman. His cricket needed to be vibrant, his physique was imposing, and his hair was dark, relatively long for the times, and the way he swept it back off his forehead became a trademark. For young women, he had definite sex appeal; for boys and young men his exploits were something out of a *Boy's Own* annual. It is remarkable how many men aged in their fifties and sixties today identify Miller as being 'my hero when I was a kid'.

BORN ON 28 NOVEMBER 1919, Keith Ross Miller was a gifted schoolboy cricketer in Melbourne. However, it seemed his future prospects would be held back by a lack of height. So small was he that for a while he considered becoming a jockey, and at senior cricket practice he had trouble getting the men to treat him seriously. Then, between the ages of 16 and 17, he shot up from five feet (152cm) short to six feet (183cm) tall, and started harbouring dreams of a career in Australian football. Indeed, he later played with some distinction in the Victorian Football League for St Kilda, but at 18 years 66 days, in February 1938, he was in the Victorian cricket XI, scoring 181 against Tasmania, and dreaming of a long career at the top of the cricket tree.

For a long time, the War killed those ambitions, but after serving with distinction as a fighter pilot, Miller was drafted into the Australian Services team for the 'Victory Tests' in England and made a huge impression with both bat and ball. That he was now a new-ball bowler stunned enthusiasts of the game back home, who recalled him solely as a promising batsman. When first-class cricket in Australia shut down in 1941, Miller had played 14 first-class matches for two centuries, two fifties … and one wicket, from the grand total of seven overs.

Miller's contribution to the Victory matches was considerable. In the first 'Test' he scored 105. In the second match, he had annoyed the Sheffield crowd by bowling quickly and bouncing the English

batsmen, especially Hutton and Washbrook, to the point that some in the crowd yelled out, 'Get off, Larwood!' Still, he had only six wickets in the series to his name when he dramatically took the new ball for England's second innings of the third match and, with sheer speed, took three wickets, before scoring 71 not out as Australia won by four wickets. Thereafter, he was an opening bowler. Meanwhile, he made another century in match four, and 77 not out in the decider to leave him with the highest series runs aggregate on either side.

Even then, his greatest triumph of that memorable season was still to come. A match was scheduled between England and a 'Dominions XI' led by Learie Constantine and featuring players from the West Indies, Australia, New Zealand and South Africa. Miller was the star. Coming to the wicket with 75 minutes left on the second day, he was 61 not out at stumps, having hit one ball onto the top of the pavilion. The following morning he continued in the same vein, with a style that had the former England captain Sir Pelham Warner celebrating: 'In an experience of first-class cricket of nearly 60 years I have never seen such hitting.'

In an hour and a half, Miller slammed 124 runs, including seven sixes. He and Constantine added 117 in 45 minutes. His score of 185 was made out of a total of 336, not enough to give the Dominions team victory, but it sealed his reputation. *Wisden* reckoned Miller 'outshone even Hammond', while the great writer Denzil Batchelor described the innings as being 'a schoolboy's dream'. The respected Australian cricket writer AG 'Johnnie' Moyes later described the knock as 'one of the most masterly seen for a generation'. Thirty-five years later, Miller called it 'my best innings ever'. At this point, we must remember, he was yet to appear in a Test match.

When the Services team returned to Australia for a series of matches against the states, Miller produced another fine knock in Sydney — an unbeaten 105 out of 204 against Bill O'Reilly and Ray Lindwall, which O'Reilly thought was one of the finest innings ever played against him.

In his book *Australian Cricket: A History,* Moyes wrote of the Miller he observed playing that season: 'During this series Australians saw Miller bowling for the first time in big cricket and they liked what they saw. It was perfectly obvious that another Test player had been developed by a Services' team, a

IAN CHAPPELL: As a kid growing up in the early 1950s, Keith Miller was my idol. There couldn't have been a better cricketer to watch for a young bloke. He was so aggressive and such a charismatic player that I just ate up everything I saw Keith Miller doing.

batsman of quality and a fast bowler with real speed and clever skill as well.'

Despite his selection for an Australian team that played New Zealand in Wellington in March 1946 (a match that was not given Test status until March 1948, in which Miller scored 30 and took 2–6 from six overs) Miller went into the 1946–47 season a likely, but not quite certain selection in the Australian XI. The country was rich with talent, and stars such as Bradman and Morris had been unavailable for the New Zealand tour. Still, Miller was seen by most enthusiasts as a vital member of the national side, a jewel too valuable to be ignored. The former NSW captain Alan Kippax said of him in the lead-up to the Ashes series: 'Probably a greater all-rounder even than Jack Gregory. Very few batsmen I have watched have his rare ability to blend beauty with power.'

How good a batsman Miller could be was amply demonstrated in a Sheffield Shield match against South Australia in November 1946. South Australia had batted for all of the opening day for 270, and by stumps on day two, Saturday, Victoria had first-innings points, having reached 3–285. Miller was 56 not out, and with Lindsay Hassett, unbeaten on 43, had provided the most exciting cricket of the match. On the Monday, the pair went on to centuries, Miller 188 and Hassett 114. The 1948 *Wisden* described Miller's effort as 'one of the finest batting displays ever seen at Adelaide'.

Victoria finally won the match outright, by nine wickets, despite Don Bradman and Ron Hamence scoring second-innings centuries. On the final afternoon, South Australia lost their last six wickets for 36, to give their opponents 35 minutes to score 79. Hassett and Miller opened the batting, and in a torrent of fours and quick singles, the target was achieved with two minutes to spare. Miller was out in what proved to be the final over, when four runs were needed and five minutes remained.

Keith Miller the batsman was an entertainment package. He liked to get on the front foot, to drive hard and on the up, but he could also hook and pull, and cut hard through point or delicately fine. Moyes, in 1954, described him this way: 'He always looks the complete batsman when he takes up his stance, and often plays that way, for his cover drive came out of the pages of the best text-book, his hits for six leave no doubt as to where the ball will go, while his forcing shots between mid-on and mid-wicket are a sight to make old men young.'

ALAN DAVIDSON: We played the Englishmen here in Sydney in one of the early matches of the '50–51 tour and I can still remember Keith straight driving Alec Bedser, first ball with the second new ball, straight back over his head, first bounce into the Sydney Showground wall beyond the boundary. It went like a two iron shot — Tiger Woods couldn't hit a two iron better. It was the most incredible shot.

As a bowler, Miller's strongest trait was his unpredictability. 'I'm sure he often had no preconceived idea what he intended to bowl even as he turned to start his run,' claimed Denis Compton. 'As a batsman you never knew what was coming. It could be as fast a ball as anyone was entitled to expect on this planet, a slow leg-break, a bouncer or a fast back-break off an immaculate length, which would land outside the off-stump and, if missed with the bat, would smack the legs.' The Rev. David Sheppard, a Test opening bat of considerable ability, was once bowled by a Miller wrong 'un at Lord's. Len Hutton, who reckoned he never saw a bowler who cared less about where his bowling mark was, also commented that, 'I never felt physically safe against him.'

'He had the perfect action for a fast bowler,' Hutton continued, 'delivering the ball with his right hand high above his left hip, thereby obtaining the maximum amount of effort at the last possible moment. This enabled him, so it appeared to me, to gain more pace off the wicket than most other fast bowlers are capable of doing. A grand sportsman in every way, he constituted with Ray Lindwall the most hostile combination of fast bowlers it has been my misfortune to face.'

Alan Davidson's view of the Lindwall-Miller partnership is this: 'Ray Lindwall was the best bowler I ever saw of any type. His control was just perfect. At the other end you had Miller, who was unpredictable, you just didn't know what was going to come next. It really was a perfect team.'

Two months after that Shield match in Adelaide, Miller produced further evidence of his skill and daring with the bat, a powerful second-innings double century against NSW in Sydney that featured some of the biggest hits ever seen at the Sydney ground. Victoria batted most of the first day for 356. On the second, NSW fell 27 short, and at stumps Victoria were 0–33. Miller came in at 2–118, after just

Cyril Washbrook is caught behind by Don Tallon off the bowling of Keith Miller, as England crash to a heavy defeat in the first Test of the 1948 Ashes series, at Trent Bridge.

over 100 minutes of cricket on the third day, and by stumps was unconquered on 206, having hit 15 fours and three sixes in 232 minutes of glorious sport.

His sixes were phenomenal. The first was a mighty swing off the leg-spinner Fred Johnston that finished on the roof of the old Members Stand. The second was off the part-time bowling of Arthur Morris, and went exactly straight, about three metres above the sightboard at the Paddington end. The third was a powerful heave off Ernie Toshack that ended in the depths of the Ladies Stand beyond square-leg.

At times Toshack had three men on the fence in the arc from long-on to long-off, so frightening were Miller's drives. Old-time members could not recall

seeing a cover field so far away from the wicket yet still preventing singles. One bullet struck the pickets on the full and rebounded almost back to the bowler Morris. The great fast bowler Ray Lindwall was reduced to operating with an outfield and a single slip; it is unlikely a cricket ball has ever been struck with such power on the Sydney Cricket Ground.

In 1947, Miller transferred his employment to Sydney, a move that would have excited no group more than the NSW fieldsmen, who no longer had to dive at those brutal drives. He would become the most popular Victorian to ever play in Sydney, a glamorous figure who would continue to strike sixes that revived memories of the longest hits everyone had ever seen.

By this time, Miller was on the threshold of a dazzling international career. He was an established Test batsman and Test bowler, as distinct from a batsman or bowler who could also bowl or bat a bit. But, to the disappointment of Bradman, among others, he appeared to lack the focused ambition

ALAN DAVIDSON: Keith Miller was a magnificent athlete. If you ever saw him kick a football, or hitting a golf ball ... he'd hit a golf ball miles further than anybody could imagine.

IAN WOOLDRIDGE: KR Miller is the most vivacious sportsman in any sport that I've ever seen anywhere, ever. He's my hero, the hero of all the kids in my generation. I remember when I was a kid and I had hair, I used to do what Miller did — flick my hair back every time. When I went out to bat, I'd pull on the batting gloves with my teeth as Miller did. The sight of Miller coming out to bat at Lord's, just walking out there, was fantastic.

He could do one of two things — he could get nought or he could get a big score at high speed, and it didn't worry him. I got to know Keith very well later because we were going on cricket tours together. I'd talk to him about this and he said, 'Look, those Test matches, I don't know why they take them all so seriously.' His reason for this was that he'd been a night fighter pilot over Europe during the War. Your life expectancy there was about three weeks, and he crashed once but he got away with it. I don't think he worried about anything ever again in his life.

necessary to climb to the very top of every facet of the game. He seemed happy to be no more than an involved and key member of every team he was a part of. Perhaps his Australian teammate Sid Barnes summed up Keith Miller the cricketer as precisely as any critic has when he wrote: 'If Keith had had the same outlook as Bradman or Ponsford he would have made colossal scores. He could, if he desired, have become the statisticians' greatest customer.'

EVEN SO, MILLER DID enough throughout his career to confirm that he was, and still is, the greatest all-rounder Australia has ever produced, superior to any of George Giffen, MA Noble, Warwick Armstrong, Jack Gregory, Alan Davidson, Richie Benaud and Adam Gilchrist. As we have seen, he first emerged as a brilliant batsman who surprised people by bowling as well as he did. By the end of his career he was a superb bowler whose batting, while still brilliant on occasions, was unreliable.

His Test statistics reflect this. In his first full series, against England in 1946–47, he averaged over 70, but although he played a number of famous innings in the years that followed, by the time he retired that average had fallen to 36.97, which hardly reflects his enormous talent. In contrast, his bowling returns improved to the point that, on his last tour of England in 1956, he bowled more balls and had a better strike rate and a better average than on either of his two previous tours there, in 1948 and 1953. In the seasons immediately after the War, his great days with the ball at Test level occurred spasmodically. His strike rate of 58.62 on his third and last Ashes

tour was superior to his strike rate in any of his first three Test series, between 1946 and 1949.

As one of the Invincibles in England in 1948, Miller found himself restricted somewhat by a back injury, but his batting was important, especially at Leeds where he launched an assault on Jim Laker that set back the English off-spinner's career for years. Later

Never one to knock back an interesting invitation, Miller steps out of a London cab for a celebrity function in Chelsea during the 1956 Ashes tour.

KEITH STACKPOLE: I can remember reading a book, called *From the Grandstand*, which he wrote in the late 1950s. In it he said that what cricket really needed in addition to Test cricket, the five-day game, was a shorter version. Of course, now we have limited-overs cricket, but back in the late '50s Keith Miller was one of the few who could see that cricket needed something else to keep it moving along. He could see one-day cricket was essential to make cricket really viable all around the world. A great visionary.

in the same innings he guided the teenage Neil Harvey to a century in the Victorian teenager's first Ashes Test. When Miller did take to the bowling crease, he formed a superb partnership with Lindwall, though there were suggestions that at least once or twice they bowled too many bouncers, especially at England's star batsmen, Hutton and Compton. There was also an occasion at Lord's, when Bradman threw

Getty Images

Miller, the swashbuckling batsman, during Australia's opening match of the '56 tour, against the Duke of Norfolk's XI at Arundel.

the ball to Miller to bowl and Miller lobbed it straight back to him, claiming later that he had told his captain in the dressing room that his back was too sore for him to bowl.

Some thought this incident might have been a key factor in the decision of the selectors, of whom Bradman was one, to leave him out of the 1949–50 tour of South Africa. Others blamed it on Miller bowling a bouncer at Bradman in a testimonial game in Sydney. Throughout his career there was an edge to his relationship with The Don. Most likely, the selectors were simply responding to the fact that the great all-rounder seemed to have fallen out of love with the game. Since the War, he had played in the Victory Tests, then played three Test series at home and gone on the '48 Ashes tour. He had confided to more than one teammate that he was fed up with cricket. If this was so, the sacking revitalised him. Miller later went to South Africa as a replacement after Bill Johnston was injured in a car accident, and played in all five Tests. Back home, he topped the Australian batting averages in the 1950–51 Ashes series — the highlight being an unbeaten century in Sydney — and took 17 wickets as well. Against the West Indies a season later, he managed another century, again at the SCG, and also took five wickets in an innings twice, but was criticised again for bowling bouncers at the Windies batsmen, most notably at Everton Weekes.

In his next three Test series, at home against South Africa and then in Ashes encounters at home and away, Miller scored only one century — 109 at Lord's in 1953 (in eight other innings in that series he scored just 114 runs) — and never managed to take five wickets in an innings. But then came a runscoring blitz in the West Indies that featured three centuries, including his highest Test score of 147 in the first Test, at Kingston, followed by an impressive beginning to the 1956 Ashes tour. A magnificent 281 against Leicestershire came a month before a stirring bowling performance at Lord's, when — leading a much-weakened Aussie attack — he completed the only 10-wickets-in-a-match performance of his Test career (5–72 and 5–80) and won Australia their only Test victory of the series.

The remainder of that series was dominated by Laker, who on dusty, ill-prepared pitches spun Australia to heavy defeats in the third and fourth Tests, and by constant media conjecture about whether Miller would replace Ian Johnson as

Australian captain. In the end, Johnson — a mediocre bowler at the end of his career — stayed in 'command', but the circumstances behind his original appointment and continued presence in the role between 1954 and 1956 remains one of cricket's strangest controversies. Richie Benaud, in his autobiography, reckoned the Board of Control couldn't come to grips with Miller's 'personality and extrovert nature, and his popularity with the public'. There have been claims that Bradman, whose influence was considerable, was worried that Miller might not be a good enough cricket diplomat for the job. Did Hassett share that view? Others whispered that in some circles, especially at the South Melbourne club where Miller had played with Hassett and Johnson, there remained a disappointment that he had not stayed in Victoria. In Sydney, Miller had questioned where all the money generated by big-time cricket was going, which many Board members didn't like at all. Perhaps it was a combination of some or all of these things …

While the reason for his non-selection as captain remains unclear, what is indisputable is that just about every cricketer who played under Miller contends he was one of the finest captains of their experience. Chief among his supporters is Benaud, who thought him the best captain he ever played under.

Stories of Miller's cavalier attitude to the game are legion, a spirit, it is said, that came from his luck (as he saw it) in surviving the War. Many of his comrades, of course, did not. On a number of occasions he publicly made clear that he deplored Bradman's win-at-all-costs approach to Test cricket. Against Essex in 1948, when Australia scored 721 runs in a day, Miller reputedly had such little taste for the carnage that he deliberately got out first ball. 'He'll learn,' said Bradman, who was batting at the other end, but he never did. Denis Compton claimed that during a Test at Lord's Miller arrived for a day's play still wearing his dinner suit. Elsewhere, when captain of NSW, he reduced the science of field settings to a new level by telling his charges, flatly, to 'scatter', or words to that effect. In a game against Cambridge University early on the 1953 Ashes tour, Hassett promoted Miller to open the batting, ostensibly to give him every chance to score heavily, as he was in line to achieve the rare feat of compiling 1000 first-class

runs in May. Miller responded by getting himself out early, because he had a tip for the races at nearby Newmarket. Unfortunately, the horse lost, and Miller stayed on at the track until late in the day; when he returned to the cricket he discovered that, rather than batting all day, Australia were just going out to field.

A couple of years later, in a Sheffield Shield match in Sydney, Miller — the NSW captain — stayed out all night to celebrate the birth of his son, forgot to pick up his teammate Peter Philpott, doubled back to get him, arrived at the ground as the players were due to go out on the field, and then took 7–12 as South Australia were bowled out for 27. 'Few batsmen could have withstood him today,' commented the former Test batsman Johnny Taylor. 'What a debt post-war cricket owes him.'

Soon after, in Melbourne, Miller chose to keep his team out on the field despite steady rain falling. His opposing captain, Johnson, could hardly have denied a request from NSW to come in, but Miller did not want to disappoint the 10,625 people who had come to the ground. Tom Goodman, in the 1957 *Wisden*, called Miller's decision: 'One of the most remarkable gestures to a sporting crowd made in Australia.' Eventually, the match was abandoned after the last two days were lost completely.

Miller led his sides as he batted and bowled and took catches in the slips — with a bold impulsive flair that reflected his personality. Once, after losing the toss on a sweltering day in Brisbane, he brought on Benaud's leg-breaks in the first hour and saw him take 5–17 before lunch. Ian Chappell remembers him at the Adelaide Oval, running back to try to catch a skier, but then deliberately dropping it because he had heard the umpire's no-ball call. The batsman who chanced a second run when the ball spilled free was run out and embarrassed when Miller quickly had the ball back to the bowler's end. He was never a reckless captain, rather a sensible man who would trust his instincts rather than procrastinate, was prepared to gamble if the odds or situation demanded it, and would never

DAVID FRITH: Keith Miller in the 1950s was the pride of Sydney. When NSW won nine Sheffield Shields on the trot he was the hero, but none of us kids dared to emulate him because he was too 'big'. He was a god.

ARTHUR MORRIS: He would have been a marvellous one-day cricketer because you'd get two cricketers for the price of one. He was tall and able to drive brilliantly, so in the one-day stuff, with the ball pitched up all the time, he would have been a magnificent hitter of the ball. And as a bowler? Well, he was one of the greatest bowlers I've ever seen.

let a game become mundane, for his team's sake as much as the crowd's. When he retired, following the 1956 Ashes tour, his captaincy ideas were evident in the approach taken by future NSW and Australian captains Ian Craig and Richie Benaud.

The cricket writer Philip Derriman has commented that if Miller had been born in a later era he would have made a fortune. 'Miller might have become a millionaire within a few years,' he wrote, 'for his good looks, his personal style, his brilliance as a player — these would have made him

irresistible to the advertising industry.' He noted that Miller did appear as the Brylcreem man in advertisements in magazines and on advertising hoardings throughout Australia in the late 1950s, and 'for a time his handsome features seemed to be on the side of every second London bus and on the walls of every London Underground station'. For this big promotion, Miller was paid the grand total of £600.

Imagine him if he was a superstar today, promoting sunglasses or cars or any of the multitude of goods and merchandise that delight in attaching themselves to the modern game. Imagine him in one-day cricket, as dynamic batsman, bowler, fieldsman, captain. 'I think that Keith Miller's impact was far greater than anybody appreciates today,' is how Mark Nicholas sees it. 'The modern comparison would be Ian Botham, in terms of the way in which they play the game and the way in which they approach life. But they were different. Botham would be a pop star, Miller a movie star.'

Miller, former England keeper Godfrey Evans and Sir Donald Bradman share memories at a Lord's Taverners function in London in 1974.

Getty Images

WG GRACE
Legend No. 14
Colossus of England

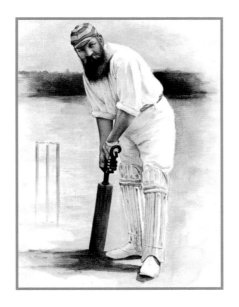

IN JULY 1923, THE Grace Gates were erected at the members' entrance at Lord's, with this inscription:

TO THE
MEMORY OF

WILLIAM GILBERT GRACE

THE GREAT CRICKETER
1848–1915

THESE GATES WERE
ERECTED BY THE MCC
AND OTHER FRIENDS
AND ADMIRERS

Simply: 'The Great Cricketer'. The idea had come, it is said, from The Hon. FS Jackson, the outstanding Yorkshire and England player, later President of the MCC, Governor of Bengal and Chairman of the Conservative Party. In his view, and all others quickly concurred, there was nothing more that was needed to be said.

Of all the men considered for *ESPN's Legends of Cricket*, there is no doubt that Dr WG Grace is the hardest to rank. In the 1860s, when he began his first-class career, cricket was hardly a sport for the masses, and prepared batting wickets were very much a thing of the future, and the distant future at that. Such uneven surfaces should have brought a champion batsman back to the field, but Grace's

The young WG Grace: the best batsman in the land, outstanding cover fieldsman and an accomplished track athlete.

record in first-class cricket in England is so far above any of his contemporaries that there can be no doubt he was, as Bradman would be in the 1930s, the cricketing king of his day.

WG's résumé is not flawless, however. Although his Test record is excellent, it is hardly beyond compare, even with the other cricket giants of the late 19th century. But he did not play his first Test match until he was 32. In Australia, after two tours, nearly 20 years apart, he was recognised as a great batsman but reviled in parts as a pretentious, arrogant bore. Still, the fans, rich and poor, flocked to see him. Back home, he was the most famous sportsman of his day; his grand grizzled beard as synonymous with cricket as were Prime Minister William Gladstone's elaborate whiskers with politics. He *made* the English game, luring athletes to the sport, spectators to the grounds, fans to the culture. Had he played today, he would have made millions; his runs, his beard and his cunning a spectacular English counter to Shane Warne's wickets and bleached blond hair.

WG Grace played first-class cricket for 43 years and was clearly the dominant player and personality in the game for more than 30 of them. As an illustration of his class and longevity, consider that in 1871, he scored 10 centuries and 2739 first-class runs at 78.25. No one else scored more than one century or averaged more than 37.66. He turned 23 during that season. Thirty-one seasons later, when Grace scored 1187 first-class runs at an average of 37.09, Victor Trumper averaged 48.49. This was Trumper's finest season in England, the year he made his reputation as the greatest batsman of his era. He was 24, three decades younger than WG.

In 1865, when Grace made his first-class debut, the game was a rural pastime enjoyed by the upper classes. But as industrialisation turned country towns into urban centres, and commercial railways offered unprecedented mobility, cricket's stature as a national sport gradually took hold. By 1908, the season of his farewell, cricket had become, with football, the sporting thread that in many ways bound the country together — a form of a mass entertainment, a source of national pride and an endeavour all young boys yearned to excel at. Despite his age and his girth, the mere appearance of WG at games in the early 20th century would touch off bouts of frenzied excitement usually reserved, in these reserved times, for the Royal Family.

Throughout his career, he scored runs on all wickets, fast and slow, spinning and dangerous, against all-comers, when young and old. To make runs in the 21st century he would, no doubt, have had to adapt his technique, perhaps work on his fitness, forget his medical practice. The video replays would catch out his custom of pushing the cricket laws to the limit. Clashes with authority would be inevitable, as would the odd uncomplimentary newspaper headline. But he would have more than coped, for his career was one where he was always adapting as the game evolved into something like what we see today.

THE SHEER SCALE OF WG Grace's runscoring efforts in cricket's early years is quite phenomenal. Born on 18 July 1848, he scored his first century — 224 not out for England against Surrey — when aged 18 years and 12 days. During that match, quite quaintly, his captain allowed him to dash off to Crystal Palace to win a quarter-mile hurdles championship. Much later, he would become the finest lawn bowler in all England. Back to 1866, he finished second in the first-class averages, making 581 runs at 52.81. Between 1868 and 1880 (the year of his Test debut), he topped the first-class averages 10 times, including seven years straight to 1874. Between 1868 and 1876 he scored 54 first-class hundreds in England. No one else scored even 10. In the decade 1871 to 1880, Grace averaged more than 49 in first-class cricket when no one else could do better than 26, or total even a third of Grace's runs. He also took a little matter of 1174 wickets in those 10 years, second highest across the country behind Alfred Shaw.

In 1873, WG became the first man to achieve the 'double' in an English first-class season — 1000 runs and 100 wickets — by scoring 2139 runs and taking 106 wickets. He promptly did it again the following year, and every year until 1878, then twice more in the 1880s. No other player managed the feat until 1882; no one else scored 2000 runs and took 100 wickets in a season until 1899.

And WG was no fair-weather cricketer. In the same year, 1870, that the wicket at Lord's claimed the life of the unfortunate George Summers, Grace scored 66 for the Gentlemen against the Players at the ground, against, among others, two intimidating pace bowlers from Yorkshire, George Freeman and Tom Emmett. Years later, Freeman, who Grace thought was the best fast bowler he ever faced, had this to say of Grace's courage that day: 'A more wonderful innings was never played. Tom Emmett and I have often said it was a marvel the Doctor was not either maimed or unnerved for the rest of his days, or killed outright. I often think of his pluck on that day when I watch a modern batsman scared if a medium ball hits him on the hand.'

Grace's influence on the art of batting was considerable, as he stuck to principles of batsmanship that we now take for granted but at the time had hardly been thought of. 'I have always believed in footwork,' he explained to disciples. He was neither a stylist, a magician nor a pure hitter; he was a technician, his game built around a well-constructed, well-rehearsed technique, an ability to see the ball early and always choose the correct shot. His was a wicket that couldn't be bought. Like all the truly great ones, he was always balanced when he batted, whatever was bowled at him. No batsman at the time or since played with the bat closer to the pad, and when he went back, which he mostly did, he went right back, and across, his head over the line. In his autobiography, Grace suggested this was something that evolved from his early days, explaining that his uncle 'took special pains with me, and helped me a great deal, by insisting on my playing with an upright bat, even as a child'. His mother, who won great renown as a cricket expert (to the extent that she earned an obituary in *Wisden*), also played a key role, badgering him to practise hard, often and early, play straight and sensibly, and score prolifically. WG had only just turned 15 when he made 32 against an All-England XI; two years later he took 13 wickets for the Gentlemen against the Players of the South, and opened the batting for the Gentlemen at Lord's.

Grace stood tall at the crease, strong, bronzed and athletic in his youth, more burly as he approached middle age, and, though he had a high backlift, he could get the bat down on shooters quicker than anyone. The willow always looked tiny in his massive hands. He knew where the gaps in the field were (which was handy when playing against opposing teams of 15, 18 or even 22) and, if you believe the legend, the quicker the bowling, the more he liked it.

IAN BOTHAM: He was the father figure of cricket, the first superstar of the game ...

Grace goes right back and across, head over the ball, technique far superior to most of his contemporaries.

He certainly preferred the solid drive to a defensive push or a mere deflection. 'Games aren't won by leaving the ball alone,' he once said. 'I hate defensive strokes, you can only get three off 'em.' He hit powerfully, but was nimble and dexterous, even when he bulked up in his later years. His timing was such that one opponent glumly suggested that he used 'a bat that seemed all middle'. The Australians of 1884 went as far as to protest at the width of his bat, to which Grace replied with a chuckle, 'Let 'em shave off as much as they want. All I want is the middle!'

The Hon. RH Lyttleton, writing in *The Badminton Book of Cricket* in 1900, was one who thought Grace's timing was his secret. 'He got the full weight of bat, arms, shoulders and body onto the ball at the very

ROBIN MARLAR: The significance of Grace is that he made cricket into a popular game. He was the No. 1, and remains to most of us, I think, the greatest hero in the story of cricket.

right second,' Lyttleton commented, 'and if a player does this, though his muscular development may be very small, still it is surprising how hard the ball will be hit. Grace, however, is a man of enormous stature, muscle and weight; and when these gifts are added to perfect timing the result is complete, not to say brutal, effectiveness.'

One imagines, on reading descriptions of the way he played, that WG would have made an ideal one-day cricketer, being able to hit the ball hard and into gaps, to bowl tightly and field well. 'As a bowler,' the esteemed cricket historian HS Altham wrote, 'WG belonged to the "high, home and easy" school of a much earlier day; with a round-arm action he varied skilfully the arc of his slows, worked them in from leg, and was a magnificent catcher of the hardest drives hit back at him.' Grace was a fine cover field in his youth, moved mainly to point later on, and a sure catch. He is reputed to have once thrown a cricket ball 122 yards, and definitely threw it 116, 117 and 118 yards in an exhibition at the Oval in 1868 that also involved the Australian Aboriginal touring side. Some whispered that his best fielding was done off his own bowling.

But it was the runs that made the legend. The great all-round sportsman CB Fry, an England cricket captain, football international and once holder of the world long jump record, recognised Grace's enormous influence on the game. 'He revolutionised batting,' Fry wrote. 'He turned it from an accomplishment into a science. He turned the old one-stringed instrument into a many-chorded lyre. Where a great man has led, many can go afterwards, but the honour is his who found and cut the path. The theory of modern batting is, in all essentials, the result of WG's thinking and working on the game.'

Grace had an insatiable appetite for runs, and strength and stamina to go with it. In August 1871, he became the first man to score 1000 first-class runs in one month. In one week in August in 1876 he hit 344 for the MCC against Kent at Canterbury, travelled by train the next day back home to his county Gloucestershire, where he made 177 not out against Nottinghamshire and 318 not out against Yorkshire. All up, 839 runs at 419.5. The following month he made 400 not out (folklore says he actually only got 399, but the scorer kindly gave him an extra run) against XXII of Grimsby, with all 22 fielding, on what was described as a 'slow and grassy' outfield.

In the 1890s a perception grew that the 'Old Man' was slowing down, that he wasn't what he'd once been, but such theories seemed deluded when he went on an orgy of runscoring in 1895. Grace began the season on 9 May with 13 and 103 against Sussex at Lord's, then 18 and 25, then what was recognised as his 100th first-class hundred against Somerset in Bristol, then 52, then 257 and 73 not out against Kent (being on the field for every ball of the match), then 18 and, finally, needing 153 runs on 30 May to be the first man to ever make 1000 runs in May, he scored 169 before a crowd of 7000 at Lord's. In cricket history, only three men have scored 1000 first-class runs in May, and only eight have scored 1000 runs in an English first-class season before 1 June. Five more hundreds helped him to an aggregate of 2346 for the season, the highest by any batsman that year, and the third best in his career. When he reached his 100th hundred, he had been obliged to stop, make a speech to the big crowd and then toast the occasion with champagne. And then he went on to 288.

CHRISTOPHER MARTIN-JENKINS: He was supposed, on one occasion when he was bowling, to have drawn the batsman's attention to a flock of birds passing in front of a low sun. The batsman looked up and was dazzled and WG quickly slipped in the next ball and bowled him. That was the sort of thing he was capable of.

In his 40s, despite the physical slowdowns brought on by middle age, Grace was able to adjust by reworking his approach. The great ones could adapt to the conditions and strategies of any era. Ever gradually, he could not thrust out his front foot to the offside as he had in his younger days, so he decided to get back on the back foot even more than he previously had. His hand-eye co-ordination was still sharp, the balance and timing still there and after hours of practice he had the confidence to play the pull shot whenever he wanted. The great left-armer, Wilfred Rhodes, who made his Test

Grace at the Crystal Palace ground in London in the early 1900s, in the company of his good friend, the former Australian captain Billy Murdoch (far right).

debut in Grace's last Test, was one who commented on Grace's ability to hit the ball hard to leg. Perhaps more than any other season, 1895 proved just how good WG Grace was.

Nowhere in his career did Grace dominate the sport more than in the time-honoured Gentlemen v Players matches. In the years before Test cricket, this was the English game's premier fixture. In the 35 years before his first appearance in these matches, the amateur Gentlemen had won just seven times; of their next 50 games they won 31 and lost seven to their professional rivals. Over 41 years Grace made 15 hundreds for the Gentlemen, and took 271 wickets. Of all his hundreds in these matches, perhaps his first was his finest — 134 out of 201 in 1868, in an innings in which none of his comrades was able to reach double figures.

THOUGH AN 'AMATEUR', THERE is no doubt WG made a huge amount of money out of the game. Once established as the sport's No. 1 player, he became proficient at driving a hard bargain, and thought nothing of pushing cricket officials to the brink. It appears the men of the MCC ignored Grace's money-making, on the basis that they needed him more than he needed them. A 21st birthday gift had been membership of the MCC, granted because of the acclaim for his cricket, and despite his lack of a public school education, and given to him a full decade before he finally qualified as a doctor. This was an era when amateur and professional sportsmen often sat uneasily besides each other, and there was always potential, as happened in rugby football, that the two would split. Had this occurred in cricket, and Grace had thrown his lot with the pros, the future for the MCC as the game's controlling body may well have been doomed. So, as ridiculous as it now looks, he was often very well paid to represent the Gentlemen against the Players, and he received a sizeable cheque, and perhaps tickets and accommodation for his wife and children, and a locum for his medical practice, before agreeing to

go on tour. During his fantastic season of 1895, he received nearly £10,000 after three testimonials were set up for him. When he started the London County team, he was paid £600 a year, plus expenses.

In the 1897 *Wisden*, editor Sydney Pardon wrote, 'Mr WG Grace's position has for years, as everyone knows, been an anomalous one, but "nice customs curtsey to great kings" and the work he has done in popularising cricket outweighs a hundred-fold every other consideration.'

It must be said that WG was not the only amateur making a pound out of the game, and that in reality he was much more pragmatic than greedy. If a sign went up outside the ground informing patrons that admission was sixpence if Grace played, threepence if he didn't, you could hardly blame him for seeking his share. And it is said that he rarely refused a request to appear at a fellow cricketer's testimonial match, or dismissed a patient because he or she might not be able to pay.

In 1872, Grace took a team to North America, and a year later made the first of his two tours to Australia. Both trips down under were successes financially and did much to help the game in the colony, but Grace did have trouble with the locals. He thought the umpiring appalling, did not care (especially on the first tour) for some of the primitive long-distance travelling into the bush, and while he enjoyed fine dining with Sydney and Melbourne's establishment, thought little of the crude behaviour, incessant insults and widespread betting of barrackers — in the outer *and* in the members' enclosures. On both tours, Australians, initially, were thrilled that the game's No. 1 man was in their midst. 'Mr Grace represents and typifies cricket to us just as the Archbishop of Canterbury may be said to represent theology,' wrote one Sydney scribe at the start of the 1891–92 tour. But the relationship soured.

One correspondent reckoned Grace 'had differences' with the umpires during every game on that second tour. In one game in western Sydney, Grace refused to play until he was allowed to bat 12 against a team of 20. He publicly criticised the dress sense of one Sydney umpire, refused to use his front-line bowlers in a game in Tasmania in protest at the poor pitch, and even stopped the Australian captain Jack Blackham using his 'lucky' penny at the toss to start the third Test, instead insisting on tossing it himself. Worst of all, he got himself

DAVID FRITH: When you look back at all the stories of WG Grace, of how he bullied umpires, bullied opponents, used to bluff batsmen out, used to talk to them, I think, well, more fool them for falling for it.

JACK BANNISTER: As a man he was a giant. He was a very hard man to play, stories abound of his sharp practice and everything else, but that's the way of the game. My first coach was the former England wicketkeeper, EJ 'Tiger' Smith, who started playing at the very end of WG's career. Tiger always said to me, 'Never mind that they say he averaged 31 or 32. He is No. 1.'

For me, too, he's No. 1, WG, because I don't think there's been a man other than Bradman who has been so far ahead of all his contemporaries — under conditions that were by far the most difficult to bat on in this country. When he started, there weren't any six hits, the overs were four-ball overs so the bowlers stayed fresher, the pitches were absolutely unspeakable at times, yet despite that he did everything he did.

involved in a public argument in Sydney that led to the umpire refusing to continue. Press reports claimed Grace had told the umpire he was blind; the Englishmen reckoned Grace had said no more than, 'You really must play more attention to the game.'

To call Grace a cheat is probably too strong (though some did, including one or two Australian umpires), but there is ample evidence that he played the game very hard, sometimes arguing that because the crowd had come to see him bat it was impertinent of his opponents to appeal and wrong for umpires not to give him the benefit of the doubt. This was undoubtedly cheeky, but it was also true. The fast bowler CJ Kortright once thought he had Grace lbw, then caught behind. Finally, with the third ball, he knocked over the champion's middle and leg-stumps. 'Surely you're not going, Doctor?' Kortright famously sneered. 'There's still one stump standing!'

Once an umpire is reputed to have had the last laugh, after Grace was bowled by a ball that just flicked the bails on the way through to the keeper. 'Windy today, isn't it umpire?' said Grace, standing his ground.

'Very windy indeed,' replied the official. 'And mind it doesn't blow your cap off on the way back to the pavilion.'

Similarly, David Frith tells a story related to him by Wilfred Rhodes. In a match in 1898, Rhodes had Grace lbw, but not only did the umpire have to raise his finger to signify the out, he also had to shout down the pitch, 'You're out, you're out, you have to go.' Only then did WG set off reluctantly for the pavilion.

To balance Grace's ledger, many friends and admirers spoke fondly of him as a decent, charitable man. Arthur Porritt, who patiently helped Grace with his life story, wrote that: 'About Dr WG Grace

there was something indefinable — like the simple faith of a child — which arrested and fascinated me … A wonderful kindliness ran through his nature, mingling strangely with the arbitrary temper of a man who had been accustomed to being dominant over other men.'

Most believed he never deliberately went beyond the rules, but was happy to bend them as far as they would go. At The Oval in 1882, in the Test that

The most famous beard in cricket; arguably the most famous beard in all of sport.

ALAN DAVIDSON: The first person who gave cricket an identity in society was WG Grace. He was recognised everywhere, he was adored everywhere. I think every cricketer should salute what he did all those years ago.

inspired the birth of The Ashes, Grace ran out the youngster, Sammy Jones, by sneaking up to the stumps while Jones was down the pitch repairing a divot. Billy Murdoch, the Australian captain batting at the other end (who would later move to England and become one of Grace's most admired friends), was appalled and complained there and then. The London sporting paper, *Bell's Life*, described the run out as 'legal and fair' but suggested that it 'may not have been a particularly courteous or generous action'. The Australians, and the 'Demon' Spofforth in particular, were still seething when they came out to knock England over for just 77, to win the Test by seven runs.

Grace's Test record is 22 matches, 1098 runs at 32.29 with two centuries. He scored a hundred on debut, at The Oval in 1880, England's first Test at home, a game in which EM and GF Grace also made their debuts (the first instance of three brothers playing in the same Test), and he also shared in the first century partnership in Tests (120 for the second wicket with AP Lucas). His innings

of 152 was a Test record for just two days, with Murdoch scoring 153 not out in Australia's second innings, but Grace regained the record when he made 170 at The Oval in 1886, a total that remained the highest by an Englishman in Tests for eight years.

As captain, he led England in 13 Tests, all against Australia, for eight wins and just two losses (despite winning only four tosses). At 50 years and 320 days, he remains the oldest man to captain his country in a Test, in his farewell match — the first Test, at Trent Bridge, in 1899.

Grace retired ostensibly because he recognised that his body was slowing down, even if his cricket brain and technique were still firing. Heckled by a section of the crowd after failing to bend enough to reach hard-hit shots that slipped through for four during his final Test, he commented ruefully, 'The ground is getting a bit too far away.' Only now did the pressures of *having* to succeed for his public seem to be nagging at him. Grace's fabled association with Gloucestershire ended sourly that same year — in his resignation letter he wrote: 'I have the greatest affection for the county of my birth, but for the committee as a whole, the greatest contempt.' — and his final seasons of first-class cricket were spent with London County, for whom he made 166 on the day after his 56th birthday. Two years later, precisely on his 58th birthday, he made 74 for the Gentlemen against the Players, his final major knock at the first-class level, though he continued to play club cricket for another decade. His final recorded game at any level occurred a week after his 66th birthday, and he scored 69 not out. Unbeaten to the end!

Grace died on 23 October 1915, four months after Victor Trumper, of a heart attack after an air raid during the Great War. The chapel for his funeral service was packed with mourners from cricket and wider society, many of them in uniform; it was somewhat stunning the way the country, conditioned as it was at this time to the pain and suffering of real battle, should so mourn the passing of a truly great cricketer. To Old England, he meant that much.

Getty Images

The Grace Gates at Lord's, opened in 1923, pictured here in 1930 during the Ashes Test in which Don Bradman scored a near-flawless 254.

GRAEME POLLOCK
Legend No. 15
South Africa's No. 1

ACCORDING TO THAT OLDEST of benchmarks, the batting average, if you take Sir Donald Bradman out, Graeme Pollock was the greatest batsman of all time. Of all cricketers to bat 20 times in Tests, Bradman leads the field by the proverbial mile, at 99.94 runs per dismissal. Next best, at 60.97, from 2256 runs in 41 innings, is Pollock.

Bill Lawry called Pollock the 'finest dispatcher of a loose ball I have ever seen'. 'I don't know if there is a Graeme Pollock Fan Club in existence,' Richie Benaud wrote in 1969, 'but I think I'd probably qualify for President.' Denis Compton thought him a 'giant in every respect', adding that he had 'the rare capacity to make even the finest of his contemporaries look modest by comparison.' Such tributes seem to come from everyone who ever saw Pollock bat.

However, attempts to precisely measure Pollock's greatness have to be tempered to a small degree by the fact that his international career was prematurely terminated by the sporting bans placed on South Africa because of the apartheid policies of the South African government. At the age of 26, he played the last of his 23 Tests. His 19th Test ended the day after his 23rd birthday. From then on, he played first-class cricket until he was almost 43, still good enough to plunder headline-generating centuries, but there is no guessing how imposing his Test record might have been had he been able to play the plethora of internationals available to modern-day stars.

BORN IN DURBAN ON 27 February 1944, family folklore has it that he was walking before his maiden Christmas. From an early age, Graeme, like his elder brother Peter, was recognised as a fine talent, and scored his first hundred at the age of nine, playing in the under-11s. At the same age he took all 10 wickets in one innings. At age 13 he was in the first XI at Grey High School in Port Elizabeth, and at 16 was a top-order batsman with Eastern Province in the Currie Cup, South Africa's equivalent of England's county championship and Australia's Sheffield Shield.

'Our school firsts side played in a men's first-grade league,' Pollock remembers, 'so I was playing in men's cricket from the time I was 13 years old. I was a fan of Australian cricket — I've always backed them from day one — and the guy I really followed was Neil Harvey, a left-hander who got so many runs against us. It was like a challenge — that's what I would like to do for South Africa. He was my role model, without a doubt.'

Pollock's Currie Cup career started with a half-century against Border in East London, but the highlight of his maiden first-class season was his first century, 102 against Transvaal B in Johannesburg. At 16 years 335 days, he was then the youngest man to make a Currie Cup century (a record since beaten by Daryll Cullinan), and by season's end was recognised across South Africa as the most promising young batsman in the game.

When he made a century in 88 minutes for the South Africans against a Combined XI in Perth in 1963, on his first tour with the South African Test team, Sir Donald Bradman told him, 'If you ever score a century like that again, I hope I'm there to see it.' A remarkable aspect of Pollock's career was

his propensity for memorable knocks, which inspired a wide range of tributes that always seemed to include the sentiment that his was an innings unlike anything seen before. In their own way, each of his greatest efforts demonstrated why he became regarded as one of the legends of the game. Here are five of them …

209 for an Eastern Province Invitation XI v the International Cavaliers, 1963

The Cavaliers bowling attack included Australian Test players Richie Benaud, Graham McKenzie, Des Hoare and Johnny Martin, and when Pollock came to the crease in the second innings they were well on top. The Eastern Province XI were 3–41 in the second innings, trying to make up a first-innings deficit of 138, but as Pollock later put it, 'It was one of those days when all bowlers came alike to me.' He had his century by lunch, and went on to make a double hundred that included three sixes and 34 fours, in 201 minutes. At one stage, the West Australian paceman Hoare went for six fours in six balls. Hoare was no slouch; he had been good enough to play in a Test match against Frank Worrell's West Indians at the Adelaide Oval just two years before.

'I have not seen a batsman of his age play an innings of such sustained aggression,' remarked the famous journalist Ron Roberts, who was manager of the Cavaliers. Richie Benaud described trying to marshal the fielding side as being 'a slightly unnerving experience', and called Pollock's display 'exhilarating'. Pollock, 19 days past his 19th birthday, became the youngest South African to score a first-class double century.

175 for South Africa, fourth Test v Australia, Adelaide, 1963–64

Pollock made his Test debut in the opening Test of this series, and after failing to get past 25 in the first two Tests scored his maiden Test century in the third. At 19 years 318 days he became the youngest South African to score a Test century. But it was in the fourth Test that he made his reputation, joining Eddie Barlow at the wicket when South Africa were 2–70 in reply to 345, and with Barlow adding a South African record 341 for the third wicket. Barlow was out for 201, Pollock for 175, and South Africa went on to 595, then their highest ever innings total against Australia.

> **DICKIE BIRD:** Graeme Pollock was one of the greatest left-hand batsmen I've ever had the pleasure to watch. When he got in he just took full control. He could turn a game. Awesome when he got going, awesome.

IAN CHAPPELL: In 1970, when we played against Eastern Province, Ashley Mallett was really annoyed. He'd got five wickets in the first Test and then got dropped from the side. So every time he played in a tour match he really tried to impress the tour selectors. And this day he was bowling really well to Graeme Pollock, for five or six overs he'd kept him pretty quiet. Graeme hadn't really looked like getting out, but it wasn't a bad effort just to keep him quiet. Then, suddenly, Graeme hit the first five balls of his next over for four and then hit a single to long-off.

Mallett hadn't suddenly started bowling badly. Graeme had just decided: Yeah, I've had a good look at him, now I'm going to let him know who is in charge. Five fours! Magnificent batting!

The Australian keeper Wally Grout thought Pollock was 'superb', acknowledging his brilliant hitting through the offside. He wondered, though, about the batsman's legside play, and noted with interest the time Pollock spent in the nets having his elder brother (now the spearhead of South Africa's bowling attack), throwing ball after ball at his pads as he sought to bolster his technique. In the press box, veteran cricket writer RS Whitington wrote of how the Adelaide faithful reacted to Pollock's wonderful innings: 'The main subject for debate in the George Giffen Stand was whether Garry Sobers, then representing South Australia, or Graeme Pollock was the more talented and attractive left-hander.'

125 for South Africa, second Test v England, Nottingham, 1965

This was the innings that made Pollock's reputation in England. He had struggled in the early Tests of England's 1964–65 tour of South Africa before making 137 and 77 not out in the fifth Test, becoming the second batsman, after the West Indies' George Headley, to score three Test centuries before his 21st birthday. However, on the South Africans' tour of England that followed straight after, Pollock was often in imperious form, scoring 1147 runs at 57.35, including one knock of 203 not out against Kent that had the locals thinking back wistfully to the glory days of their local hero, Frank Woolley.

But the highlight of Pollock's tour, South Africa's whole tour in fact, was his innings at Trent Bridge. By the numbers, the effort is impressive enough: South Africa were 4–43 and 5–80 on the first morning before Pollock scored 125 and steered them to 269 all out. However, it was the way he batted, the manner in which he dominated while those around him struggled, that was most impressive. He scored 125 runs out of 160 in 140 minutes, on a pitch that Richie Benaud said was 'soft like Plasticine and reckoned by many experts to be too slow for strokeplay'.

'There was not a single blemish, from what I can remember, in that innings,' says Ian Wooldridge. 'It was just perfect. He was such a wonderful judge of length. You never saw Graeme go forward and then come back or go back and then have to come forward; he'd have the absolute length of the ball judged perfectly. And he was hitting this ball with ferocious power. In terms of pure cricket, I think that's technically the best innings I've ever seen.'

'The knock at Nottingham was Graeme's very best,' is the opinion of South Africa's wicketkeeper Denis Lindsay. 'Tom Cartwright was virtually making the ball talk, and he made us look like a

The young Graeme Pollock. Even by his 21st birthday he was recognised as just about the finest batsman South Africa had ever produced.

Eddie Barlow (left) and Pollock at the Adelaide Oval in 1963–64, when they added 341 — Barlow 201, Pollock 175 — for the third wicket in 283 minutes.

bunch of second-class students. Graeme came in and patted the ball all around the park, hardly missed a ball. It was a tremendous innings.'

'If ever one innings stamped its maker among the greats this was it,' wrote the esteemed writer EW Swanton.

The match was a triumph for the Pollock brothers. Not only did Graeme follow up with 59 in the second innings, Peter took 10 wickets (5–53 and 5–34) as South Africa won by 94 runs.

209 for South Africa, second Test v Australia, Cape Town, 1966–67

Pollock's batting played a key part in South Africa's triumphant series win. He scored 5 and 90, 209 and

> **DENIS LINDSAY:** Who was the better of Graeme Pollock and Barry Richards? They were two different players. Barry was the class player, the more majestic player. Graeme just tore attacks apart.

4, 2 and 67 not out, 22, 105 and 33 not out: 537 runs at 76.71. His 90 in the first Test was scored at a run a minute, but it was the double century, ironically made as part of a losing cause after Australia had scored 542, that was his most exciting innings.

Australia had lost the first Test heavily, the first time they'd lost a Test in South Africa, so in Cape Town they were delighted to not only make their huge total but then reduce the home team to 5–85. Handicapped by a bruised toe and a strained thigh muscle, but seemingly as unflustered as ever, Pollock batted against the tide just as he had at Trent Bridge. Only his captain Peter van der Merwe (50) and brother Peter (41) stayed with him for any length of time, while he batted in all for 350 minutes.

He also showed that the habit bowlers had got into in previous years, of bowling at his pads to avoid his offside power, had turned him into an excellent onside player. 'He is now as close to a complete all-round batsman as one is likely to find,' wrote Richie Benaud.

274 for South Africa, second Test v Australia, Durban, 1969–70

South Africa did not play another Test series until the Australians returned in early 1970, for four Tests. Pollock's first five scores in the series were 49, 50, 274, 52 and 87, before he failed twice in the last Test, as South Africa won the series 4–0.

The 274 in Durban came after Barry Richards had scored his maiden Test century, and people who were there talk about the batting of the young opener and the great left-hander after lunch as perhaps the greatest hour in South African cricket history. 'That hour after lunch on the first day was unbelievable,' remembers their teammate Lee Irvine. 'We talk about one-day cricket now and how people hit the ball. What happened that day was not hitting, it was strokeplay, and it was the most brilliant cricket I've ever seen in my life. Two greats of the game trying to outdo each other in some way.'

'Everything went for me that day,' Pollock recalls. In all, he batted for 417 minutes, faced 401 balls, and hit a five and 43 fours. That 274 was the highest score ever made by a South African in Test cricket until Daryll Cullinan made 275 not out against New Zealand in 1999 (a score matched by Gary Kirsten against England in 2000).

At lunch, Richards was 94, and Pollock was due to replace Ali Bacher, who'd been dismissed just before the break. 'This is Barry Richards' home ground, Old Kingsmead,' Ian Chappell remembers of that break in play, 'and the place is buzzing. And the only word that you can hear is "Richards … Richards … Richards …"'

'We came out after lunch and Graeme Pollock is in, and I think there were four balls remaining in Alan Connolly's over. And he whacked two or three of them for four — bang! bang! bang! — through the offside.

'At the end of the over he just leant back on the handle of his bat and looked around. I was standing next to Keith Stackpole in the slips, and I said, "Stacky, we're in trouble here."

'He said, "What do you mean?"

'I said, "This so and so, he's heard the buzz about Richards and he's come out here to prove that there's another bloke in the South African side who can bat a bit. He's going to have a look at Richards, see how many he makes and he's going to make double that score."

'I was wrong. Richards made 140, Pollock only made 274.'

Another Australian player, Paul Sheahan, recalled of the carnage: 'You could understand how a bloke like Sobers hit so hard, because his backlift was this enormous arc, but Pollock never seemed to lift his bat up and hardly followed through. At one stage "Garth" McKenzie was bowling with four in the covers and Pollock was still beating them. The only good thing about it was that you didn't have to run far, because the ball would career back off the fence.'

Two Tests later, and Pollock's Test career was over, though he could not have believed it at the time. After South Africa's scheduled tour of England in 1970 was cancelled, Pollock was permitted to join a Rest of the World team that took part in a five-match series that served as a substitute for the originally programmed Tests. He managed one century, in the final international, a performance he matched in Australia in 1971–72 when again a South Africa tour was cancelled and replaced with a tour by a Rest of the World combination.

FOR THE NEXT 15 years, Pollock's career was restricted to Currie Cup cricket in South Africa, plus occasional series against rebel

> **GRAEME POLLOCK:** I think that people get a bit over-technical. As long as you're balanced and your head is still and you watch the ball, then you've got a good chance.

teams from Sri Lanka, England, the West Indies and Australia, and also private touring teams such as the 'International Wanderers' side that Richie Benaud brought to the republic in early 1976. How lethal he might have been in international one-day cricket was indicated by his fastest century in first-class cricket, made from 52 balls for the International Cavaliers against a Barbados XI in Scarborough (England) in 1969.

He resisted the temptation to sign up for county cricket, a decision he explained in his 1968 autobiography. 'I live for the game. It is as much a part of me as breathing,' he wrote. 'Yet I do not want to play all the time, nor depend upon it for my

Getty Images

Pollock in England in 1965 was superb, most notably in the Test match at Trent Bridge where he played one of the finest innings ever seen at the ground.

livelihood. I fear that playing under the pressure of championship conditions for six days a week might have weakened even my great enthusiasm for the game.'

The cocktail of politics and sport that kept South Africa out of world cricket from 1970 to 1992 proved especially cruel to Pollock in 1977, when he and leg-spinner Denys Hobson — unlike their countrymen Mike Procter, Barry Richards, Eddie Barlow, Clive Rice and Garth le Roux — were barred from World Series Cricket. Understandably, Pollock had been one of the first players approached. The reason for his eventual absence was an intriguing interpretation of the ban on sporting contacts with South Africa, which allowed contact with South African players who were also county cricketers, on the principle that these were individuals plying their trade, but would not allow contact with those who weren't. So Pollock, having arrived in Australia hoping to play again against the world's best, had to fly home. A week before he arrived, he'd scored a century in both innings for Eastern Province against Rhodesia.

This peculiar reasoning had a sequel a decade later, six months after Pollock had retired from first-class cricket, when an invitation to play in an MCC v Rest of the World XI at Lord's had to be withdrawn for the same reason he was barred from WSC.

IAN CHAPPELL: They had a competition in South Africa called the Gillette Cup, one of the very early one-day competitions in the world. He was playing for Eastern Province against Border, who played in Section B of the Currie Cup. He came in in the 12th over and at the end of the 60 overs he was 222 not out. In a one-day game! If I hadn't seen it in *Wisden* I would never have believed it.

I remember talking to Graeme about it and I said, 'How the hell did you make 222 not out in a one-day game?'

He said, 'Oh mate, I got a bit lucky. The opposition captain cocked up his arithmetic.'

I said, 'What do you mean?'

He said, 'Well, he got to the end and he didn't have any frontline bowlers left, and I hit 74 off the last four overs.'

WHAT MADE POLLOCK so good? His coach back at Grey High School, George Cox, said his greatest asset was his 'instant and infallible judgment of length'. Consequently, he was rarely ruffled, always balanced, always with time to swing through the line. He had an unshakeable confidence in his own skill, and an unerring ability to hit the bad ball for four. Denis Lindsay remembers that Pollock 'hated getting out'. Mike Procter put it this flatly: 'Graeme just put his foot down the wicket and hit it.'

'He kept things very, very simple,' confirms Ian Chappell, 'didn't move his feet a hell of a lot but he was never unbalanced when he played. He got into that same position and was so well balanced that he could just play everything from there. I remember one day — this is long after we had all retired and we were chatting about batting — somebody said "this" is a good idea and "that" is a good idea and Graeme said, "In the end, you should remember this is a see-the-ball, hit-the-ball game."'

Pollock was immensely strong in the wrists and forearms, which allowed him to use a bat much heavier than the average. His weighed 3lbs, almost a pound heavier than the willow Bradman used. Some cynics thought he might have had a weakness against pace, but a century scored against the International Wanderers in 1976 when Dennis Lillee was near his fastest, set that myth straight. In the second innings of that same game, Lillee actually took 7–27, as if to prove he was fair dinkum. Pollock, despite not being far from his 40th birthday, also scored two hundreds against the West Indies rebels in the early 1980s, against two lively quicks in Franklyn Stephenson and Sylvester Clarke.

Pollock ended his career amid great fanfare in 1987 with Currie Cup records for most runs (12,409) and most catches (157). In all, he'd made an imposing 20,940 first-class runs, at 54.67 with 64 centuries, despite never playing county cricket. He'd thought seriously of giving it away after the second rebel West Indies tour, in 1983–84, but played on when word reached him of an Australian rebel tour.

'I started my career against the Australians in Australia in 1963–64 and I thought it would be nice to finish against an Australian team,' he explained at the time. Then, when asked how he was batting, he said, 'I'm not putting away the half-volley and the full toss like I used to straight away. Now I stick

JONTY RHODES: The highlights packages of Graeme Pollock's knocks are almost his whole innings. He hit a lot of boundaries, I don't remember him scampering too many singles. That's the kind of player that he was — he found the gap really, really well.

He once came and spoke to the South African side and said, 'It's vital that if a guy bowls you a bad ball it must go to the boundary.' And judging by what I saw of highlights packages on him — it didn't even have to be a bad ball — most of the time he pierced the gap and made sure the ball got to the boundary.

around for 10 to 15 minutes before I play those shots. Fifteen years ago I could do it. Now it's frustrating that bowlers, some of them mediocre, can get away with bad balls to me.'

Pollock's last five-day match was at St George's Park in Port Elizabeth, an appropriate venue for his farewell given that that was where his first-class career had begun in 1960–61. He said goodbye in style.

144 for South Africa, fourth 'Test' v Australians, Port Elizabeth, 1986–87

The stage was set after Kim Hughes declared the Australians' first innings at 9–455. It was a Sunday,

1 February 1987, and Pollock came out with the score at 2–64 to a rapturous reception from a crowd of around 10,000. First ball, he was nearly caught behind off Rodney Hogg, but after that he settled in to perform one last masterpiece. Two hundred and sixty three minutes later, after hitting 22 fours and one six, his international career (bar for a couple of one-day games) was over.

It was not a poor attack that he overwhelmed this day. And Pollock was 42, nearly 43 years old. Opening the attack with Hogg was Terry Alderman, who in 1989 would take 41 wickets in an Ashes series. Rod McCurdy, the first change, had originally

A view through the barbed wire, as groundsmen prepare the square at The Oval before the start of the 1970 English season. The wire was needed to keep anti-apartheid protesters at bay. At this stage the South African tour of England had not been cancelled, but it soon would be, and Graeme Pollock would be barred from Test-match fields around the world for the rest of his career.

Getty Images

> **GRAEME POLLOCK:** If isolation meant changing South Africa's politics, if it played a part, then I am quite happy that I missed out.

been picked for the 1985 Ashes tour, but declined that trip to go to South Africa. Trevor Hohns, a leg-spinner with 15 years' experience in first-class cricket, would be Australia's first choice spinner through 1989.

'Pollock scored mostly fours or singles,' local cricket writer George Byron wrote. 'Like so many captains, Hughes appeared to have decided on a defensive field in the hope of tempting Pollock into a rash shot. But the Australians soon found they were dealing with a master of the stolen single — especially off the last ball of the over — and that if he beat the fielder there was no chance of catching the ball before it reached the fence.'

Pollock on the attack against the rebel West Indians in early 1983, reviving memories of the glory days.

Pollock's last 41 runs, from 103 to 144, involved 10 boundaries (mostly off Alderman) and a single, before he played a tired shot 10 minutes before stumps and was bowled. As he walked off the ground, to a prolonged standing ovation, McCurdy walked over and said quietly, 'Well done, mate …

'And thanks.'

THE FOLLOWING DAY, WHILE accepting plaudits from across the cricket community — and from government ministers — Pollock gave an interview in which he pleaded for immediate political change in his country. Pollock had been among the high-profile players who walked off the field in a 1971 selection trial, in protest at merit *not* being the only criterion for selection in South African cricket teams. Sixteen years later, after his last great innings, he was widely quoted as saying, 'I can see the justice of our cricket isolation now, though it was hard at the time. The changes [now] will have to be political, because cricket itself has done a great deal. Pressure for change in South Africa will now have to come by way of international trade and political sanctions rather than through sport.'

In July 2000, his nephew Shaun, son of Peter, became the South African captain. South Africa is back in the international game, after those political changes he craved finally occurred. And Graeme Pollock has been named his country's cricketer of the century, crowned in an emotional ceremony in Cape Town in January 2000.

South Africa have had some fine wicketkeepers, including Johnny Waite, Denis Lindsay and Mark Boucher. Bowlers such as Neil Adcock, Hugh Tayfield, Allan Donald and Shaun Pollock sit at the top of South Africa's career bowling aggregate and average tables. But they do not dominate the batting lists as the great left-hander does. We come back to that statistic — his batting average of 60.97. This figure does not tell of the way he batted, the precision or the power, but it does confirm his consistency, and reflects his genius. Only one other South African batsman, AD Nourse (2960 runs at 53.81) has scored 2000 Test runs and averaged more than 50. Just as Sir Donald Bradman was clearly Australia's finest batsman of the 20th century, so too was Graeme Pollock the No. 1 man for South Africa.

MALCOLM MARSHALL
Legend No. 16
The Complete Fast Bowler

AT HEADINGLEY, IN JULY 1984, Malcolm Marshall was responsible for one of the most astonishing performances ever produced by a fast bowler. Earlier in this series, he'd wrecked the fledgling Test dreams of Andy Lloyd, who was struck on the helmet, had to spend several days in hospital with blurred vision, and didn't play again all season. However, on day one of the third Test, Marshall smashed his own left thumb while fielding and everyone assumed he was out of the game, perhaps gone for the season. Thus, when the ninth West Indian first-innings wicket fell, the players began to head for the dressing rooms, only to head back to their positions when Marshall walked out onto the ground, to bat one-handed long enough for Larry Gomes to reach his century. Then, with his lower arm encased in plaster, Marshall took 7–53, bowling scarcely below top speed, swinging the ball like an artisan in the overcast conditions. The batsmen even complained that the white plaster was putting them off, so Marshall covered it with pink elastoplast, which made it sort of skin-coloured. As it turned out, he missed just one Test and was back at The Oval to claim five wickets in an innings for the seventh time in 10 Tests, a run he extended to 11 in 14 when he dominated the 1984–85 Test series in Australia.

'I remember when he broke his hand at Leeds and we thought he wouldn't play,' says Clive Lloyd, like a proud father recalling a son's graduation with honours. 'But I said, "Would you like to play?" And he was surprised that I'd asked him.

'He bowled, took seven wickets, batted in a good partnership, and we won the Test match. And it just shows you the type of spirit that we had in those days. That's what we were all about. We were very good professionals, very good family and we wanted to win.'

Marshall's Test record — number of wickets (376), bowling average (20.94) and strike rate (a wicket every 46.77 deliveries) — is quite superb. But what is perhaps most telling is the fact that of all the fast men who were a part of that West Indian 'family', he is by a substantial majority recognised as being the best, superior to Roberts and Holding, Garner and Croft, Ambrose and Walsh.

He was that good.

WHAT SET HIM APART? Consider these comments:

Wasim Akram: 'He used to identify batsmen's mistakes very quickly. Some bowlers can judge in, say, half an hour, but by that time the batsman is set. Malcolm Marshall could make this judgment in the first two minutes. A complete bowling master.'

Carl Hooper: 'I thought he was a complete fast bowler, he could do everything with the ball. He'd swing his outswingers, if it wasn't swinging he could seam it off the deck, he had good pace and above all he was smart. That's why I give him the edge over everybody else.'

Roger Harper: 'Malcolm was a complete fast bowler in the sense that he was capable of swinging the ball at tremendous pace, he was capable of bowling on very flat wickets, rolling his fingers over, trying to cut

> **MARK NICHOLAS:** Marshall was an unbelievably intelligent bowler; that and stamina were his strengths. He remembered everything about his opponents. He needn't play against someone for five years and when he stood and faced them again he would immediately pinpoint their weaknesses and home in on them.

it. He knew exactly what to do for different conditions and different batsmen. And, apart from all that, he was willing to work for his wickets.'

Martin Crowe: 'He was one of my favourite bowlers, not to face but to admire. He had a wonderful attitude and, obviously, a very strong ability to get the ball to kick and climb. He worked players out, he was very intelligent and knew exactly what he was trying to achieve. I thought he was the most complete fast bowler to come from the Caribbean.'

The *complete* fast bowler. 'Marshall stood out,' wrote *Wisden* in its obituary of the great fast bowler in 2000. 'He allied sheer pace to consistent excellence for longer than anyone else; he was relentlessly professional and determined; and he was also the best batsman of the group [of great West Indian fast men], coming nearer than any recent West Indian to being an all-rounder of the quality of Garry Sobers.'

MALCOLM MARSHALL HAD DIED, aged just 41, from colon cancer on 4 November 1999. Born in St Michael, Barbados in 1958, he began his schoolboy cricket career as an opening batsman, but was able to overcome the fact that he, unlike many of his fast-bowling contemporaries, was less than six feet tall to become a strike bowler before his 20th birthday. He yearned to be a Test cricketer from the day he saw a fellow Barbadian, Garry Sobers, score a century against New Zealand in Bridgetown in 1972. In fact, he continued to want to be Sobers throughout his career, to the point where captain Clive Lloyd would say, 'Come on "Sobie", come and have a bowl.' Marshall would then stroll to the bowling crease, collar often upturned as Sobers used to do, and explode into action.

After a solitary first-class appearance for Barbados as a 19-year-old, Marshall was selected in the West Indies team that toured India without its World Series Cricket stars in 1978–79. He made his Test debut in the second Test of that series, in Bangalore, bowling first change behind Sylvester Clarke and Norbert Phillip for one wicket (Chetan Chauhan) and batting No. 9 for 0 and 38. Though he had little success, he did enough elsewhere for Hampshire in England to take him on as successor to Andy Roberts, and for the once again full-strength Windies to include him in their squad for the 1979 World Cup.

Marshall toured Australia and New Zealand in 1979–80 but hardly played, though he still made an impact. 'I remember playing in a game, his first game for the West Indies on that tour,' says Michael Holding, 'and he was quick. First time I'd actually seen him bowl outside of the nets and he bowled extremely quickly. We all said to ourselves, "How can a little man like this bowl this fast?" Marshall then went to England in 1980, where, at Old Trafford, he had a major impact on a Test match for the first time in his life. The home team had reached 3–126 before the young fast bowler, who had come on after Roberts, Holding and Joel Garner, precipitated a collapse that saw seven wickets fall for just 24 runs. Marshall himself took three wickets in 14 balls, and *Wisden* noted that he 'had as much pace as any'.

Even so, such was the competition for places in the West Indies top side, that it took him another two-and-a-half years to establish himself at Test level. In the meantime, he forged a reputation in county cricket, making his mark in 1982 when he took 134 first-class wickets — a total beyond any other bowler in the last 32 years of the 20th century — at an average of 15.73. However, it wasn't until the home series against India in early 1983, when he took 21 wickets in the five Tests, including 5–37 at Port-of-Spain, that he truly cemented his place on the frontline. Many rated him the fastest bowler at the 1983 World Cup, where he also gave notice of his batting ability, most notably in the final when a late stand with Jeffrey Dujon almost saved the day.

Rather than being a drawback, Marshall's lack of height allowed him to skid through at the batsmen in a manner that made him extremely awkward, and very different from his partners in fast-bowling crime. His bounce was ultra-accurate and as a consequence lethal, and he developed an outswinger to go with his scare tactics. The England all-rounder Vic Marks described his bowling this way: 'He sprinted up to the wicket, barely stopping at the crease to deliver the ball, slightly open-chested but with supple fingers delicately controlling the seam.' In his early days Marshall raced in from a Holding-like long approach, but later he cut his run-up, though never the bustling nature of his sprint to the crease, which ended with the ball being whipped with plenty of wrist down towards the batsman. 'So quick is his action,' Michael Manley wrote in his *A History of West Indies Cricket*, 'that you might miss the perfection of

COLIN CROFT: Marshall was a real student of the game, he learnt as he went. In his mind, he was never perfect, he was always trying to get better.

his delivery stride, left [front] leg kicking and body laid out almost horizontal to maximise the whip effect of the delivery itself.'

Marshall learnt to vary his pace after observing the champions, and was taught how to bowl an inswinger by the great Dennis Lillee (later, Marshall passed on to Imran Khan what Lillee had showed him; the fast bowlers' union knows few boundaries). He could move the ball off the pitch too, especially the leg-cutter, and few fast men have used the full width of the bowling crease better. And he was as effective from around the wicket as he was over, whether the purpose was to give his bouncer more potency or to give a new angle to his inswinger.

'All good fast bowlers are intelligent, they've got a streak of cunning when it comes to their bowling,' says Greg Chappell. 'And Malcolm Marshall was up

Malcolm Marshall in Pakistan in 1980, surprisingly quick but not yet a certain selection in the West Indies Test XI.

Ian Botham is caught behind by Thelston Payne off Marshall in Bridgetown in 1986. Viv Richards, with arms raised, joins in the celebrations.

there with the best. My career ended before his really started, so I didn't bat against him a lot. I was fortunate that I didn't.'

Indeed, Chappell's career ended in 1983–84, the same season in which Marshall snared 33 wickets in a six-Test series in India, as the West Indies gained ample revenge for their shock loss in the recent World Cup. Viv Richards described his bowling in this series as 'ferocious, his pace and accuracy were just mesmerising'. In one spell on a green pitch in Kanpur, he knocked the bat out of Sunil Gavaskar's hands before dismissing him, stunning the local fans and players. At the conclusion of his opening spell that day his figures read 4–9 from eight overs. With the bat, Marshall scored 240 runs in that series,

IAN BOTHAM: He bowled a slippery, skiddy bouncer, which caused all batsmen problems. He could swing it at a high pace. On his day he was unplayable.

including 92 in the first Test (the closest he came to scoring a Test century), and became the first West Indian to score 200 runs and take 25 wickets in one Test series. Back home, he overwhelmed Kim Hughes' over-matched Australians, taking 5–42 when they were 97 all out at Bridgetown, 5–51 at Kingston and 22 wickets for the series, despite having missed the opening Test.

In Adelaide in 1984–85, he produced a spell that, when all things are considered, might have been his finest ever. The pitch was lifeless, and for once his fellow bowlers were struggling, but Marshall rose to the occasion, taking 5–69 and 5–38. It was not just the fact he took 10 wickets, it was the way he got them. Allan Border remembers: 'Malcolm Marshall bowled a spell between lunch and tea — non-stop, we're talking two hours of bowling — in 100-degree heat. He just rushed in, having decided that he had to really have a red-hot go, bowled real good pace and broke the back of our batting. That, to me, sums up what he was all about. Other bowlers, even the other great bowlers that the West

Indies had at their disposal, wouldn't have been able to sustain their performance like Malcolm Marshall did that day.'

When Marshall followed up with 5–86 in the first innings of the fourth Test, at the MCG, he had taken five wickets in an innings on four straight occasions.

Two weeks earlier, in the second Test of that Australian series, at the Gabba, the Tasmanian batsman David Boon made his debut, and marked the occasion with a brave half-century in the second innings. During that knock, Marshall walked up to the Test debutant and said, 'Boonie, I know this is your first Test match, but are you going to do the right thing and get out or do I have to come around the wicket and kill you?' Later Marshall did go round the wicket and bowled Boon a bouncer, which was hooked away for four, to which Boon's batting partner, the tailender Rodney Hogg (who was unaware of the earlier conversation) exclaimed, 'What are you trying to do? Get us killed?'

Such was the impact of the West Indian fast bowlers in the 1980s. They knew they had it over opposing teams.

At the end of his career, Boon named Marshall as the best fast man he faced. 'There are a huge number of pacemen who earned my enormous respect,' he wrote, 'men such as Sir Richard Hadlee, who made you play at nine out of 10 balls, Michael Holding and Curtly Ambrose, the Pakistani duo of Wasim Akram and Waqar Younis, and South Africa's Allan Donald. But Malcolm Marshall was just that little bit better. He had one of the best brains of any bowler I faced (which he coupled with a wicked sense of humour), and could bowl *that* quick and swing it both ways. Inevitably, you found yourself in trouble.'

Then Boon added: 'In hindsight, the story from my first Test match, when Malcolm offered to come around the wicket and kill me, was an example of his wit. It was just him taking the mickey out of someone making their debut, but at the time, from where I was quivering, there was nothing even remotely funny in it.'

From 1984 to 1986, Marshall was irresistible. In consecutive home series against New Zealand (four Tests) and England (five) he twice took 27 wickets, and took his 200th Test wicket, too, the sixth West Indian to do so, and in the shortest time, in terms of Tests, of anyone to reach that mark. Away from the record books, the most brutal image he left was the

MARK NICHOLAS: The reason Marshall was the greatest of all fast bowlers was that he could adapt to all conditions. I would call him a bowler for all seasons and all places, in that he could get on the flattest wickets of, say, the sub-continent, and bowl as effectively as he could on green tops in England or fast tracks in Western Australia. It was the West Indies' 1983 tour of India that confirmed him in the eyes of many people as so special, when he competed to such a degree that he was almost winning matches on his own.

horrendously bruised and battered face of England's Mike Gatting, who was struck a fearful blow during a one-day international in Kingston in February 1986. The pitch was two-paced and slightly corrugated, and Gatting tried to pull a typically skidding bouncer. 'It flew off the track after it pitched and I can remember seeing it come over the

Getty Images

England's Andy Lloyd fails to avoid a Marshall bouncer and is struck a fearful blow during the 1984 Test series in England. Lloyd, who was making his debut, never batted in Test cricket again.

IAN SMITH: Marshall was a very difficult bowler for me, because he bowled so aggressively and was so often so accurate. There was never any let-up. His bouncer, for me, was the most dangerous bouncer I faced because it was always threatening, at times life-threatening.

top of my bat,' is the batsman's memory of the blow. 'The helmet I was wearing only had side flaps and so the only obstacle in the ball's path was my nose. I felt like I had walked into a brick wall …'

Many who saw that ball reckon it was the fastest over Marshall ever bowled. Gatting was left with two very black eyes and a two-centimetre cut on the bridge of his flattened nose, while his team, psychologically, was shattered, going on to lose every match in the Test series that followed.

Unlike many other pacemen of recent times, Marshall was superb on the sub-continent. Take Lahore in November 1986, when he took 5–33 from 18 overs as the West Indies won by an innings. In that three-Test series he took 16 wickets at 16.63. Eighteen months later, in England, he grabbed a West Indies series record 35 wickets at just 12.65. Five of them came in an hour at Manchester where he took 7–22 as England floundered to 93 all out. In Australia in 1988–89 he took his 300th Test wicket, in his 61st Test, the ninth bowler and second West Indian to do so, and produced his best bowling of the series in Sydney, on a spinner's wicket, by taking 5–29 from 31 overs in Australia's first innings. 'The king of fast bowlers,' Australia's Merv Hughes called him, recalling that summer. 'Whenever Viv Richards wanted something done, he would bring Marshall back.'

Against India at Port-of-Spain in early 1989 Marshall took 11–89 (5–34 and 6–55), the fourth and final time he managed 10 wickets in a Test, and continued on until his fourth Test tour of England, in 1991. His final Test bowling average remains the lowest of all those to take 250 Test wickets.

CURRENT WEST INDIES CHAMPION Brian Lara remembers his first encounter with Marshall, which occurred when Lara's Trinidad and Tobago played Marshall's Barbados in 1988. 'The first delivery I faced in the match was from Malcolm and, of course, his reputation with the ball preceded him. I was scared, my heart was pumping and I was out caught down the legside first ball. As he went past me with his hands in the air he stopped and touched me on the shoulder and said, "Tough luck!"'

He played hard but fair, and was always competitive, wherever he was playing. Joel Garner reckoned that Marshall's real strength was that 'he never gave less than 100 per cent for any team he played or was involved in'. Greg Matthews, the former New South Wales and Australian all-rounder, was a teammate when Marshall played a season for Waverley in the Sydney grade competition. He remembers Marshall shouting for a caught behind decision and being shocked when the umpire turned him down. 'He finished the over and went down to fine-leg, and you could hear him complaining from there,' Matthews explained. 'That was because he was so competitive. Some other sportspeople take a step back when they come down from a higher level but he was never like that.'

Marshall finished his career with 157 wickets in one-day internationals, fifth highest when he retired, though it is fair to say that even though he played some important late-order cameos with the bat, his overall impact was not as great in one-day cricket as it was in Test matches. The rules curtailing short-pitched deliveries tended to blunt the West Indians' firepower, bringing them back to the field. Even so, they remained almost unbeatable at home, not losing a one-day series until the Australians defeated them 4–1 in 1991.

Marshall continued playing for Hampshire until 1993, and returned to the club as coach in 1996, the same year he also became West Indies' coach, following the team's defeat in the semi-finals of the World Cup in India, Pakistan and Sri Lanka. As well, he played and coached in South Africa following the dismantling of apartheid in the early 1990s, after his Hampshire teammate, the South African-born Robin Smith, recommended him to Natal. 'He had a huge effect on my career,' says current South African captain Shaun Pollock, who made his debut for Natal while Marshall was there. 'He had so much knowledge and feel for the game.' In his third season in South Africa, as captain for most of the season while regular leader Jonty Rhodes was playing for South Africa, Marshall led Natal to the Castle Cup title. In the process, he took

35 wickets at 16.17 and averaged almost 30 with the bat, and was named one of South Africa's cricketers of the year.

For all his strengths, Marshall recognised his limitations as a tutor. 'While coaching and technology are all good things,' he said, when asked about the failings of the West Indies batsmen of the late '90s, 'the only things that matter when a batsman crosses the boundary ropes on his way to the crease are ability, guts, determination and flexibility. If a batsman does not have at least three of those, he will fail, regardless of whatever coaching or technological devices he uses.'

One sensed he was frustrated by the approach of the West Indies teams he coached, which paled in comparison with the great teams he played with a generation before.

By the time he was taken ill during the 1999 World Cup, Marshall's coaching methods were being criticised, even though Lara's team had squared a memorable home series against the all-conquering Australians earlier in that year. Chemotherapy treatment after the Cup was not successful, and he returned to Barbados to marry his long-time girlfriend Connie just before he died. At his funeral, five West Indian captains were among the pallbearers.

'It is an amazing phenomenon of his short life that opponents everywhere, from Barbados to Bombay, from Sydney to Southampton, loved him so,' said Mark Nicholas when giving the eulogy. 'Let's face it, he was a lethal bowler — who could forget that skidding bouncer homing in on its target like a Scud missile — and also a brilliantly, skilful bowler capable of all kinds of swing and cut and subtle changes of pace.'

Wes Hall, a fellow Barbadian and hero of many a West Indian Test victory in the 1960s, said that Marshall was the greatest of all fast bowlers. Then, after a pause, he added, 'And the one thing Wesley Hall knows about is fast bowling.'

The reaction to Marshall's death was a sombre reminder of the status that cricket, and great cricketers, retain in the psyche of the people of the West Indies, particularly of Barbados. The global response, with tributes from so many notable players of his and other eras, showed just how much he was respected. In Brisbane and Harare, where Test matches were being played, teams of other countries paid tribute with a minute's silence.

Marshall never made a Test century, but did enough at the highest level to suggest that, had he concentrated more on his batting, he could have made significant Test runs.

Like many before him, Marshall rose from modest beginnings to climb to the top of the cricket tree. He lost his father at an early age, as Sir Garfield Sobers had done before him, but like his idol became a symbol of Barbados' cricket strength.

'For everyone who lives here, on this magical island,' said Nicholas, 'the name of Malcolm Marshall is synonymous with the style of the place:

ALAN DAVIDSON: Malcolm Marshall was the best West Indian bowler that I've ever seen. He had a wonderfully competitive nature, and no matter what the pitch conditions, he could bowl on it. You have a look at Malcolm Marshall's record: he toured everywhere and he performed in every country. He had superb control, he bowled superb line and length, and his variations were tremendous.

Marshall on the balcony at Lord's, acknowledging his supporters after Hampshire won the Benson & Hedges Cup final in 1992.

with the game of cricket in its purest calypso form, but also in its more modern professional form; with fun and sun; with the good and simple living that is typical here; and with the honesty and generosity of spirit that characterises the people of Barbados.'

Tony Cozier reflected on his own special memories of Marshall. One was of Marshall the batsman, and one shot in particular — the 'flourishing flick through mid-wicket' that carried the hallmark of another of Marshall's childhood heroes, the outstanding Barbados batsman of the 1960s, Seymour Nurse. Another memory was of Marshall winning for Barbados a Shell Shield match in Grenada bowling leg-spin, when it had appeared that the Windward Islands would hold out for a

draw. 'He really could do anything with the ball,' Cozier said.

The complete fast bowler. And on top of all that, he loved the game and appreciated his place in it. 'For me,' says Jonty Rhodes, 'the most endearing thing about Malcolm was how humble he was. He was prepared to give. He was the first guy to the net, he was the last guy to leave and he had a lot to offer everyone. I was so impressed by a person who had almost reached the end of his career and who could easily have just sat back and said, "Well, I've done it, I'm here to take a last pay out and then I'm out of here." Instead, he gave so much back.

'It was just a privilege to play with a guy who had such an absolute zest for cricket.'

ALLAN BORDER: Who's the best West Indies paceman? You've probably got 10 champion fast bowlers to choose from, but I think that, day in, day out, in all conditions, Malcolm Marshall is my pick. He was something special.

GREG CHAPPELL
Legend No. 17
Elegance Personified

REG CHAPPELL PICKED QUITE a way to leave Test cricket. In the fifth Test of the 1983–84 Australian summer, against Pakistan at the SCG, Chappell bid farewell to the international stage by scoring 182 and taking three catches. The century made him the first batsman to score a century in his first and last Test innings, and the sixth man and first Australian to score 7000 Test runs. The second catch was his 121st in Tests, breaking Colin Cowdrey's previous record for most catches by a non-wicketkeeper. Completing the occasion, the great bowler-keeper combination, Dennis Lillee and Rod Marsh, who had both begun their Test careers in the same season as Chappell (1970–71) also decided that this would be their final Test.

It was certainly the end of an era; Australian cricket would take many seasons to recover from the loss.

All these aggregate records have since been beaten, by batsmen such as Allan Border, David Boon, Mark Taylor, and Steve and Mark Waugh, and fieldsmen such as Border, Taylor and Mark Waugh, but the memory of Chappell's skill and style remain vivid for fans who became hooked on Australian cricket during the tempestuous and sensational 1970s. Also of great significance is his

Greg Chappell in England in 1972, his first overseas tour as a Test cricketer.

Test batting average of 53.86, from 87 Tests and 151 innings. Of all those to score 2500 runs, only Bradman among Australians and 10 batsmen in all have averaged more. His medium-pace bowling was serviceable, good enough to get him 47 Test wickets and even one spell of 5–61 against Pakistan in Sydney in 1972–73. And his magnificent catching, especially in the slip cordon, was foolproof; he ranks with Bob Simpson and Mark Waugh as the best catcher of flying edges Australia has ever had.

Chappell never gave the impression of chasing records, but in his 13-year career in international cricket — 11 in 'traditional' cricket and two in World Series Cricket — he set quite a few:

JEFF THOMSON: He was the best batter in my time and that encompasses a lot of blokes — Javed Miandad, Barry Richards, Clive Lloyd, throw 'em all in. Greg Chappell was an absolute machine.

• Most runs scored by an individual in a Test match — 380 (247 not out and 133) against New Zealand at Wellington in 1973–74. This was later beaten by England's Graham Gooch, who scored 456 (333 and 123) against India at Lord's in 1990, and by Mark Taylor when he scored 426 (334 not out and 92) against Pakistan at Peshawar in 1998.
• Most catches by a non-wicketkeeper in a Test — seven against England at Perth in 1974–75. This has since been equalled by India's Yajuvendra Singh, Sri Lanka's Hashan Tillekeratne and New Zealand's Stephen Fleming.
• First man to score hundreds in both innings of his first Test as captain — 123 and 109 not out against the West Indies in Brisbane in 1975–76 — and the first Australian to score a hundred in each innings of a Test twice. When Chappell returned as Australian captain after WSC, he resumed with scores of 74 and 124 against the West Indies at the Gabba in 1979–80.
• First man to captain Australia in 40 Tests. Chappell's last Test as captain, the inaugural Australia-Sri Lanka Test match, in Kandy in April 1983, was his 48th in charge, nine more than the previous highest, Bob Simpson. Since Chappell's retirement, Allan Border has led Australia in 93 Tests, Mark Taylor in 50.
• First batsman to score four double centuries in Test cricket after World War II. As at 31 March 2002, the men to make four or more Test scores of 200 or more are Sir Donald Bradman (12), Wally Hammond (7), Javed Miandad (6), Marvan Atapattu (5), Chappell (4), Len Hutton (4), Sunil Gavaskar (4), Gordon Greenidge (4), Brian Lara (4) and Zaheer Abbas (4).

Greg Chappell was the younger brother of Ian Chappell, who played 75 Tests for Australia between 1964 and 1980 and led Australia with distinction between 1971 and 1975. In 1972, at The Oval, they provided the first instance of brothers both scoring a century in the same Test innings. Eighteen months later, in Wellington, they provided the only instance of brothers scoring centuries in each innings of the same Test. Their grandfather, Victor Richardson, captained Australia to South Africa in 1935–36, and played 19 Tests between 1924 and 1936. Their younger brother, Trevor, played three Tests for Australia in 1981, but is best remembered for bowling the infamous 'underarm' in a one-day international against New Zealand earlier in that same year. More of that later.

Being the younger brother of an excellent cricketer guaranteed a testing upbringing. 'Our Test matches in the backyard were pretty willing affairs,' Greg remembers. 'Our father encouraged us to play our cricket seriously. He encouraged us to play with a hard ball from a very early age so we got to know what a hard ball was like. That was the good news. The bad news was he didn't provide us with any pads and gloves. So we got to find out what a hard ball felt like. But it was good. Ian's five years older, so he was bigger and stronger, and I copped a pretty good workout from a very early age.'

Ian takes great pride in his role, saying: 'Greg always says that when people ask him what Test cricket was like, he replies, "I was well prepared for Test cricket. Test cricket could never be as tough as playing against my brother in the backyard." Anything after that was a breeze ...'

GREG CHAPPELL, BORN IN Adelaide on 7 August 1948, made his Sheffield Shield debut for South Australia during the 1966–67 season. Brother Ian was away with the Australian team in South Africa at the time, so initially the attendants in the Adelaide Oval scoreboard used his nameplate when Greg was batting, but quickly they realised they'd need to make another for the following season. In seven years with South Australia, Greg scored almost 4000 runs, including 10 centuries, before heading to Queensland for the 1973–74 season.

He moved to Brisbane for many reasons, including the dollars offered by the Queensland Cricket Association, but most of all it was the opportunities on offer, in business and most importantly the chance to get captaincy experience at the first-class level. Queensland had long been the easybeats of the Sheffield Shield, but Chappell turned that around immediately, to the point that his side would have won the Shield in his first season up north had they won their last game outright (Queensland lost in Sydney by 167 runs). His influence up north was summed up by the all-rounder Phil Carlson, who said, 'He's the best cricketer in Australia and he's playing for us. He is getting the players around him performing. Batting with Greg makes an enormous difference. It's so

MAX WALKER: If you look at any of the coaching manuals, you could draw a template over Greg Chappell and work from that.

much easier with someone at the other end as good as he is. Greg is super-confident. He doesn't think there's anyone better than him. And there isn't ...'

Many critics thought Chappell should have been selected in the Australian side as early as the 1969–70 tour of India and South Africa, but instead he had to wait until the second Ashes Test of 1970–71, at the first ever Test in Perth, to make his international debut. He began in style, scoring 108 in his first innings and managing to cause a storm in the eastern states by reaching three figures — the sixth Australian to do so in his maiden Test innings — while ABC television viewers were forced to watch the main evening news rather than the first half-hour of the final session. His first 50 runs took 200 minutes, the second 58, and with Ian Redpath, who went on to 171, he took Australia from 5–107 to 6–326 in reply to 397. Redpath is a cricketer whose contribution to the Australian cause through this era is often forgotten, even though he scored more than 4700 runs in Test cricket (including eight centuries, four of them against the West Indies) and was Ian Chappell's vice-captain in 1974–75, and Greg's in 1975–76. But the players remember. 'I learnt a lot about batting in Test cricket just from batting with Ian Redpath on that day,' says Greg Chappell of his maiden ton.

Later in the series, Chappell was at the bowler's end when Terry Jenner was struck by a John Snow bouncer, and was the closest witness to the finger-pointing argument that developed soon after between Snow, England captain Ray Illingworth and umpire Lou Rowan. A few days earlier, his own captain, Bill Lawry, had been unceremoniously dumped by the Australian selectors, to be replaced by brother Ian. Greg Chappell learnt very quickly how tough and competitive Test cricket could be.

MARTIN CROWE: Greg Chappell had everything I would want as a player. He had style, grace and elegance. He had smoothness, fluency, he flowed into his strokes. He never clubbed the ball and he always placed it into the gap.

Chappell on the attack during the 1977 Ashes tour. The off-field pressures brought about by the emergence of World Series Cricket made this trip an extremely difficult one for the Australian captain.

The value of these lessons became apparent on his first Ashes tour, in 1972. He had gained valuable experience of English conditions while playing county cricket with Somerset in 1968 and 1969, but this was still only his second Test series (the 1971–72 South African tour of Australia had been cancelled, replaced by a rubber against a Rest of the World team in which Chappell played in only the final three 'Tests' and scored 425 runs at a Bradman-like 106.25). In the second Test, at Lord's, in what became known as 'Massie's Match' — Western Australia's Bob Massie, on his Test debut, took 8–84 and 8–53 — Chappell compiled a superb 131. Australia had lost the first Test, mainly because the batsmen had performed poorly against England's pacemen, and were 2–7 when Chappell found himself in the middle. 'People like Ray Illingworth and John Snow, who bowled to that 131, say it was absolutely masterly, that he was elegance personified,' comments Jack Bannister.

'Physically and mentally, I think it was as well as I played at any stage during my Test career,' says Chappell of that knock. 'The thing that I reflect on over that innings was that I didn't make a mental mistake until the ball I got out. I don't think I concentrated as well as that very often in my Test career. So, given the conditions, given the state of the game, I rate that as my best Test innings.'

In the fifth Test, at The Oval, Greg made 113 and Ian 118 as the two added 201 after coming together at 2–34. The great broadcaster and journalist John Arlott wrote enthusiastically: 'Soon Greg was standing up from his jack-knife stance to strike the ball cleanly and effortlessly off the front foot. No modern batsman has driven the ball more fluently or stylishly between mid-wicket and mid-on — the most difficult of strokes to execute orthodoxly … Greg was assessing the bowling perfectly and bending it stylishly to his will. His driving was cultured and profitable, his cutting delicately precise …'

Following the 1972 England tour, Chappell scored Test centuries at home against Pakistan and in the West Indies, where he became the first Australian to score more than 1000 runs on a Caribbean tour, and New Zealand. Against England in 1974–75, he was undoubtedly the best batsman on either side, and after a disappointing Test series in England in 1975, came back in a much-hyped series against the West

GREG CHAPPELL: Going out on the field as captain for the first time, I was excited and a little bit nervous. Ian, the previous captain, was still in the side. He's also my older brother, and he'd been pretty critical of me most of my life, so I was expecting that it would probably be no different here.

Dennis Lillee took the ball to bowl the first over, and I had five slips and two gullies, a fine-leg and a bat pad. And it was after the third ball of the over that I realised I didn't have anyone in front of the wicket on the offside. So I pretended that I intended to do that and just slipped one of the blokes out of the gully cordon and put him in the front of the wicket on the offside. I thought that might be a sensible move. How Ian stood there for three balls and let it go by, I've no idea.

DAVID LLOYD: He was a confident player and he brought that to the middle. There was no sense that he was vulnerable or hesitant when he came to the crease; there was a little bit of arrogance, which doesn't go amiss. He had absolute confidence in his own ability, he knew what he could do, and he knew that he was better than most.

Indies in Australia to put a strong case that he was the finest runmaker in the world.

This West Indies series was seen as an unofficial world championship, coming straight after Australia had dominated two Ashes series and the Windies had won the inaugural World Cup (defeating Australia in the final). The visitors' attack was led by the lethal fast bowlers, Andy Roberts and Michael Holding, but Chappell — in his first series as Australian captain — was supreme, hitting three centuries and 702 runs in the series (at an average of 117), the most runs scored by an Australian in one series against the West Indies.

Of all these innings, perhaps the unbeaten 109 in the second innings of the first Test, his second

century of the match, was the most impressive. 'He has made all sorts of scores on all wickets and against all bowlers,' Ian Chappell wrote in a post-Test newspaper column. 'But I have always thought him to be less at home on a turning wicket. On Tuesday he showed this is no longer so and he did it in his usual batting style — dominating the bowling.' Ian was Greg's batting partner throughout that innings, the pair adding an unbroken 159 to get Australia home by eight wickets.

If Chappell was clearly the best batsman in Australia at this time, it was also true that — outside his adopted Queensland at least (as well as making the Sheffield Shield team competitive, his seven Tests at the Gabba would bring him a total of

Greg Chappell would rank with Bob Simpson and Mark Waugh as the finest slips field Australia has had in the past 40 years. This one, off the bat of the West Indies' Richard Austin during a WSC SuperTest in early 1979, was a bump ball and thus wasn't out, but it still shows him at his sharpest. Two other ESPN Legends are in the photograph — the bowler, Dennis Lillee, and the batsman at the non-striker's end, Viv Richards.

1006 runs, at 111.77) — he battled for 'folk hero' status. While supporters of Dougie Walters, Lillee and Thommo, Rod Marsh and Ian Chappell had no trouble recognising Greg Chappell's phenomenal ability, the new captain's aloof, always serious onfield persona did not attract the same fervent response from the fans in the outer as did the more good-humoured, colourful, sometimes eccentric behaviour of his teammates. The fans called the others by their nicknames, reflecting how they felt close to them; Greg Chappell was the straight man, respected rather than loved.

However, it was not his style to worry about popularity stakes. In 1976–77, Australia won short series against Pakistan and New Zealand and then the Centenary Test at the MCG. But behind the scenes, players were being secretly lured to World Series Cricket. Such negotiations placed Chappell, the Australian Cricket Board-appointed Australian captain, in an extremely awkward position. When news of the WSC revolution broke early on the 1977 Ashes tour, the Board effectively froze relations with him, and gradually the tour developed into one of the most unpleasant ever undertaken by an Australian team. While his batting form was reasonable, featuring a superb century at Old Trafford in the second Test, he was unable to inspire his team to rise above the innuendo and bickering, and the Ashes were lost 3–0. Prior to the final Test, Chappell announced his retirement from Test cricket. Officials quickly pointed out he was about to be banned anyway.

For the two years of World Series Cricket, Chappell handed the captaincy back to his brother and scored 1416 runs in the SuperTests, 523 more than any other Australian. His aggregate in the one-day internationals of 1166 was also substantially higher than that of any of his comrades. The cricket was as relentless and competitive as anything he had ever played, and the camaraderie the rebels felt was unique, to the point that, while Chappell saw the many advantages in bringing the game back under one banner, he felt a sense of loss when the compromise came. 'I learnt more about myself in that period of two years — as a player, as a person — than at any other stage in my career,' he says now. 'I rate some of the innings that I played during that period as the best innings I ever played. I probably got away in Test cricket up to that point using about 75 or 80 per cent of my talent, but I had to use every ounce of it during World Series Cricket. It took me to another level as a player.'

Chappell led the Australian team in every Test he played from December 1979 until his final home season, when he handed the responsibility to Kim Hughes. Hughes had led the side on overseas tours to England (1981 and the 1983 World Cup) and Pakistan (1982) when Chappell was unavailable, for personal or business reasons. As a batsman, Chappell's Test average was slightly higher after WSC than it was before (4097 runs at 53.20 in 51 Tests between 1970 and 1977 compared with 3013 at 54.78 in 36 Tests, 1979–84), and he scored three of his four Test double centuries after his return. However, cruelly, he is remembered most of all for two darker events from the period 1979 to 1984.

The first was the underarm, the second his run of ducks in 1981–82. The underarm came during the World Series Cup finals of 1980–81, in game three, with Australia and New Zealand locked one-all in a best of five series. The Australians had already played 12 one-dayers and five Tests during the summer, after touring Pakistan and England for short tours in the off-season, after a full Australian season in 1979–80, after WSC. Throughout the '80–81 season, Chappell, as the Australian captain, had been involved in ongoing arguments with officialdom, blues that he says provoked a moment in cricket history that proved beyond doubt that one-day cricket matters to cricket fans, even to prime ministers.

'It was pretty difficult, as we all — administrators and players — came to grips with the new era of cricket,' Chappell explains. 'As Australian captain, I found it pretty onerous, the extra work that I had to do behind the scenes in discussions and so on, trying to get the administrators to include us in their discussions. The underarm incident was really a combination of all the frustration that came from arguing with the administrators about everything that was wrong with the programming, with having two touring teams and all those one-day games,

> **JEFF THOMSON:** He always gives that impression, doesn't he? Business-like, serious, as opposed to his brother, who always looked more ruffled, a real Aussie look. Greg looked more like the English gentleman. It was a wolf in sheep's clothing. Greg is one of the boys.

plus six Test matches, in one season, how it impacted against the Australian team being successful. It's not an excuse for what happened on that day at the Melbourne Cricket Ground, it's an explanation for where I was at, physically and mentally, by the time we got to that game. The easy explanation for the underarm was that it was all about not losing a game. That was probably about 10 per cent of what it was all about. Mostly, it was a cry for help. It was a statement that I had had enough.'

With a ball to go, New Zealand needed six to tie, with the rugby international, burly Brian McKechnie, on strike and Trevor Chappell to do the bowling. Greg went up to his brother and asked, 'How are you at bowling underarms?'

'I don't know, why?' Trevor replied.

'You're about to find out.'

McKechnie blocked the grubber, threw his bat in the air, and the teams walked off to a torrent of boos. A little girl ran up to Chappell and cried, 'You cheated!' Afterwards, he was condemned in the media, even by his elder brother, who asked, 'Fair dinkum, Greg, how much pride do you sacrifice for $35,000 [the size of the winner's cheque]?' Richie Benaud called the delivery 'gutless'. From across the Tasman, New Zealand Prime Minister Robert Muldoon described it as 'an act of cowardice'. But by the time of the fourth final, two days later at the SCG, people had heard Chappell apologise and considered the stress he was under, and their rage had mellowed. There were far more cheers than jeers when the Australian captain strode out to bat, and he responded with a match-winning 87 not out.

The sheer style of that innings only confirmed what critics had known ever since one-day cricket became an integral part of the cricket calendar — that Greg Chappell was Australia's finest batsman in both forms of the game. 'Greg had supreme touch and balance,' was Bob Simpson's explanation for this. 'He was the sort of player who never seemed to trash the ball and yet could hit it many a mile.'

In 74 one-dayers between 1971 and 1983 he scored 2231 runs at the very impressive batting average of 40.18, including three centuries. However, for a spell during the 1981–82 season, he couldn't take a trick, to the point where he couldn't score a run. Chappell's full sequence of scores in that Australian season, in Tests and one-dayers, was 22, 6,

> **IAN CHAPPELL:** As a batsman, Greg at his peak was the best mentally organised batsman of his time. When he was in that frame of mind he was a very tough batsman to get out.

3, 1, 201, 38, 22, 0, 0, 0, 0, 6, 12, 0, 35, 59, 61, 0, 4, 1, 0, 10, 61 and 7. The press — some of whom still believed Chappell had got away too lightly over the underarm — had a field day, and pressure mounted for Chappell to consider his place in the side.

Greg Chappell's view of this traumatic period is this: 'I was starting to get to the stage, with a young family and so on, where all of a sudden cricket wasn't the only thing in my life. It wasn't the be-all and end-all of my life, for the first time my attention was diverted from cricket. I got into a slump and then I got into this downward spiral of becoming anxious and worrying about failing, rather than thinking about being successful. It was

Chappell in Perth in 1982–83, during his final series against England. By series end, he would be only the fourth Australian captain in more than 70 years (after Warwick Armstrong in 1920–21, Richie Benaud in 1958–59 and his brother Ian eight years earlier) to regain the Ashes at home.

Chappell in February 2002, after being elected into Australian cricket's Hall of Fame.

psychologist working with the West Indian team, suggested to Chappell that he wasn't watching the ball. 'Are you picking it up the moment it leaves the bowler's hand?' Webster asked.

Chappell pondered and then replied, 'I don't think so. I am picking it up somewhere along the line but I am not watching it out of the bowler's hand. How could I forget to do something so basic? I am not watching the bloody ball!'

Chappell went into the nets to fix the problem and then to New Zealand, where he scored a superb 176 from just 218 deliveries in the third Test, including exactly 100 in the first session of the second day, on a seamer's wicket. 'We were in big trouble,' recalls Jeff Thomson, who scored 25 out of an eighth-wicket stand of 84. 'Greg just said, "Hang around with me and watch this." So I stayed there, best seat in the house, Hadlee in his heyday, and Greg just belted him …'

Back in Australia, Chappell scored two centuries in the 1982–83 Ashes series, including his first Test century in the city of his birth, as he matched his elder brother's feat of leading an Australian team that regained the Ashes at home. Then it was to Kandy, to captain his country one last time, and then home for that final series against Pakistan.

Chappell believes he retired at exactly the right time. Such was his state of mind at the finish that there was little chance that he was going to look back, years later, and wish that he'd played some more. 'I overdosed on cricket,' he says. 'I got to the stage where I wasn't enjoying it, so I knew my time was up.' This is a man who, more than a decade earlier after being dismissed in a Test at Headingley, had been so distraught at getting out that he had shaken and slammed a locker in the dressing room so vigorously that it all but fell on top of him. It had mattered that much (though, of course, he had the self-control to not show any such emotion on the field). Now, he needed to announce his retirement before his final Test, when he required 69 runs to become Australia's leading runscorer in Tests and 72 for 7000 in Tests, to give him a clear incentive when he walked out for that farewell game. As history shows, a specific target was all he needed. The acclaim he received after that game, as cricket fans acknowledged his class and his contribution, was stronger and more heartfelt than the applause he'd received at any other stage of his career.

an education process, to work my way through it and to come out the other side. I was certainly a better player and hopefully a better person and a better captain for the experience.'

Brother Ian offers this perspective: 'I always thought that Greg's best captaincy was done when he was failing as a batsman in that period when he struggled for runs. Greg was so successful for such a long time that he thought that anyone who was failing was doing so because they weren't giving it 100 per cent. But he suddenly realised that you could be trying your guts out and still be failing.'

The solution to Greg Chappell's batting woes came at summer's end, when Rudi Webster, a sports

ALLAN BORDER: I learnt a lot from observing him, the way he went about his practice routines, the way he handled himself in public, the way he controlled the cricket team and matches in general.

GEORGE HEADLEY
Legend No. 18
The One Who Led The Way

GEORGE HEADLEY BECAME KNOWN as the 'Black Bradman', but Lord Constantine, one of the great names of West Indian cricket, reckoned that was wrong. When hypothesising one day over an all-time XI, Constantine said, 'We must choose Headley first, and then we must choose Bradman, for he is the White Headley.'

Elsewhere, Headley was known as 'Atlas', because of the way he carried the West Indies side of which he was always the key player. Since World War II, the cricket world has become used to hearing of exceptional West Indies batsmen — from Weekes, Worrell and Walcott, through Sobers and Kanhai, to Lloyd, Richards, Greendige, Richardson and Lara — so it is possible to forget just how important Headley was to the story of West Indian cricket. The truth is, despite all the brilliance and style and renown of the Windies champions that followed him, it could well be that Headley was the greatest of them all.

He was a small man, finely built, who usually wore his sleeves buttoned at the wrists and his cricket cap with its peak always on a jaunty angle. First impressions, which might have suggested he was fragile and easily swayed, were wrong. His cricket proved he was tough and strong.

ALAN DAVIDSON: A little man, a tiny man, but he had the eye. George Headley's eyes had something, a sparkle. Great batsmen have got great eyes.

In 1930–31, he was in Australia, facing a buoyant Australian team still celebrating Bradman's triumphant 1930 tour of England. He began with 25 and 82 against NSW, then made 131 against Victoria, out of 212, including a hundred before lunch. Hugh Trumble, at the time Australia's greatest ever wicket-taker, was heard to remark that Headley's century at the MCG was one of the best he had ever seen.

In the lead-up to the first Test, Headley played in matches in Sydney, Melbourne and Adelaide, thus showing his considerable talents to all the major figures in the Australian game, including the NSW captain Alan Kippax, the Victorian and Australian skipper Bill Woodfull, and Australia's leading bowler, South Australia's leg-spinner Clarrie Grimmett. It wasn't too difficult to work out that Headley was the visitors' best batsman. More difficult was developing a strategy to get him out. However, by the time of the first Test, a battle plan had been settled on.

Headley's early displays in Australia proved what a wonderful offside player he was. However, it was noted that his only regular shots to the onside were a hook shot, played with authority and control, and a leg glance. Rarely did he play the ball into the area between square-leg and mid-on. And rarely, whether hitting the ball to the off or leg, did he push forward, preferring to get right back onto his stumps to play with command off the back foot. Grimmett's greatest asset was his accuracy, born, says legend, from countless hours practising with his pet fox terrier in his backyard and at the local nets. A master of flight, he could land the ball on the same sixpence whether the delivery was tossed up or pushed through. The plan was for Grimmett to relentlessly attack Headley's leg-stump. The plan worked.

After Headley failed twice against this tactic in the first Test at the Adelaide Oval — caught first ball, close-in on the legside in the first innings, and stumped for 11 in the second — he dedicated his mind to fighting back. The West Indians stayed in Adelaide long enough after the Test to attend the first day of the Sheffield Shield match between NSW

and Grimmett's South Australia, and Headley took time to closely absorb the way Bradman and Archie Jackson attacked the leg-spinner while scoring big centuries. 'They played him one way all the time,' Headley recalled years later. 'Either back and forcing him away on the onside, or, when he flighted the ball, they left the crease and gave him the full drive.'

In the second Test, in Sydney, the Windies were caught twice on a sticky pitch and Headley made just 14 and 2 in the second Test. But at least he had not fallen to Grimmett. His resolve now was even firmer.

He decided he had to overhaul his game. One of his favourite shots to this point was a cross-bat slash through the covers, aimed at anything pitched wide enough of the off-stump to allow a free flow of the bat. But that shot had cost him his wicket in Sydney, when he dragged a wide one from Alan Fairfax back onto his stumps. Too risky, it was eliminated from his repertoire. Cover drives would only be played with a straight bat, hitting through the line.

Of greater concern was the fact that he could not drive through mid-on and mid-wicket as Jackson and Bradman had done. He decided to open his stance, with his left shoulder pointing to mid-wicket. Then, it was to the nets, for practice and more practice, until he felt he was sure he had the on-drive right. 'Those who toured with Headley,' wrote Michael Manley in *A History of West Indies Cricket*, 'recounted in loving detail how they were obliged to spend hour after hour in the nets bowling at him.'

'I have to make a century against Grimmett,' Headley said to his teammate and friend Edwin St Hill, before the third Test. Which he surely did, an unbeaten 102, in 247 careful minutes, out of a total of 193 in the West Indies' first innings. In the second innings he top-scored again, making 28 out of 148, before falling to the left-arm spin of Bert Ironmonger. Grimmett took nine wickets in the Test, but not Headley's.

'Satisfied?' asked St Hill afterwards.

'Not yet,' Headley replied, 'I have to master him.'

Again, the task was completed, as Headley made a superb 105 in the final Test, scored in just 146 minutes with 13 fours. Later, Grimmett commented, 'The little West Indian, George Headley, was a magnificent player, the best onside batsman against whom I ever bowled.'

In his book, *Australian Cricket: A History*, AG Moyes wrote, 'George Headley stood head and shoulders above his fellows in skill and in achievement and there is no question that he was among the three finest batsmen in the world at that time, the others being Bradman and Hammond. This grand little man excelled in onside play, but he was thoroughly well-equipped at all points, having patience and consistency as well as skill.'

One of Australia's craftiest captains, Herbert Collins, said in the 1950s that he 'never saw a batsman whose footwork excelled Headley's.' Australia's leading umpire at the time, George Hele, rated Headley one of the three best batsmen he saw at close quarters, Bradman and Hammond being the others. 'I was not alone in my judgment,' Hele recalled in 1974. 'Headley was a sound and glorious strokemaker, mostly to the onside …'

GEORGE HEADLEY WAS BORN in Panama, the son of a Barbadian father and a Jamaican mother, on 30 May 1909. His father was part of the large Caribbean contingent who'd been lured to Panama to help construct the Canal. When George was around 10 he was sent back to the West Indies, to the place of his mother's upbringing, to get an education in Jamaica's English rather than Panama's Spanish, and, as it happened, to become totally absorbed in cricket. Growing up under the tutelage of a beloved aunt, he graduated from playing informal matches with a bat hacked out of wood and sour oranges for a ball to junior cricket, and then to senior club cricket with the St Catherine Cricket Club in Kingston. There, legend has it, the shorts he wore reminded everyone that, despite his obvious batting and fielding gifts, he was still a boy among men.

A crucial point in the teenage Headley's cricket education came in early 1927, when the former England captain Lord Tennyson brought a team to play seven matches in Jamaica. Until he was injured in a car accident after the third game of the short tour, Ernest Tyldesley of Lancashire was in superb form, scoring hundreds in each of his first three innings. 'I watched him all day,' Headley recalled nearly 40 years later, as if Tyldesley was still giving priceless batting lessons in front of him.

A year later, the 18-year-old Headley was actually on the field against an English team. This side, again led by Tennyson, included the excellent Hampshire and England batsman, Philip Mead, but was weak in bowling, and Headley quickly found that he had nothing to fear. Earlier in 1928, his parents, having moved from Panama to the US, wanted their son to join them, to study dentistry. But there was a hitch in organising the necessary visa; in the meantime George was selected in the Jamaican team, and he stayed to make 16 and 71, 211, 40 and 71 against the Englishmen. All those runs convinced him to remain in Jamaica, to make his cricket fortune. Back in the UK, Tennyson was telling friends that he had seen a teenager who might develop into another Victor Trumper.

Late in his career, Headley recalled those matches: 'When I think of the things I used to do, I tremble and marvel at myself. There was a time in my early days when I was always down the crease and hitting the sightscreen first bounce over the bowler's head. I couldn't do it now if I tried. In fact, I could not try. I suppose it was youth and inexperience.

'But I have to say this,' he added, 'I used to go down and very rarely miss …'

Despite his runs, Headley was not in the West Indies team that toured England in 1928. The selectors suggested he was too raw, but more important surely was the fact that he came from Jamaica, 1500 kilometres away from the key on and off-field players in Barbados, Trinidad and British Guiana. Furthermore, the politics of having to fit enough players from each of the islands into the touring party, combined with the inherent prejudices of the day, made it very hard for a black working-class teenager, however gifted, to get a go.

These factors were reflected in a comment from Headley after his career was over. 'What is not generally realised is the almost inseparable obstacles the average cricketer in the West Indies has to overcome,' he remarked. 'I was comfortable compared to many I knew, whose lot was unemployment, half-fed, and in dire circumstances. The powers-that-be make no attempt to help such fellows, but, when the occasion demands, they are expected to bowl or bat for five or more days.'

> **TONY COZIER:** Headley set the example for those who followed, so that after the war, in the inter-territorial tournaments back home, you had the three Ws coming through, you had JK Holt from Jamaica. Headley was the one who led the way.

CLIVE LLOYD: I once spent a couple of hours with Sir Donald Bradman and he said he was 'in awe' of George Headley. He said he was a tremendous cricketer.

Headley enjoyed no more first-class cricket until early 1929, when he made 57 and 22, 17 and 43, 41 and 143 against another team from the UK. He was not yet 21 when 12 months later the Hon. Frederick Calthorpe brought an England team over for the first official Test series in the Caribbean. The tourists were hardly England's finest, but did include the 52-year-old left-arm spinner Wilfred Rhodes and the future bodyliner Bill Voce, as well as the veteran Test batsmen Patsy Hendren, George Gunn and Andy Sandham, and a wicketkeeper/batsman destined for stardom, Les Ames, who'd made his Test debut the previous English summer. Headley clearly enjoyed their company, scoring 703 runs during the series — 21 and 176 in Barbados, 8 and 39 in Trinidad, 114 and 112 in British Guiana (spearheading the West Indies to their first-ever Test win), then, finally and gloriously back home in Kingston, 10 and 223. Headley's 176 remains the fifth-highest innings by a batsman in his first Test. He was the youngest player, at 20 years 315 days, to score a Test double century until Pakistan's 19-year-old Javed Miandad scored 206 against New Zealand in Karachi in 1976–77. The 223 is still the highest score made by an individual batsman in the fourth innings of a Test.

His feats were celebrated *throughout* the Caribbean, but he was especially revered on his home island, where he gave hope and pride to the entire black community. In the same way Viv Richards and Andy Roberts gave validity to the cricket claims of Antigua, indeed the entire Leeward Islands, in the 1970s, so Headley boosted the status of Jamaican cricket in the late 1920s and 1930s.

The West Indies team that toured England in 1933. Standing (left to right): JM Kidney (manager), Herman Griffith, Cyril Christiani, Ivan Barrow, Ellis Achong, Cyril Merry, Manny Martindale, Archie Wiles, George Headley. Front: Jackie Grant (capt), Clifford Roach, Ben Sealey, Vincent Valentine, Oscar Dacosta.

Headley at Old Trafford in 1939, making 51 out of an innings total of 133. During this series, the West Indies had five innings and Headley top-scored in three of them, and was run out for 65 in a fourth through no fault of his own.

THE STORY OF THE West Indies in Test cricket in the 1930s, following the Australian tour of 1930–31, is one of defeats in England (in 1933 and 1939) and success against the Englishmen in the Caribbean (1935). It is also the story of the maturing of George Headley to greatness.

Before any of those Tests, in early 1932, an English team, again captained by Lord Tennyson, visited Jamaica to find Headley in colossal form. He made a century in each of the three first-class matches. At lunch on the second day of the first of these games Headley had smashed 344 and was still not out. With Clarence Passailaigue, who finished on 261 not out, he added 471 before the innings was closed at 5–702. He followed up with innings of 84, 155 not out and 140 — in all 723 runs in four innings at an average of 361.50. 'I cannot recollect such perfection of timing, nor variety of shots,' remarked Tennyson. This was hardly the strongest possible English side, but all bar one of the team were county cricketers and it did include three Test England captains and seven other former, current or future Test players.

In 1933, Headley finished third on the English first-class season averages, scoring 2320 runs at 66.28, including seven centuries. No one else in the West Indies touring team averaged even 40, only three averaged 30 or more. In the second Test, at Old Trafford, Headley hit a stirring 169 not out, having come to the wicket at 1–26 to bat through the rest of the innings, but the three-match series was lost 2–0, with England winning by an innings at Lord's and The Oval. On a personal note, Headley's tour was horribly marred by news of the death of his aunt, the woman who had raised him since the age of 10, in devastating floods that ravaged Kingston.

In the Caribbean in 1934–35, the West Indies won a Test series for the first time, beating a reasonably strong English side 2–1 in four Tests. The contest began in Barbados on a diabolical pitch and involved just 309 runs, two declarations, and an eventual four-wicket win for England. But much of the talk afterwards was about brave and extraordinarily skilful displays on the sticky wicket from Hammond for the visitors (43 and 29 not out) and Headley (44 run out) for the West Indies. Hammond's reputation on wet tracks was well established; he was regarded at the time as being at least the best since Jack Hobbs on such surfaces. However, Neville Cardus, as good a judge as any, would later rate the Jamaican ahead of him. Cardus especially remembered one Headley century on a dangerous pitch at Lord's, which, in the renowned writer's majestic words, was 'of such sure judgment and aim that if ever he edged a viciously spinning ball he did so with the edge's middle'. On poor batting surfaces, Headley's astonishing powers of concentration came to the fore. 'When I am walking down the pavilion steps, going into bat, if I met my father I wouldn't recognise him,' he explained one day. 'And once I am at the wicket I am concerned with nothing else but seeing the ball from the bowler's hand.'

In the critical final Test, in Jamaica, Headley came in at 1–5 on the first morning, and batted for over eight hours to finish on 270 not out. The West Indies passed 500 for the first time in a Test, and went on to win by an innings and 161 runs. The style of the win, and the fact that at the forefront of the home team's success was a local black man, was a cause of huge celebrations in just about every corner of the Caribbean, especially, of course, in Jamaica. George Headley moved from cricket to folk hero.

Headley played no more Test cricket until 1939, when he undertook his second trip to England with a West Indies team. By this time, he was a hardened professional cricketer, having first signed with Haslingden in the Lancashire League for the 1934 season — in the process doubling his annual income — and had evolved into one of the shrewdest thinkers in the game. Jeff Stollmeyer, only 18 on that 1939 tour but destined to become one of the most powerful post-war figures in West Indian cricket, said after his career had ended that Headley 'had a greater

DAVID FRITH: I met George in '81 and I'm so glad that I did. I spent the day with him in Bridgetown watching a Test match. He had a great sense of humour but he also had a sense of fair play. One of the English batsmen was given out to a patently poor decision and George said to me, 'Man, that spoiled it for me.' I was impressed by that, because it showed that he wasn't being one-eyed. He cherished cricket. Cricket had given him a lot and he'd given a lot to cricket.

tactical sense than any other cricketer with whom I played'. There was a time when Constantine was asked a question about cricket tactics, but was not sure of the answer. 'George will know that,' was his solution, said in a way that implied that no question was too awkward for the master.

However, in 1939, West Indies cricket was far from ready for a black captain. Indeed, Headley and Constantine had to fight hard for a suitable financial deal for themselves and Manny Martindale, the other black professional in the squad. Headley's negotiating skills had already been tested in 1936 when he refused to play for Jamaica against a touring Yorkshire team unless he was paid. Local authorities reckoned he owed it to the place where he learnt his cricket to play for nothing, but Headley argued he was a professional cricketer now, and thus entitled to, at the very least, a reimbursement of his expenses. The Yorkshiremen, after all, were receiving a fee for their appearances. All he wanted was justice. The officials, ever mindful of the impact on their box office if the leading man failed to show, finally gave way.

Throughout the England tour of '39, Headley was supreme, topping the first-class averages with 1745 runs at 72.60, including a century in each innings in the opening match of the series, at Lord's, the first man to do so in a Test at the ground. No other West Indian scored 1000 runs on the tour, or averaged even half what Headley did.

'Headley was, of course, the great batsman of the side,' wrote Cardus at tour's end. 'On all wickets he proved himself as reliable a batsman as any taking part in the game at the present time. He was almost exclusively a back-foot player, and it is only because of some doubt as to whether he can jump from the back to the front with Bradman's rapidity that I rank him second to Bradman as a punishing stroke player on good pitches. Headley would take his place automatically in the best company of any period of cricket's history.'

Headley was run out for 65 in the final Test, after a mix-up with Jeff Stollmeyer's elder brother Vic, who was making his debut. Vic actually went on to miss a century by just four runs, but it was the dismissal of Headley that people remembered. Sixty years later, when he died, in otherwise glowing obituaries Vic Stollmeyer was referred to, in somewhat sinister tones, as 'the man who ran out the great George Headley'.

IAN CHAPPELL: One of the best pieces of good fortune I have ever had was to meet George Headley. At the time, in 1973, things were a bit rough in Kingston, Jamaica, and we'd been told not to go out on our own at night. On this occasion we'd gone in the team bus to an official function at the Old Pavilion at Sabina Park. And there I'd met George Headley. I called over Rodney Marsh because George was telling lovely stories, not just about cricket, but about life.

We were really enjoying the conversation when our manager, Bill Jacobs, came up and said, 'C'mon, the bus is leaving.'

And I said, 'No Bill, I'm enjoying this conversation, I'm not leaving.' Rod said basically the same thing. 'But how are you going to get home?' asked Bill.

And I replied, 'I'll worry about getting home when George Headley gets sick of talking.'

THE SERIES ENDED ON 22 August, and within days the world was at war. For 30-year-old George Headley, the best days of his cricket career were over. However, there were still rare post-war glory days to come, most notably when he scored an unbeaten double century against Barbados in 1947. Named officially as captain of Jamaica that year, he made an immediate mark by successfully asking the Jamaican Board that his black teammates be given a transport and kit allowance. He also played three more Tests, spread over six years. In the first of these, against England in Barbados in January 1948, he was named captain, the first black man to lead a West Indies Test side, but he had to miss the rest of the series because of a back complaint.

Headley was no last-minute fill-in as captain, but at the same time his appointment represented more of a tiptoe than a giant leap, because a white man had already been named as skipper for the upcoming Tests in Trinidad and British Guiana. The intention was for Headley to return to the captaincy for the fourth Test in Kingston, but he was still injured and John Goddard, a white Barbadian, retained the job. The next time a black man led the West Indies in a Test match was at the Gabba in Brisbane in December 1960.

Headley went to India as a player in 1948–49, but injury kept him out of all but the first Test. In 1950, some campaigned for him to lead the West Indies in England, but the question of a fair tour's pay became an issue. Frank Worrell and Everton Weekes, both league cricketers in England, negotiated a deal reflecting their occupation as league cricketers and Headley wanted a similar arrangement. Instead the Board offered him amateur rates, £5 a week, so he

accepted an offer from the Bacup club in the Lancashire League to replace Weekes for the season.

The third Test of Headley's post-war career, in early 1954, was a peculiar affair, which came about when Jamaicans launched a fund to raise money to bring the then 44-year-old Headley back from England, where he was coaching and playing for Dudley in the Birmingham League. Without him, his supporters

The West Indies' Manny Martindale and Derek Sealy leave the field at the conclusion of the drawn third Test, at The Oval, in 1939. In a matter of days the world would be at war.

argued, there was no way a full-strength England team could be beaten. One thousand pounds was duly raised, and the great hero came home.

England captain Len Hutton remembered the fans watching the teams rehearse in Kingston. 'Then, twirling his bat, out strode George Headley, "King George" as he is known to his own folk,' Hutton wrote in his autobiography. 'George took his place in one of the vacant nets and, in a flash, interest in the MCC players vanished. They were deserted while the chattering crowds surged around the net where George, the island hero, was preparing for his practice knock. Every time George hit the ball hard the crowd cheered excitedly. By the way they behaved you would have thought that, at that very moment, he was completing another of his illustrious Test centuries!'

Sadly, the Test comeback lasted only one unhappy match, in which he appeared ruffled by the pace of Fred Trueman and Brian Statham, and by left-arm spinner Tony Lock's quicker ball, which at that point in Lock's career was as often thrown as bowled. Still, George Headley left Test cricket with his reputation undiminished and a record that remains one of the most impressive in the game's history. Consider the following:

- In the list of batsmen who have played 20 innings in Test cricket, only Bradman (99.94) and Graeme Pollock (60.97) have higher averages.
- Forgetting Headley's three post-war Tests, his Test career batting average is 64.70.
- Of the first 14 centuries made by West Indian batsmen in Test cricket, Headley made 10 of them.
- Headley hit eight hundreds against England in 16 Tests (including those two post-war Tests). Only four men in Test history, Bradman (19 in 37 Tests), Garry Sobers (10 in 36), Greg Chappell (nine in 35) and Steve Waugh (nine in 42) have scored more centuries against England. Arthur Morris (24 Tests), Viv Richards (34 Tests) and Allan Border (47 Tests) also scored eight.
- In the 35 Test innings in which he batted before the War, Headley top-scored 15 times.

Headley is also the only Test cricketer to have a son and a grandson both play Test cricket. Ron Headley played for the West Indies in 1973, while Dean Headley first appeared for England in Test cricket in 1997.

Critics trying to identify reasons for the decline of the current West Indies team recall fondly the days when Headley and his Jamaican teammates used to travel the length and breadth of the island, tutoring potential champions. His legacy was not merely his runs and his legendary status in the game; though he spent a fair proportion of his playing career in the English leagues, he always was a man of his people. Cricket-wise, his greatest gifts were a rare understanding of the art of batting and that, like Bradman, he was able to successfully blend the intricacies of modern technique with total concentration and a spontaneity and naturalness that were there from the start.

Headley died on 30 November 1983, recognised as a truly great cricketer and a trailblazer. He was an ambassador for his country, his team, his race and his sport, and was so successfully and consistently without ever once doing anything other than all he could. His prodigious achievements amid injustices prompted by race and class say as much about the man as do his professionalism and skill with the bat. He was no more the Black Bradman than The Don was the White Headley. They were both very much their own cricketers, their own men.

MICHAEL HOLDING: He was never one to speak of himself. If you got him in a quiet moment he would tell you a little bit about the cricket that he'd played and about the fast bowlers that he'd come across and that sort of thing, but he was very quiet, very soft-spoken. He was involved at my club in Jamaica, the Melbourne Cricket Club, and also with Lucas, another club. He spent a lot of time at Melbourne, and he was a good friend of my father, so I had close contact with him at the club. As a matter of fact, I got an award from him once at a Melbourne presentation; I don't remember exactly how old I was, maybe young teens, and when he presented me with that award someone took a picture. A couple of weeks later, he presented me with a copy of that picture and on the back of it he had written, 'Play cricket and see the world.'

SIR FRANK WORRELL
Legend No. 19
Capital S, Capital I, Capital R

SIR FRANK WORRELL'S CONTRIBUTION to cricket and the West Indies goes much further than any one Test series, even one as extraordinary as the famous 1960–61 series in Australia. He was a superb batsman, one of the game's most exquisite stylists. As the West Indies' first full-time black captain, he came to the post at a time when the islands' sense of one was fracturing, but managed to keep the team together as one true symbol of the entire Caribbean. As a statesman, his influence arguably went further than that of any other cricketer in history.

'He had great vision,' remembers Clive Lloyd, West Indies captain from 1974 to 1985. 'I always respected him because he was somebody you could talk to and he was always giving you the right sort of vibes. He was very intelligent, he knew the game inside out, and he could manage people. He was a great captain, a great player and a great manager …

'I thought that my job when I became captain was to continue his wonderful work.'

Born in Barbados on 1 August 1924, by the age of 13 Frank Worrell was a schoolboy prodigy. Soon he was in the Barbados team as a slow left-hand bowler, but one effort as nightwatchman was

> **ALAN DAVIDSON:** Frank Worrell — statesman, captain, player — I don't know of any player I respected as a person more from an opposition team. I've always said that he was capital S, capital I, capital R ...
> SIR Frank!

sufficient to convince his seniors that he was good enough to succeed higher up the batting order. At age 19, he hit a first-class triple century, 308 not out, for Barbados in an inter-colonial encounter with Trinidad in Bridgetown. Two seasons later, the Trinidadians were victims again, as Worrell hit 245 not out in Port-of-Spain. It wasn't just the runs he compiled either; it was the way he made them.

Such rungetting was phenomenal for one so young, but he also possessed a brave and worldly attitude that bordered — to the white upper classes at least — on insolence. Worrell knew his place from an early age, but he didn't like it and didn't accept it. 'A proud and strong-minded man, [he] had grown up increasingly restless under the unyielding racial hierarchy that was Barbados society,' wrote Michael Manley in *A History of West Indies Cricket*. Thus, in 1947, Worrell moved to Jamaica, which he believed was an island less dominated by racial divides.

Thirteen long years later, Worrell became the West Indies first long-term black captain, not just an interim compromise, after a drawn-out battle by many to reshape the thinking of a West Indies Board of Control that appeared to retain strong ties to the Caribbean's colonial past. First up, Worrell took the team to Australia in 1960–61, to mould it to his philosophies and encourage a brand of cricket that helped revitalise the sport in Australia. Not done with that, Worrell then went to England in 1963 and he and his players did the same thing there. Never did a more popular side ever venture to the old country. The Lord Mayor of London, in a post-tour reception, stated that 'a gale of change has blown through the hallowed halls of cricket'.

In this period, the Windies won nine Tests out of 15, a statistic that reflects the fact that Worrell was more than just a diplomat. 'The point is, if you weren't winning, people from different islands could say you weren't picking him or you weren't doing this,' says Clive Lloyd. 'But if you were winning you got rid of that. I learnt a lot from him in this respect, that winning was the key to being one entity, even though we were from different islands. Winning was the glue that kept us together.'

After the 1963 tour, Worrell announced his retirement and was promptly knighted, a genuine hero for all West Indian people, for all cricket people. Any number of paths were open to him, and it seemed likely that he would play a leading role in the social and political development of the Caribbean. His reputation as a soldier for the working class did him no harm with the masses, while his faith in what he knew to be right made him potentially a leader of rare passion and perception.

It was not to be. As manager of the West Indies team, he was in India in 1966–67, but fell ill and soon after was told he had leukaemia. The disease had taken a grip, and he died on 13 March 1967. Garry Sobers commented not long after his mentor's passing, 'With his death, cricket lost one of its greatest personalities, the West Indies lost one of its greatest ambassadors and I lost a friend, whose wisdom guided me for many years. I — and countless other West Indies cricketers, both past and present — owe to him a debt which can never be repaid; and the players of the future will benefit from his greatness, too.'

The West Indies teams that followed in Worrell's wake — including Sobers' great side of the mid-1960s and the all-conquering combinations so effectively led by Clive Lloyd and Viv Richards in the 1970s and 1980s — owed much to his leadership, his courage and his ability to recognise and promote all that is extraordinary about the cricketers and people of the Caribbean.

WORRELL'S GREATEST YEARS WITH the bat were between 1948 and 1950. He made his Test debut in the second Test of the 1947–48 home series against England, making 97 and 28 not out, and then followed up immediately in Georgetown by scoring his initial Test century, an unbeaten 131. On the strength of those two appearances, the English writer EW Swanton, who covered the series, commented, 'His [Worrell's] gifts exceed those of any modern player, Bradman and Compton excepted.' In the fourth and final Test Worrell made 38 (giving him a Test average at this stage of 147), but was overshadowed by an innings of 141 by Everton Weekes that was so explosive and impressive that after the series the England captain, Gubby Allen, rated Weekes fractionally superior to Worrell. Allen also noted the strength and batting skill of the West Indies' keeper, Clyde Walcott, especially one six Walcott hit, off the back foot, which flew back over the sightscreen off the medium pace of Ken Cranston. By 1950 in England, the 'three Ws' as they became known, all born on the same tiny island of Barbados within 18 months of each other, were major stars.

Only Weekes and Walcott toured India in 1948–49. Worrell stayed behind, after a dispute with the West Indian Cricket Board. His protest was not about the decision to make the white John Goddard captain over the great George Headley, but the root cause was the same. He had joined Radcliffe in the Lancashire League in 1948 — on a contract worth £500 — and as a professional cricketer had to consider his worth, while the authorities proposed a rate of pay that reflected the fact that blacks across the West Indies were paid a relative pittance. In standing firm on this issue, Worrell established himself as a man of principle, brave and able to make a stand of behalf of not just himself, but also his comrades. And the point had been well made. When the invitations went out for the 1950 tour of England, he and other professional players were offered better deals.

Before he set sail for England, Worrell did go to India, a year after the official West Indies made their tour, with a 'Commonwealth' team made up predominantly of professionals from the Lancashire League, which meant it contained Australians as well as Englishmen, and two West Indians — Worrell and the Jamaican opening batsman JK Holt. They played five 'Tests', winning one and losing two, with Worrell magnificent. Indeed, he always thought his finest batting came on this campaign, specifically in the unofficial 'Test' in Kanpur, when he made 223 not out and 83 not out. A year later, on a similar tour, Worrell took over as captain after the former Test keeper Les Ames became indisposed, and impressed all with his knowledge of the game and ability to bring the team together, despite the players' different nationalities and disparate personalities.

When Worrell arrived in England for the 1950 tour he was 25 years old, but his solitary official Test experience was those three home Tests back in

early 1948. He started the tour with a polished two-hour 85 at Worcester, but in the early weeks of the trip was overshadowed by Weekes, who made a double century against Surrey and then 304 not out against Cambridge University (in 325 minutes). However, while Weekes would score two more double centuries before the tour was through, the man recognised as the West Indies' No. 1 batsman by season's end was Worrell, largely on the back of a wonderful innings in the third Test, at Trent Bridge.

England had won the first Test on a turner at Old Trafford, but the visitors responded with some style at Lord's. Now, in the third Test, after England had been dismissed for just 223, Worrell took charge in a way that had Neville Cardus nostalgically dreaming of cricket's Golden Age. 'When Worrell played his wonderful innings of 261 at Nottingham,' he wrote at the conclusion of the series, 'many young onlookers were probably seeing for the first time some of cricket's greatest strokes; grand or brilliant or graceful in turn, with the fieldsmen helpless, even though placed defensively in far-flung positions …'

What Worrell did was totally dominate a day's cricket as few batsmen have ever done before or since. He came to the wicket early on day two with the score 2–95 and left early on day three at 4–521, having scored 261 runs out of 426 while for the most part Weekes, one of the most powerful hitters in history, was at the other end. Worrell was in after the nightwatchman Christiani was dismissed, and batted through the day, his team losing only one more wicket — opener Rae for 68 at 3–238 — before the close. At stumps, the score was 3–479, Worrell 239 not out.

Wisden was exhilarated by his 'scintillating style'. At one stage, the Englishmen tried to contain him by bowling well wide of the off-stump, so he stepped to the offside as the ball was delivered and pulled it through mid-wicket. The legside was strengthened, so Worrell stepped back and drove off the back foot, easy as you like, for four more.

ARTHUR MORRIS: Frank Worrell was a good strokemaker, beautiful cover driver. A very good player, very good batsman and a very handy bowler, too. And a first-class bloke.

MICHAEL HOLDING: A lot of the politics went out of cricket when Frank Worrell took over the captaincy. People learnt from Frank Worrell that it was more important for people in the Caribbean to think about the West Indies instead of thinking about the respective islands that they were from.

The West Indies won that Test by 10 wickets, and the fourth, too, by a prodigious innings and 56 runs, with Worrell making 138. This was the first time the West Indies had won a Test series in England, and to the people back home, cricket fans or not, it was proof that they were coming of age. Worrell's Test batting average, after seven Tests (all against England), was now a Bradman-like 104.13.

By the time his Test career was over, 13 years later, that figure had dropped to 49.48, but in that time the region he represented had moved dramatically towards independence and his reputation, as a leader and statesman, had flourished.

Frank Worrell and Everton Weekes resume their fabulous partnership at Trent Bridge in 1950. They would not be parted until they had added 283 runs for the fourth wicket. Worrell made 261, Weekes 129.

IN 1951–52, WORRELL FOUND himself in Australia, for the first series between these two teams in more than 20 years. Unfortunately, many of the Windies batsmen found it hard to come to terms with the pace of Lindwall and Miller. The series was closer than the eventual 4–1 result implies (Australia won one Test by one wicket, another by three), but the three Ws were restricted to just one century — Worrell's 108 in the fourth Test — and Australia's cricket writers were reserved in their praise. AG Moyes did describe a brief innings in Sydney as being of 'rare beauty', but also wrote, 'Worrell, classed as probably the most accomplished player in the world, took too long to realise that he had to fight to get runs. Not until he was twice out without scoring against South Australia did he settle down and fight. When he did he was grand. His century in the Melbourne Test was both skilful and plucky. His second innings of 30 was even better as an exhibition of batting …'

Through the remainder of the 1950s, Worrell played some but not a lot of Test cricket. At the same time, he continued in the Lancashire League, with Radcliffe and then Norton, and studied at Manchester University, where he obtained a degree in sociology. He began that course after the 1952–53 home series against India, when he made one score of 237 in Jamaica but averaged only 49.75 for the five-Test series. Against England at home in early 1954 he made another big hundred, this time 167 in Trinidad in the fourth Test, but was unproductive otherwise. Against Australia in the Caribbean in 1955 he hardly scored a run. It seemed his priorities had changed.

In England in 1957, under the leadership of John Goddard, he topped the tour batting averages, performing gallantly in the Tests, where he opened the batting and bowling in the final three matches. In the third Test, at Trent Bridge, he was on the field for the first 20-and-a-half hours of the match, bowling 21 overs, then batting studiously through his team's innings for 191 not out, then bowling seven more overs. He was a more defensive batsman now, because that is what the team's needs demanded. It seemed he may have refocused on Test

Worrell on his way to 160 against Cambridge University, early on the 1950 tour.

cricket, but after the tour he remained in England to concentrate on his studies — in essence taking an extended leave of absence from the first-class game. The inexperienced wicketkeeper, Gerry Alexander, succeeded Goddard as captain for the home series against Pakistan that followed, which featured some extraordinary performances from names soon to become household — Garry Sobers, Wesley Hall, Rohan Kanhai and Conrad Hunte. Sobers went past Len Hutton's world record Test score when he made 365 not out in Jamaica. Hunte scored a hundred in his first Test, 260 in his third. Hall took 46 Test wickets on a tour of India and Pakistan in 1958–59, in which Kanhai hit two Test double centuries and Sobers made hundreds in three consecutive Tests.

Sir Learie (later Lord) Constantine, the electric all-rounder of between the Wars, had always argued, though the results on the field often suggested otherwise, that the West Indies team was as good as any other. Why then, did they not win more often? The reason, in Constantine's eyes, was the quality of generalship. 'We need a black man as captain,' he would argue; not, he stressed, because a black man was automatically a better leader but simply because he felt the team, made up predominantly of gifted black players, needed a captain who understood them and could mould them into one unit.

Worrell was a man of grace and dignity, but he was also an ultra-tough character who believed totally in his judgment and sense of justice. He knew the value of winning, and he knew how to win. He was Sir Learie's captain. Gradually, the authorities were coming to the same conclusion. The fact that elsewhere in the community the black population was becoming more agitated accelerated this revolution.

Worrell had been invited to go to India and Pakistan as skipper in 1958–59, but was so engulfed in his studies at Manchester University that he could not go. When an English team came to the Caribbean in 1959–60, Worrell had been away from the first-class game for two years, but felt that with his degree completed he was now able to return to Test matches. That he was not offered the captaincy did not matter. Short of practice at the first-class level, he was still able to score 197 not out, adding 399 with Sobers (226) in the first Test, in Barbados. During a series that featured some acrimonious moments on and off the field, he must have absorbed the sense of rebellion against colonial rule and demand for change throughout the islands. By the time the team was picked for the Australian tour in 1960–61, the demands for Worrell to be handed the reins were irresistible.

IN CRICKET TERMS, THE series in Australia was a thriller, which went right down to the very last ball. More important than any result, though, the teams reminded the cricket world of how the game should be played.

Worrell had become West Indies captain at a time when cricket appeared to be in serious decline. Too many captains seemed preoccupied with avoiding defeat. Since Len Hutton had won a series in Australia in 1954–55, at least partly by slowing over-rates, paying spectators were seeing fewer deliveries in

Worrell bowling spin against Surrey in May 1950. Later, he would become a medium pacer sometimes called upon to open the bowling in Test matches.

a day. In 1957, Peter May and Colin Cowdrey had saved a Test against the West Indies spinners, Sonny Ramadhin and Alf Valentine, by using their pads rather than their strokes. In 1958–59, Ashes cricket reached its lowest ebb when England's Trevor Bailey batted 458 minutes for 68, and then Jim Burke, the Australian opener, sought to outdo him, making 28 in more than four hours. As sport entered the television age, cricket seemed headed for the dark ages. Into this environment stepped a new West Indian leader, who decided that his team would play Test cricket in the same spirit that had invigorated the game of his youth, not just for entertainment's sake but also because, in his eyes, this was the most likely way to win. In Richie Benaud, he found an Australian captain equally as pragmatic and ambitious. As a consequence, the 1960–61 series in Australia quickly evolved into the most exciting in history.

Most importantly for the future of West Indian cricket at the highest level, Worrell transformed the way the West Indies team approached its task. Early reports of the 1960–61 tour suggest that the Windies team lacked cohesion and discipline. They were entertaining, but hardly competitive. Matches were lost against Western Australia and NSW. Catches were dropped, field placements changed by all and sundry, absurd shots played.

'Gradually Worrell harnessed all this enthusiasm and put it to good use,' wrote AG Moyes in his book of the tour. 'He alone became the leader and his word was accepted. He had the affection and confidence of his team and gradually they began to improve. They began to play as a team, they learnt to fight as a team. There were no divisions in the side. But to the end they did not leave their laughter at the gate as they took the field. They took it with them. The spare parts came together to form a machine which could function efficiently under the guidance of a master mechanic.'

Worrell had the misfortune to make a pair in one day during the second Test, at the MCG. However, at other times his batting was superb. Often forgotten amid all the excitement of the Tied Test is that Worrell himself made 65 in both innings, the first a crucial knock that gave Garry Sobers great support on the first day after Alan Davidson had reduced the West Indies to 3–65. In Sydney, he made a sparkling 82, playing one drive that Davidson remembers to this day. 'It went between cover and extra cover for four,' he explains. 'The follow-through … he finished on one knee! Gerry Alexander still says that that is the greatest moment he's ever known in cricket. "I've seen it all," he said.'

For his captaincy, his batting, but most of all for his dignity, integrity and approach to the game, the Australian Cricket Board of Control introduced 'The Frank Worrell Trophy' at the end of the series, for future competition between the two teams.

In the last over of the Tied Test, perhaps the most famous over in cricket history, two episodes say much about the character of the West Indies captain. With an over to go and Wes Hall to bowl it, Australia needed six to win with three wickets in hand. The first ball struck Wally Grout just below the stomach, fell at his feet, and Richie Benaud ran though for a very painful 'leg' bye. Five to win. Worrell went up to his fast bowler and said quietly but firmly, 'Wes, whatever you do, I don't want you to bowl a bouncer to Benaud.'

Hall ran and bowled, straightaway, a bouncer, 'delivered,' Benaud wrote later, 'with every bit of speed and power the big fella could muster'. The Australian captain went for the hooked four that would have all but won the game, but edged a catch through to Alexander. The game was back on an even keel. A slightly thicker edge, though, and the ball would have flown over the keeper's head. The excited West Indians gathered around, anxious to assure each other they could still win this amazing game. Hall, adrenalin pumping, accepted the joy and congratulations of his teammates, until Frank Worrell spoke, like a schoolmaster about to discipline a wayward student: 'Wes, what did I say about not bowling a bouncer?'

Four balls later, and the scores were tied. One run would give Australia victory. As Hall walked slowly back to his mark Worrell came over from mid-on. He knew Hall would give his all to the next delivery, his job was simply to make sure his bowler was focused on the job at hand. 'Remember, Wes,' Worrell said quietly, 'if you bowl a no-ball, you'll never be able to go back to Barbados.' Hall recalls that this reminder so terrified him that he made sure to put his foot a good yard behind the crease. Worrell had, through that not-so-gentle advice, reinforced to his fast bowler that he was doing this for more than just himself, and in the process removed any negative thoughts from Hall's mindset — other than the possibility of a no-ball, which was easily prevented. The ball was bang on line, Kline,

Worrell on the attack at Edgbaston during the 1957 Test series. He made 81.

the No. 11 batsman, turned it to Joe Solomon at square-leg, who made the throw that made history.

The immortal photograph of the final dismissal of the Tied Test shows a scene of great excitement. Bails are flying, arms are punching the air, joy is mixed with pandemonium. Except at the bowler's end, where Worrell, calm as you like, has run in to take a throw, should it come to that end. Solomon's throw hit the stumps 22 yards away, so the captain could objectively survey the scene. Nothing fazed him.

It was the same at the Lord's Test of 1963, which again came down to the final over, when England's second-last pair reverted to sneaking short singles wherever they could find them. But then they pushed their luck too far, as Derek Shackleton prodded a ball to Worrell close in on the legside and took off. A run out seemed certain, but how overpoweringly tempting must it have been for Worrell to impulsively shy at the stumps? Instead, he calmly gathered the ball and outran Shackleton to the bowler's end.

'I go back to 1951, when they were in Sydney, and I was collecting autographs,' says David Frith today.

IAN WOOLDRIDGE: I remember during that 1963 tour, the way he looked after his team. Basil Butcher had made a very big hundred at Lord's, and I'd been talking to a West Indian journalist who told me that Butcher was the son of a cane cutter. I wrote this in a story, not realising the implications. What I'd done was actually very offensive to the West Indians. That evening, middle of the evening, I got a phone call from Frank. He said, 'We've got a bit of a problem here, can you come up to the hotel?'

I don't know another captain who would do this. When I got to the hotel, Frank said, 'Let's go up to Basil Butcher's room.'

And he left me there with Butcher, to sort it out. Butcher explained that I had inadvertently been extremely rude. And I apologised. That's how Frank settled the problem. It didn't go on, it didn't fester. He had that wonderful wit about him.

'They [the West Indies tourists] got into the team bus and I thought I'd missed him. I had Weekes and I had Walcott, but I badly needed Worrell. It's fifty years ago now, but I can still picture that dreamy face looking down from the high window of the bus. I just stretched up with my book and he reached down and he wrote, "With best wishes, Frankie Worrell", and then he handed it back down with another dreamy smile. I was won from that moment on.'

Frank Worrell, soon to be Sir Frank, always made it look easy, but it rarely was. Purely on talent, runs and wickets, there is no doubt there have been greater cricketers. Not too many, but enough to keep him outside a Top 25 as elite as *ESPN's Legends of Cricket*. But add up all that he was and all that he did in his 42 years, when you consider his God-given cricket ability *plus* his strength, his personality and his influence, and a strong case can be put that Sir Frank Worrell was *the* most notable cricketer of the 20th century.

Worrell and the England captain Ted Dexter (left) wait to be interviewed by Peter West on the *Sportsview* TV program at the conclusion of the 1963 series in England, which the West Indies won 3–1.

Getty Images

SIR LEONARD HUTTON
Legend No. 20
Born to Bat

YORKSHIRE IN THE 1930s was the finest provincial cricket team in all England. It might have been the best in the world; certainly a match against NSW or Victoria would have been a beauty. So powerful were they, and so gritty was their brand of cricket, that the acclaimed writer Neville Cardus suggested only half-jokingly in 1938 that the Yorkshire team should be picked to represent England.

As assured as the county's form in this decade was its place in cricket history: 14 times county champions before 1930 and the birthplace of champions such as Bobby Peel, the Hon. FS Jackson, George Hirst, Wilfred Rhodes and Herbert Sutcliffe. Yorkshire won the county championship seven more times between 1931 and 1939, on the back of grand performances from a host of full England caps, including Sutcliffe, Maurice Leyland, Bill Bowes, Hedley Verity and, from 1934 on, a right-handed opening batsman named Leonard Hutton.

Long before he made his first-class debut at age 17, the old sages and champions who saw the boy Hutton in the Headingley nets knew he was going to be a good 'un. Sutcliffe, for example, wrote with excitement, 'He is a marvel — the discovery of a generation.' They can be a conservative lot in the north of England, so there was little chance such praise was going to be wasted.

For 20 years in big-time cricket, Len Hutton confirmed time and again that he was just about the most technically-correct batsman in history. He allied his technique to a natural Yorkshire grit and a great hunger for runs and success. Hutton was a batsman with all the shots, but he played the attacking ones less often than a Bradman, a Headley or a Compton. On the rare occasions when he did throw caution to the wind, such as at the Sydney Cricket Ground in 1946–47, he produced cameos that left eyewitnesses grasping for precedents. Through the immediate post-war years he carried a weak English batting line-up, and then became the pivotal figure in England's return to cricket pre-eminence in the mid-1950s. In doing so, he became one of the most important figures in the history of the game.

Fred Trueman called him 'a batsman whose bat had no edges'. There was often such a certainty about Len Hutton's batting that when he did fall short his supporters were gobsmacked. When Ray Lindwall knocked Hutton over second ball with a fast yorker at Headingley in 1953, the start of a day's play that ended grimly at 7–142, the talk at stumps was not of the dire batting or England's poor position, but simply, still, of that first over. Jack Fingleton wrote of the quiet as Hutton walked off: 'This silence reminded me of the one at Melbourne when Bradman was out first ball to Bowes in 1932.' Only the great ones make that sort of impact when they fail.

In 79 Tests, Hutton scored 6971 runs at 56.67. That puts him sixth on the all-time English Test batting averages (based on a minimum of 20 innings played), behind Sutcliffe, Eddie Paynter, Ken Barrington, Wally Hammond and Jack Hobbs. He did all this even though he lost six years of his career to World War II, and was hampered by injury thereafter. When international cricket resumed in 1946, Hutton's left arm was three centimetres shorter than his right, and he was forced into premature retirement a decade later by a chronic back injury that had caused him pain for years.

W HEN HUTTON FIRST ARRIVED at Headingley, he was met by Hirst, then the Yorkshire chief coach. 'You're the boy from Pudsey, aren't you?' he said. 'Keep your eyes open and you'll be all right.' In actual fact, he was from a little village called Fulneck, near Pudsey, but Pudsey (the birthplace of Sutcliffe) was close enough. Early on, young Len was hopelessly overawed by his seniors in the Yorkshire XI. Bowes described the teenager as 'a slow-speaking, naïve lad who found it hard to believe what he was watching'. Patrick Murphy, in his book *The Centurions*, tells the story of 81-year-old Bobby Peel slowly advising, not long after Hutton had made his Test debut against New Zealand in 1937, 'Once you start thinking about getting quick runs you're finished. We don't expect fireworks from an opening batsman.'

In his debut Test, Hutton scored 0 and 1, but he set things straight in the second Test, at Old Trafford, when he made an even 100. Twelve months later, he started his Ashes career with another century, in a Test in which he was one of four Englishmen to get to three figures and Australia's Stan McCabe made his immortal 232. Hutton then failed at Lord's, missed the Leeds Test,

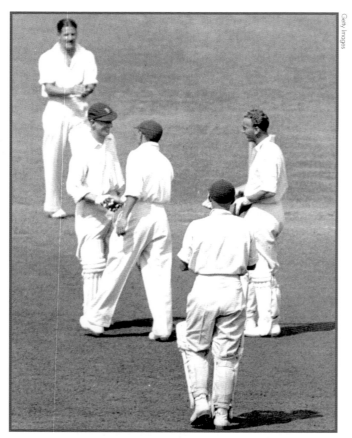

Australian captain Don Bradman is the first to congratulate Len Hutton after the Englishman passed Bradman's previous record score in Ashes Tests of 334. Soon after Hutton broke Wally Hammond's Test record of 336 not out.

but came back at The Oval to compile one of cricket's most famous long innings.

Hutton had been at Headingley in 1930 to see Sir Donald Bradman make 334. He could scarcely have believed then that he would be the batsman to break that Ashes record score, or when he did surpass it that the first person to shake his hand would be The Don. The previous Test record was actually 336 not out, made by Wally Hammond in New Zealand in 1933, but everyone seemed to focus on Bradman's innings as the one to beat. Hammond, Hutton's captain here, reputedly sent him to the middle with orders to 'stay there forever'. The wicket at The Oval, it must be said, was as flat as the track on which Mark Taylor made 334 at Peshawar in 1998, which is very docile indeed, and the Australian attack, O'Reilly and Fleetwood-Smith apart, was hardly Test class. McCabe, a great batsman who bowled medium pace a bit, opened the bowling, and his partner was Mervyn Waite, who took one Test wicket in his life. But though England batted for 335.2 overs, and the ball refused to turn, O'Reilly was relentless, and at the end Hutton felt as if he'd earned every run. He wrote later of having nightmares about O'Reilly after batting for two days for exactly 300. On the third day, just before he passed Bradman's record, he walked slowly down the pitch to his partner, Joe Hardstaff, and asked to be protected from the great Australian leg-spinner, while O'Reilly, for his part, never forgot how, with Hutton closing on 334, he deliberately bowled two no-balls. The logic was that the idea of a free hit might break Hutton's concentration — the score was long past 700, so anything was worth a try — but Hutton played a straight, defensive bat. His focus could not be disturbed, not even by charity.

In all, he batted for 13 hours and 17 minutes for 364 until he hit an exhausted catch to cover. 'Every day we went out there Hutton was batting,' remembers the Australian opening bat Bill Brown. 'Or that's what it seemed like. He was very watchful, didn't play any risky shots, he played steadily up and down the line, handled O'Reilly very well. He was there all of the first day, all of the second day and part of the third day.'

England went on to 7–903 before Wally Hammond declared not long after Bradman was carried off with a suspected broken ankle. With both the Australian captain and Fingleton disabled, Australia disintegrated to be all out for 201 and 123,

ALAN DAVIDSON: He had the most relaxed stance, and as the bowler ran in he didn't move. But just as you were about to deliver the ball his back foot would start to go back and across, back into a position where he gave himself that extra half a yard to watch the ball. Len had so much time to play shots. He was the most technically correct player I've ever seen.

leaving England with the biggest winning margin in Test history.

Cardus described the immediate reaction after Hutton went to 336: 'The scene which now occurred moved even the hardened critics. Thousands of happy people stood up and cheered. Somebody with a cornet began to play "For he's a jolly good fellow" and the crowd took up the refrain in that evangelical tone which the British public invariably adopts when it lifts up its heart to rejoice in song.'

The attention that innings won did not sit easily with the shy Yorkshireman, and he was unable to produce big scores on the tour of South Africa that followed; instead, he kept making promising starts then getting out. It took a while, too, to overcome the unsettling effect of being knocked unconscious by a bouncer in the lead-up to the first Test. Back in England, though, against the West Indies, Hutton played a Test innings of a very different kind from that Oval marathon, sharing a glorious stand of 248 with Denis Compton in just 140 minutes. Reflecting the fact that Hutton was now cast in a defensive mould, the rave reviews were for Compton, even though it was Hutton who did the bulk of the scoring during the partnership.

This problem he faced was purely about image; no one doubted Hutton's ability to make runs. By the end of that Windies series, he'd made 1345 Test-match runs in 13 Tests at 67.25, a better average than Sutcliffe or Hammond, better even than George Headley. 'In 1939 he was said to be batting as well as any Englishman, or possibly any batsman, could ever have batted,' reflects David Frith. Of course, the war came at a bad time for everything, but from a cricket perspective it came at exactly the worst time for 23-year-old Len Hutton. The loss of potentially the best six years of his cricket life was one thing; the physical disability he carried afterwards was another.

JACK BANNISTER: Technically, he was England's best batsman post the Second World War. In the 1950s he was regarded as head and shoulders above anybody.

'After my arm was fractured, I had to move my left hand farther round the handle of the bat, so that the back of the hand faced cover-point,' Hutton wrote in his autobiography. 'I never played so well again. In 1939 I could play every stroke in the book as and when I wished. After my disablement, I could not play certain shots the way I would have liked.'

Eventually, after trying lighter bats and various methods, Hutton accepted that he would have to eliminate the hook and the pull shots from his game, which left him short-handed to confront the twin fast-bowling threats of Lindwall and Miller. In Australia in 1946–47 he was also hampered by the chronic back complaint that had first annoyed him in 1938, but that did not prevent him playing one of the finest short innings in Test history. In 24

minutes, just before lunch, after Australia had declared their first innings at 8–659 (including innings of 234 from Bradman and Sid Barnes), Hutton scored 37 in a manner that had the old-timers in the SCG Members Stand recalling the days of Trumper. AG Moyes, wrote, 'It was a glorious piece of batting, a choice miniature that I shall carry with me always. The Hutton who scintillated that day was one of the masters.' The revelry ended when, forgetting himself, Hutton tried to hook a Miller bouncer, but he could not hold onto his bat, and it slipped away and hit the stumps.

In 1947, he scored a century in his first Test at Leeds. The fact that it took a decade for him to play a Test on home turf in Yorkshire underlines the opportunities he missed because of the War. Twelve months later, he was dropped from the England XI, in a decision as absurd as any made by a cricket selection committee. Apparently, there was some disquiet at the way he coped with Miller and Lindwall's bouncers at Lord's, but no one stopped to acknowledge why that barrage had come in the first place: Hutton's wicket was always the one the Australians wanted most. He

Hutton jogs up the steps of The Oval pavilion in 1938 after being caught at cover for 364.

Getty Images

The Australians race in for souvenirs at the end of the first Ashes Test of 1950–51. At the bowler's end, the undefeated Len Hutton looks on, having played one of the finest innings in Ashes history.

missed only one Test and at The Oval, in Bradman's farewell, top-scored in both innings, including a superb lone hand in the first when he was first in and last out for 30, in an innings total of 52.

'I should hate to think,' Hutton wrote after he retired, 'any batsmen in future might have to stand up to the number of bouncers Cyril Washbrook and I had to cope with during our partnerships in the 1946–47, 1950–51 series in Australia and against the Australians in England in 1948.'

From the other end, Miller conceded, 'I must say that when I bowled at Len I felt a sense of personal grudge I have never known against any other batsman. Ray [Lindwall] did too. I suppose Len suffered a greater barrage from the two of us than any other player in the world. We both put in that little bit extra against Len, and he had to take it time after time.'

It probably wasn't until 1950 that, from the perspective of his technique, Hutton truly came to terms with his war injury and was confident in his ability to handle the short ball. With the retirement of Bradman, and despite the claims of the Australians, Morris and Harvey, the West Indians, Worrell and Weekes, and his countryman, Compton, in most people's eyes Hutton was now the best, most dependable batsman in the world. His ability to watch the ball right onto the bat, his perfect balance,

ARTHUR MORRIS: Hutton had a great ability to push the rising ball between mid-wicket and square-leg and get his single. One day in 1946, on a wet pitch in one of the Test matches, Cyril Washbrook was up the batting end, having to play the other seven deliveries. Balls were flying all over the place, up about his head, and Cyril was hooking at them. At one point, Len pulled me over and said, 'Cyril can't get ones …'

and skill as an opener in letting the ball come to him, finding the gaps, getting the ones, piercing the field, made him No. 1. 'He picked the length of the ball up remarkably quickly,' recalled his young Yorkshire teammate Ray Illingworth. Hutton rarely left his crease to play the spinners — inspiring future generations of English batsmen to do the same — but his mastery of them was amply demonstrated against the West Indies' Ramadhin and Valentine at The Oval, when he batted through England's first innings for 202 not out. In Australia straight after, he was easily the batsman of the series, averaging more than double that of any other batsman on either side.

His 62 not out in Brisbane was perhaps his most notable innings of that 1950–51 tour, though he also became the first Englishman to bat through a Test innings twice when he made 156 not out, out of 272, in Adelaide. The knock at the Gabba was made batting at No. 8, out of an innings total of 122, circumstances brought about by a shocking wet pitch which made batting impossible for everyone else. Held back until what proved to be the last day, but in at 6–30 chasing 193 to win, he made some spectacular strokes (including driving Lindwall, cool as you like, over cover's head for four) and added 45 for the last wicket with Doug Wright, of which Wright scored 2. 'England lost, in the final analysis, because they only had one Hutton,' wrote Fingleton. 'Just half another Hutton would have been sufficient.'

This was the eighth Ashes Test England had lost since the War, out of 11 Tests. By series' end they'd lost three more times, but in the final encounter of the summer, in Melbourne, England finally achieved their first win against Australia since The Oval in 1938. Hutton, unbeaten on 60 out of 2–95, hit the winning runs.

By the time the Australians returned to England in 1953, Hutton was England captain. He was clearly the best candidate for the captaincy, but no professional had ever been appointed to the post. In the late 1930s, Hammond had become an amateur so he could take the job, but Hutton quietly but firmly informed the powers-that-be that he had no intention of doing likewise. He was appointed anyway, though one imagines that at least some of the MCC committeemen would have agreed to the move grudgingly, while one or two long-departed former Presidents would have been turning rather furiously in their graves.

He brought to the captaincy the pragmatism, caution and desire to win that typified his cricket. The pace salvos he faced immediately after the war seem to have made him a strong advocate of fast bowling, and as young firebrands such as Trueman, Brian Statham and Frank Tyson emerged, Hutton's tactics quickly revolved around them, to the point that in Australia in 1954–55 he even cast aside the medium pace of Alec Bedser, who had, for much of the previous decade, been England's primary bowling hope.

Hutton also, unashamedly, slowed his team's over-rate, which conserved his bowlers' energies, frustrated his opponents and, because he won, bred a generation of imitators who robbed spectators of overs for decades. But the critics of Hutton as a captain had to focus on the downside of his methods, because his results were outstanding. He never lost a series, from the home series against India in 1952 until his retirement from Tests after the 1954–55 tour of Australia and New Zealand; his career record as a Test captain reads 23 matches for 11 wins and only four losses.

There is no doubt that the pressures of the captaincy played hard on Hutton, especially in the Caribbean in 1953–54 and in Australia a year later. The West Indies tour took place amid a backdrop of political agitation and crowd disturbances, and he was not helped by some ill-judged antics from his own men, and his inability or desire to play the diplomat, but he still led his team back from 0–2 down to square the five-Test series. He led from the front, scoring 169 in Georgetown, as England won the third Test by nine wickets, and 205 in Kingston in the final Test, which was won by exactly the same margin. This was the first time an England captain had scored a double century away from home.

In Australia, Hutton won some notoriety by sending his opponents in at the Gabba in the first Test, after going into the match with an all-pace attack, and losing by an innings and 154 runs. Still, he held his nerve, refused to lose faith in his fast-bowling strategy, and was able to sit back and watch his pacemen, led by Tyson, win the next three Tests.

Though he came home with the Ashes retained, there is no doubt that this tour wore Hutton down completely. His batting fell away noticeably, as the stress ate away at him. In Sydney, having made the agonising decision to drop Bedser after years of loyal service, he forgot to tell him. In Melbourne, with the series now level at one-all but the captain pleading exhaustion, he had to be talked into playing. Then in Adelaide, when his men needed only 94 in the last innings to win, he could not be shaken from his despondency after Miller snared a couple of early wickets. He was sure his team was going to lose, but the always more cavalier Compton told him not to worry and then went out and got England home.

Hutton was a serious cricketer, and cricket was to him a serious business, but perhaps at least some of his hardness was simply shyness, misconstrued. He was a better player and strategist than communicator. Keith Miller told the story of an English player complaining about Hutton on the 1954–55 tour. 'It's not what he's said,' the player said, 'it's what he hasn't said.'

'There was a lot of the Bradman in Hutton's cricket make-up,' Miller reckoned. 'He made up his mind quietly on his own and took few people into his confidence. He believed — as did "Braddles" — that when you get your opponents down you should drive them into the ground. When he was out in the middle he rarely spoke to an opponent. It was not in him to give his opponent an inch on the field.'

Yet if Hutton was often dour, he wasn't always dry. Compton recalls batting with him amid great tension against the Australians at Lord's in 1953: 'When Len called me down the wicket I thought it was to point out a trap being laid for me, or to watch for Lindwall's yorker, a word of encouragement, or at least a tactical profundity from that shrewdly analytical cricket brain of his. Instead, I was surprised to hear, "What are we doing here? Surely we could have got better jobs than this?"'

Hutton made 145 in that match, an innings Cardus thought 'one of the most regal and highly pedigreed ever seen in an England-Australia Test match'. That 1953 series, which ended in an emotional English triumph in the year of Queen Elizabeth II's coronation, was the highlight of Hutton's career. Batting-wise, he was dominant again, averaging 55.37 in a series in which no other batsman from either side could do better than 40. The only Ashes series England had won since 1928–29 was the controversial bodyline engagement of 1932–33, and the joy felt when Compton and Bill Edrich steered the home side to victory at The Oval spread across the land. At the ground, the playing area was covered by a sea of humanity within minutes of the winning run being hit, and as the

Hutton leads England onto the field at The Oval in 1952. This was the first season in which England were captained by a professional.

players gathered on the pavilion balcony, the crowd chanted for the England captain. From a team perspective this time, it was 1938 all over again.

'Ladies and gentlemen,' Hutton responded nervously, 'it is very difficult to know what to talk about on these occasions. But I must say how happy and thrilled I feel about it all today. And, of course, for it to happen here at The Oval, which has always been a happy hunting ground for me, is marvellous …'

Lindsay Hassett, the beaten but dignified Australian captain, followed with a much more entertaining speech, but Hutton would not have cared for being beaten in the public-speaking stakes.

> **ARTHUR MORRIS:** What Len did was decide to slow the game up and not take any risks. I can understand that a bit because he was the first professional captain of England and I think a few people at Lord's were just waiting for him to make a decision that could have been a disaster.

DAVID FRITH: Hutton was born to bat. I saw him in Sydney on two tours and he quickly became a hero because he batted so artistically and, of course, there was the underlying story that he was a frail man who'd been damaged during the war with that broken left arm. And he was taking a lot of very fast, hostile bowling. The interesting thing about Len, as I got to know him, was his personality. He was by nature very reticent, reluctant to talk in almost all situations. But I loved the man and to me he was the greatest batsman England ever produced. I didn't see some of the others but I saw him and I've got memories still.

A Test earlier, he'd been criticised for his negative tactics, when he had Trevor Bailey bowl wide down the legside to curtail a late Australian run chase. Hutton argued that in this instance he was merely doing what the Australians had done in the past — 'One side cannot afford to be magnanimous in Test cricket if their opponents are not prepared to be the same,' he said. But it did look ugly. However much he enjoyed the cheering of the crowd, Len Hutton preferred success over popularity.

Though Hutton sought no fanfare on his retirement in 1956, he was almost immediately knighted, purely for his services to the game, the second Englishman — after Sir Jack Hobbs — to be so honoured. He finished his career with 40,140 first-class runs at 55.51, while his Test aggregate included 19 centuries but only two sixes. His Test record score survived until 1958, when Garry Sobers went one run better (Brian Lara went on to 375 in 1994). Sir Leonard also had the pleasure of seeing his son Richard play five Tests for England, in 1971.

Despite the knighthood, despite all the runs, the stress, the controversy and the glory, throughout his career and life Len Hutton remained very much his own man. In his tribute to Hutton in the 1991 *Wisden*, following the great batsman's death on 6 September 1990, the veteran writer John Woodcock wrote, 'Hutton retained until the end the unassuming manner which marked his apprenticeship.' He was still, in many ways, the boy from Pudsey.

Sir Leonard Hutton with Lady Hutton and sons Richard (left) and John, after the former England captain was knighted at Buckingham Palace in July 1956.

Getty Images

WASIM AKRAM
Legend No. 21
They Called Him King

*I*N THE EYES OF so many, from Sir Donald Bradman to Sachin Tendulkar, Wasim Akram is the greatest left-arm fast bowler the game has ever seen. Certainly, cricket has never had a *great* bowler with as quick and deceptive an arm-action as Wasim. The only man to take 400 wickets in Tests and one-day internationals, Wasim burst onto cricket's international stage in 1984 as a teenager and stayed there — swaggering, brilliant, imposing and controversial — for the following 16 years.

From a short run, he would bustle into the wicket, to deliver the ball with a whippy whirr of an action that had the ball at the batsman quicker than could be believed. If speed was his surprise, swing was his art; no bowler in history has been better at getting the old ball to swing, or more adept at swinging the new or old ball at pace. He was made for one-day cricket. With the bat, left-handed again, he was a colossal hitter, holder of the record for most sixes in a Test innings, but able to bat for long periods if the game demanded it. Like all the great bowling all-rounders, there seems little doubt that he could have been a successful Test batsman if he had devoted himself to that craft. The downside of his career was that he was often a focus of controversy, with

> **SACHIN TENDULKAR:** Wasim Akram is an exceptionally talented all-rounder who can change the game with his bat and the ball.

unsubstantiated accusations thrown at him in regard to ball tampering, match-fixing, undermining captains, feigning injury. Yet he kept bouncing back, never beaten, to play more than 100 Tests and more than 300 one-day internationals. Wasim Akram led Pakistan in 25 Tests, for 12 wins.

Two episodes, a decade apart, say much about Wasim's approach to his sport. The first occurred at the Adelaide Oval in early 1990, when he scored his maiden Test century. To do so he had to overcome the tireless and outstanding Australian paceman, big Merv Hughes.

'I was cocky as a batsman and that would annoy Merv,' Wasim told Hughes' biographer Patrick Keane in 1997. 'I decided to play my shots, and everything I was hitting was going for four and Merv was getting very annoyed. We wanted him annoyed and I hit him for a three and he was standing right in the middle of the pitch. He didn't move and I had the bat up I so I just banged into him, with the bat under his ribs. He was very strong and didn't move, and there were a lot of words exchanged. It was quite funny.'

Test cricket is a tough, competitive arena, but the battles are there to be enjoyed. And its traditions and its heroes are to be respected. In November 1999, at the Gabba in Brisbane, the local crowd gave the recently retired Ian Healy a long and heartfelt reception when he was paraded around the ground during the tea interval of the first Test. Wasim led his team out onto the field, to publicly acclaim the great wicketkeeper. The two teams had had their spats on and off the field over that decade, but they had enjoyed many tough games as well and Wasim wanted to acknowledge another battle-hardened warrior. The gesture said something of the respect for Healy in the world game, and much about Wasim Akram too.

Wasim Akram, not long past his 21st birthday, at the 1987 World Cup.

WASIM HAS BEEN A performer of the highest skill, a remarkable entertainer and prolific wicket-taker. That he managed to step out of his mentor Imran Khan's considerable shadow and forge his own reputation on cricket's loftiest stage is proof of his greatness. Yet above all else was his resilience, which came through time and again, whatever the hurdles put in front of him. There is no better way to illustrate Wasim Akram's cricket greatness than to journey through his long, astonishing and tempestuous career . . .

Born on 3 June 1966, a year and a day after the Waugh twins, Wasim's first-class debut came in the opening match of New Zealand's tour of Pakistan in late 1984. He was conscripted from a training camp for talented teenagers to play for a Pakistan Cricket Board Patron's XI and marked his first appearance by taking 7–50 and 2–54. Kiwi opener John Wright remembers him well: 'We played a President's XI in Rawalpindi and it was Wasim's first first-class match. They had another young fellow, who was their big hope, who ran in off the sightscreen. But who we took notice of was this young 18-year-old who had a pair of sandshoes on, was very thin, ran off about 15 paces and hit the bat a lot harder than the other fellow. How could he get the ball through so quickly with such little apparent effort? He was just a left-arm natural.'

With that, he was in Pakistan's one-day team, for a match against the tourists in Faisalabad, but his impact was negligible — four overs for 31 runs, after Zaheer Abbas had given him the first over, in a match reduced to 20 overs a side. That was Wasim's only clash with the New Zealanders during their tour, but straight after he was facing them on their turf, where the two teams played Test and one-day series in January and February, and it was here that he really began developing his reputation. He was, though, surviving purely on talent.

'The only thing I knew about bowling was to run in and bowl line and length, and that was all I was trying to do when I got some wickets on my first outing for Pakistan,' Wasim recalls of his early days as an international cricketer. Rather sheepishly, he confesses that he did not know what a yorker was. Still, while his Test debut, in the second Test, in Auckland, passed almost without notice, a fortnight later, in Dunedin, he announced himself to the cricket world by becoming the youngest bowler to take 10 wickets (5–65 and 5–72) in a Test.

From there it was on to Australia for the World Championship of Cricket, a one-day tournament featuring all the then Test-playing teams, staged to celebrate the 150th birthday of Victoria. Wasim had not bowled in any of the one-day internationals in New Zealand, and had no success in Pakistan's opening match in Melbourne, but against Australia at the MCG he was magnificent, taking the first five wickets of the home team's innings (including Kepler Wessels, Dean Jones, Allan Border and Kim Hughes) and finishing with 5–21 from eight overs. He was four months short of his 19th birthday.

Scoring runs and taking wickets against the powerful West Indies at home in 1986 and against England away in 1987 boosted Wasim's ever-growing reputation, while his significant role in Pakistan's dramatic first-ever series win in India in 1987 was rewarded with a popstar-like reception back home. Throughout, he absorbed the nuances of the game from hardheads such as Imran and Javed Miandad, and observed how tough and bitter Test cricket can be, especially in series home and away against England that were rife with personal clashes and umpiring controversies. Of Imran, he says today, 'Obviously, he had a lot of influence on my cricket. I met him at the right time of my career and learnt a lot from him. He has been with me all the way through, and still is.' When Wasim made an

immediate impact at Lancashire after signing with the county for the 1988 season, his rating as one of world's most influential cricketers was assured.

In 1989, Wasim took his first hat-trick in international cricket in a Champions Trophy match against the West Indies at Sharjah. Within 12 months, he'd done it again, in the final of the Austral-Asia Cup against Australia, a game in which he also hit 49 from 35 balls. His batting prowess was evident again in the Nehru Cup final, against the West Indies in Calcutta in 1989, when he slammed Viv Richards high over the mid-wicket fence to give Pakistan a thrilling victory with one ball to spare.

One memory Wasim, the free spirit, retains of his maiden Test century against Merv Hughes and co. in Adelaide in 1989–90 is of hitting the off-spinner Peter Taylor for a big six one ball after Imran had told him to be careful. Others are of his utter mental exhaustion after batting for four hours, and his admiration for his captain, who batted twice as long. Trailing by 84 runs on the first innings, Pakistan slumped to 5–90 before Imran and Wasim added 191 in a minute more than four hours, to help force a draw. Wasim's 123 came from 195 balls. At season's end, *The ABC Australian Cricket Almanac* thought Wasim to be the 'world's premier all-rounder', which echoed an opinion Imran stated often during the tour. And it definitely wasn't just about scoring runs. A decade later, Ian Healy rated Wasim as the fastest bowler he ever faced, based purely on one spell he survived during that 1989–90 season.

In five Tests at home in 1990–91 (he missed one through injury), Wasim took 31 wickets, including one remarkable spell in Lahore against the West Indies when he became the third bowler in Test history to take four wickets in five balls. Then in 1992, he played a key role in Pakistan's triumph in cricket's fifth World Cup, in Australia and New Zealand. He was the leading wicket-taker in the competition, with 18 at 18.78, and in the final, after Pakistan had reached 6–249 (Wasim 33 from

ALLAN BORDER: Wasim Akram's the cricketer I'd like to come back as if I had another go at it — six foot four, running in and bowling with a real good pace, being able to field as well and also being able to handle the bat.

The man of the match in the 1992 World Cup final, straight after the game with Javed Miandad.

Of Lamb's dismissal, Wasim reflects, 'That was the wicket to remember for me. We played the match of our life.'

To this point, Wasim's career was relatively controversy-free. He had been fined £1000 by Lancashire after an on-field temper tantrum in 1991, while suggestions of ball-tampering had been raised after a New Zealand tour of Pakistan in 1990. Things were about to change. The 1992 World Cup was Imran's farewell, and Javed Miandad was in charge when Pakistan returned to England for a five-Test series later in the year. This was an often bitter series, marred by a whispering campaign that culminated in Lamb making a specific ball-tampering complaint via a newspaper article. Wasim and his fast-bowling partner Waqar Younis had mastered the art of 'reverse swing', of getting an old ball to swing with even more effect than any new one. To do so, the bowling side worked on the ball, to moisten one side with spit and sweat while keeping the other as dry, and thus as light, as possible. The allegations centred on the means used to roughen one side of the ball, but no official charges were laid and the Pakistanis strongly maintained their innocence. Pakistan won the series 2–1, and Wasim was named one of *Wisden*'s five cricketers of the year.

Dickie Bird remembers a discussion he once had with the late Peter Burge, Australian batsman of the 1950s and 1960s and later ICC match referee. Burge had seen all the great fast bowling duos from Lindwall and Miller and Tyson and Statham to Lillee and Thomson, Roberts and Holding, and Ambrose and Walsh, and he rated the Wasim and Waqar show the best of them all. There are many across the cricket world, and especially in England, who share this view. In the 49 Tests they bowled in tandem between 1989 and 2001, the partnership of Wasim and Waqar took 472 wickets, almost 10 wickets per match.

In a one-off Test in Hamilton in the first week of 1993, Wasim (5–45) and Waqar (5–22) bowled Pakistan to a stunning 33-run victory after New Zealand had been set only 127 to win on a flat batting wicket. Wasim rates this one of the two best Test victories he has been involved in, alongside the thrilling 16-run defeat of India in Bangalore back in 1987. He passed 1000 Test runs in Hamilton, a match played in the middle of Pakistan's involvement in the one-day World Series tournament in Australia, where they performed dismally. Afterwards Javed Miandad

19 deliveries), he dismissed Ian Botham for 0, then came back for a second spell to get Allan Lamb and Chris Lewis with successive deliveries, to earn the man-of-the-match award. All fans of Pakistan cricket remember those wickets of Lamb and Lewis. With England fighting back at 4–141, Imran asked his strike bowler to bowl as quick as he could. 'Forget about wides and no-balls,' he said to his protégé, 'bowl as quickly as you can.' Wasim charged in, and bowled Lamb with a ball that swung from the leg to hit the off bail as the batsman tried to defend, and then embarrassed Lewis with a cruel, inswinging yorker which rebounded off the batsman's pads to hit the off-stump.

BOB WILLIS: To generate that amount of pace off a 15-yard run-up is almost unheard of; his control of both seam and swing is quite remarkable.

DAVID LLOYD: I was very privileged to work with Wasim Akram at Old Trafford as coach of Lancashire. He was the overseas player and I made him captain as well. I could see this guy as a natural leader. The Lancashire players had a nickname for him, they just called him 'King'.

He had a magnificent team meeting the first time he was captain. We're out there doing the prelims, a bit of catching here and there, and warming up generally, when he said to me, 'Get the team in the dressing room, I want to talk to them.'

So I said, 'Everybody in the dressing room, everybody in, sit down. Right captain, over to you.'

And his only words were, 'Come on, I have a dream.'

He just left it at that. There's a pause and I've gone, 'Right then, well come on.' And out they went. They'd follow him anywhere. He was a great leader.

was sacked as captain for a one-day tournament in South Africa and tour of the West Indies that followed and Wasim was his replacement. However, the new leader's reign started badly in Grenada when he was one of four players arrested and charged (but later cleared) with 'constructive possession' of marijuana.

Leading Pakistan is the toughest assignment in international cricket. In less than three years, from the start of 1993 to late 1995, Javed Miandad, Wasim Akram, Waqar Younis, Salim Malik, Ramiz Raja and then Wasim again captained the national side in a Test match. He had lost the captaincy initially after a number of team members mutinied; his reinstatement came after Ramiz had been held responsible for an embarrassing home loss to Sri Lanka. Wasim's shoulder injury, which prevented him bowling in the second innings of the second

England opener Alec Stewart avoids a Wasim riser at The Oval in 1996.

TIM DE LISLE: A lot of professional bowlers are excited about Wasim Akram in a way that they're not excited by people of equal excellence, such as Glenn McGrath or Shaun Pollock. There's a fire and a genius about him, so skilful, and an excellent batsman as well when he puts his mind to it. A really compelling figure.

Test after Pakistan had gained a 110-run first-innings lead, and forced him to miss the decider, was a key factor in that loss.

Wasim began his second stint as captain in Australia in 1995–96, where he was forced to play diplomat as the Australian media focused on Salim Malik's alleged attempts to bribe Shane Warne, Tim May and Mark Waugh when the Australians were in Pakistan in 1994. The cricket itself was not encouraging for the tourists, at least early on, but they did come back to win the third Test, at the SCG, and then won a one-off Test in New Zealand, where Wasim took five wickets in a Test innings for the 20th time in his career, in his 67th Test. However, immediately after came the World Cup in India, Pakistan and Sri Lanka, which turned into something of a personal disaster for Wasim. He strained a side muscle while batting in the final group game, against New Zealand, and did not recover in time to play in the quarter-finals. When that match was lost — to India, to the grave disappointment of all Pakistanis — by 39 runs, many angry patriots turned on their side. Wasim was accused, by one of his neighbours among others, of betting on his side not to retain the Cup, and distraught fans burned an effigy of their captain when the team's plane was diverted to Karachi to avoid the angry mob who had turned up at Lahore airport to make their displeasure known. Others went to his home, to throw rocks and eggs, and one man tried to file charges in the Lahore High Court, accusing the team of deliberately losing.

'When you lose, especially in our part of the world, lots of people don't realise it's only a game,' Wasim explains. 'You're trying your best, but somebody has to win, somebody has to lose. Believe me, whenever I go out, it doesn't matter if I'm playing for a club side, if I'm playing a game of table tennis, a game of golf, I love to win. Everybody loves to win, nobody wants to lose, and — especially if you play for your country — how can you even think of losing purposely?

'Obviously the pressure was there at the time. I was down very low at the time but my family came in, my parents, my wife, they were really backing me up. They know what sort of person I am, they know how much I used to enjoy playing for my country. They just said, "It doesn't matter, don't read the press, just go on, try your best, work hard." I've been through a lot, but in the end it was worth playing for Pakistan even with all the controversy I have been through.'

Wasim dropped out of one-day tournaments in Singapore and Sharjah after that World Cup letdown, but came back to lead Pakistan to a 2–0 series win in England. This was the third straight time Pakistan had beaten England in England. In the third and final Test, he became the 11th bowler and second Pakistani (after Imran) to take 300 Test wickets. Then, back home, he smashed one of Test cricket's most memorable innings, against Zimbabwe in Sheikhupra, breaking a number of records. He scored 257 not out, his highest score in first-class cricket and the highest ever made by a No. 8 in Test cricket. His 12 sixes were the most ever hit by an individual in one Test innings, breaking Wally Hammond's old mark (10, for England v New Zealand in 1933). And his eighth-wicket partnership of 313 with Saqlain Mushtaq was a Test record. As if to emphasise his all-round greatness, he followed up by taking 6–48 and 4–58, his fourth 10-wicket haul in Tests, in the second Test of the series. Unfortunately, things then turned sour for the great all-rounder. When the shoulder injury flared again, Wasim opted for surgery, which fixed the damage but in the process he learnt that he was suffering from diabetes. His ailments meant he could only play one first-class match for Lancashire in 1997, and when he finally returned to the Pakistan Test XI in October of that year he was no longer captain, that role now being held by Saeed Anwar.

Meanwhile, the match-fixing controversy bubbled along and then came to a raging head. Having regained the captaincy for the November-December home series against the West Indies, Wasim led his charges to a 3–0 series whitewash, the first two Tests being won by an innings. But in the Singer Champions Trophy in Sharjah that followed straight after, Pakistan lost to England after appearing to be in control, and Wasim was slandered across the country. Fed up with the innuendo, Wasim resigned the captaincy and announced he was contemplating retirement. The Pakistan selectors showed their hand when they dropped him for the tour of South Africa and Zimbabwe, on 'fitness grounds'. In reality, an inquiry had been instigated by the Pakistan Cricket Board, which eventually saw Wasim cleared of all match-fixing charges, and at that point he was recalled for the latter part of the African tour.

Through 1998, Wasim played Tests under a succession of captains — Rashid Latif, Aamir Sohail, Saeed Anwar and Moin Khan — before once again the Pakistan Cricket Board turned to him. He was given the job for the away series in India, a potentially explosive contest, and immediately led Pakistan to a thrilling 12-run victory in Chennai.

The home team came back to level the series in the second Test, but that match was notable for Wasim because he surpassed Imran as Pakistan's leading wicket-taker in Tests by taking his 363rd wicket in his 85th Test.

Originally, this was to be a three-Test series, but instead the third match, in Calcutta, became the opening encounter of an 'Asian Test Championship'. It attracted a record estimated attendance of 465,000 over the five days, and featured some ugly crowd scenes generated by the controversial run out of Sachin Tendulkar and then by the fans' awful realisation that their heroes were tumbling to defeat. The final of the championship was played in Dhaka in Bangladesh, and Pakistan defeated Sri Lanka by an innings, with Wasim becoming the third bowler to take a second hat-trick in Test matches, and the first to take Test hat-tricks in more than one country. He had snared his first Test hat-trick against Sri Lanka earlier in the championship, in Lahore, becoming the first bowler from the Indian sub-continent and the first captain to do so.

After Pakistan won a one-day tournament in Sharjah, thrashing India in the decider, Wasim was assured of the captaincy for the 1999 World Cup, where he led his team all the way to the final. Unfortunately, they played poorly in this match, losing to Australia by eight wickets, and slurs were cast on the team's commitment and stones were

Wasim at Lord's in 1998, after leading Lancashire to victory in the NatWest Trophy final.

thrown at the captain's house in Lahore. There was a sad predictability about it all. The team was obliged to sneak back into Pakistan amid high security, and yet another inquiry was established to probe the team's performance.

Pakistan played well under Wasim's captaincy in one-day tournaments in Toronto and Sharjah late in 1999, but were then outclassed by Steve Waugh's team in Tests and one-dayers in Australia in 1999–2000. Wasim's only personal highlight came in Sydney during a one-dayer, when he took his 400th ODI wicket, the first man to do so.

After this, he quit as captain and dejectedly asked the Pakistan Cricket Board to never consider him for the job again.

> **JOHN WRIGHT:** He probably had a bigger repertoire of what he could do with the ball than anyone else that I've ever struck. He could swing it and seam it, and he did it at pace.

Getty Images

Wasim traps Nick Knight lbw in the second Test of the short England–Pakistan series in 2001. This was the great Pakistani's final Test at Old Trafford, where he had developed such an affinity with the Lancashire faithful over so many years.

but could not prevent Jimmy Adams and Courtney Walsh adding 19 runs for the last wicket to give the Windies a 1–0 series win. Then came his 100th Test and his 400th Test wicket.

'I rate him higher than Courtney Walsh, Sir Richard Hadlee and Kapil Dev,' remarked Imran, when asked at the time to compare Wasim to the other three bowlers who had broken the 400-wicket barrier at that time. 'He is like Hadlee, but has more variety than any of these three greats of world cricket.'

Through the second half of 2001 and into 2002, the signs were strong that Wasim's career was winding down. He was no longer a certain selection in either the Test or one-day side, so it came as little surprise when he announced in late April 2002 that he had decided to retire after cricket's eighth World Cup, scheduled to be held in early 2003.

'I don't think there can be a better occasion to hang up my boots,' he told the *Dawn* newspaper. 'It is my dream to help Pakistan regain the Cup and return home with pride.'

The wickets in Pakistan are rarely pace-bowling friendly but Wasim Akram has prevailed over them. Of all the men to play 100 Tests, he was clearly the fastest; this fact, and all his runs and one-day international performances are a wonderful tribute to his durability. He might have suffered a number of injuries, many hastened no doubt by his unique bowling action, but they never stopped him for long. Though the match-fixing allegations were never proven, the pressure they created was often relentless, as was the impact of the complicated politics that lurk just below the surface of Pakistani cricket, but they did not detract from his greatness as a cricketer, nor his toughness — mental and physical — as a sportsman. India's Ravi Shastri is another who rates Wasim the best left-arm paceman of them all. He goes even further. 'I know there is Tendulkar, there's Lara, there's the likes of Steve Waugh and Shane Warne,' he says. 'But Wasim Akram, for me, was the cricketer of the 1990s.'

The stress seemed never-ending. In the next 18 months, Wasim had to suffer the indignity of being fined for failing to co-operate fully with Pakistan's major anti-corruption inquiry, a charge he denied and a fine he immediately appealed against. When asked why he kept playing, given the strains of the scandal, he replied flatly, 'I have not done anything wrong.'

On the field, he was still capable of outstanding performances, such as in the pivotal third and final Test of Pakistan's tour of the West Indies in 2000, in Antigua, when he took 11 wickets (6–61 and 5–49),

ANDY FLOWER: We've had quite a few tussles. I think he is a superb performer. He has a great skill of swinging the ball prodigiously at pace, without any discernable change of action. And he's equally good with the new ball and the reverse-swinging old ball.

He has all the skills and the power to take a wicket at any stage of a match. Even on a flat deck, even with a 40-overs-old ball, he's still dangerous. He's always dangerous.

KAPIL DEV
Legend No. 22
Lionheart

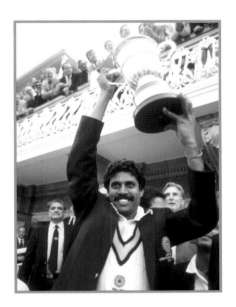

EFORE KAPIL DEV, INDIA did not produce great pace bowlers. Batsmen, yes. Spinners, absolutely. Occasionally, you might see a pace bowler worthy of the adjective. But *great* pace bowlers, never. The general consensus was that the hot and dusty conditions in India would not allow it. Until, suddenly, in the late 1970s a genuinely talented opening bowler came to the fore. Fans and teammates could not believe it. When, in November 1994, Kapil Dev became the leading wicket-taker in Test history, many rated his greatest achievement as being the 217 wickets he'd taken on home soil. That certainly will be his most enduring pace-bowling record.

'My effort should disprove that India can't produce fast bowlers,' Kapil said with a weary smile when he took over from Sir Richard Hadlee at the top of the Test wicket aggregates.

He'd been born nearly 36 years earlier, on 6 January 1959, in Chandigarh. Having first emerged in local cricket at age 13, at 15 he was one of 24 teenagers invited to a live-in coaching camp at the Cricket Club of India in Bombay. Conditions were hot and sultry and the boys were asked to labour long and hard. At lunch on day one of the camp, Kapil was astonished to discover that the menu involved no more than two dry chapattis and some vegetables. 'I am from the North,' he angrily told organisers. 'I work hard and bowl fast. I am hungry when I finish. I could eat a horse and all you can give me is two chapattis.'

Officials could not believe it. One asked, like Mr Bumble in Dickens' *Oliver Twist*, if he wasn't happy with the arrangements. 'No sir,' the young Kapil stood his ground, 'I am a fast bowler and I need more nourishment.'

'This is India, young man,' the official shot back. 'There are no fast bowlers in India.'

For more than 20 years, Kapil Dev used that remark as a spur. He'd prove them wrong.

HE MADE HIS FIRST-CLASS debut in November 1975, seven weeks before his 17th birthday, taking 6–39 for Haryana against Punjab in a North Zone Ranji Trophy match. Kapil received early rave reports for his bowling, though it was also noted that in a university match he scored a triple century. By the start of the 1978–79 season, he was recognised as the most promising all-rounder in all India.

Thus, his Test selection was not unexpected. Kapil made his Test debut in October 1978, in the opening Test of the first India–Pakistan series for 17 years. To their countrymen's great joy, Pakistan had much the better of the rubber (when Pakistan won the second Test their government declared a national holiday) but even though Kapil was only 19 years old he was not overawed as India's counter to Imran Khan and Sarfraz Nawaz.

Initially, Kapil was a little tentative, and failed to take a wicket in Pakistan's first innings of the series, which only ended when Mushtaq Mohammed declared at 8–503 (Kapil 0–71 from 16 overs). India closed their innings too, at 9–462 (Kapil 8). But then, as if to announce his arrival to the world, the teenage fast man let his inhibitions go, firing in a

bouncer at Pakistan's opening bat, the old pro Sadiq Mohammed, brother of the Pakistani captain. This was no ordinary Indian bouncer, such as Sadiq had seen in the first innings, but a fizzer that whooshed past Sadiq's frantic, late duck out of the way, after which the batsman looked quickly up with that where-on-earth-did-that-come-from look on his startled face that all quick bowlers love. He called for a helmet. Which was lucky, too, because next over another quick one clattered into it with a clang that echoed around the ground.

The slips fieldsmen fought hard to contain their glee, while the keeper, Syed Kirmani, not a man prone to get over-excited, clapped his gloves and called out, 'One More!' And why not? It was so nice not to be on the receiving end.

It was a sight, as Sunil Gavaskar explained years later, 'Not only one for sore eyes, but also for cracked fingers and the badly bruised chests and thighs that we had suffered over the years.'

Not long after, Sadiq edged Kapil to second slip, where Gavaskar took the catch to give his young firebrand his first Test wicket. 'The sting of that catch stayed on the palm for a couple more overs,' Gavaskar recalls. This was happening, remember, on a wicket that had given up nearly 1000 runs at more than 50 runs a wicket. And Sadiq was a seasoned campaigner who had scored Test centuries against, among others, Lillee, Thomson and Richard Hadlee.

In the third Test, Kapil smashed a half-century from 33 balls. Then, in the home series against the West Indies that followed straight after, he cemented his reputation. The fourth Test, on an unusually bouncy wicket in Madras, developed into what *Wisden* called a 'bumper war'. But whereas in the past India had gone into such battles hopelessly undermanned, this time they held their own, and won the match by three wickets, thanks to Kapil's belligerence, seven wickets and 26 not out at the death. In the fifth Test, he hit his first Test century, a blazing 126 not out from 124 balls. The series ended 1–0 in the home side's favour; India had a new hero.

When, less than 12 months later, Kapil took his 100th Test wicket, he'd been a Test cricketer for just a year and 105 days. He was the youngest to get to this mark (21 years, 25 days, beating Australia's Graham McKenzie), and the quickest (beating Ian Botham, who'd taken two years, nine days). Two days later, he became the youngest to score 1000

Test runs (eclipsing Javed Miandad). He was playing in his 25th Test. More important than all these statistics was the pride he gave his countrymen; India had a fast bowling all-rounder to match the likes of Botham, Imran and Hadlee.

'My philosophy is simple,' Kapil once said. 'Play to win. Attack. Get your runs and your wickets. Never stop trying. Hit the ball, over the slips, over the ropes. Runs on the board count.'

'A great cricketer, a lionhearted cricketer,' says Ravi Shastri. 'The kind of pitches we played on in India in the 1980s were flat, tailor-made for batsmen, but Kapil never once complained. He just bowled over after over. He would come in day after day and deliver the goods for India. If you were talking about 80 overs before the new ball, rest assured that Kapil would bowl 25, even 35 of them, and then he would come back again.

'If you saw him fielding in the outfield, he was a real natural. Of the four great all-rounders of the '80s — Kapil, Botham, Imran and Hadlee — I think Kapil was the most naturally talented.'

The famous Kapil Dev leap, a feature of international cricket throughout the 1980s.

ON HIS RETIREMENT, KAPIL was asked to nominate his most fondly remembered bowling efforts. He came up with five, as follows:

India v Pakistan, fifth Test, Madras 1979–80

India won this Test by 10 wickets, giving them a 2–0 series win. It was their first success in a rubber against their neighbours since the inaugural confrontation between the countries in 1952–53 (when India won 2–1). The victory in January 1980 was due in no small part to Kapil, who took 11 wickets in the match (4–90 and 7–56) on a wicket that was by all accounts placid. As well, he scored 84 from 98 balls in India's first innings.

India v Australia, third Test, Melbourne 1980–81

India had been thrashed in the first Test, and almost lost the second, before coming back in stunning fashion at the MCG to square the series. Australia led by 182 on the first innings, eventually needed only 143 to win and Kapil was apparently out of the Test with a groin injury. But on the fifth morning, after the home team lost 3–18 on the fourth evening, Kapil demanded a pain-killing injection and then strode out to take 5–28 from 16.4 overs, bowling unchanged for nearly three hours, as Australia crashed to 83 all out.

India v England, first Test, Lord's, 1986

This was the first time India won a Test at Lord's, in their 11th Test at the ground. It was also the first time India had won a Test under Kapil's captaincy, in his 21st Test as leader. He had sent England in, seen his batsmen glean a first-innings lead of 47,

RAVI SHASTRI: He hit the ball as hard as anyone I've seen in world cricket and, when on fire, would pull out shots that were out of the ordinary. We'd see him sometimes batting in the nets and practising defence and we would all laugh. Because this is something that he's just not going to do when he goes out in the middle the next day.

and then bowled magnificently to take 4–52 as England crumbled to 180 all out. The target was 134, and at 5–110 there were some jitters in the Indian dressing room. But the captain came out to slam 23 not out and the game was won, fittingly with a big six from the captain.

India's tour of Australia, 1991–92

Many believed that by the early 1990s Kapil had lost his outswinger. Some blamed the delivery's demise on his advancing years, others thought the constant grind of one-day cricket — where the lack of a slip field and the need for economy makes the inswinger more useful — might be the cause. But in Australia the outswinger returned, and Kapil took 25 wickets, including the 400th of his career (Mark Taylor in the fifth Test in Perth).

India v Sri Lanka, second Test, Bangalore, 1993-94

The final wicket of this match, won by India by an innings and 95 runs, was the 431st of Kapil's career, bringing him level with Sir Richard Hadlee as the

Kapil at Tunbridge Wells in 1983, playing arguably the greatest innings in World Cup history.

game's highest wicket-taker. It was the 27,056th delivery of his Test career, in his 129th Test. Nine days later, in Ahmedabad, at 10.34am and with all of India either watching or listening, he dismissed Sri Lanka's Hashan Tillekeratne to go past Hadlee. After one more Test, in New Zealand, and two more wickets, the great adventure was over.

Surprisingly, Kapil's top five does not include his best innings return in a Test — 9–83 at Ahmedabad against the West Indies in 1983.

Kapil was never express in the way of Andy Roberts, Jeff Thomson or Michael Holding, but in the first half of his career at least he was more than fast enough and had that rare ability to hit the bat surprisingly hard. His greatest asset was that late outswing, which came from a side-on action that could grace any cricket textbook, and the nous to effectively vary pace and length. He was a much better batsman than his final Test-match average (31.05) suggests. And, most certainly, he was one of the most courageous and durable of the great Test cricketers: from 1978 to 1994 he never once missed an international match because of injury.

To some degree, Kapil's fast bowling reputation was tarnished by the latter stages of his career, when he was more medium pace than strike force. Years of carrying the load had worn him down — he never had a Thomson, a Miller, a Holding or a Waqar Younis at the other end. Instead, he shared the new-ball with 20 different partners during his Test career, none of whom threatened to take the first over off him. His 300th Test wicket arrived in Sri Lanka in January 1987, but it was five more years before he reached 400 and two more before he broke the world record.

'THE CROWN SITS PRECARIOUSLY on the head of a king,' Kapil wrote in 1985. As brilliant, devout, loyal and popular as he was, he could not stay clear of the sense of intrigue that often pervades Indian cricket. This sometimes had him in conflict with the other legend of the game in India in the 1980s, Sunil Gavaskar, and more than once through the 1980s the duo swapped the captaincy. Kapil, aged 24, took over from Gavaskar in 1983 and almost immediately led India to their most famous triumph, in the World Cup final at Lord's. Before 1984 was out, Gavaskar was back in charge.

Andy Roberts is lbw to Kapil, the West Indies are nine wickets down, and the 1983 World Cup final is almost won.

But when the Sri Lankans came to India in August 1985, Kapil was again tossing the coin, Gavaskar having quit of his own accord after leading India to victory in the World Championship of Cricket one-day series in Australia. Kapil kept the captaincy until India narrowly lost a five-Test home series against Pakistan in early 1987, after which Dilip Vengsarkar took over. From then until his retirement, Kapil played under Vengsarkar, Ravi Shastri, Kris Srikkanth and Mohammad Azharuddin.

Though India won few Tests during his time as captain, his time at the helm was not without its glory days. In his first series as captain, in the West Indies in 1982–83, he became the youngest man to that point to take 200 Test wickets and complete the 200 wickets/2000 runs Test double. He did this in Port-of-Spain, in his 50th Test, and marked the occasion by scoring a century from 95 balls.

Four years later, 10 weeks after becoming the first man to captain India to a series victory in England, Kapil was the Indian captain in cricket's second Tied Test, against Australia in Madras in September

1986, and his role in the drama was significant. First, he scored a blazing hundred in India's reply to Australia's 7–574 (declared), racing from 50 to 100 with only 16 scoring shots. Then, on the final day, his team played in a manner befitting their captain's approach to batting, pursuing the imposing 348 run target with gusto, only to fall a solitary run short.

Even this memorable moment in cricket history, however, could not come close to his role in India's famous win in the 1983 World Cup. In the final at Lord's, his leadership as India defended a total of 183 was superb, his 11 overs for just 21 runs were

WASIM AKRAM: He knew everything — outswing, inswing, how to bowl on a slow wicket, slower ball, yorkers, everything. He was a complete bowler. And helped me. We would talk about bowling, batting, attitude. Whatever Imran demanded from Pakistan, Kapil wanted for India. Every youngster looks up to him as one of the greatest cricketers that the sub-continent has ever produced.

important, and his beautifully judged running catch of Viv Richards at mid-wicket, 20 metres from the boundary, was perhaps the single most critical moment of the match.

Within a year, however, he was replaced as skipper. 'The powers that be had decided that I was too headstrong to be leading India; this same man who a year ago could do no wrong,' he lamented. 'I had been showered with gold coins and now I was being asked to play for silver. I accepted it philosophically; that's my make-up but I was angry. It was not the fact of losing the captaincy but the reasoning behind it.'

Worse still, in the home series against England in 1984–85, Kapil was dropped for the only time in his career, after failing somewhat recklessly in the second Test, in Delhi. In his autobiography, England's Mike Gatting recalled that Kapil and Gavaskar 'were having a few cross words for some reason'. When Kapil went in midway through the final day, most observers thought the game was safely drawn, but they would not have known of an alleged conversation between captain and star all-rounder in the Indian dressing room. The story goes that Kapil had indicated he was going to have a slog, rejecting Gavaskar pleas for caution.

Out in the middle, Kapil belted a big six and was then caught, third ball, at long-on for 7. From there, the innings disintegrated to 235 all out and England were left to score 125 in 59 minutes and 20 overs, which they did with eight wickets in hand and time to spare. Despite the fact he'd top-scored in the first innings, Kapil's uninterrupted run of 65 Tests was brought to an end — for 'disciplinary reasons' announced the selectors.

The Indian public was irate at Kapil's sacking, and such was their anger that the selectors were forced to issue a public statement explaining that his omission would only be temporary. Many suspected Gavaskar was behind it, though neither he nor Kapil ever suggested this. Clearly, though, there was at least some rancour between the two. Just as clearly, the two were both gifted, single-minded cricketers, whose strong characters and ability to back their skills and have faith in their judgment were part of their make-up and key factors in their success. Kapil carried the Indian bowling, Gavaskar the batting: given the adulation that both enjoyed and the fact that for spells in the mid-1980s the national team was not winning, occasional disharmony was inevitable.

To Kapil's fans, the rare indiscriminate shot was simply an offshoot of the way he played. Indeed, his career is littered with some of the game's most dynamic innings. 'He was a destroyer,' reckons Maninder Singh. 'He would just attack the bowlers to the extent that I've seen bowlers lose their concentration, lose their confidence. That is what Kapil Dev thrived on. He was a very attacking batsman, I would say destructive.'

On his first tour of England, in 1979, he'd smashed 102 in 74 minutes against Northants in the opening first-class game of the trip. So much for getting acclimatised. Back home, in a charity match in Bangalore, he clobbered a spectacular century in 33 minutes with 10 sixes and eight fours. Then to Australia, where in a one-day international against New Zealand at the Gabba in Brisbane, Kapil hit one of the biggest sixes ever seen at the ground. The blow flew over the Clem Jones Stand and landed in Stanley Street outside the ground. 'I will always remember one of our bowlers, Jeremy Coney, taking out the white handkerchief at one stage and surrendering to him because he hit the ball so hard and so often,' says then Kiwi keeper Ian Smith.

Some would argue that the best example at Test level of Kapil Dev's pure hitting skill occurred in the sixth and final Test against England, in Kanpur, in 1981–82. The match was certain to be drawn and the series decided in India's favour, so Kapil put on

Jack Bannister: In trying to save the match in Bombay, he holed out to deep long-off when he was under instructions to block, so they dropped him for the second Test. He came back in Madras and Chris Cowdrey was bowling. Kapil walked out to a huge reception. Everybody wondered — now, how do you play your first ball after you've been dropped? Are you going to make a gesture, or are you going to say, 'Let's have peace and I'll play properly.'

First ball from Cowdrey was as near a wide as you can ever get without being called and Kapil launched himself at it and smashed it through Norman Cowans' hands at wide mid-off. And then he turned and waved his bat to the dressing room. That was his gesture at what had happened. He was a terrific character and, in his own country, an absolute legend.

a show, racing to his century in 84 balls. Or perhaps that was outdone by his performance in Kanpur in 1986–87, when he scored 163 against Sri Lanka. The 100 that day was reached in 74 balls, equal fourth fastest of all time. Kapil also recorded three of the swiftest Test fifties ever made — one in 30 balls (the fastest ever recorded, against Pakistan in Karachi in 1982–83), two more in 33 balls.

India's tour of England in 1982 was advertised as something of a clash of the all-rounders, between Ian Botham in the English corner and Kapil Dev representing India. From a batting perspective, at least, the battle was sensational, with Botham hitting scores of 67, 128 and 208 in his three innings in the series, and Kapil making 41 and 89, 65, and 97. Of Kapil's four knocks, perhaps the first two, at Lord's, were the most impressive. His 41 was a careful knock; he was one of only two men to reach double figures as Botham and Bob Willis reduced India to 125. In the second innings, Kapil smashed 89 out of the 117 added for the last four wickets of the innings. *Wisden* called his batting 'spectacularly violent'.

'Hitting thirteen 4s and three 6s, with his bat making the sound of gunfire,' the Almanac's correspondent continued, 'he was soon on course for the fastest Test century of all time. When he was caught at short mid-wicket, he had received only 55 balls.'

In all, he'd batted for 77 minutes. When England batted again, needing 65 to win, Kapil quickly took three wickets in eight balls, to reduce England to 3–18, but the close of play interrupted his magic spell and Allan Lamb rushed his side to victory on the following morning.

FOR ALL THIS PHENOMENAL firepower, Kapil Dev's greatest innings came not in a Test match, but — of all places! — at Tunbridge Wells. An occasional venue for Kent in southern England, it was host in 1983 to a World Cup match between India and a Zimbabwean side that had surprised Australia earlier in the competition. India came into the game having won only two of their first four qualifying matches so they could not afford to falter if they wanted to reach the semi-finals. As it turned out, they needed Kapil Dev at his absolute best to get this vital win (by 31 runs). Without him, the colossal celebrations at Lord's seven days later would never have happened.

DEAN JONES: In 1991–92, I was really looking forward to getting into these guys because they weren't super quick. I remember the first ball, Kapil Dev bowling, I played and missed because it swung *that* far. Allan Border's looked at me from the other end and gone, 'Phew, what was that?' Then the next one, I saw it start to swing, so I played a little bit outside the line but it didn't swing as much as the first one. Through the gap between bat and pad … bowled!

Coming from India, he had to be a brilliant player to get over 400 Test wickets. His bowling suited Australian conditions, or English conditions, but he just had this ability to get wickets when it counted.

The first ball of the day at Tunbridge Wells kicked at Gavaskar off a length and the last had him lbw. One for none. By the 10th over, Kapil Dev was in the middle, at 4–9. By the 13th over it was 5–17. From this unlikely launching pad, Kapil unleashed one of one-day cricket's greatest fightbacks. First he added 60 with Roger Binny, who scored 22. Shastri fell almost immediately to make it 7–78, but Kapil was undeterred, and in the 36th over he reached his 50 and India their 100. At lunch it was 7–106, and afterwards Kapil and Madan Lal took the score to 140 in the 44th over before David Houghton took his fourth catch of the innings.

As well as being one of the finest keepers of his generation, Syed Kirmani was also an underrated batsman, and he resolved to keep the Zimbabweans out while his captain launched a final assault. Even he could not have believed how well this strategy would work. Kapil's century came in the 49th over, not long after the century stand between Kapil and Kirmani came in 13 overs, when the 60th over ended Kapil was 175 not out (six sixes and 16 fours), Kirmani 24 not out, the innings total 8–266

'He was a fighter to the core,' says Maninder Singh, reflecting on that innings. 'He would accept challenges. The more the challenge the better he would perform. I think that's a quality in any great player and that's a quality that Kapil had.'

The last of Kapil's eight Test hundreds, 129 against South Africa at Port Elizabeth in 1992, was made out of a total of 188, after India had fallen to 6–31. Two years earlier, he had produced perhaps his most famous cameo at the batting crease. With India nine

GREG CHAPPELL: I put him down as a great fighter, somebody who persevered, someone who never gave in. You know he might have had figures of none for a hundred but he still kept running in and still kept trying to get wickets the same way he always did. I don't remember ever playing against him when he was bowling conservatively. He was always trying to get you out and that's why he was so successful.

wickets down and needing 24 to avoid the follow-on at Lord's, Kapil hit the off-spinner, Eddie Hemmings, for four straight sixes, all of them over the boundary near the Nursery-end sightscreen. Easy.

Sadly, Kapil's star status in India took a battering when match-fixing and bribery allegations were rife through 1999 and 2000. Although eventually cleared, he had to suffer the indignity of being accused by former comrades of bribing teammates to underperform and then the ignominy of having his home raided by government tax officials. The sight of the great champion breaking down awfully during a much-publicised television interview was one of the saddest moments of the whole,

horrendous saga. 'I will die. I will commit suicide before I take a bribe. I have not taken money. I have not offered any money to anybody,' he wept. Making matters worse, allegations and rumours had been put about at a time when the Indian national team, then coached by Kapil, was performing poorly. After a reasonable start in Test and one-day series at home against New Zealand, the team was humbled in Australia and then lost at home to South Africa. Kapil resigned as coach, to avoid the public eye and concentrate his resources on rebuilding his reputation as the people's champion.

'Kapil is a guy I have always admired,' Sir Vivian Richards commented at the height of the bribery scandal. 'I have always thought he was that one person who carried the Indian flag to the cricket field, and he was one of the few Indians who showed it. He took great pride in representing his country. And I in the opposition saw it and admired it.'

This, surely, is the memory cricket fans need to retain — of the great warrior blazing away with the bat no matter how precarious his team's position and carrying his country's bowling attack in a way no Indian paceman had ever done before.

Team coach Kapil Dev with his captain Sachin Tendulkar during India's ill-fated tour of Australia in 1999–2000.

Getty Images

STEVE WAUGH
Legend No. 23
The Pros' Pro

STEVE WAUGH WAS BORN to sport. A prodigiously gifted schoolboy cricketer and highly talented footballer, he was one of those rare young athletes who could have turned his sporting hand to just about anything. Fortunately for cricket, this was the game that won his heart and, most importantly, his soul. Today, it is possible to argue that only Grace, Hobbs and Bradman in the history of the sport have had as good an understanding of and appreciation for the game while they played; that no one today knows more about what it takes to succeed, to score runs, to know when to attack and when to defend, to have an edge over your opponents.

As a boy, he played cricket because he loved it, a natural who trusted his instincts and tried to score off every ball. Having a twin as gifted as himself meant his competitive instincts were honed from a very early age. As a young Test cricketer in an ordinary side, he had to first learn to survive before he could prosper. Then, when dropped from the Australian side in the early '90s, he decided that it wasn't how flash you look that matters, it's how many runs you make. With every stage in this development, his hide got tougher, his ambition to make the absolute most out of his ability gradually evolving into an obsession.

DICKIE BIRD: If I was in a war, going over them trenches, I would want Steve Waugh on my right-hand side and Ian Chappell on my left-hand side, and I think I would win a few wars, I'll tell you that now.

Today, to his comrades in the Australian squad he is a hero, their strongest backer, a captain who values loyalty to a fault. 'He's taken us to the next level,' says Glenn McGrath. Never a fan of change for change's sake, Waugh sees himself as a good judge of talent and character, and if a player has his support he has it unconditionally, to the point that Waugh has sometimes come into conflict with selectors and commentators. The justification for this unqualified backing of his men is elementary: Waugh wants his players relaxed, confident and aware that they are worthy of their place in the side. If this happens, he reasons, they are most likely to contribute. It has certainly worked for him.

One of Waugh's greatest achievements in runscoring came in a Sheffield Shield match against Western Australia in Perth in December 1990, when he and twin Mark put together a phenomenal partnership. It was the largest fifth-wicket partnership in history, 464 runs, and was compiled in 407 minutes against an attack that included four international pace bowlers — Bruce Reid, Terry Alderman, Chris Matthews and Ken MacLeay. Steve made 216 not out, Mark 229 not out. Rod Marsh, who was at the WACA that day, had been behind the stumps the day Barry Richards had played his most famous innings in Australia, 356 for South Australia against WA in 1970–71. Marsh thought the Waughs were superior.

Mike Whitney, the NSW fast bowler, tells the story of the brothers coming into the dressing room after the Blues captain, Geoff Lawson, had declared to end the partnership, as soon it went past the previous for the highest stand in Shield history. Mark, as Whitney, tells it, was unconcerned, happy to take the pats on the back and quietly revel in the moment. Steve, on the other hand, sat angry in his corner, ripping his gloves and pads off.

'What's wrong with you?' Whitney asked.

'You probably wanted to declare as well,' Steve spat back, 'so you could have a bloody bowl.'

'That's a pretty selfish attitude, isn't it?' replied the fast bowler, 'you've just broken the world record!'

'But we could have put on 600,' said Steve, without a hint of a smile.

He meant it, but he wasn't being selfish, merely reflecting his attitude to the game. Those extra runs, in his view, would have helped the team. Never give your opponent a chance is his mantra. When you've got 'em down, keep 'em down. And never get satisfied.

If you're good, try to be great.

STEPHEN WAUGH WAS BORN in the south-western suburbs of Sydney on 2 June 1965, four minutes ahead of brother Mark. Drafted into a star-studded NSW team in December 1984, to bat No. 9 and bowl second change in his first match, he marked his maiden first-class season with a glittering innings of 71 in that summer's Sheffield Shield final. Just nine months later he was in the Australian side, to play India in the Boxing Day Test at the Melbourne Cricket Ground. Australia's Test team was at perhaps its lowest ever ebb, having lost four series straight — to the West Indies, West Indies, England and New Zealand — since the retirement of Dennis Lillee, Rod Marsh and Greg Chappell. On top of the loss of those great players, a rebel Australian team to South Africa had further drained the available talent pool. Six months short of his 21st birthday, Waugh was the bright new hope. But he had played only 11 first-class games, and by his own admission was unprepared for the big time.

'I was a selector when he first got picked, and he did get picked before he was ready,' reflects Greg Chappell. 'We were going through difficult times, and a decision was taken that we had to pick players who had the right mental make-up to be able to withstand the tough times and come out the other side of it and be good cricketers. Steve went through that tough initiation period and has come out the other side, as we expected, as a very tough individual.'

Three and a half years on, when Waugh arrived in England for the 1989 Ashes series, he was yet to score a Test century. But he had not missed a Test for Australia since his debut — a run of 26 matches in which he had scored 1099 runs at 30.53, hardly the stuff of champions. There were times when it appeared that it was only his medium-paced bowling — good enough to three times get him five wickets in a Test innings — and his superb fielding that kept him in the team. Australia had won just four of those 26 Tests, none of Waugh's first 12. He'd toured New Zealand, India and Pakistan without winning a Test away from home.

The one glorious achievement during this time was Australia's stunning upset victory in the 1987 World Cup. Waugh was a pivotal figure in this triumph, sometimes scoring crucial runs (such as in the semi-final win over Pakistan in Lahore, when he smashed 18 runs, the eventual winning margin, from the 50th and last over of Australia's innings) and often bowling with nerveless efficiency in the final overs. Twice in the qualifying rounds, against India and then New Zealand, Waugh was required to bowl the last over with the odds against the Aussies, and twice he came through. Against the Indians, the home team needed six runs with one man left, but Waugh got that wicket with the fifth ball of the over. Against the Kiwis, the equation was seven to win with four wickets remaining, but Waugh got two wickets, there was a run out, and the Australians got home by three runs. He was also outstanding in the final, where he took 2–37 from his nine overs, including the vital wicket of Allan Lamb. His nerve and poise earned him the sobriquet, 'The Iceman'.

Waugh had enjoyed a season of county cricket with Somerset in 1988 so much that *Wisden* named him one of their five cricketers of the year. And for much of the Ashes Tests of '89 he was unstoppable, especially in the first two encounters, when he made 177 not out, 152 not out and 21 not out, as Allan Border's suddenly indomitable side went two-up in the series. His Test average for the rubber finished, Bradman-like, at 126.50. Back home in Australia, the team were greeted as all-conquering heroes.

'Watching Waugh, I became convinced that I was observing a future Australian captain in the making,' reckoned the great left-hander Neil Harvey. 'I'll treat the "New Bradman" newspaper posters with the disdain they deserve; a far closer model for Steve Waugh is Dougie Walters.'

This would have suited Waugh just fine. As a student of the game, his curiosity spurred by kinships with former Test players such as 'Stork' Hendry and the great leg-spinner Bill O'Reilly, he knew that comparisons with Bradman were ridiculous. As a child, Doug Walters had been his hero, so to be mentioned in the same breath was rewarding, even inspiring.

Disappointingly, Waugh's exploits in England that golden summer were a false dawn. They did not, in

Steve Waugh in England in 1989, when he suddenly went on a runscoring sequence that at one stage, immediately before he was dismissed in the fourth Test, gave him a batting average for the series of 485 (177 not out, 152 not out, 21 not out, 43 and 92).

the short term at least, herald the arrival of Australian cricket's next superstar. For the next four seasons, he rarely dominated in the Test arena, though he remained one of the most effective all-round one-day players in the world. He even missed a season and a half of Test cricket through 1991 and 1992, when, ironically, his place in the side was taken by his twin.

In then Australian coach Bob Simpson's view, when Waugh first emerged on the first-class scene he played with very stiff knees, which meant he still needed to learn to get his head right over the ball, to

ANDY FLOWER: A couple of things stand out about Steve Waugh: his determination to succeed and the fact that he can come through under pressure. There are not many batsmen in world cricket or through history of whom you can confidently say, 'I'd like this guy to bat for me.'

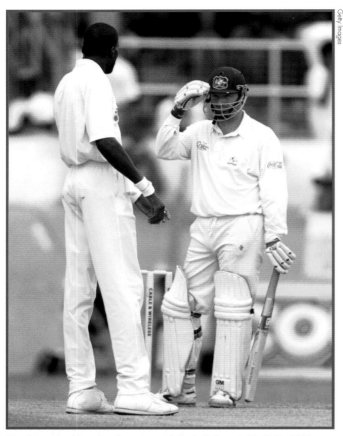

Waugh's much publicised confrontation with Curtly Ambrose in Trinidad in 1995.

Younis peppered him with bouncers but he remained brave, defiant and made 98. It was the same against the West Indies in the Caribbean in 1995. The cricket tutorial Waugh went through was brutal and comprehensive, but when he graduated he was a man armed with an enormous knowledge about the game and extraordinary confidence in himself, his strategies and his technique.

To at least a degree, Waugh had owed his selection for the 1993 Ashes tour to the memory of his fantastic performances of four years before. Although most critics had him in their sides when the touring party was announced, either of the omitted Dean Jones or Justin Langer could have been picked instead. His Test batting average at the time stood at a far-from-impressive 36.28, from 80 innings with 11 not outs. Once in England, Waugh did enough to make the first Test team, but didn't confirm his place in the side until the second innings of the third Test, when he made a crucial 47 not out to help force a draw. In the fourth Test he made the second big hundred of his career at Leeds, this time 157 not out in an undefeated fifth-wicket partnership of 332 with his captain, Allan Border. Australia won that Test, giving them an unbeatable 3–0 lead in the series, and never again was Waugh's place in the Australian Test XI in jeopardy.

Thus, the story of Steve Waugh's Test career is one of two halves. Until that 1993 Ashes series he was a moderate Test cricketer, a batting all-rounder capable of the occasional outstanding performance. Since 1993, he has built a reputation as one of the greatest batsmen of his generation. At the conclusion of Australia's series in South Africa in 2002, his career batting average stood at exactly 50.00; it has been around and usually above 50 — the measure of the truly great players — consistently since 1996. Yet, when asked in 2002 what a 50-plus Test batting average indicated, he replied flatly, looking at it purely from his perspective, 'Resilience.' From the start of the 1993 Ashes series to the end of the Australians' series in South Africa in early 2002 — during which time he played in 96 Tests and had 153 innings (with 30 not outs) — Waugh scored 7097 runs at an average of 57.70.

At 1 May 2002, only three men — Sunil Gavaskar, Sir Donald Bradman and Sachin Tendulkar — had scored more career Test centuries than Waugh's 27 (Allan Border also has 27). Only Border has played more Tests or scored more runs for Australia.

'smell it' as the old timers used to say. That he made the Test team with such a defect in his technique speaks wonders for his natural talent. He worked to overcome that problem, and also decided to eliminate the 'low percentage' shots, such as the hook against the fast men, from his repertoire. In England in 1989 his back-foot cover drive was a feature of the series, but the cricket world perceived that he had a difficulty with short-pitched deliveries, and he began receiving them in bulk. Another re-assessment of his technique, an acceptance that patience is a virtue and that it didn't matter how you coped so long as you did, and hours of hard yakka in the nets fixed the problem. That he was cured was clearly demonstrated in Rawalpindi in 1994, when Wasim Akram and Waqar

GLENN MCGRATH: He's a tough cricketer. When the pressure is on you know you can always count on him. He goes out there, he plays it tough, it means a lot to him. And he has a lot of respect and honour for the game.

Of those Australians who scored over 2500 Test runs, only Bradman, Greg Chappell and Border have a higher batting average. Only India's Mohammad Azharuddin has played more one-day internationals.

Beyond statistics, the true measure of the man has been the way he has observed, absorbed and applied lessons learnt on the international cricket stage, and the circumstances in which he has made his most important Test-match contributions. Take, for example, the Caribbean in 1995, when Australia beat the West Indies in a Test series for the first time in 20 years. 'Despite being subjected to an illegal amount of the short stuff, he was the best batsman around,' is Simpson's widely-shared view. Waugh's brave 200 in the series-deciding fourth Test in Jamaica was the crucial innings of the rubber. Just as significant was the manner in which he stood up to the leader of the much vaunted West Indies pace attack, Curtly Ambrose, on a dangerous wicket in the third Test, in Trinidad. During his innings of 63 not out (out of 128), Ambrose fired down a particularly wicked flyer that caused Waugh to jerk his head back out of the way. As the bowler stared his quarry down, Waugh nonchalantly asked him what he was looking at; affronted, Ambrose stepped closer and angrily told him he couldn't say that; nerveless, Waugh suggested he go back to his bowling mark. It needed the Windies captain, Richie Richardson, to drag an angry Ambrose away.

'That incident added considerably to the Steve Waugh legend,' Ian Healy commented years later. The Windies did win that Test, but Australia won 11 of the next 15 played between the two countries.

In the 1997 Ashes series in England, the home side led 1–0 after two Tests before Waugh scored a century in each innings of the third Test, at Old Trafford. He became the third Australian and first Australian right-hander to achieve this feat in an Ashes Test, but perhaps more significantly he scored his hundreds on a pitch on which only one other batsman passed 55, and on which no one else could reach three figures. Especially important was his batting on the first day, when he made an undefeated 102 out of 7–224, which justified captain Mark Taylor's decision to bat first and gave Shane Warne sufficient runs to bowl Australia into a commanding position on the second day.

Waugh's greatest triumphs came in 18 months of cricket, from the World Cup in England in mid-1999 through the 1999–2000 and 2000–01 Australian seasons. In the World Cup, Australia were on the brink of an early departure, but crept into the second round and as a result gave Waugh, the one-day captain since December 1997, an opportunity to add considerably to his cricket status. In the final match of the second round — for the Australians, in essence, a knockout match — he scored an unbeaten 120 from 110 balls, as his team achieved a successful chase of South Africa's imposing 7–271 with two balls to spare. Australia had been 3–48. It can be argued, considering the state and status of the match, that Waugh's remarkable effort was one of the greatest one-day centuries ever made. 'This was not an innings for the faint-hearted. It was an innings that few cricketers could possibly have played,' wrote Mark Nicholas. Four days later, in a semi-final at Edgbaston, Waugh scored 56 and then led his men superbly as the South Africans' final batsman, Allan Donald, was run out off the game's last ball, to miss the final by one run. From there, the Australians went to Lord's to rout Pakistan and win the tournament.

A very rare instance of Steve Waugh hooking in a Test match. He was batting here with No. 10 Stuart MacGill, at the MCG in an Ashes Test in 1998–99, and the shot enabled him to reach a dramatic hundred.

JONTY RHODES: He's been the hardest man in international cricket for a while. I can't think of anyone else in his league. He has perfected the art of gutsing things out in tight situations, for being the man for a crisis. He's thrived on that, developed his reputation. Every time that the chips are down, he's produced the goods. There are some really good players around but no one who values their wicket as much as he does. He bats and bats and carries on batting and batting. Like a barnacle, he's stuck to the crease and he won't move.

Had Waugh not made that hundred against South Africa, Australia would have been eliminated and Waugh might easily have been sacked as captain of the Australian one-day side. Instead, he returned home to a hero's welcome, after which he and his Test and one-day teams set off on an unprecedented run of success. After a hiccup in Sri Lanka, the Test team won 16 Tests in a row — one against Zimbabwe, then three against each of India, Pakistan and New Zealand, five against the West Indies, and one against India. The previous best such run is 11. Meanwhile, the one-day team won 13 matches straight in January–February 2000.

The Test team had been slow to get going when Waugh first took over as captain (from Mark Taylor

Getty Images

Waugh at Headingley during the 1999 World Cup, playing the innings of his one-day life against South Africa to get Australia into the semi-finals.

after the 1998–99 Ashes series), but now they clearly shared his insatiable appetite for success. 'When he took over, I don't think he was letting his instincts control his captaincy,' says Allan Border. 'He was doing things by the book. We had this conversation where I said to him, "Mate, you have got great instincts for the game, it looks to me that you are not letting them flow through."'

One of his favourite axioms is 'back yourself', and indeed this is what he did as he and his team grew to greatness. 'Test-match cricket is exactly what the title suggests,' Waugh commented in 2000. 'It is a test of many skills and attributes, that can be exposed or eroded if you are not up to the challenge at any given time. Many people think it's a test of just your natural talent, which, of course, forms a piece of the overall jigsaw. But to me Test cricket also entails words such as dedication, sacrifice, commitment, unselfishness, camaraderie, courage, pride and passion. To win, you must have all these plus more. You have to be able to handle pressure better than your adversary over a sustained period of time. You have to be able to seize the moment when a game is in the balance, but more importantly know when this moment is upon you.'

In Waugh's eyes, a verbal crack at your opponent is part of the battle, provided the intention is to win a psychological edge, rather than just to hurl cheap abuse. Less combative types call it 'sledging'; he sees it as a form of acceptable gamesmanship, as trying to cause some 'mental disintegration' in the opposition camp. Perhaps his most famous onfield one-liner came during his great century at the 1999 World Cup. Dropped by Herschelle Gibbs on 56, with his team behind on run-rate, he looked the South African square in the eye and said, 'I hope you realise you've just lost the game for your team.'

From that moment on, an Australian victory always seemed more likely. A psychological imbalance between the two teams whenever they meet — the Australians assured and dominant, South Africa unsure, almost submissive — remains to this day.

Waugh's Australians with the Frank Worrell Trophy after sweeping the West Indies at home in 2000–2001. This win was the team's 15th consecutive Test victory, a run they extended to 16 soon after in India. Back row (left to right): Justin Langer, Colin Miller, Ricky Ponting, Jason Gillespie, Glenn McGrath, Matthew Hayden, Andy Bichel. Front: Stuart MacGill, Michael Slater, Steve Waugh, Adam Gilchrist, Mark Waugh.

'It is a measure of the man that he has turned a good Australian side into a really good Australian side by his presence and his attitude towards cricket,' says Gibbs' longtime teammate Jonty Rhodes. The Indian skipper, Sourav Ganguly, a prickly opponent in 2001, rates him 'probably the best captain around in the world today, and a great, great player'.

In his first 25 Tests as Australian Test captain, he hit eight centuries. Eighteen of those Tests were won, five lost. And just two, both rain-ruined Tests in Sri Lanka, were drawn, reflecting the aggressive, play-to-win-whatever-the-circumstances strategy his team adopts.

In this regard, the team is simply mimicking their leader, for he is the master of the counter-attack. Take, for example, Rawalpindi in 1998, when he came in with Australia 3–28 and scored 157, adding 198 for the fourth wicket with Michael Slater. In the West Indies in 1999, he arrived at the crease in Kingston with Australia 3–46 and made 100, and two weeks later in Bridgetown he was in again at 3–36 and scored 199, this time adding 281 with Ricky Ponting. And not only is Waugh able to make runs in difficult circumstances, he is also able to inspire his comrades to go beyond their call of duty. In the Boxing Day Ashes Test in Melbourne in 1998–99, Waugh scored 122 not out and added 88 for the ninth wicket with the batting duffer Stuart MacGill. Similarly, in Calcutta in 2001, against India, he fashioned a stirring rearguard action with the pace bowler Jason Gillespie, as they added 133 for the ninth wicket after Australia had slumped to 8–269. Gillespie made 46, his highest Test score, while Waugh went on to one of his most treasured centuries.

CLIVE LLOYD: Steve Waugh is like a Gavaskar. He has great concentration, he's a good thinker. In a tight situation, you'd want him to bat for you, because he has that steely resolve. He's a real pro, the pros' pro.

'If I had to choose a city to manage this feat it would definitely have been Calcutta, a city I love, and if I had to choose a ground it would have been the Eden Gardens, one of the game's most hallowed grounds,' said Waugh after that innings. His comments reflected his passion for the history and integrity of the game, and also his love of India and the fact that a cause close to his heart is based in Calcutta. 'You have to earn the support of the crowd at the Eden,' he continued. 'When you walk out to bat as an opposition player the atmosphere is hostile but, as you move towards three figures, that animosity

Steve Waugh with his brother Mark before they played their 100th Test together, against South Africa in late 2001. Note Steve's battered Australian cap — his pride in the 'baggy green' is reflected in the resolute way he plays, and has rubbed off on his teammates.

gradually evolves into a genuine appreciation for your play. And, to make the innings even more important to me, there are the little children in Udayan who live here and make this city a special place for me.'

In Calcutta in 1998, after Australia had been thrashed in the second Test, Waugh had been asked by charity workers to visit the decrepit part of the city where the leprosy sufferers and their families are forced to exist. Throughout his career, he has made a point of exploring unfamiliar surroundings, of getting away from the grind of touring to discover something new. Here, it was explained to him that there was a way out for the poverty-stricken children, through the building of a special home and the development of healthcare and education facilities, but funds were desperately needed to make this happen. Work was being done for the sons of some leprosy sufferers, but nothing for the daughters. Waugh agreed to become involved as a patron of the cause, and then, typically, approached the task with the same commitment he has shown to his hundreds. The first stage of the Udayan home for girls was opened in 2000, and extensions were operating by the time of Waugh's return on the Australians' tour in 2001. There is still a great deal to be done, as Waugh freely admits, but much has already been achieved, for which the Australian captain can take significant credit.

The 20-year-old Test debutant from Sydney's south-west could hardly have imagined himself taking on such a responsibility. Then, the primary objective was simply to play a second Test. Sixteen years on, he is a much wiser, more pragmatic, more worldly man. The veteran cricketer in his mid-30s sees no problem in trying to win every Test, to win it all. Very few cricketers in history have believed so totally in this philosophy.

When it was decided in 2002 that Waugh was no longer worth his place in the Australian one-day side, it seemed a pity the selectors didn't wait to see what he had absorbed from his mediocre (by his standards) form during the 2001–02 domestic season. After all, it had been his first personally unproductive Australian season in a decade. The story of his career suggests that, had he kept his place — and maintained his desire — he would have come back an even smarter, shrewder, more effective cricketer than before. Significantly, for Steve Waugh, there was no thought of retirement. The job, in his eyes, was not yet completely done.

BARRY RICHARDS
Legend No. 24
Coaching-book Perfect

OF ALL THE LEGENDS featured in this book, none has played fewer Tests than South Africa's Barry Richards. His entire Test career amounted to four matches, all against Australia at home in early 1970. Yet, many who saw him bat suggest he was as good as any batsman of his era. 'Technically, he's probably as good as anybody who's played,' reckons Graeme Pollock. 'Once in two or three generations there comes a virtuoso batsman who beguiles even his opponents. Such is Barry Richards,' wrote the late John Arlott, the doyen of English commentators. Mike Procter, a colleague of Richards since schooldays, says, 'If I had to choose someone to bat for my life, I'd choose Barry.' The renowned writer Henry Blofeld considered Richards to be 'undoubtedly the supreme batsman of his generation and arguably the best the game of cricket has ever known'.

'It is inconceivable,' Blofeld continued, 'that any other batsman of any period could have reduced the art of batting to such absurdly simple dimensions.'

Blofeld made these comments in 1977. Seven years earlier, Richards had walked out for his first Test innings already recognised as an outstanding batsman, a rating the result of his excellent performances in South Africa's first-class competition, the Currie Cup, and in English county cricket.

South Africa's opponents in this series, Australia, arrived having won their two previous series, against the West Indies at home and India away. South Africa had not played in a Test series since 1966–67, when they had thrashed Bob Simpson's Australian team. To some, this series was a battle for the cricket world title. In the end, it was no contest. It was, as we said, to be the only Test series of Barry Richards' career.

South Africa won Richards' debut Test by 170 runs. The 24-year-old's contribution was 29 and 32, not the start he wanted, but he did take what proved to be his only Test wicket, John Gleeson bowled for 10. Less than two weeks later, in Durban, he made his mark.

In the long history of Test cricket, only four men — Trumper, Macartney, Bradman and Majid Khan — have scored a century before lunch on the first day of a Test. Here in Durban, in his *second ever* Test, Richards was magnificent from the jump, totally dominating an opening partnership of 88 with the veteran Trevor

Barry Richards, a batting genius who — because of circumstances that were entirely out of his control — played in only four Tests.

Goddard. The score at lunch was 2–126 and Richards, despite defending throughout the session's penultimate over, was 94 not out. At the time, Richards cared little for the hundred before lunch, being concerned only about reaching his maiden Test century. This he did four balls after the break. Had he known his Test career was nearly over, he admitted years later, he might have had a real go at that magical figure.

As we have already noted in the story of Pollock's career, the batting in the hour after lunch, until Richards was dismissed, is celebrated today in South Africa as the greatest ever seen in that country. There was a kaleidoscope of strokes, the two trading moments of genius, and 103 runs were added before Richards' masterpiece ended when Eric Freeman bowled him for 140. Pollock went on to slaughter the attack for 274.

Doug Walters, who fielded through the carnage, reckoned it was 'as good an innings as I have seen anywhere'.

Walters continued: 'He's one of the most confident players I have ever watched. It is nothing at all for Richards to dance down the pitch to medium-pace bowlers as well as slow bowlers.'

Richards hit 65 and 35 in the third Test and 81 and 126 in the fourth, giving him 508 runs for the series, at 72.57. Keith Miller, the great all-rounder, was in South Africa covering the Tests for Australian newspapers. Part of his report of that second (and last) Test century of Richards' career was as follows: 'He took two little skips down the pitch to sweep Gleeson effortlessly over square-leg to bring up his fifty, then he took to Walters, hitting a sizzling hook for four, then lifting him into the packed stand for six. Next in line for the slaughter was McKenzie, when Richards stood up straight and banged the ball screaming to the mid-off boundary. Then came the golden stroke of his innings. The next ball from McKenzie was just a fraction short but Richards with amazing reflexes was across and hit him into the identical spot where he had slammed Walters. This was the stroke of a truly great batsman. He even hit Connolly with an overhead tennis smash to rocket the ball against the mid-on fence …'

BARRY RICHARDS WAS BORN on 21 July 1945, in Durban. From around the age of 12, when he made an impression on the touring

Australians during practice before the third Test of 1957–58, he seemed destined for the top, a fact that was underlined by a series of excellent displays on a South African schoolboys tour of the UK in 1963. An innings of 79 at a run-a-minute against the Hampshire second XI caught the attention of officials there. 'This is the best young batsman I have ever seen,' was the opinion of Hampshire's then coach, Leo Harrison.

Two years later, Richards returned with Procter to play a season on the Gloucestershire staff, and made 59 in his one first-class match. Then, in 1966, Richards, Procter and another former schoolboy star, Lee Irvine, stayed in the UK briefly after a private cricket tour, and managed to scrounge some work at The Oval during the final England-West Indies Test of the summer, as attendants in the Windies dressing room. For young ambitious cricketers, this was an unbelievable chance to get a taste for Test cricket while watching champions at close quarters.

'We read about these fellows — Garry Sobers, Rohan Kanhai, Basil Butcher, Seymour Nurse and so on — and suddenly there they were,' Richards remembers. 'It was just a tremendous experience to be able to view them from the balcony, which is obviously the best view in the house, to be part of it and to get the atmosphere of a Test-match dressing room. I mean, "Sobie" was the premier all-rounder, probably of all time, one of the greatest. Just being in his company was inspiring. It inspired me to say, "Hey, this is where I want to be, in a Test-match dressing room. I'm going to put my head down and try to do it."'

A few months later, Procter was playing in Tests against Australia, but Richards was not, left out as a disciplinary measure after he angrily kicked a flowerpot into a swimming pool when he was refused entry into a nightclub. Still, Richie Benaud, who saw Richards during that tour, described him this way: 'A brilliant right-hander who plays very straight and hits the ball very hard with perfect timing. He is one of the best young players I have ever seen.'

Overseas players were admitted to the English county championship by special registration in 1968, and Richards joined Hampshire. His first county innings was at Sussex, and he started with a duck, bowled by the lethal fast man, John Snow. His first home match, against Glamorgan two

GRAEME POLLOCK: Without a shadow of doubt, the best two batsmen I played with or against were BA Richards and Sir Garfield Sobers.

weeks later, yielded four runs in two innings. However, between these two, he played an innings that established his reputation. He remembers it this way: 'My second game for Hampshire was against Yorkshire. We had to go from Hove, with no motorways, all the way up to Harrogate. During the night the covers had blown off and it was like there was a little 'S' marked down the wicket, a wet/dry scenario, and they had some pretty hard heads in the Yorkshire side. I remember getting 70 out of 122, which, from a skill point of view, factoring in the conditions, was as good a knock as I ever played.'

For most of the decade that followed, Richards was one of county cricket's finest players. Between 1968 and 1976, Richards was never out of the top 20 in the competition batting averages, in all scoring 15,607 first-class runs for the county at an average of 50.51, including 38 centuries. When Hampshire won the county championship in 1973, *Wisden* specifically commented that there was no happier dressing room in England. The opening partnership of Richards and Gordon Greenidge was a key to the triumph. This one title (the second in the county's history) could in fact have been three, as only rain robbed them in 1974 and one or two poor results against lowly sides proved costly in 1975. The county also won the John Player League in 1975. Richards' final complete season for the county, his benefit year of 1977, was disappointing, and after six matches in 1978 he departed — to devote himself to World Series Cricket and then play out his first-class career for Natal.

GREG CHAPPELL: Barry Richards was one of the most stylish players I ever saw, and almost coaching-book perfect in everything that he did. You could take a young player down to the cricket ground and sit him down, and say watch Barry Richards and try to learn from him.

DICKIE BIRD: He had so much time in which to play the ball. He had all the time in the world. I've seen the ball leave a bowler's hand and, through the air, he still hasn't moved. I'm thinking, when is he going to move? But by God, when he moved, he picked the line and length up so quickly. Whether it was on the back foot or on the front foot. A tremendous player.

RICHARDS, A FRACTION MORE than 180cm in height, stood erect at the crease, and used a lengthy backlift as if to emphasise his high grip of the bat. He thought nothing of lofting the ball away from the infield, even over the turning heads of cover and mid-off. While he hooked in the air, encouraging captains and bowlers, rarely, if ever, was he trapped at fine-leg. The legendary Australian cricket writer, Ray Robinson, was one of a number of observers who suggested that Richards often left onlookers feeling that they had just been shown how the game should be played.

John Arlott described his style this way: 'When he sets out to play himself in, no one in the world has a straighter bat. His footwork then is calmly fast; he is in position for his stroke so early that he has time to play it with an air of apparent boredom … He sees and identifies the length and line of the bowled ball that moment faster than others, which enables him to play at leisure where they must hurry.'

As Richards' seasons of exile blended one into another and it became less and less likely that South Africa would be readmitted to the Test arena, he became less and less motivated by the daily grind of first-class cricket. He needed significant moments to inspire him, and one such opportunity came against the touring Australians in England in 1975. Richards was captaining Hampshire for the first time, while Jeff Thomson was at full pace, desperately trying to get his run-up right before the start of an Ashes series. Richards was respectfully careful against Thommo, who *Wisden* reported bowled 'well without any luck', but against Australia's support bowlers, the

Richards, England's former batting champion Denis Compton and Pakistan's Mushtaq Mohammed shelter from the rain during a charity match in London in 1974.

quick Alan Hurst and leggie Jim Higgs, he was brutal. At one point in his first innings he took 34 from just two Hurst overs. Twice, Higgs was hit for six but, four short of his century, Richards was caught on the boundary. In the second innings, he raced to 69 in exhilarating style, before Thomson struck him a painful blow in the groin and he had to retire hurt.

Six months later, in Durban, Hurst knocked Richards cold with a bouncer, which he ducked into after a contact lens came loose. A few hours later, Richards returned to bat in his usual style. 'He played as though nothing had happened,' Hurst commented years later. 'Players you see hit, usually the last place they want to go near is the ground.'

Hurst was playing for an international 'Wanderers' team that featured stars such as Dennis Lillee and Ian Chappell and was managed by Richie Benaud. They were in South Africa for a series of matches designed to give cricket visionaries such as Chappell, Lillee and Benaud a first-hand look at the situation, to give the South African players some top-class cricket, and to hopefully boost the development of multi-racial cricket in the republic. However, Richards and two of his colleagues, Lee Irvine and Graeme Pollock, refused to play in the first 'international', on the basis that they deserved to be paid exactly the same as the tourists. Benaud, for one, was seriously disturbed by the South Africans' stance, which many critics tagged 'mercenary'.

But as one of the best in his field, Richards felt that he deserved to be paid accordingly. In fact, he went further, believing he was entitled to the same sort of rewards as the finest performers in tennis and golf. But there was more to it than this. The events of the previous five years, which had shunted him out of the international game through no fault of his own and cost him financially as a result, had made him wear what he bitterly called his 'professional hardness' on his sleeve.

The South African cricketers, Richards high-profile among them, had tried to initiate change. In 1971, with a scheduled tour of Australia under

Richards wearing his World Series Cricket colours during a single-wicket competition at The Oval in September 1979.

threat and fast approaching, the South African Cricket Association asked the South African government if two black players could be included in the touring party. The government said no, a decision announced just before the final selection trial at Newlands in Cape Town. The players decided to make a public protest. Procter bowled the first ball of the match to Richards, and then all the players downed tools and walked off, going via the press box to deliver a statement, which read: 'We cricketers feel that the time has come for an expression of our views. We fully support the South African Cricket Association's application to include non-whites on the tour to Australia if good enough

CHRISTOPHER MARTIN-JENKINS: County cricket watchers at Southampton probably didn't realise how immensely lucky they were to have Barry Richards and Gordon Greenidge opening the batting. When the game was really tough, Richards found it easier than the average mortal to play the ball that was moving all over the place.

> **DENIS LINDSAY:** If the challenge was there he was tremendous. If there was no challenge, then he would get to 50 or get to 100 and just toss it. One day, when we were playing in Durban. Barry got to about 40 and he turned around to me and said, 'Come on, let's have a little bit of fun here.' And he played for the next half hour with the edge of the bat and was still hitting balls through the covers for four. That's how great Barry was.

and furthermore, subscribe to merit being the only criterion on the cricket field.'

Eventually, the game was resumed. But the players' views were ignored and the tour was cancelled. South Africa would not officially return to international cricket until the early 1990s.

Elsewhere the politics was confused. In 1974, the Indian government refused Richards and Procter entry into India to participate in a charity match for flood victims. Inside South Africa, the cricket authorities rejected proposals for tours by mixed-race Rest of the World sides and an English XI featuring Basil D'Olivera, a 'coloured' South African who had been obliged to go to England to enjoy a Test career. For an exasperated Barry Richards, everything was going nowhere fast.

'The feeling of futility has increased since I reached my 30th birthday in 1975,' Richards wrote in his autobiography. 'I watched in 1976 the uninhibited joy of the West Indies, including my county opening partner Gordon Greenidge, exhibiting again the thrill of winning a Test rubber. Television pictures captured the elation on the faces of England's players at regaining the Ashes the following year. I have had to envy the accolades poured upon players who I know in my heart of hearts, in all modesty, have never been as good as me.'

From 1970, Richards was obliged to score his runs without any challenge beyond that of scoring enough to justify the contracts he had signed. In 1976–77, instead of scoring more runs in the Currie Cup, he played grade cricket for Midland-Guildford in Perth, also servicing sponsorships and doing commentary work on radio and television. It was here that he was approached to join World Series Cricket. 'Kerry Packer and his associates found doing business with me an extremely straightforward task,' Richards remembered. And then he added, significantly and happily, 'The money was only incidental to a last

opportunity to play in the company of world-class cricketers again.'

In his story of WSC, *The Cricket War*, Gideon Haigh quoted Richards' World XI teammate Alan Knott, the English wicketkeeper, who realised how much the challenge of playing against the very best meant to the South African. 'He [Richards] practised and trained with 100 per cent dedication, always continuing when others had finished. You were always worried that if you agreed to throw and bowl to him in practice you would be there all day, because he just wanted to bat and bat.'

At Gloucester Park, a Perth venue better known as a trotting track, against a high-class Australian attack, Richards played one of his finest hands. The match was a SuperTest between Australia and the World XI in early 1978, the temperature that day reached 42°C, and Ian Chappell, the Australian captain, lost the toss.

Richards opened with Gordon Greenidge. At Hampshire, Richards would often let the always aggressive Greenidge take the lead. But not here. Richards took 30 fewer deliveries to reach his hundred, and when Greenidge reached 114 the West Indian had to retire hurt, to be replaced at the crease by Viv Richards.

One aspect that had been heavily promoted throughout this first WSC season was the comparison between the two Richards. Australian fans had seen Viv in the 1975–76 Test series, remembered him from the 1975 World Cup final, knew that he'd blasted two double centuries against England in 1976, and seen him smash two hundreds in earlier SuperTests that summer. Barry's reputation down under revolved around that one Test series against Australia and a season in the Sheffield Shield. Most Australians, if asked who was the better, would have plumped for the West Indian. On this day, at least, they were wrong.

In 90 minutes, Viv scored 41 runs, while Barry hit 93 before he miscued Ray Bright to Greg Chappell at long-off to be out for 207. In all, 136 of Richards' score had come in boundaries. The scoreboard read 1–369, after 60 overs. 'It was one of those days,' wrote Henry Blofeld, 'when Barry Richards could have done anything he liked with every ball that was bowled to him.'

A little more than 12 months later, Richards produced his second great innings in WSC, a superb 110 not out. In the 1978–79 SuperTest final in

Sydney, as tough a cricket test as has ever been played in Australia, Richards' batting proved the difference. For most of the game the bowlers were in charge, and the World side were left to score 224 to win. 'The pitch,' recalled Haigh, 'was crumbling underfoot.'

'Today, they don't regard it as first-class cricket,' says Richards of WSC. 'I can't imagine why not. It's not in any record books or in *Wisden* or anything like that. You and I know how hard it was.'

Richards and Procter, both literally playing the game of their lives, had come together at 4–84 and added 91 before Procter was bowled by Bright. Still a tricky 49 to get, but Richards was supreme as he launched an assault on Gary Gilmour and Lillee that quickly and brutally won what had to that moment been a tight, tense affair.

While most cricket fans were delighted with the settling of the cricket war after that 1978–79 season, for the South Africans it was a disaster. They were sent back into exile; for Richards the only 'international' matches would be five-day and one-day games against rebel English, West Indian and Sri Lankan teams in the early 1980s. He continued on with Natal until 1982–83, before retiring to take up administrative positions in Australia, first in Perth and then Brisbane, from where he saw Queensland win its first Sheffield Shield and South Africa re-enter international cricket. When asked how he felt about South Africa's return he comments: 'It's quite difficult, you know. We could not play anybody and nobody played us for 21 years. Those 21 years for me were between ages 22 and 43, and that finished off my cricketing career. But when South Africa came back to international sports, nobody wanted to look back at our era. All the players from my generation have almost been scrapped out of the record books. We paid the price twice. First, when nobody played us, and the second time round, when nobody wanted to remember the players in the era when South Africa's history was not a good one.'

I N ALL, RICHARDS SCORED 28,358 first-class runs, at 54.74, with 80 centuries. Four times he scored four centuries in one season for Natal. At Hampshire, against Nottinghamshire in 1974, he batted through the innings unbeaten for 225 out of just 344, one of three times he batted through a first-class innings. He scored a hundred before lunch nine times, five times on the first day. Twice he scored a century in both innings of a county match. But the most amazing innings of his career was played not in England or South Africa, but in Australia — the highest score of his first-class cricket life, 356 for South Australia against Western Australia in Perth in 1970–71.

Richards had arrived in South Australia on a complicated agreement. Coca-Cola supplied him with a vehicle, a salary and promised him a dollar for every first-class run scored, and 10 dollars for every wicket taken. This was to prove an expensive exercise, for Richards finished the first-class season with 1538 runs, including scores of 224, 356, 146, 155, 178 and 105, at an average of 109.86.

The WA bowling attack for the match in Perth featured five past, present or future internationals, including Dennis Lillee, Graham McKenzie and the captain, Tony Lock, formerly of Surrey and England. Behind the stumps was Rod Marsh, still recovering from the shock of being selected as Australia's new wicketkeeper.

The following breakdown of Richards' innings reveals something of the consistent, brutal nature of his batting.

Runs	Minutes	Fours	Sixes
50	70	7	–
100	125	13	–
150	176	21	–
200	209	28	1
250	268	30	1
300	317	39	1

IAN CHAPPELL: It got to the point, late in the afternoon on that day Barry slaughtered Western Australia, when he was just hitting every ball downwind. Where they bowled it had absolutely no relevance to where Barry hit it. He just decided that he wasn't going to run any more. He was just going to hit fours. If McKenzie bowled at his legs, but he had to hit it through the covers to go downwind, then he went through the covers.

I remember looking at the scoreboard and thinking, 'What a bummer, he's going to fall just short of 300. I've never seen 300 scored in a day before.' I'm looking at the board and working it out, thinking, 'Oh, he'll probably get 280.'

Pretty good judge I am. He finished the day on 325.

Richards in full flight for Hampshire.

In all, Richards hit 44 fours and one six during the day's play, and faced 322 deliveries. He was the third man to score 300 in one day in an Australian first-class match. Only five men in the history of first-class cricket anywhere had scored more runs in one day than his 325 (the most ever is 345 by Charlie Macartney for Australia against Nottinghamshire in 1921). At stumps South Australia were 3–513. The runs had come as follows: 135 in the 110-minute pre-lunch session; 211 in the two hours between lunch and tea; and 167 in the 100 minutes before stumps. SA captain Ian Chappell had scored 129, in a partnership of 308 that ran for 170 minutes.

'I was at the height of my powers,' Richards says today. 'The eye was still young, the body still supple. It all just gelled.' He had played at and missed the first ball of the day, an outswinger from McKenzie, and heard Marsh snigger to first slip John Inverarity, 'Geez, I thought this bloke was supposed to be able to play a bit.' After the last ball of the day was driven to the sightscreen, Inverarity turned to his weary keeper and muttered: 'I suppose he can play a bit.'

Later that season, in Sydney, Richards scored 178 and attracted a healthy crowd to the SCG, even though an Ashes Test was being played in Melbourne and televised into Sydney homes. NSW won the match on the first innings, 7 (declared) for 441, to 316. On the last day NSW batted again, and were bowled out for 133, the final wicket falling just before game's end. Throughout that final session the spectators continually barracked their own batsmen, especially the NSW captain Brian Taber. What they wanted was a declaration, however token, so that South Australia would have to bat again. On that sunny afternoon, the fans cared not for the outright points, or even the Sheffield Shield. What they craved was one more glimpse of the batting of Barry Richards.

ALLAN BORDER
Legend No. 25
A Tough Nut to Crack

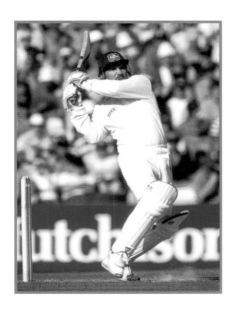

STEVE WAUGH REMEMBERS THE fourth Ashes Test of 1993: 'At the end of play the previous evening, we were in the impregnable position of 4–613. Allan Border was 175 not out, while I was unbeaten on 144, and our stand had brought 292 runs. Our captain announced we would be batting on for 30 or 40 more minutes "to cause further mental and physical disintegration of the opposition". That one statement sums up for me the killer instinct that has made AB such a champion player and competitor throughout his career.'

Of Border's batting, the outstanding New Zealander Martin Crowe comments: 'He knew his game inside out. He had some limitations, but in some ways that was his great strength, because he was able to stick with those limitations. A great puller of the ball, a very good cutter. He had a very good punch drive and nuggetty defence.'

All Border's teammates speak with admiration about the example he set. The great keeper, Ian Healy, reckons few men he encountered during his career loved the game of cricket more than Allan Border. Michael Slater fondly recalls a partnership against South Africa at the SCG in 1993–94 when his captain showed him how to tough out a difficult situation. Merv Hughes reckoned Border 'always saved his best for when the team most needed it'. Paul Reiffel valued his commitment to the team. 'The one thing I will always remember is the loyalty he showed to the team,' he reflected in 1998. 'It was so obvious. He gave 100 per cent to the team and he expected 100 per cent back …

'If you did that, he was with you all the way.'

ALLAN BORDER, BORN ON 27 July 1955 in the Sydney suburb of Cremorne, had the misfortune to make his Test debut in the summer in which Australia suffered its biggest ever series defeat. He came into the side for the third Ashes Test of 1978–79, the only Test Graham Yallop's much weakened Australian team won that summer. By his own admission, he wasn't ready for Test cricket, but in his second Test, at the SCG, Border scored 60 not out in the first innings and then 45 not out in the second, displaying deft skill on a turning pitch. However, that was not enough to save him being dropped for the sixth Test, despite the fact the match was in Sydney. 'When we did see him at the crease,' England's David Gower recalls, 'everyone to a man in our side thought, this man is going to be around for a while.' Realising the error of their ways, the selectors had Border back for Australia's next Test, batting at No. 3 against Pakistan in Melbourne, and he immediately scored his first Test century. He was never dropped again. A mere 15 years and 152 Tests later, he retired as the leading runscorer in the history of Test cricket.

Among the Test records he held when he retired were most matches (156), most innings (265), most runs (11,174), most fifties (63), most scores of at least 50 (90), most catches by a non-wicketkeeper (156), most matches as captain (93) and most successive Test appearances (153). Eight years on, only the catches record has been broken (by Mark Taylor and Mark Waugh).

IAN BOTHAM: AB was one of the gutsiest players I played against. I must have bowled to him probably four or five times when he had a broken finger, but he kept on playing. I'd try to hit him on the hand, used to say, 'Which one is it?' And he'd tell me where to go and to just get on with my bowling.

After having little success at the 1979 World Cup in England, Border's first overseas tour as an Australian Test player was to India in the second half of 1979. There, he scored 162 in the first Test, but the tourists were beaten in the six-Test series 2–0. Back in Australia for the first Test series after the reunion of 'traditional' and 'Packer' cricket, he was one of three non-World Series Cricket players chosen first-up in the Australian XI, pitched in at the deep end at No. 3. 'I was sitting around, the new kid on the block, with all these legendary names that, through my teenage years, I'd watched play cricket on television and read about,' he says of his first day in an Australian XI with Dennis Lillee, Greg Chappell, Rod Marsh and company. 'All of a sudden I was in the same dressing room. That felt a little more daunting than actually being involved in my first Test match.'

In his second overseas tour, to Pakistan in 1980, Border became the first, and to this day only, player to score 150 in both innings of a Test match. By this time, it was acknowledged that he was more at home batting between four and six, using a style of batting that was becoming known throughout the world. He stood upright as the bowler approached and then crouched slightly as the ball was delivered. A master in nudging the ball into the gaps and working the bowlers for ones and twos, he drove often and effectively through the covers and played horizontal bat shots such as the pull and the cut quite fiercely. He was masterful against the spinners, always eager to use his feet to drive through the offside or past mid-on. After the 1981 Ashes series, in which he scored a century in each of the final two Tests despite fracturing a finger, Sir Leonard Hutton called him the best left-handed batsman in the world.

At the end of 1981, after 33 Tests, Border's Test batting average was 51.86. Three years later, on the eve of the 1985 Ashes tour having now played 61 Tests, his average had barely dropped, to 51.59. His consistency was a trademark. In the early '80s he played a number of impressive innings, such as at the Adelaide Oval in 1981–82, when he made 78 and 126 against the West Indies, and in Melbourne in 1982–83, when he and Jeff Thomson staged a memorable last-wicket fightback against England. Needing 74 to win late on the fourth day, the pair had scored half of them by stumps. The next day 18,000 spectators came to the MCG to see a finale

Border in India in 1979, his first overseas tour as an Australian Test cricketer.

that might have lasted one ball; instead the Australians inched towards their target until, with four runs required, Thomson edged Botham to the slip cordon. Border was left 62 not out.

Border believed his performance in Trinidad in 1984, against Joel Garner and Malcolm Marshall, was his greatest batting effort. 'I didn't have all the flamboyant shots, and I probably played better at other times in different games,' he explains. 'But when you talk about the wicket conditions, it was a bit wet and greasy, we lost the toss, we were inserted, we were playing against the West Indies of 1984 with their awesome bowling attack. To make those runs under those circumstances, it was probably as good as I've played.' In the first innings he made 98 not out; in the second, unconquered again, he went two runs better.

Border went past 4000 runs during that series in the Caribbean, in which he scored 521 runs at 74.42. No other Australian batsman scored even half that many, or averaged more than 26. At career's end he was to lament that he was in the absolute best form of his career in a period, 1984 to 1987, when the Australian team was ordinary.

WHEN BORDER TOOK OVER as Australian captain in December 1984, the Australian team was in crisis. Greg Chappell, Marsh and Lillee had retired at the end of the previous season. His new team had lost its previous five Tests, and few observers believed the change of captain from Kim Hughes to Border would suddenly turn things around. Under these circumstances, the fact his leadership tenure started with a loss, a draw and a win was encouraging. However, any thoughts that the team might get on a winning roll evaporated in England, where after a promising beginning and despite the captain's 597 runs and two centuries, Border's Australians lost the Ashes after being thrashed in the final two Tests. The team in England had had to make do without

DICKIE BIRD: I thought he was a fine captain. He had the respect of the players, you see. They worshiped Allan Border and they'd do anything for him, and that is the sign of a great captain, when you're getting the respect of your players.

many of the country's most talented and experienced cricketers, who had signed to play with a rebel team in South Africa, and were thus banned from Test cricket.

'When he took over the captaincy, he probably wasn't ready for it,' Greg Chappell says. 'He was ready for it from the point of view of cricket knowledge, but I don't think he was emotionally and mentally ready for it. It came to him perhaps a bit quicker than he would have liked.'

This became apparent through the 1985–86 season, which evolved into one of the least productive in the history of the Australian team. In nine Tests, three at home against New Zealand and

The first big win as captain. Border with Dean Jones (left) and Craig McDermott after the 1987 World Cup final.

India, and three away against the Kiwis, Australia won no series and only one Test. Border scored four centuries, but his great innings were saving games, not winning them, and during the New Zealand tour at the end of this long, frustrating summer, Border poured his angry heart out to reporters.

'I've said everything I can say to that bunch,' he complained about his players. 'If they don't know now how I feel, they never will. It's up to them now to show they want to play under me as captain and for Australia.'

The appointment of Bob Simpson as coach for that New Zealand trip was an important one, and the team appeared to be toughening up during its next series, in India. Although they did not win a Test on tour, the opening encounter ended in a dramatic tie, and players such as Dean Jones, David Boon, Geoff Marsh and Greg Matthews seemed to be on the improve. Border's declaration (unusually bold for him at this stage in his captaincy career), setting the home side 348 to win on the final day of the first Test, was the key factor in making the event so memorable. Whatever the positive impressions created on the field, however, critics still pointed out that in his first 21 Tests as captain, Australia had won just three times. In that time, his supporters countered, the captain had scored seven centuries. As a batsman he was certainly doing his bit.

'If I had a chance to do it all again, there wouldn't be too much I'd change, except my approach to captaincy,' Border says today. 'Given the opportunity again, I'd go for it in a lot more positive fashion than I did.'

He really wasn't seen at his best as a Test skipper until 1989, though his tide had begun to turn when the Australians won the 1987 World Cup. They went into that tournament as outsiders but captured the ultimate prize thanks to a plan developed by Border and Simpson that deliberately separated Australia's style of cricket from that of other nations. In doing so they changed the way *all* teams approached one-day cricket.

'We did actually sit down and start to have specific tactics,' Border remembers. 'We'd never done that before, which is quite extraordinary; before that we had a lot of talented players, particularly in the early '80s, and we just went out and played.' The formula revolved around opening batsman Geoff

Marsh anchoring the innings, as more aggressive batsmen around him tried to keep the run-rate moving. The hope was that wickets could be kept for a dash in the final 10 overs, while throughout the batsmen adopted a bolder approach to running between wickets. Bowlers had a strong idea at which point of the innings they would be required, which helped them focus on when they would be needed. Most important of all, endless hours of hard work made the Australians the fittest and the best fielding team in the world. Border, lurking at mid-wicket and deadly when throwing at the stumps, became a symbol of this excellence in the field.

In 1987–88, Australia won a Test series for the first time under Border's captaincy, though it was a close-run thing: No. 11 Mike Whitney had to keep out Richard Hadlee in the third and final Test at the MCG to give his captain a draw and a 1–0 series win. In the second Test, Border scored 205, his highest Test score, during which he passed 7000 Test runs and then Greg Chappell's Australian record 7110. This was his 22nd century in his 91st Test.

DURING THE EARLY WEEKS of the 1989 Ashes tour, the English tabloids reckoned Border's team to be the worst Australian side to ever arrive in the UK. England had won the last three Ashes series in England, the previous Ashes series in Australia and also dominated the Bicentenary Test at the SCG in January 1988. Border's team had just completed a difficult series against the West Indies, with their only victory being on the turning track in Sydney where the West Indians always struggle. Most astonishing about that win, the destroyer had been Border's left-arm spin — his match figures of 11–96 (7–46 and 4–50) were the best ever by a captain in a Test. In 155 other Tests he took 28 wickets. Earlier in that series he had played his 100th Test match, the first Australian to do so.

The way Border's men turned the tabloids around in 1989 is mind-boggling. Australia's 4–0 victory — it could have been six but for rain — was to be the first of three consecutive Ashes series victories for Border, a captaincy record matched only by Joe Darling at the start of the century (and afterwards by Mark Taylor in the following three rubbers). Unlike 1981 and 1985, Border did not manage a Test century on this tour, but he still averaged 74 and scored six half-centuries. And most critics reckoned

Border soaks up Ashes glory at Old Trafford in 1989. To his right, vice-captain Geoff Marsh chants the Aussie team's victory song.

the first of these, an innings of 66 on the first day of the series, at Headingley, was the most critical knock of the summer. Put into bat, Australia were 2–57 when Border came in to attack the bowling and seize an initiative the Australians hold to this day.

It was during this series that Border and his men began plotting strategies on opposition players that were often less than conventional but which proved remarkably effective. A classic example was the placing of two fieldsmen at short mid-wicket, about 10 metres from the bat, for Graham Gooch, which appeared to destroy the Englishman's confidence to the point that he asked to be excused late in the series. The value of such strategies were on display between 1989 and 1992, when the Australian team enjoyed a

IAN BOTHAM: AB got the 'Captain Grumpy' tag because he was fed up with Australia losing. He took losing as a personal insult and decided to do something about it.

MARTIN CROWE: At the end of the day, Allan Border just wanted to play cricket to the best of his ability. He wasn't born to be in the spotlight, he was very down to earth, a great bloke, wonderful to have a beer with or a game of golf with. And, at the same time, he was really good to play against, because you knew exactly where you stood.

For me, he personified the true spirit of an Australian cricketer. Never gave an inch. Never gave a mug an even break, mate. He carried on the tradition of Ian Chappell, Greg Chappell, Dennis Lillee and Rod Marsh.

run of success, the only hiccups being in the Caribbean in 1991 and at the 1992 World Cup. Border went through a spell of 61 Test innings without a century during this time, but such was his consistency that he kept his Test batting average above 50 throughout. Against the West Indies in 1991, a clash advertised as a fight for the world championship of Test cricket, Border and his men battled manfully, but were outplayed in crucial sessions and could only win the final Test match (in which the captain played with a fractured thumb). They did, though, beat the West Indians in the one-day international series, a feat no visiting team had done before.

The shot that took Border past Sunil Gavaskar as the highest runscorer in Test history.

While his creativity evolved, his fundamental philosophy never changed. Border didn't think it was his job to motivate or educate Test players, other than through his own example on the field and in the nets. The logic was typically blunt: I never needed this sort of inspiration from others. Yet if asked, his teammates have all said that his advice was invariably spot-on. Meanwhile, on the field, his leadership became uncompromising.

'I formed a pretty good friendship with David Gower, Ian Botham, Mike Gatting and a lot of the English guys,' Border says of his early days as Australian captain. 'We got on well, had traditional after-day's-play drinking sessions. In this regard, England in 1989 was a watershed for me. The side had shown glimpses of turning things around. We had a few young players who were just starting to make their marks for Australia and I could see that there was a lot of potential in the team. But I needed to change my captaincy. I had to be a little harder, had to go into the game better prepared, had to plan things a lot better. The captain in 1989 had a lot harder edge.'

For Gower, this change of attitude was stark. 'Allan Border made no bones about it,' he reflects. 'He felt he was a little bit soft in 1985 and a bit too friendly, which is his natural nature, so he came back in '89 and made a simple point of talking to no one on our side, except to say 'heads' or 'tails' at the start of a game. I used to get on very well with him. I still do, actually, now that we have had that little hiatus. But I hardly had a civil word from him until August on that tour, by which time they had won the Ashes.'

The selectors made a point of giving Border tough cricketers — recalled 'veterans' Terry Alderman and Geoff Lawson, plus emerging talents such as Steve and Mark Waugh, Mark Taylor, Merv Hughes, Craig McDermott and Ian Healy — who wouldn't back down when things got difficult. Throughout all this, as the team improved and his captaincy got stronger, his batting stayed exactly the same: reliable, unpretentious, effective. And he stayed totally loyal to those prepared to fight by his side.

This loyalty led to his most infamous spat with officialdom. It came late in the 1991–92 home Test series against India, which Australia eventually won 4–0, when the selectors decided to drop Geoff Marsh. A dead-set battler, a 'Border-type' of cricketer, Marsh had had a greater influence on the Australian team than his Test batting average of 33 implied. He was a guy everyone liked and got along with, brave and dogged against the quickest bowlers, a strong backer of his leader, and an effective 'middle man' when Border was angry. In return, Border was eternally grateful for Marsh's support.

Before play on the final day of the fourth Test, in Adelaide, Border was told that his mate was gone. He was ropeable; in his eyes, this decision was heartless, disloyal and wrong, and he expressed his disapproval by not going onto the field at the start of play. Instead, he made an angry phone call to chairman of selectors Laurie Sawle in Perth — and then chose not to travel straightaway to the WACA for the final Test, preferring to stay in Adelaide overnight with his rejected allies.

Episodes such as this earned Border the 'Captain Grumpy' tag. His occasional blow-ups only reflected the fact he was human and that he was never completely comfortable with the pressures and off-field duties that came with the leadership. He was also a victim of his habit of keeping his emotions locked away until things came to a head. The eruption that eventually came could be ugly. 'The truth was that his "dark" days normally only occurred when he believed the team was not giving enough of themselves and when individuals were not doing everything in their power to perform at their peak,' Steve Waugh says.

In Sri Lanka in 1992 his captaincy came to the fore. In the first Test, in Colombo, Australia recovered from a first-innings deficit of 291 runs to win, the greatest revival in Test history. On the last day, Sri Lanka, chasing 181 for victory, reached 2–127 before Border took a stunning catch, running backwards from mid-on to dismiss Aravinda de Silva. From there, the home team's innings started to stumble, and at seven down with 31 still needed, the Test was back on an even keel. At this point, Border threw the ball to his young leg-spinner, Shane Warne, whose Test career bowling figures to that point were 1–335 from 90 overs. His only over to that point in

Border reaches 200 at Headingley, fourth Ashes Test, 1993.

the innings had gone for 11 runs. Healy, behind the stumps, remembers thinking, 'Geez, that's a gutsy move.' But Border knew his young man. Warne promptly took 3–0 and the Test was over.

Border's greatest ambition was for his men to win a series against the mighty West Indies. He came so close, just two runs from glory. In the fourth Test of 1992–93, a last-wicket partnership between Tim May and Craig McDermott inched Australia to within one run of a tie, two of a win. Australia led the five-match series 1–0. As always in tight situations, Border had a cricket ball in his possession, which he tossed from hand to hand. He and his teammates knew that ball well. They called it his 'worry ball'.

CLIVE LLOYD: Nothing ruffled Allan Border. He went out with this real Australian attitude that he wanted to stay out there no matter what was happening. He was a true professional, and a tough, tough nut to crack.

Sadly, the precious Australian victory was not to be. McDermott gloved a short ball from Courtney Walsh through to the keeper, and television cameras captured the Australian captain in the viewing area of the home dressing room, slamming the worry ball into the concrete floor so angrily it bounced up and hit the roof. A week later, the Australians were decimated in Perth, Border made the only pair of his first-class career, and the dream was gone.

BORDER ANNOUNCED HIS RETIREMENT on 11 May 1994, after taking his men to South Africa for the first tour by an Australian team after the dismantling of *apartheid*. Five years later, the Australian Cricket Board decided to introduce an award to be given to the official Australian cricketer of the year, and named it the 'Allan Border Medal'. Such an award could have been named after any of the truly great Australian cricketers of the past, yet there wasn't a word of protest when Border was the champion selected for the honour. It seemed so appropriate; he captured so much of what all young Australian cricketers yearn to be.

In the third Test of 1992–93, Border had scored his 10,000th Test run. During a brief New Zealand tour soon after, he went past Sunil Gavaskar's Test aggregate record, which prompted Sir Donald Bradman to issue a statement. 'Not only does this [the new record] recognise his skills as a batsman, it is also a tribute to his physical fitness and tough character.'

In England in 1993, Australia were as ruthless as they'd been in 1989, winning by four Tests to one. Warne, blossoming under his captain's faith, strength and guidance, had evolved into the most exciting and effective spin bowler in many years. At Headingley, Border ended up with 200 not out, sharing that long unbroken stand of 332 with Steve Waugh that gave Australia enough runs to win by an innings and 148 runs, and take an unassailable 3–0 lead in the series. In the years since, Australian teams have been remarkably successful, and one of Border's comrades, Dean Jones, sums up this revolution this way: 'AB effectively made a cricket team. He put it together. He taught the new rules, the new culture, he lifted the baggy green cap out of the mud, dusted it off, made it pristine again and put it on the heads of kids who were proud to wear it.

'I have great respect for the wonderful deeds that Mark Taylor did as a captain and for the magnificent work that Steve Waugh, who I think will be remembered as the most successful Australian captain of all time, has done. But if it wasn't for Allan Border they wouldn't be anywhere.'

Border toasts Steve Waugh, winner of the Allan Border Medal in January 2001 as Australia's cricketer of the year.

STATISTICS
Legends of Cricket
Career Records (as at 1 May 2002)

Sir Donald George Bradman (Australia)
Born: 27 August 1908; *Died:* 26 February 2001

TEST CRICKET (1928–1948)

Tests	Inn	NO	HS	Runs	Avge	100	50	Ct	Balls	Runs	Wkts	Avge	Best	5W	10M
52	80	14	334	6996	99.94	29	13	32	160	72	2	36.00	1–8	–	–

FIRST-CLASS CRICKET (1927–1949; NSW & South Australia)

Mat	Inn	NO	HS	Runs	Avge	100	50	Ct	Balls	Runs	Wkts	Avge	Best	5W	10M
234	338	43	452*	28067	95.14	117	69	131	2114	1367	36	37.97	3–35	–	–

Sir Garfield St Aubrun Sobers (West Indies)
Born: 28 July 1936

TEST CRICKET (1954–1974)

Tests	Inn	NO	HS	Runs	Avge	100	50	Ct	Balls	Runs	Wkts	Avge	Best	5W	10M
93	160	21	365*	8032	57.78	26	30	109	21599	7999	235	34.03	6–73	6	–

FIRST-CLASS CRICKET (1952–1974; Barbados, South Australia & Nottinghamshire)

Mat	Inn	NO	HS	Runs	Avge	100	50	Ct	Balls	Runs	Wkts	Avge	Best	5W	10M
383	609	93	365*	28315	54.87	86	121	407	70789	28941	1043	27.74	9–49	36	1

ONE-DAY INTERNATIONAL CRICKET (1973)

ODI	Inn	NO	HS	Runs	Avge	100	50	Ct	Balls	Runs	Wkts	Avge	Best	4W
1	1	–	0	0	0.00	–	–	1	63	31	1	31.00	1–31	–

Sir Isaac Vivian Alexander Richards (West Indies)
Born: 7 March 1952

TEST CRICKET (1974–1991)

Tests	Inn	NO	HS	Runs	Avge	100	50	Ct	Balls	Runs	Wkts	Avge	Best	5W	10M
121	182	12	291	8540	50.23	24	45	122	5170	1964	32	61.37	2–17	–	–

WORLD SERIES CRICKET SUPERTESTS (1977–1979)

Mat	Inn	NO	HS	Runs	Avge	100	50	Ct	Balls	Runs	Wkts	Avge	Best	5W	10M
14	25	3	177	1281	58.23	4	4	18	106	51	–	51.00	–	–	–

FIRST-CLASS CRICKET (1971–1993; Combined Islands, Leeward Islands, Somerset, Queensland & Glamorgan)

Mat	Inn	NO	HS	Runs	Avge	100	50	Ct	Balls	Runs	Wkts	Avge	Best	5W	10M
507	796	63	322	28067	49.40	114	162	464	23220	10070	223	45.15	5–88	1	–

ONE-DAY INTERNATIONAL CRICKET (1975–1991)

ODI	Inn	NO	HS	Runs	Avge	100	50	Ct	Balls	Runs	Wkts	Avge	Best	4W
187	167	24	189*	6721	47.00	11	45	101	5644	4228	118	35.83	6–41	3

Shane Keith Warne (Australia)
Born: 13 September 1969

TEST CRICKET (1992–)

Tests	Inn	NO	HS	Runs	Avge	100	50	Ct	Balls	Runs	Wkts	Avge	Best	5W	10M
101	139	13	99	2091	16.59	–	7	83	28346	11935	450	26.52	8–71	21	5

FIRST-CLASS CRICKET (1991–; Victoria & Hampshire)

Mat	Inn	NO	HS	Runs	Avge	100	50	Ct	Balls	Runs	Wkts	Avge	Best	5W	10M
192	257	34	99	3930	17.62	–	14	153	48496	21350	803	26.58	8–71	38	5

ONE-DAY INTERNATIONAL CRICKET (1993–)

ODI	Inn	NO	HS	Runs	Avge	100	50	Ct	Balls	Runs	Wkts	Avge	Best	4W
178	99	27	55	914	12.69	–	1	72	9837	7019	273	25.71	5–33	13

Sir John Berry Hobbs (England)
Born: 16 December 1882; Died: 21 December 1963

TEST CRICKET (1908–1930)

Tests	Inn	NO	HS	Runs	Avge	100	50	Ct	Balls	Runs	Wkts	Avge	Best	5W	10M
61	102	7	211	5410	56.94	15	28	17	376	165	1	165.00	1–19	–	–

FIRST-CLASS CRICKET (1905–1934; Surrey)

Mat	Inn	NO	HS	Runs	Avge	100	50	Ct	Balls	Runs	Wkts	Avge	Best	5W	10M
826	1315	106	316*	61237	50.65	197	270	340	5169	2666	107	24.92	7–56	3	–

Dennis Keith Lillee (Australia)
Born: 18 July 1949

TEST CRICKET (1971–1984)

Tests	Inn	NO	HS	Runs	Avge	100	50	Ct	Balls	Runs	Wkts	Avge	Best	5W	10M
70	90	24	73*	905	13.71	–	1	23	18467	8493	355	23.92	7–83	23	7

WORLD SERIES CRICKET SUPERTESTS (1977–1979)

Mat	Inn	NO	HS	Runs	Avge	100	50	Ct	Balls	Runs	Wkts	Avge	Best	5W	10M
14	24	6	37	226	12.56	–	–	3	3441	1800	67	26.87	7–23	4	–

FIRST-CLASS CRICKET (1969–1988; Western Australia, Tasmania & Northamptonshire)

Mat	Inn	NO	HS	Runs	Avge	100	50	Ct	Balls	Runs	Wkts	Avge	Best	5W	10M
198	241	70	73*	2377	13.90	–	2	67	43265	20695	882	23.46	8–29	50	13

ONE-DAY INTERNATIONAL CRICKET (1972–1983)

ODI	Inn	NO	HS	Runs	Avge	100	50	Ct	Balls	Runs	Wkts	Avge	Best	4W
63	34	8	42*	240	9.23	–	–	10	3593	2145	103	20.82	5–34	6

Sachin Ramesh Tendulkar (India)
Born: 24 April 1973

TEST CRICKET (1989–)

Tests	Inn	NO	HS	Runs	Avge	100	50	Ct	Balls	Runs	Wkts	Avge	Best	5W	10M
93	149	15	217	7869	58.72	29	31	63	1962	1037	25	41.48	3–10	–	–

FIRST-CLASS CRICKET (1988–; Mumbai & Yorkshire)

Mat	Inn	NO	HS	Runs	Avge	100	50	Ct	Balls	Runs	Wkts	Avge	Best	5W	10M
182	282	29	233*	15740	62.21	52	73	127	5171	2845	49	58.06	3–10	–	–

ONE-DAY INTERNATIONAL CRICKET (1989–)

ODI	Inn	NO	HS	Runs	Avge	100	50	Ct	Balls	Runs	Wkts	Avge	Best	4W
286	278	26	186*	11069	43.92	31	55	92	5999	4950	105	47.14	5–32	4

Imran Khan Niazi (Pakistan)
Born: 25 November 1952

TEST CRICKET (1971–1992)

Tests	Inn	NO	HS	Runs	Avge	100	50	Ct	Balls	Runs	Wkts	Avge	Best	5W	10M
88	126	25	136	3807	37.69	6	18	28	19458	8258	362	22.81	8–58	23	6

WORLD SERIES CRICKET SUPERTESTS (1977–1979)

Mat	Inn	NO	HS	Runs	Avge	100	50	Ct	Balls	Runs	Wkts	Avge	Best	5W	10M
5	8	2	24	127	21.17	–	–	1	999	521	25	20.84	4–24	–	–

FIRST-CLASS CRICKET (1969–1992; Lahore, Dawood, Worcestershire, Oxford University, Pakistan International Airlines, Sussex & NSW)

Mat	Inn	NO	HS	Runs	Avge	100	50	Ct	Balls	Runs	Wkts	Avge	Best	5W	10M
382	582	99	170	17771	36.79	30	93	117	65224	28726	1287	22.32	8–34	70	13

ONE-DAY INTERNATIONAL CRICKET (1974–1992)

ODI	Inn	NO	HS	Runs	Avge	100	50	Ct	Balls	Runs	Wkts	Avge	Best	4W
175	151	40	102*	3709	33.41	1	19	37	7461	4845	182	26.62	6–14	4

Walter Reginald Hammond (England)
Born: 19 June 1903; Died: 1 July 1965

TEST CRICKET (1927–1947)

Tests	Inn	NO	HS	Runs	Avge	100	50	Ct	Balls	Runs	Wkts	Avge	Best	5W	10M
85	140	16	336*	7249	58.45	22	24	110	7969	3138	83	37.80	5–36	2	–

FIRST-CLASS CRICKET (1920–1951; Gloucestershire)

Mat	Inn	NO	HS	Runs	Avge	100	50	Ct	Balls	Runs	Wkts	Avge	Best	5W	10M
634	1005	104	336*	50551	56.10	167	185	819	51449	22389	732	30.58	9–23	22	3

Sunil Manohar Gavaskar (India)
Born: 10 July 1949

TEST CRICKET (1971–1987)

Tests	Inn	NO	HS	Runs	Avge	100	50	Ct	Balls	Runs	Wkts	Avge	Best	5W	10M
125	214	16	236*	10122	51.12	34	45	108	380	206	1	206.00	1–34	–	–

FIRST-CLASS CRICKET (1966–1987; Bombay & Somerset)

Mat	Inn	NO	HS	Runs	Avge	100	50	Ct	Balls	Runs	Wkts	Avge	Best	5W	10M
348	563	61	340	25834	51.46	81	105	293	1953	1240	22	56.36	3–43	–	–

ONE-DAY INTERNATIONAL CRICKET (1974–1987)

ODI	Inn	NO	HS	Runs	Avge	100	50	Ct	Balls	Runs	Wkts	Avge	Best	4W
108	102	14	103*	3092	35.13	1	27	22	20	25	1	25.00	1–10	–

Ian Terence Botham (England)
Born: 24 November 1955

TEST CRICKET (1977–1992)

Tests	Inn	NO	HS	Runs	Avge	100	50	Ct	Balls	Runs	Wkts	Avge	Best	5W	10M
102	161	6	208	5200	33.54	14	22	120	21815	10878	383	28.40	8–34	27	4

FIRST-CLASS CRICKET (1974–1993; Somerset, Worcestershire, Queensland & Durham)

Mat	Inn	NO	HS	Runs	Avge	100	50	Ct	Balls	Runs	Wkts	Avge	Best	5W	10M
402	617	46	228	19399	33.97	38	97	354	63547	31902	1172	27.22	8–34	59	8

ONE-DAY INTERNATIONAL CRICKET (1977–92)

ODI	Inn	NO	HS	Runs	Avge	100	50	Ct	Balls	Runs	Wkts	Avge	Best	4W
116	106	15	79	2113	23.21	–	9	36	6271	4139	145	28.54	4–31	3

Sir Richard John Hadlee (New Zealand)
Born: 3 July 1951

TEST CRICKET (1973–1990)

Tests	Inn	NO	HS	Runs	Avge	100	50	Ct	Balls	Runs	Wkts	Avge	Best	5W	10M
86	134	19	151*	3124	27.16	2	15	39	21918	9612	431	22.30	9–56	36	9

FIRST-CLASS CRICKET (1971–1990; Canterbury, Nottinghamshire & Tasmania)

Mat	Inn	NO	HS	Runs	Avge	100	50	Ct	Balls	Runs	Wkts	Avge	Best	5W	10M
342	473	93	210*	12052	31.71	14	59	198	67519	26998	1490	18.11	9–52	102	18

ONE-DAY INTERNATIONAL CRICKET (1973–1990)

ODI	Inn	NO	HS	Runs	Avge	100	50	Ct	Balls	Runs	Wkts	Avge	Best	4W
115	98	17	79	1751	21.61	–	4	27	6182	3407	158	21.56	5–25	6

Keith Ross Miller (Australia)
Born: 28 November 1919

TEST CRICKET (1946–1956)

Tests	Inn	NO	HS	Runs	Avge	100	50	Ct	Balls	Runs	Wkts	Avge	Best	5W	10M
55	87	7	147	2958	36.97	7	13	38	10461	3906	170	22.97	7–60	7	1

FIRST-CLASS CRICKET (1938–1959; Victoria, NSW & Nottinghamshire)

Mat	Inn	NO	HS	Runs	Avge	100	50	Ct	Balls	Runs	Wkts	Avge	Best	5W	10M
226	326	36	281*	14183	48.90	41	63	136	28405	11087	497	22.30	7–12	16	1

Dr William Gilbert Grace (England)
Born: 18 July 1848; *Died:* 23 October 1915

TEST CRICKET (1880–1899)

Tests	Inn	NO	HS	Runs	Avge	100	50	Ct	Balls	Runs	Wkts	Avge	Best	5W	10M
22	36	2	170	1098	32.29	2	5	39	666	236	9	26.22	2–12	–	–

FIRST-CLASS CRICKET (1865–1908; Gloucestershire & London County)

Mat	Inn	NO	HS	Runs	Avge	100	50	Ct	Balls	Runs	Wkts	Avge	Best	5W	10M
872	1493	105	344	54896	39.55	126	254	887	126157	51545	2876	17.92	10–92*	246	66

* 12-a-side match

Robert Graeme Pollock (South Africa)
Born: 27 February 1944

TEST CRICKET (1963–1970)

Tests	Inn	NO	HS	Runs	Avge	100	50	Ct	Balls	Runs	Wkts	Avge	Best	5W	10M
23	41	4	274	2256	60.97	7	11	17	414	204	4	51.00	2–50	–	–

FIRST-CLASS CRICKET (1960–1987; Eastern Province & Transvaal)

Mat	Inn	NO	HS	Runs	Avge	100	50	Ct	Balls	Runs	Wkts	Avge	Best	5W	10M
262	437	54	274	20940	54.67	64	99	248	3743	2062	43	47.95	3–46	–	–

Malcolm Denzil Marshall (West Indies)
Born: 18 April 1958; Died: 4 November 1999

TEST CRICKET (1978–1991)

Tests	Inn	NO	HS	Runs	Avge	100	50	Ct	Balls	Runs	Wkts	Avge	Best	5W	10M
81	107	11	92	1810	18.85	–	10	25	17584	7876	376	20.94	7–22	22	4

FIRST-CLASS CRICKET (1977–1996; Barbados, Hampshire & Natal)

Mat	Inn	NO	HS	Runs	Avge	100	50	Ct	Balls	Runs	Wkts	Avge	Best	5W	10M
408	516	73	120*	11004	24.83	7	54	145	74645	3180	1651	19.10	8–71	85	13

ONE-DAY INTERNATIONAL CRICKET (1980–1992)

ODI	Inn	NO	HS	Runs	Avge	100	50	Ct	Balls	Runs	Wkts	Avge	Best	4W	
136	83	19	66	955	14.92	–	2	15	7175	4233	157	26.96	4–18	6	

Gregory Stephen Chappell (Australia)
Born: 7 August 1948

TEST CRICKET (1970–1984)

Tests	Inn	NO	HS	Runs	Avge	100	50	Ct	Balls	Runs	Wkts	Avge	Best	5W	10M
87	151	19	247*	7110	53.86	24	31	122	5327	1913	47	40.70	5–61	1	–

WORLD SERIES CRICKET SUPERTESTS (1977–1979)

Mat	Inn	NO	HS	Runs	Avge	100	50	Ct	Balls	Runs	Wkts	Avge	Best	5W	10M
14	26	1	246*	1416	56.64	5	4	19	346	155	6	25.83	5–20	1	–

FIRST-CLASS CRICKET (1966–1984; South Australia, Somerset & Queensland)

Mat	Inn	NO	HS	Runs	Avge	100	50	Ct	Balls	Runs	Wkts	Avge	Best	5W	10M
321	542	72	247*	24535	52.20	74	111	376	20950	8717	291	29.95	7–40	5	–

ONE-DAY INTERNATIONAL CRICKET (1971–1983)

ODI	Inn	NO	HS	Runs	Avge	100	50	Ct	Balls	Runs	Wkts	Avge	Best	4W	
74	72	14	138*	2231	40.18	3	14	23	3108	2096	72	29.11	5–15	2	

George Alphonso Headley (West Indies)
Born: 30 May 1909; Died: 30 November 1983

TEST CRICKET (1930–1954)

Tests	Inn	NO	HS	Runs	Avge	100	50	Ct	Balls	Runs	Wkts	Avge	Best	5W	10M
22	40	4	270*	2190	60.83	10	5	14	398	230	–	–	–	–	–

FIRST-CLASS CRICKET (1928–1954; Jamaica)

Mat	Inn	NO	HS	Runs	Avge	100	50	Ct	Balls	Runs	Wkts	Avge	Best	5W	10M
103	164	22	344*	9921	69.86	33	44	76	3845	1842	51	36.11	5–33	1	–

Sir Frank Mortimer Maglinne Worrell (West Indies)
Born: 1 August 1924; Died: 13 March 1967

TEST CRICKET (1948–1963)

Tests	Inn	NO	HS	Runs	Avge	100	50	Ct	Balls	Runs	Wkts	Avge	Best	5W	10M
51	87	9	261	3860	49.48	9	22	43	7141	2672	69	38.72	7–70	2	–

FIRST-CLASS CRICKET (1940–1964; Barbados & Jamaica)

Mat	Inn	NO	HS	Runs	Avge	100	50	Ct	Balls	Runs	Wkts	Avge	Best	5W	10M
208	326	49	308*	15025	54.24	39	80	139	26740	10115	349	28.98	7–70	13	–

Sir Leonard Hutton (England)
Born: 23 June 1916; Died: 6 September 1990

TEST CRICKET (1937–1955)

Tests	Inn	NO	HS	Runs	Avge	100	50	Ct	Balls	Runs	Wkts	Avge	Best	5W	10M
79	138	15	364	6971	56.67	19	33	57	260	232	3	77.33	1–2	–	–

FIRST-CLASS CRICKET (1934–1960; Yorkshire)

Mat	Inn	NO	HS	Runs	Avge	100	50	Ct	Balls	Runs	Wkts	Avge	Best	5W	10M
513	814	91	364	40140	55.51	129	177	400	9774	5106	173	29.51	6–76	4	1

Chaudhry Wasim Akram (Pakistan)
Born: 3 June 1966

TEST CRICKET (1985–)

Tests	Inn	NO	HS	Runs	Avge	100	50	Ct	Balls	Runs	Wkts	Avge	Best	5W	10M
104	147	19	257*	2898	22.64	3	7	44	22627	9779	414	23.62	7–119	25	5

FIRST-CLASS CRICKET (1984–; Pakistan Automobiles Corporation, Lahore, Lancashire, Pakistan International Airlines)

Mat	Inn	NO	HS	Runs	Avge	100	50	Ct	Balls	Runs	Wkts	Avge	Best	5W	10M
252	348	39	257*	7106	22.99	7	24	97	49272	22046	1022	21.57	8–30	70	16

ONE-DAY INTERNATIONAL CRICKET (1984–)

ODI	Inn	NO	HS	Runs	Avge	100	50	Ct	Balls	Runs	Wkts	Avge	Best	4W	
331	261	50	86	3328	16.37	–	6	85	16972	10966	459	23.89	5–15	21	

Kapil Dev Nikhanj (India)
Born: 6 January 1959

TEST CRICKET (1978–1994)

Tests	Inn	NO	HS	Runs	Avge	100	50	Ct	Balls	Runs	Wkts	Avge	Best	5W	10M
131	184	15	163	5248	31.05	8	27	64	27740	12867	434	29.64	9–83	23	2

FIRST-CLASS CRICKET (1974–1994; Haryana, Northamptonshire & Worcestershire)

Mat	Inn	NO	HS	Runs	Avge	100	50	Ct	Balls	Runs	Wkts	Avge	Best	5W	10M
275	384	39	193	11356	32.91	18	56	192	48853	22626	835	27.09	9–83	39	3

ONE-DAY INTERNATIONAL CRICKET (1978–1994)

ODI	Inn	NO	HS	Runs	Avge	100	50	Ct	Balls	Runs	Wkts	Avge	Best	4W	
225	198	39	175*	3783	23.79	1	14	71	11202	6945	253	27.45	5–43	4	

Stephen Rodger Waugh (Australia)
Born: 2 June 1965

TEST CRICKET (1985–)

Tests	Inn	NO	HS	Runs	Avge	100	50	Ct	Balls	Runs	Wkts	Avge	Best	5W	10M
148	233	41	200	9600	50.00	27	44	102	7193	3197	89	35.92	5–28	3	–

FIRST-CLASS CRICKET (1984–; NSW & Somerset)

Mat	Inn	NO	HS	Runs	Avge	100	50	Ct	Balls	Runs	Wkts	Avge	Best	5W	10M
315	486	80	216*	21127	52.03	67	88	248	16636	7799	243	32.09	6–51	5	–

ONE-DAY INTERNATIONAL CRICKET (1986–)

ODI	Inn	NO	HS	Runs	Avge	100	50	Ct	Balls	Runs	Wkts	Avge	Best	4W	
325	288	58	120*	7569	32.90	3	45	111	8883	6761	195	34.67	4–33	3	

Barry Anderson Richards (South Africa)
Born: 21 July 1945

TEST CRICKET (1970)

Tests	Inn	NO	HS	Runs	Avge	100	50	Ct	Balls	Runs	Wkts	Avge	Best	5W	10M
4	7	–	140	508	72.57	2	2	3	72	26	1	26.00	1–12	–	–

WORLD SERIES CRICKET SUPERTESTS (1977–1979)

Mat	Inn	NO	HS	Runs	Avge	100	50	Ct	Balls	Runs	Wkts	Avge	Best	5W	10M
5	8	1	207	554	79.14	2	2	1	–	–	–	–	–	–	–

FIRST-CLASS CRICKET (1963–1983; Natal, Gloucestershire, Hampshire & South Australia)

Mat	Inn	NO	HS	Runs	Avge	100	50	Ct	Balls	Runs	Wkts	Avge	Best	5W	10M
339	576	58	356	28358	54.74	80	152	367	6120	2886	77	37.48	7–63	1	–

Allan Robert Border (Australia)
Born: 27 July 1955

TEST CRICKET (1978–1994)

Tests	Inn	NO	HS	Runs	Avge	100	50	Ct	Balls	Runs	Wkts	Avge	Best	5W	10M
156	265	44	205	11174	50.56	27	63	156	4009	1525	39	39.10	7–46	2	1

FIRST-CLASS CRICKET (1977–1996; NSW, Gloucestershire, Queensland & Essex)

Mat	Inn	NO	HS	Runs	Avge	100	50	Ct	Balls	Runs	Wkts	Avge	Best	5W	10M
385	625	97	205	27131	51.38	70	142	379	9750	4161	106	39.25	7–46	3	1

ONE-DAY INTERNATIONAL CRICKET (1979–1994)

ODI	Inn	NO	HS	Runs	Avge	100	50	Ct	Balls	Runs	Wkts	Avge	Best	4W	
273	252	39	127*	6524	30.63	3	39	127	2661	2071	73	28.37	3–20	–	

Statistics for WG Grace and Sir Jack Hobbs

The question of which 19th-century matches were and weren't first-class — and even which scores were correct — has been an awkward one for cricket statisticians, in part because the definition of what constituted a first-class match was not agreed upon until 1947, more than 30 years after WG Grace's death and more than a decade after Jack Hobbs retired. For many years, the most reputable record of Grace's career was the one published in *Wisden* in 1916, to supplement his obituary. However, in the 1950s, the accuracy of these statistics was questioned, with specific reference to some scores that had been wrongly recorded and a few games that seemed to be classed as 'first-class' purely because Grace was playing. Then, in 1973, the Association of Cricket Statisticians (ACS) was formed, with one of its first objectives being to formalise the list of first-class matches. The result of their analysis was an updated record for WG, which reduced the number of first-class matches he played by nine, his first-class total runs by 685 and the number of centuries he scored by two.

In Hobbs' case, the ACS did not include one match from England's 1909–10 tour of South Africa which had previously appeared in his first-class record, but did include a private tour of India and Ceylon in 1930–31 on which Hobbs played in nine matches and scored two centuries. Thus, the ACS has Hobbs scoring 61,760 first-class runs and 199 first-class centuries during his career.

There is no doubt that the ACS's figures are precise. However, by using them the significance of some famous cricket moments — events that were much celebrated at the time — is greatly diminished. For example, when that huge crowd turned out at Taunton in 1925 to see Hobbs equal WG's 126 first-class centuries (see the photograph on page 56), they were, if we now accept the 'modern' figures, actually a few weeks late. Consequently, in this book we have followed the lead of the master statistician Bill Frindall, who continues to use the traditional figures — incorporating corrections to scores without discarding games of questionable standing — while noting the ACS's revised numbers. Frindall's more detailed explanation for his approach is included in the appendix to Simon Rae's definitive biography of WG, *WG Grace*, which was published in 1998.

Test Records (as at 1 May 2002)

Most Runs

R	Batsman	Inn	Runs	Avge
1	AR Border	265	11174	50.56
2	SM Gavaskar	214	10122	51.12
3	SR Waugh	233	9600	50.00
4	GA Gooch	215	8900	42.58
5	Javed Miandad	189	8832	52.57
6	IVA Richards	182	8540	50.23
7	DI Gower	204	8231	44.25
8	G Boycott	193	8114	47.72
9	GS Sobers	160	8032	57.78
10	ME Waugh	205	7949	42.28
11	SR Tendulkar	149	7869	58.72
12	MA Atherton	212	7728	37.69
13	MC Cowdrey	188	7624	44.06
14	CG Greenidge	185	7558	44.72
15	MA Taylor	186	7525	43.49
20	BC Lara	150	7320	50.13
21	WR Hammond	140	7249	58.45
22	GS Chappell	151	7110	53.86
23	DG Bradman	80	6996	99.94
24	L Hutton	138	6971	56.67
38	JB Hobbs	102	5410	56.94
44	Kapil Dev	184	5248	31.05
46	IT Botham	161	5200	33.54

Highest Batting Average

R	Batsman	Inn	Runs	Avge
1	DG Bradman	80	6996	99.94
2	RG Pollock	41	2256	60.97
3	GA Headley	40	2190	60.83
4	H Sutcliffe	84	4555	60.73
5	AC Gilchrist	44	2160	60.00
6	SR Tendulkar	149	7869	58.72
7	K Barrington	131	6806	58.67
8	ED Weekes	81	4455	58.61
9	WR Hammond	140	7249	58.45
10	GS Sobers	160	8032	57.78
11	JB Hobbs	102	5410	56.94
12	CL Walcott	74	3798	56.68
13	L Hutton	138	6971	56.67
14	GS Chappell	151	7110	53.86
15	AD Nourse	62	2960	53.81
17	Javed Miandad	189	8832	52.57
19	SM Gavaskar	214	10122	51.12
20	AR Border	265	11174	50.56
22	IVA Richards	182	8540	50.23
23	BC Lara	150	7320	50.13
25	SR Waugh	233	9600	50.00

1. Qualification: 40 innings.

In all tables 'R' stands for Ranking. Best performers in each category are listed, plus any of ESPN top 50 Legends who are ranked highly.

Most Wickets

R	Bowler	Balls	Wkts	Avge
1	CA Walsh	30019	519	24.44
2	SK Warne	28346	450	26.52
3	Kapil Dev	27740	434	29.64
4	RJ Hadlee	21918	431	22.30
5	Wasim Akram	22627	414	23.62
6	M Muralitharan	24511	412	23.38
7	CEL Ambrose	22103	405	20.99
8	GD McGrath	20149	389	21.91
9	IT Botham	21815	383	28.40
10	MD Marshall	17584	376	20.94
11	Imran Khan	19458	362	22.81
12	DK Lillee	18467	355	23.92
13	Waqar Younis	15109	353	22.94
14	AA Donald	15519	330	22.25
15	RGD Willis	17357	325	25.20
18	FS Trueman	15178	307	21.57
21	BS Bedi	21364	266	28.71
23	J Garner	13175	259	20.97
25	MA Holding	12680	249	23.68
26	R Benaud	19108	248	27.03
31	GS Sobers	21599	235	34.03
33	RR Lindwall	13650	228	23.03
35	CV Grimmett	14513	216	24.21
37	AME Roberts	11135	202	25.61
43	JC Laker	12027	193	21.24
45	SF Barnes	7873	189	16.43
47	AK Davidson	11587	186	20.53

1. Bowlers from pre-1920 dominate a 'Best Test Bowling Averages' table. Of all to bowl at least 3000 deliveries in Tests, GA Lohmann (18 Tests between 1886 and 1896) has the lowest average — 112 wickets at 10.75. Next best is SF Barnes, then CTB Turner (101 wickets at 16.53, between 1887–1895) and R Peel (101 wickets at 16.98, 1884–1896). Of post-World War II Test players to bowl more than 5000 deliveries, the lowest career bowling average belongs to JH Wardle, with 102 wickets at 20.39. Next best are AK Davidson, SM Pollock (261 wickets at 20.72), MD Marshall, J Garner and CEL Ambrose.

2. MJ Procter (Legend No. 32) played in only seven Tests, taking 41 wickets at 15.02. This is the fourth lowest average of all bowlers to take 25 or more Test wickets, behind Lohmann, JJ Ferris (61 wickets at 12.70) and AE Trott (26 wickets at 15.00). Procter's strike rate of a wicket every 36.92 balls is the third best of all bowlers to take 25 or more wickets in Tests, after Lohmann and Trott.

3. WJ O'Reilly (Legend No. 30) took 144 Test wickets in 27 Tests between 1932 and 1946, at an average of 22.59. Of Australian bowlers since World War I to take 100 Test wickets, only AK Davidson and GD McGrath have a better bowling average.

Most Centuries

R	Batsman	Inn	100s
1	SM Gavaskar	214	34
2	DG Bradman	80	29
2	SR Tendulkar	149	29
4	SR Waugh	233	27
4	AR Border	265	27
6	GS Sobers	160	26
7	GS Chappell	151	24
7	IVA Richards	182	24
9	Javed Miandad	189	23
10	WR Hammond	140	22
10	M Azharuddin	147	22
10	MC Cowdrey	188	22
10	G Boycott	193	22

1. The highest score made in Tests is 375 by BC Lara (for West Indies v England, St John's, 1994). Next best is 365* by GS Sobers (for West Indies v Pakistan, Kingston, 1957-58), then 364 by L Hutton (for England v Australia, The Oval, 1938), 340 by ST Jayasuriya (for Sri Lanka v India, Colombo, 1997-98), 337 by Hanif Mohammed (for Pakistan v West Indies, Bridgetown, 1957-58), 336* by WR Hammond (for England v New Zealand, Auckland, 1933), 334* by MA Taylor (for Australia v Pakistan, Peshawar, 1998) and 334 by DG Bradman (for Australia v England, Leeds, 1930).

2. VT Trumper (Legend No. 46) scored 3163 runs in 48 Tests between 1899 and 1912, at an average of 39.04. His eight centuries was the most scored by an Australian in Tests until DG Bradman scored his ninth Test hundred in 1931.

Most Five Wickets in an Innings

R	Bowler	Tests	5WI
1	RJ Hadlee	86	36
2	M Muralitharan	73	33
3	IT Botham	102	27
4	Wasim Akram	104	25
5	SF Barnes	27	24
6	DK Lillee	70	23
6	GD McGrath	84	23
6	Imran Khan	88	23
6	Kapil Dev	131	23
10	Waqar Younis	79	22
10	MD Marshall	81	22
10	CEL Ambrose	98	22
10	CA Walsh	132	22
14	CV Grimmett	37	21
14	SK Warne	101	21
16	AA Donald	72	20
19	FS Trueman	67	17
21	R Benaud	63	16
27	AK Davidson	44	14
27	BS Bedi	67	14

All-rounders with 1500 Test Runs and 150 Test Wickets

R	Player	Tests	Runs	Avge	Wkts	Avge
1	GS Sobers	93	8032	57.78	235	34.03
2	Imran Khan	88	3807	37.69	362	22.81
3	KR Miller	55	2958	36.97	170	22.97
4	SM Pollock	63	2242	31.57	261	20.72
5	RJ Hadlee	86	3124	27.16	431	22.30
6	IT Botham	102	5200	33.54	383	28.40
7	CL Cairns	55	2853	32.79	197	28.80
8	Kapil Dev	131	5248	31.05	434	29.64
9	MH Mankad	44	2109	31.47	162	32.32
10	Wasim Akram	104	2898	22.64	414	23.62
11	RR Lindwall	61	1502	21.15	228	23.03
12	R Benaud	63	2201	24.45	248	27.03
13	MD Marshall	81	1810	18.85	376	20.94
14	RJ Shastri	80	3830	35.79	151	40.96
15	SK Warne	101	2091	16.59	450	26.52

The ranking is determined by dividing the player's batting average by his bowling average, the higher the result the better.

1. The first man to score 2000 runs and take 100 wickets in Tests was W Rhodes (Legend No. 28), who — in a career that ran from 1899 to 1930 — scored 2325 runs (at an average of 30.19) and took 127 wickets (at 26.96).
2. MJ Procter (Legend No. 32) played in only seven Tests (1967–70), scoring 226 runs (at 25.11) and taking 41 wickets (at 15.02). In first-class cricket, Procter scored 21,936 runs (at 36.01) and took 1417 wickets (at 19.53) between 1965 and 1988.

Most 10 Wickets in a Match

R	Bowler	Tests	10WM
1	M Muralitharan	73	10
2	RJ Hadlee	86	9
3	SF Barnes	27	7
3	CV Grimmett	37	7
3	DK Lillee	70	7
6	DL Underwood	86	6
6	Imran Khan	88	6
8	GA Lohmann	18	5
8	AV Bedser	51	5
8	Abdul Qadir	67	5
8	Waqar Younis	79	5
8	SK Warne	101	5
8	Wasim Akram	104	5
14	MD Marshall	81	4
14	IT Botham	102	4

1. The most wickets taken by a bowler in one Test is 19, by JC Laker (9-37 and 10-53 for England v Australia, Manchester, 1956). Next best is 17, by SF Barnes (8-56 and 9-103 for England v South Africa, Johannesburg, 1913-14); then 16 by ND Hirwani (8-61 and 8-75 for India v West Indies, Madras, 1987-88), RAL Massie (8-84 and 8-53 for Australia v England, Lord's, 1972) and M Muralitharan (7-155 and 9-65 for Sri Lanka v England, The Oval, 1998).

Most Dismissals by a Wicketkeeper

R	Keeper	Tests	Ct	St	Total
1	IA Healy	119	366	29	395
2	RW Marsh	96	343	12	355
3	PJL Dujon	79	265	5	270
4	APE Knott	95	250	19	269
5	Wasim Bari	81	201	27	228
6	TG Evans	91	173	46	219
7	MV Boucher	52	196	5	201
8	AC Parore	67	194	7	201
9	SMH Kirmani	88	160	38	198
10	AJ Stewart	64	184	11	195

1. These figures only include catches taken when keeping wicket.

Most Catches by a Non-Wicketkeeper

R	Fieldsman	Catches
1	ME Waugh	173
2	MA Taylor	157
3	AR Border	156
4	GS Chappell	122
5	IVA Richards	122
6	IT Botham	120
6	MC Cowdrey	120
8	RB Simpson	110
8	WR Hammond	110
10	GS Sobers	109

Most Appearances

R	Player	Tests
1	AR Border	156
2	SR Waugh	148
3	CA Walsh	132
4	Kapil Dev	131
5	SM Gavaskar	125
5	ME Waugh	125
7	Javed Miandad	124
8	IVA Richards	121
9	IA Healy	119
10	GA Gooch	118
21	Wasim Akram	104
24	Ian Botham	102
25	SK Warne	101
27	CEL Ambrose	98
29	APE Knott	95
31	GS Sobers	93
31	SR Tendulkar	93
38	Imran Khan	88
40	GS Chappell	87
41	RJ Hadlee	86
44	WR Hammond	85
44	BC Lara	85
46	GD McGrath	84

One-Day International Records (as at 1 May 2002)

Most Runs

R	Batsman	Inn	Runs	Avge
1	SR Tendulkar	278	11069	43.92
2	M Azharuddin	308	9378	36.92
3	DL Haynes	237	8648	41.37
4	ME Waugh	236	8500	39.35
5	Inzamam-ul-Haq	249	8459	39.71
6	PA de Silva	266	8430	35.12
7	Saeed Anwar	227	8348	39.75
8	SR Waugh	288	7569	32.90
9	SC Ganguly	185	7522	43.98
10	A Ranatunga	255	7456	35.84
11	Javed Miandad	218	7381	41.70
12	ST Jayasuriya	249	7365	30.68
13	BC Lara	189	7257	42.43
14	Salim Malik	256	7170	32.88
15	IVA Richards	167	6721	47.00
17	AR Border	252	6524	30.62

Note: SR Tendulkar has scored 31 ODI hundreds. Next best is Saeed Anwar (19), then ME Waugh (18), SC Ganguly (18), DL Haynes (17), BC Lara (14), G Kirsten (12), NJ Astle (12), PA de Silva (11), ST Jayasuriya (11), IVA Richards (11), CG Greenidge (11) and Ijaz Ahmed (10).

Most Wickets

R	Bowler	Balls	Wkts	Avge
1	Wasim Akram	16972	459	23.89
2	Waqar Younis	11465	375	23.55
3	A Kumble	12035	290	29.15
4	M Muralitharan	10276	276	24.08
5	J Srinath	10637	276	28.78
6	SK Warne	9837	273	25.71
7	Saqlain Mushtaq	8071	271	21.07
8	Kapil Dev	11202	253	27.45
9	AA Donald	7515	238	21.57
10	GD McGrath	8228	235	23.13
11	SM Pollock	8364	228	23.35
12	CA Walsh	10822	227	30.47
13	CEL Ambrose	9353	225	24.12
14	WPUJC Vaas	8741	222	27.63
15	ST Jayasuriya	9557	216	35.40
18	SR Waugh	8883	195	34.67
20	Imran Khan	7461	182	26.61
26	RJ Hadlee	6182	158	21.56
27	MD Marshall	7175	157	26.96
31	J Garner	5330	146	18.84
32	IT Botham	6271	145	28.54
33	M Holding	5473	142	21.36
44	IVA Richards	5644	118	35.83

World Cup (1975–1999): Most Runs

R	Batsman	Inn	Runs	Avge
1	Javed Miandad	30	1083	43.32
2	SR Tendulkar	21	1059	58.83
3	IVA Richards	21	1013	62.31
4	ME Waugh	22	1004	52.84
5	SR Waugh	30	978	48.90
6	A Ranatunga	29	969	46.14
7	GA Gooch	21	897	44.85
13	BC Lara	19	708	44.25
16	Kapil Dev	24	669	37.16
17	Imran Khan	24	666	35.05

World Cup (1975–1999): Most Wickets

R	Bowler	Balls	Wkts	Avge
1	Wasim Akram	1662	43	25.81
2	AA Donald	1164	37	21.08
3	Imran Khan	1017	34	19.26
4	SK Warne	977	32	19.50
5	CZ Harris	956	30	24.40
6	IT Botham	1332	30	25.58
8	Kapil Dev	1422	28	31.85
8	CA Walsh	948	27	20.25
9	SR Waugh	1039	27	30.14
10	AME Roberts	1021	26	21.23

Further Reading

Among the biographies, tour books, histories, almanacs and statistics books consulted for *ESPN's Legends of Cricket* were the following:

ABC Australian Cricket Almanacs 1990–1994

John Arlott, *The Ashes 1972*; Pelham, London, 1973

John Arlott, *John Arlott's Book of Cricketers*; Angus & Robertson, Sydney, 1979

Trevor Bailey, *The Greatest of my Time*; Eyre & Spottiswoode, London, 1968

Richie Benaud, *A Tale of Two Tests*; Hodder & Stoughton, London, 1962

Richie Benaud, *Willow Patterns*; Hodder & Stoughton, London, 1969

Richie Benaud, *On Reflection*; Collins, Sydney, 1984

Richie Benaud, *Anything But… An Autobiography*; Hodder & Stoughton, London, 1998

Scyld Berry (ed.), *The Observer on Cricket*; Unwin Hyman, London, 1987

Dickie Bird, *My Autobiography*; Hodder & Stoughton, London, 1997

Henry Blofeld, *The Packer Affair*; Collins, London, 1978

Mihir Bose, *A Maidan View: The Magic of Indian Cricket*; Allen & Unwin, London, 1976

David Boon, *Under the Southern Cross*; HarperSports, Sydney, 1996

Allan Border, *Beyond Ten Thousand: My Life Story*; Swan Publishing, Perth, 1993

Ian Botham, *The Incredible Tests 1981*; Pelham Books, London, 1982

Ian Botham, *My Autobiography*; Collins Willow, London, 1994

Don Bradman, *Farewell to Cricket*; Hodder & Stoughton, London, 1950

The Bradman Albums (Vols 1 & 2); Weldon, Sydney, 1987

Ian Brayshaw, *End of Play: Caught Marsh Bowled Lillee*; ABC Books, Sydney, 1984

Mike Brearley, *The Return of the Ashes*; Pelham Books, London, 1978

Mike Brearley, *The Ashes Retained*; Hodder & Stoughton, London, 1979

Mike Brearley, *Phoenix From The Ashes*; Hodder & Stoughton, London, 1982

Keith Butler, *Howzat: Sixteen Australian Cricketers talk to Keith Butler*; Collins, Sydney, 1979

Neville Cardus, *Cardus on Cricket*; Souvenir Press, London, 1977 (first printed 1949)

Neville Cardus, *Cardus in the Covers*; Souvenir Press, London, 1978

Neville Cardus, *Play Resumed With Cardus*; Souvenir Press, London, 1979

Neville Cardus, *A Fourth Innings With Cardus*; Souvenir Press, London, 1981

Neville Cardus, *A Cardus For All Seasons*; Souvenir Press, London, 1985

Greg Chappell, *The 100th Summer*; Garry Sparke & Associates, Melbourne 1977

Ian Chappell, *Chappelli*; Hutchinson, Melbourne, 1976

Ewen Chatfield, *Chats*; MOA Publishing, Auckland, 1988

CD Clark, *The Record-breaking Sunil Gavaskar*; David & Charles, London, 1980

Denis Compton, *Compton on Cricketers*; Cassell, London, 1980

Tony Cozier, *The West Indies: Fifty Years in Test Cricket*; Angus & Robertson, Brighton UK, 1978

Philip Derriman, *True to the Blue: A History of the NSW Cricket Association*; Richard Smart Publishing, Sydney, 1985

Jack Fingleton, *Cricket Crisis*; Cassell, Sydney, 1946

Jack Fingleton, *Brightly Fades The Don*; Collins, London, 1949

Jack Fingleton, *The Ashes Crown The Year*; Collins, Sydney, 1954

David Foot, *The Reasons Why*; Robson, London, 1996

Bill Frindall, *The Wisden Book of Test Cricket 1876–77 to 1977–78*; Queen Anne Press, London, 1979

Bill Frindall and Victor H Isaacs, *The Wisden Book of One-day International Cricket 1971–1985*; John Wisden, London, 1985

Bill Frindall, *The Wisden Book of Cricket Records*; Headline Book Publishing, London, 1998

Bill Frindall, *The Wisden Book of Test Cricket (Volume 2) 1970–1996*; Headline Publishing, London, 2000

Bill Frindall, *The Wisden Book of Test Cricket (Volume 3) 1996–2000*; Headline Book Publishing, London, 2000

David Frith, *The Fast Men*; Transworld, London, 1975

David Frith (ed.), *Cricket Gallery*; Rigby, London, 1976

David Frith, *The Slow Men*; Horwitz Grahame Books, Sydney, 1984

Mike Gatting, *Leading From The Front*; Queen Anne Press, London, 1988

Sunil Gavaskar, *Idols*; Allen & Unwin, London, 1984

David Gower, *Gower: The Autobiography*; Collins Willow, London, 1992

WG Grace, *WG: Cricketing Reminiscences & Personal Recollections*; The Hambledon Press, London, 1980 (first published 1899)

Anna Grimshaw (ed.), *CLR James: Cricket*; Allison & Busby, London, 1986

Richard Hadlee and Dick Brittenden, *Hadlee*; AH & AW Reed Ltd, Auckland, 1981

Richard Hadlee, *Rhythm and Swing*; Collins, Auckland, 1989

Gideon Haigh, *The Cricket War*; Text Publishing, Melbourne, 1993

Gideon Haigh, *The Summer Game*; Text Publishing, Melbourne, 1997

Chris Harte, *Two Tours and Pollock*; Sports Marketing, Adelaide, 1988

Ian Healy, *Hands & Heals*; HarperSports, Sydney, 2000

Sir Jack Hobbs, *My Life Story*; The Hambledon Press, London, 1978 (first published 1935)

Gerald Howat, *Walter Hammond*; Allen & Unwin, London, 1984

Len Hutton, *Just My Story*; Hutchinson, London, 1956

Imran Khan, *Imran*; Pelham Books, London, 1983

Imran Khan, *All Round View*; Chatto & Windis, London, 1988

CLR James, *Beyond a Boundary*; Stanley Paul, London, 1963

Kapil Dev, *By God's Decree: The Autobiography of Kapil Dev*, Harper & Row, Sydney, 1985

Patrick Keane, *Merv: The Full Story*, HarperSports, Sydney, 1997

Malcolm Knox, *Taylor & Beyond*; ABC, Sydney, 2000

Allan Lamb, *My Autobiography*; Collins Willow, London, 1996

Bridgette Lawrence, *Masterclass: The Biography of George Headley*; Polar Publishing, Leicester, 1995

Adrian McGregor, *Greg Chappell*; Collins, Sydney, 1985

Arthur Mailey, *10 For 66 And All That*; Phoenix Sports Books, London, 1958

Ashley Mallett, *Clarrie Grimmett*; University of Queensland Press, Brisbane, 1993

Michael Manley, *A History of West Indies Cricket*; Andre Deutsch, London, 1988

Christopher Martin-Jenkins, *The Complete Who's Who of Test Cricketers*; Orbis Publishing, London, 1980

Keith Miller, *Cricket Crossfire*; Oldbourne Press, London, 1956

AG Moyes, *Bradman*; Angus & Robertson, Sydney, 1948

AG Moyes, *A Century of Cricketers*; Harrap, London, 1950

AG Moyes, *Australian Bowlers*; Angus & Robertson, Sydney, 1953

AG Moyes, *Australian Batsmen*; Harrap, London, 1954

AG Moyes, *Australian Cricket: A History*; Angus & Robertson, Sydney, 1959

AG Moyes, *With the West Indies in Australia, 1960–61*; Angus & Robertson, Sydney, 1961

Patrick Murphy, *The Spinner's Turn*; JM Dent & Sons, London, 1982

Patrick Murphy, *The Centurions*; JM Dent & Sons, London, 1986

Patrick Murphy, *Botham: A Biography*; JM Dent & Sons, London, 1988

Peter Philpott, *A Spinner's Yarn*; ABC Books, Sydney, 1990

Graeme Pollock, *Down The Wicket*; Pelham Books, London, 1968

Mike Procter, *Mike Procter and Cricket*; Pelham Books, London, 1981

Simon Rae, *WG Grace*; Faber & Faber, London, 1998

Barry Richards, *The Barry Richards Story*; Angus & Robertson, Sydney, 1978

Viv Richards, *Hitting Across the Line: An Autobiography*; Pan Macmillan, Sydney, 1991

Ray Robinson, *On Top Down Under*; Cassell, Sydney, 1975

Irving Rosenwater, *Sir Donald Bradman*; Batsford, London, 1978

Gordon Ross, *A History of West Indies Cricket*; Arthur Barker Ltd, London, 1976

Bob Simpson, *The Reasons Why*; HarperSports, Sydney 1996

Terry Smith, *Bedside Book of Cricket Centuries*; Angus & Robertson, Sydney, 1991

John Snow, *Cricket Rebel*; Hamlyn, London, 1976

Garry Sobers, *Cricket Crusader*; Pelham Books, London, 1966

Garry Sobers, *King Cricket*; Pelham Books, London, 1967

Garry Sobers, *Garry Sobers' Most Memorable Matches*; Stanley Paul, London, 1984

Sir Garfield Sobers, *Sobers: Twenty Years At The Top*; Macmillan, Melbourne, 1988

EW Swanton, *As I Said At The Time: A Lifetime in Cricket*; Collins Willow, London, 1983

EW Swanton, *Cricket From All Angles*; Michael Joseph, London, 1968

EW Swanton, *Gubby Allen, Man of Cricket*; Hutchinson/Stanley Paul, London, 1985

Donald Trelford, *WG Grace*; Sutton Publishing, Stroud UK, 1998

AA Thomson, *Cricket: The Golden Ages*; Stanley Paul, London, 1961

Shane Warne, *My Own Story*; Swan Publishing, Perth, 1997

Wasim Akram, *Wasim*; Judy Piatkus (Publishers) Ltd, London, 1998

Steve Waugh's tour diaries; Pan Macmillan (1993–94), HarperSports (1995–2001), Sydney

Ray Webster & Allan Miller, *First-Class Cricket in Australia (Volume 1, 1850–51 to 1941–42)*; Published by Ray Webster, Glen Waverley, Australia, 1991

Rudi Webster, *Winning Ways*; Fontana, Sydney, 1984

Wisden Cricketers' Almanacks

RS Whitington, *Simpson's Safari*; William Heinemann, Melbourne, 1967

RS Whitington, *Time of the Tiger: The Bill O'Reilly Story*; Hutchinson, Melbourne, 1970

RS Whitington, *Captains Outrageous?*; Hutchinson, Melbourne, 1972

RS Whitington & George Hele, *Bodyline Umpire*; Rigby, Adelaide, 1974

RS Whitington, *Keith Miller: The Golden Nugget*; Rigby, Adelaide, 1981

Mike Whitney, *Quick Whit*; Ironbark Press, Sydney, 1994

Simon Wilde, *Caught: The Full Story of Corruption in International Cricket*; Aurum Press, London, 2001

Charles Williams, *Bradman*; Little Brown & Company, London, 1996

Bob Willis, *The Cricket Revolution: Test Cricket in the 1970s*; Sidgwick & Jackson, London, 1981

Peter Wynne-Thomas, *The Complete History of Cricket Tours*; Hamlyn, London, 1989

As well, numerous newspapers and websites were consulted, most notably cricinfo.com and the sites of the *Sydney Morning Herald*, the *Times of India* and the *Daily Telegraph* in London, and *The Referee*, which was published in Sydney between 1886 and 1939.